JUNG
IN MODERN
PERSPECTIVE

Edited by Renos K. Papadopoulos
and Graham S. Saayman

PRISM · UNITY

JUNG IN MODERN PERSPECTIVE

First published in 1984 by Wildwood House Ltd

This edition published in Great Britain 1991 by:
PRISM PRESS
2 South Street
Bridport
Dorset DT6 3NQ

and distributed in the USA by:
Avery Publishing Group
120 Old Broadway
Garden City Park
NY 11040

Published in Australia by:
UNITY PRESS
Lindfield
NSW 2070

ISBN 1 85327 064 4

Printed by The Guernsey Press Ltd, The Channel
Islands.

Contents

Contributors

Dr M. V. Bührmann, after medical studies at the University of Cape Town, specialized in public health in Johannesburg and psychiatry in London, where she also trained as a Jungian analyst. Later she practised as an analyst and lectured in the Department of Psychiatry at the University of Cape Town. Now most of her time is spent on research into transcultural psychiatry (on which she has published extensively) and supervising psychotherapists.

Dr H. Dieckmann is a leading Jungian analyst who lives and practises in Berlin and works at the University of Berlin. He is a founder and former President of the C. G. Jung-Institut there and editor of *Zeitschrift für Analytische Psychologie*. He has published many books and papers on analytical psychology.

P. A. Faber is a lecturer in the Department of Psychology, University of Cape Town, and a clinical psychologist. He has been involved in research on archetypal psychology for a number of years.

Dr Marie-Louise von Franz is one of Jung's foremost living disciples. She has published prolifically in many languages. Her books in English include: *C. G. Jung: His Myth in Our Time* (1975), *Number and Time* (1974) and *Alchemy: An Introduction to the Symbolism and the Psychology* (1980). One of her special interests in recent years has been the relationship between the realms of physics and depth psychology.

Professor J. W. de Gruchy is Associate Professor and Head of the Department of Religious Studies, University of Cape Town; also founder editor of the journal *Theology in South Africa* and author of the book *The Church Struggle in South Africa* (1969).

Dr J. L. Henderson was born in Egypt and educated at the universities of Oxford and London. He has lectured extensively in various countries and was Senior Lecturer in the History of International Affairs at London University, Institute of Education. His published work includes: *Education for World Understanding* (1968), *A Bridge Across Time: An Assessment of Historical Archetypes* (1975), and *The Unbridled Ego* (1980).

Dr E. G. Humbert, a prominent Jungian analyst, author and lecturer, lives and practises in Paris. He is editor of the French Jungian journal *Cahiers de Psychologie Jungienne*, former president of the French Society for Analytical Psychology and published a synthesis of Jungian theory, *Jung*, in 1982.

Dr L. Jadot was until recently Professor of Psychology at the Catholic University of Louvain in Belgium and is a practising analyst.

Professor M. T. Kelsey is Professor of Religion at the University of Notre-Dame and the author of many books and articles on the Christian experience, Christian approaches to dreams and the relationship between Christianity and Jungian psychology.

Dr G. Maffei is Libero Docente in Psychiatry at the University of Pisa and a practising analyst. A member of the Associazione Italiana per lo studio delle psicologia analitica, he is the author of numerous articles on analytical psychology and psychiatry and books including *I tics* (1969) and *Il Mestiere il Uomo* (1977).

Dr Renos K. Papadopoulos, born in Cyprus and educated at the universities of Belgrade and Cape Town, is a Jungian analyst. Formerly a lecturer in the Department of Psychology at the University of Cape Town and currently the Director of Psychological Services to children, young people and their families in the London Borough of Redbridge.

Dr A. Plaut was born in Germany, received his medical training in South Africa and England and then specialized in psychiatry. A leading training analyst and author, and chairman of the Society of Analytical Psychology, Dr Plaut lives and practises in London. His special interest in recent years has been the relationship between maps and mapmaking and archetypal images.

G. H. Pulvermacher was born in Germany and studied musicology, philosophy and Indology at the University of Breslau. He has been Professor of Music, Dean of the Music Faculty and Director of the South African College of Music at the University of Cape Town.

Professor L. Rauhala is Associate Professor of Psychology at Helsinki University and Senior Lecturer in Philosophy at the University of Turku, Finland. He is also the author of many articles and books on clinical psychology, psychotherapy and the philosophy of psychology, including *The Unconscious and the Problem of Intentionality* (1969).

Professor J. F. Rychlak holds the Maude C. Clarke Chair in Humanistic Psychology, Loyola University of Chicago, and is a fellow of the American Psychological Association and former President of its Philosophical Division. Professor Rychlak has published extensively. His books include *The Psychology of Rigorous Humanism* (1977), *Discovering Free Will and Personal Responsibility* (1979), and *A Philosophy of Science for Personality Theory* (2nd ed., 1981).

Dr Graham S. Saayman was formerly Professor and Head of the Department of Psychology at the University of Cape Town and now at Sudbury Algoma Hospital, Ontario, Canada. He was the founder of the research group in Jungian psychology at the same university and has published studies on ethology, archetypal psychology, family therapy and experimental psychology. He is on the editorial board of *Archives of Sexual Behaviour* and *Carnivore,* acts as a corresponding associate commentator on *The Behavioural and Brain Sciences* and also practises as a family therapist.

Dr S. de Voogd was born in the Netherlands and educated there and at New York University. She now teaches philosophy at the University of Amsterdam. Her book of essays, *A Transparent World* (in Dutch), was published in Amsterdam in 1979.

Preface and Acknowledgements

This collection of readings offers a representative sample of modern approaches to Jungian thought, its implications for and applications to a variety of disciplines and viewpoints today. Eight of the articles are printed here for the first time, whereas the other nine are republished with the kind permission of the authors and the original publishers, which we gratefully acknowledge.

'Tentative views on Dream Therapy by Xhosa Diviners' by M. Vera Bührmann first appeared in the *Journal of Analytical Psychology*, 1978, vol. 23, pp. 105–121; 'The Favourite Fairy-Tale of Childhood' by Hans Dieckmann appeared in the *Journal of Analytical Psychology*, 1971, vol. 16, no. 1; 'The Jungian Interpretation of History and its Educational Implications' by J.L. Henderson in *New Era*; 'Active Imagination According to C.G. Jung' by E.G. Humbert appeared as 'L'imagination Active d'après C.G. Jung' in *Cahiers de Psychologie Jungienne*, 1977, no. 13, pp. 1–24; 'From the Symbol in Psychoanalysis to the Anthropology of the Imaginary' by L. Jadot appeared as 'Du Symbole en Psychoanalyse à l'Anthropologie de l'Imaginary' in *Le Langage et l'Homme*, 1976, no. 31, pp. 11–19; 'Jung as Philosopher and Theologian' by M. Kelsey in *The Well Tended Tree*, ed. Hilde Kirsch, New York, G.P. Putnam's Sons, pp. 184–196, copyright 1971 by the C.G. Jung Foundation for Analytical Psychology; 'Archetypal Structures, Primal Repression and the Therapeutic Relationship with Psychotics' by G. Maffei in *The Annual of Italian Analytical Psychologists*, 1977, vol. 1, pp. 203–224; 'Jung and Rebirth' by A. Plaut in the *Journal of Analytical Psychology*, 1977, vol. 22, pp. 142–157; 'The Basic Views of C.G. Jung in the Light of Hermeneutic Metascience' by L. Rauhala in *The Human Context*, 1973, vol. 5, no. 2, pp. 254–267. 'Meaning and Order: Concerning meeting points and differences between depth psychology and physics' by Marie-Louise von Franz was first given as a talk and is printed here by permission of Billy Jack Enterprises, Inc., CBS Studio Center, 4024 Radford Avenue, Studio City, California.

Introduction

*Not for a moment dare we succumb to the illusion that an
archetype can be finally explained . . . Even the best attempts at
explanation are only more or less successful translations into
another metaphorical language. (Indeed, language itself is only
an image). The most we can do is to dream the myth onwards
and give it a modern dress . . .*
          C.G. Jung *(The Psychology of the Child Archetype).*

The theme of this book was conceived at a symposium at the
University of Cape Town, commemorating the centenary of Jung's
birth. The response of both students and public led to the organization
of a larger event, richer in both scope and depth in 1977. Appropriately
then, Alfred Plaut, one of the participants, spoke on the pivotal theme
in Jungian thought, that of Rebirth. It indeed became apparent that the
Jungian opus was now experiencing a rebirth, entering into a period of
a more mature and objective appraisement of its contributions, not
only to psychology, but also to a variety of other disciplines. This
rebirth follows the somewhat extreme reactions of scepticism, if not
incredulity, of the early days and of the almost equally uncritical
euphoric adoptions of the hippie era. It is also true that we have
encountered an increasingly mature approach in our University-
Academic experience.

Thus, the need for a text representing this attitude became apparent.
Moreover, this experience has shown us that much of the Jungian
literature remains inaccessible to many who are not well versed in his
system. We see, in other words, that the existing distance between
Jung and many readers is due not only to prejudice but also to the
realistic difficulties in grasping a psychological system of such breadth
and scope, formulated in Jung's own individualistic terminology. In
order to assimilate any psychological language, it is essential to digest
it in its entirety or else to run the risk of losing sight of its organic
coherence. This is particularly true of Jung's enormous tapestry,
dealing as it does with so many issues which have direct, experiential
relevance to modern man. His system, therefore, is particularly
vulnerable to uncritical and mechanistic compartmentalization,
consequent distortion and hence to either noncomprehending
rejection, or equally uncritical adoption and imitation. What is thus
ideally needed is an approach to his entire psychology which does not

seek merely to reiterate or paraphrase its concepts in terms diluted from the language he himself employed. We hope that this book takes a small step towards offering such an approach, from a variety of modern perspectives.

Jung frequently stated that his was not a theory, but a set of meaningfully inter-related observations derived from his personal experiences and comparative researches. His remark to the effect that he was glad to be Jung and not a Jungian reflects the profound emphasis he placed upon the sanctity of the individual. However, at the same time, he stressed the importance of the wider human collective. This seeming paradox might be resolved by the consideration that the person who is truly in contact with his own unique individuality is able to account adequately for his own experiences in the language of a wider social context. Thus, Jung's essential message 'know yourself' should lead not to an isolated and egotistic state, but to a recognition of universal structural and developmental processes. It was Jung's telling insight that this realization might be achieved by means of an inner dialogue, translated into meaningful action in the lived world.

It is his emphasis upon the *process* set in motion by this dialogue which we have tried to stress here. Jung was averse to dogma, in keeping with his formulation of the individuation process and its unique development in each individual. He frequently repeated that he had no one theory of dreams, no single method of psychotherapy. In so doing his dialectical method drew the central distinction between content and process while at the same time allowing for their meaningful interrelationship in clinical practice, thus anticipating contemporary trends in psychotherapy theory and research. We note this distinction in one of his most fundamental contributions – his concept of the archetype. Jung repeatedly emphasized the constant renewal of the contents of the archetypal structures in the context of the social, cultural and historical moments in the life of the individual. Indeed, his work might be read as a description of constantly recurring themes and developmental processes in the history of consciousness.

The articles presented here constitute yet another set of attempts at reformulation in 'modern dress'. We are aware that our list of contributions is not exhaustive and that, consequently, we are open to the criticism we ourselves have mentioned above – namely, that of compartmentalization. However, we have attempted to present a genuinely broad coverage of works, adequate to Jung's own wide sweep of interests, at the same time focussing not on isolated aspects of his work but rather on some of his central themes. These essays represent perhaps the most important facets of the contemporary perspective within which Jung's contribution to psychology and culture is currently re-appraised. They also indicate possible directions that Jungian studies might follow in the future.

More specifically, it seems that Jung's writings will always have a significant impact on any mature understanding of religion. Naive conceptions of a God 'out there', unrelated to the constitution of our own psyche and our knowledge of ourselves, others and the world, will of course continue to give rise to accusations against Jung of, for instance, mysticism, occultism and animism. It is not surprising therefore that, by extension, an emerging new and serious appraisal of religious systems and the spiritual practices of other cultures has turned to Jung for inspiration and deeper understanding. These studies range from experimental and laboratory investigations of meditation, dreams, sleep and other altered states of consciousness to more phenomenological assessments of various nuances of the human condition. Jungian attempts to understand other cultures have received substantial impetus from the recent pioneering work of Dr Vera M. Bührmann in South Africa. Humanistic psychology, the so-called third force in psychology (the other two being psychoanalysis and behaviourism), seems to have settled down after a frantic period of adolescent omniscience, and appears now to afford the acknowledgement that Jung spoke about 'self realization' half a century earlier than the humanistic psychologists. This admission has led to a re-evaluation of such matters and has prompted a detailed re-reading of Jung. A similar trend seems to have taken place in Feminism. After the period of slogans subsided, a fresh examination of Jung's work on psychological androgyny and its ramifications became imperative. A further exciting development is found in the study of the themes of popular culture and modern mythology from a Jungian standpoint, such as the phenomena of mass fascination with hobbits, space exploration, unidentified flying objects, dragons and the like. However, the final testing ground of the survival of Jungian thought may in the long run prove to be the philosophy of science, epistemology, and methodology. Psychology itself appears at last to have caught up with developments in science in general, by gradually abandoning the restrictive and outdated models of causal, positivistic and mechanistic approaches. Theorists find much value in Jung's dialectical and holistic direction. The future of Jungian psychology (with all its implications) may ultimately depend on the ability of a science reappraised in Jungian terms to build alternative, viable and meaningful models. 'The most we can do is to dream the myth onwards . . . '

Cape Town   RENOS K. PAPADOPOULOS
                                               GRAHAM S. SAAYMAN

CHAPTER 1

Jung and Rebirth

BY ALFRED PLAUT

I. Introduction

I have asked myself why it is that we should wish to celebrate the anniversary of someone who was born a hundred years ago and is no longer with us. A naïve question perhaps, but the answer is not all that obvious, for many famous men have lived and died without figuring in the calendar of people in different parts of the globe a hundred years later. What kind of achievement is most likely to qualify for these ritualistic observances? If we were to take the Christian calendar with its anniversaries of the birth, death and resurrection of its founder, and some saints as testimonies to their spiritual impact on the world, we could, I believe, arrive at one conclusion: pioneers in the art of living and dying stand, among famous people, the best chance to be honoured by ritualistic celebrations.

It seems as if by such observances on these occasions the dead person were again with those who wanted to acknowledge their debt of gratitude. While this may be a reasonable assumption, it still remains odd that those who feel that they have benefited from the work and example of a pioneer, should want to celebrate the recurrence of his birth. Unless, of course, we believe that by our deep respect he is reborn in the spirit. Celebration of his birthday could then lead to a renewal of knowledge, a renaissance.

Whether in the case of Jung a hundred years from now we may still think so is a matter of speculation – another question, more pertinent to my theme, would be how many times and in what ways a man can be said to have been reborn during his life-span. Before taking a closer look at this question, I should like to remind ourselves of the vast difference between an unquestioning acceptance of a religious leader and the appreciation which is due to a pioneer in the field of psychology who loathed anything approaching discipleship or adulation.

II. The theme of rebirth among other leitmotifs

In his paper 'On synchronicity' Jung quotes Wilhelm Stekel[1] who drew attention to some whimsical connexions which seemed to exist between a man's name and his peculiarities or profession. Thus Freud (meaning joy) championed the pleasure principle, Adler (eagle) stood for the will to power, and Jung (young) for the idea of rebirth. Stekel intimates that the name has a compelling effect and Jung asks himself whether these names could be meaningful coincidences. The answer is not important here. What matters is that 'rebirth' played a significant part in Jung's ideology. Stekel's allusions remained only partially true: Freud revised his libidinal theory when he wrote *Beyond the pleasure principle* and Jung's interest in all psychological phenomena and transformation cannot be captured by a single word like 'rebirth', which may be used in so many different ways that I shall have to be strictly selective. And yet Stekel's early recognition of Jung's characteristic concept which was to play an important part in his *Transformations and symbols of the libido* (later known as *Symbols of transformation*) first published in 1912, is remarkable enough to serve as an introduction to my theme. Stekel's article preceded the publication of that book by about one year. So he must have known about Jung's great interest in the topic. We do know that this book contains a long chapter 'Symbols of the mother and of rebirth'. Twenty-seven years later, in 1939, Jung gave an Eranos lecture entitled 'On different aspects of rebirth' which (re-edited in 1950) appears in *C.W.* vol. 9 part I as 'Concerning rebirth'.[2] One may take it therefore that the thoughts he had put together 'on the spur of the moment', as he informs us, had been at the back of his mind for forty years.

There are other recurring themes, or leitmotifs, in Jung's work, of which the four most prominent are:

1. Special rebirth symbolisms, as pointed out in 'Psychology and alchemy'[3] and in 'The psychology of transference'.[4] Here images of incest, death and decay are essential preludes to the whole-making process.

2. His discovery of the relationship between the context of psychoses and of myths from 'The psychology of dementia praecox', 1907,[5] to 'Schizophrenia' in 1958.[6]

3. The enduring interest Jung showed in paranormal or supernatural phenomena, from his M.D. thesis 'On the psychology of so-called occult phenomena', 1902[7], via 'On synchronicity', 1951[8], to an essay 'Flying saucers: a modern myth', 1958.[9]

4. Jung's concern with religions and the image of God in man's psyche from the time when, as a schoolboy of eleven, prayer to God satisfied him because 'it was without contradictions', to his quarrelling with God in his 'Answer to Job', 1952.[10]

These lasting and controversy-arousing interests, or, more truly, fascinations were balanced, one might say, by Jung's vast intellectual abilities, his manual skills, his wide travels, systematic recording and classifying of observations, as well as his ability to hold a variety of audiences and to empathize with people of all sorts. It was a balance to which Jung himself referred when he wrote 'I always knew that I was two persons'. He called his No. 1 personality the son of his parents to whom his mother referred as a good boy, which he regarded as egotistic and mean, separated from God, yet needed to get by in the world. The other he called confusingly his No. 2 personality. I say confusingly, because it corresponded to his true nature, but he discovered it only gradually as he grew up. Nothing could persuade this No. 2 personality that only man was created in the image of God.[11] He thought that nature all around him represented it more truly. When we consider the subjects which fascinated Jung as well as the temporary separation of his parents during his childhood, we begin to understand the boy's need to carry his soul-stone in his trouser pocket and the man's life-long search for reconciling symbols. It was a need for permanence to which repeated cycles of loss and separation followed by gains and discovery added their share.

We lesser mortals are also constantly losing and discovering or re-discovering ourselves and I shall therefore take these minor forms of rebirths which take place during our life-span and perhaps more particularly under the focus of analysis as an essential point of my reflections. But first let us look at certain episodes in Jung's life. I shall call these rebirths although Jung never referred to them as such. It would have been pompous had he done so and in any case during the heat of battle one does not think that way.

III. Three rebirth episodes in Jung's life

Perhaps 'crisis' would do to express an important turning point in a person's life. But then we would impoverish the event of all that led up to it and what came out of it and, above all, it would lose the characteristics of the person to whom it seemingly had to happen when it did. What is more, crisis orientates one towards contingency planning and problem solving rather than toward the feeling of having undergone a lucky or even miraculous transformation of death, recovery and renewal. At any rate, the three episodes which follow demonstrate that inevitably painful separations tend to precede a creative breakthrough.

When Jung broke with Freud between 1912 and 1913 it was an event which had been gradually building up. 'After the parting of the ways with Freud, a period of inner uncertainty began for me'. With these words the chapter 'Confrontation with the unconscious' (in *Memories, dreams, reflections*) opens. The description of dreams and visions and other events which followed make the self-diagnosis 'I suspected there was some psychic disturbance in me' sound like an understatement. The healing discovery and transformation occurred when he submitted himself to impulses from the unconscious, all attempts to pay attention to childhood memories having proved futile. 'I have never fully unwound the tangle of my earliest memories', he wrote at the age of 83. Anyway, during this period of profound turmoil he began to play with bottles, stones and mud. It is hard for us in our day and age to imagine what it must have meant in 1912 – when regression as a respectable concept and potential therapeutic aid was unknown – to dare to submit himself to the impulses of the unconscious as this then thirty-six year old highly respected doctor did. 'This moment', writes Jung, 'was a turning point in my fate, but I gave in only after endless resistances and with a sense of resignation'.[11] It was a 'painfully humiliating experience' that there was nothing to be done except play childish games. Nevertheless, he tells us how this game reconnected him with the dream of his childhood of the underground phallus. He had, by chance, so it seemed, found a way of re-entering an important area of his mental life and he wrote: 'This connection gave me a feeling of satisfaction'.

But having gained access was only the first step. It was like discovering that he was in an unknown part of the world and he now had to set about orientating himself in relation to it. Almost fifty years later he wrote that 'Everything that I accomplished in later life was already contained in the dreams and phantasies which began in 1912'. We may therefore feel certain that without his own near-psychotic episode combined with remarkable self-discipline the *Symbols of transformation* would never have been written. Although the breakdown after separating from Freud is the best documented, two others must be recounted here.

When I was a novice in the Jungian circle an episode called 'When Jung nearly died' was still referred to in hushed voices. The looks which accompanied the voices reminded me of the way grown-ups used to talk when I as a child was supposed either not to understand or, if I did, to keep that knowledge to myself. I came to the conclusion (which still has to be disproved) that Jung's heart attack was preceded or complicated by an affair of the heart. My usually reliable source at the time added significantly: 'The only person who was allowed to see him was Mrs Jung.' Whatever the facts, Jung's own account only tells us how in 1944 he broke his foot and that the mishap was followed by a heart attack. In a state of unconsciousness he experienced visions and hallucinations. These, combined with the medication he received, made him conclude that he was close to death. His nurse told him afterwards, 'It was as if you were surrounded by a bright glow', and added that she sometimes observed this phenomenon in the dying. Jung at that time had a series of visions, some of great beauty, accompanied by a feeling of detachment. He felt weightless and floating in space; at least three weeks passed before he could truly make up his mind to live again. This had been hard as there had been moments of ecstasy and bliss night after night; his sleep rhythm had altered in that he fell asleep in the evening and woke at midnight when the glorious experiences started while he was lying awake 'in an utterly transformed state'.[11] He wrote: 'We shy away from the word "eternal", but I can describe the experience only as the ecstasy of a non-temporal state in which present, past and future are one'. And further 'after the illness a fruitful period of work began for me' . . . 'The insight I had had or the vision of the end of all things, gave me the courage to undertake new formulations'. This resolution resembles the decision he made when at the age of twelve his fainting spells were diagnosed as epilepsy: 'Why then, I must get to work', he had said to himself.

The third episode to which I am referring happened after his wife's death in 1955 after fifty-three years of marriage. He had a dream in which the same calm objectivity emanated from her image which signified detachment 'from valuations and from what we call emotional ties'. Once more he resorted to stone sculptures. Once again this was followed by a fruitful period of writing. But 'it cost me a great deal to regain my footing and contact with stone helped me.'

IV. Rebirth – controlled

It is all too tempting to subsume under a single heading a multitude of psycho-dynamic processes. We could think of self-realization, integration and individuation and other words which mean to indicate the specifically Jungian concepts of the healing or whole-making therapeutic aim of analysis. To these rather comprehensive terms one could add various steps or stations on the way to this desirable end of all transformations thus bearing out Jung's major thesis. But this would be too large an undertaking for a single lecture. By using rebirth as my theme I could easily fall into the trap of applying just another large cover word in order to do a package deal. Instead, I should like to restrict myself to a personal statement on '*What of Jung is most in need of rebirth today?*' – more prosaically put: which are the areas of his work that I would like to review critically and see develop further?

In my limited answer I shall concentrate on some basic principles. In the first place, I must prune the term rebirth of some of its many meanings, such as transmigration of souls, reincarnation, resurrection and participation in rituals as in initiation and healing through birth ceremonies. What is even more relevant, I am going to concentrate on the positive and hopeful, even idealistic (the word has a pejorative ring in the ears of some analysts) potentialities. But in so doing I shall remain mindful of the dangers which surround every change and transformation whether it concerns an individual or large social groups. Here I am thinking of what Jung in the language of 'primitive psychology' refers to as loss of soul and states of possession including mass-enthusiasms. Analysis, like revolutions, cannot be embarked on without risk of serious damage. Such anxieties about changes and uncertain outcomes differ, however, from the feeling that one is dying because everything seems hopeless. When lethargy and depression as well as anxious resistance to change are the order of the day and sleep is disturbed by night it is hard to be receptive to a new richness of mind which may be waiting just around the corner. In such states we usually cling to our material possessions and everything else which we take for granted as if our lives depended on it, when just the opposite is the case: life may depend on giving up so-called security.

There are times in analysis when I find it impossible to say whether I am dealing with a temporary deathly state preceding a fruitful change or irreversible damage. I suppose without some cautious optimism it would be impossible to proceed: as therapists we have to hold the hope that has vanished from our patients' minds.

In order to further limit the usage of the word 'rebirth' let us cast our minds back to the three episodes in Jung's life and consider the common pre-conditions, as well as the differences and similarities in manifestation and result. Loss in the form of separations is, of course, the outstanding common factor preceding the breakdowns, both in the sense of ideological separateness and on a deep emotional level as the Freud–Jung letters clearly demonstrate. The death of his wife typifies the loss of a condition of life, a permanent background and material security Jung had come to take for granted. The heart condition can probably not be dissociated from Jung's intimate and important relationship with Toni Wolff, although some of Jung's followers ascribed it to the effect of World War II. At all events, the omission of her name from *Memories, dreams, reflections* is, for me, the one serious flaw of that book. But it will help me when I come to discuss what is for me the most pertinent aspect of rebirth, namely the repeated crossing of thresholds between superego and self as guidelines to our ways of conduct.

Regression, as we now call it, with its varied symptomatology such as leaden inertia, or alternatively, oceanic blissful states and infant-like play and rhythmic activity can be, as is now common knowledge among analysts, a precursor to new developments and insights and outlooks, in short, rebirth. What remains unique in Jung's personal achievement is the wholeheartedness with which he went along with these predicaments and impulses arising from within himself to which one has to add – or perhaps it is the same thing – his vitality which made him take the initiative after setbacks, thus turning what appeared to be the end into a new beginning.

The other common element in Jung's rebirth which will bring us to my personal view, is the reconnection, in Jung's example with the help of stone, within himself, of present and past, the strong synthesizing trend which characterises Jung's life and work. Another clinical feature which we regularly encounter in regressions is curiously missing from Jung's accounts: there is no reference to dependency. Maybe Mrs Jung could have told us something on that subject! However, it is also possible that the relation to a stone or stones, which were for him highly animated even 'numinous' objects that would not let him down and yet connect him with the past – his and theirs – may have replaced dependence on another human being to some extent.

V. *Personality factors of the re-born or twice-born*

The need for synthesis in a personality as divided as Jung's is not very surprising if we bear in mind the chapter entitled 'The divided self', and the process of its unification in William James's *The varieties of religious experience*. The psychological basis of the sick souls who must be twice born in order to be happy 'seems to ascertain discordancy or heterogeneity in the native temperament of the subject, an incompletely unified *moral* and intellectual constitution' (italics mine).[12] Well, I don't know about twice, nor about 'happy', but I do see the difference between the constitution James is describing and the other which he calls 'healthy minded', corresponding roughly to 'God's in his Heaven, all's right with the world', or, to quote James: 'The once born with their sky-blue optimistic gospel'. On the other hand, he writes: 'It is indeed true that the outlook upon life of the twice born – holding as it does more of the element of evil in solution – is the wider and completer'. Their need for what James calls a 'higher synthesis' is so much greater and there is no doubt at all that Jung belonged to their company, especially with his No. 2 personality. Yet he defends himself stoutly against a 'split' or dissociation and emphasizes that the interplay between a No. 1 and 2 personality happens in every individual. However, this may be a question of degree and few people can have been more aware of their duality than Jung was.

In order to get quickly to the Jung who lived in constant touch with his unconscious I should like to recall my first meeting with him in

1952. When I came into the room he asked me about my name, which he apparently had not come across before. He added almost at once that when he read it he had thought: 'Oh, that is Plautus coming to see me!' (i.e. Titus Maccius Plautus: see Hammond and Scullard[13]). This was said in a bantering sort of way and led to our talking about the places where some of his family and mine had come from. Nevertheless, by the time I had left I found myself wondering whether my ancestry could in some way have been connected with that Roman joker. Next, we talked about parts of Africa which we both knew and where only a few white people lived. His major point was how the white man's psychology was influenced by the black man's Africa. Words like 'primitive psychology' and terms derived from anthropology all indicate how much he was at home with the impulsive emotional reactions, including dangerous rages, arising straight from those blind layers of our minds which we call irrational. The personification of the unconscious, to be in touch (literally) with it was, I believe first, not second nature to him.

To harness and structure these inner perceptions and initial outpourings into thoughtful views which could be presented within a given context was a highly necessary discipline which he imposed on himself, aiming at a synthesis with varying degrees of success, but never so completely that the two components of his personality did not show through. At any rate these transformations and elaborations of his libido were a vital necessity to him. When I read how his daughter had been afraid of her father's outbursts and rages – which *he* was quite quickly able to forget – I knew the significance of the lowering of the mental threshold for him which he so frequently refers to by the term *abaissement du niveau mental*. It is the contact with this vital layer of our minds which can renew the mainsprings of energy. But it is also a force of nature dangerous to encounter without the necessary ritualistic precautions. The manifestations and quanta of energy, represented by archetypes, as such, are, like nature, totally uncaring as to the effect on the life of humans.

There are some special consequences for a person who lives so near to his instincts and the unconscious in general, but is also aware of it: he must let neither the source of this energy, nor his ability to give it shape and form, get the upper hand. In addition, such people frequently shy away from a resolution of this conflict in the form of success. Both Freud and Jung seemed to have belonged to those who would have been wrecked by success. Ernest Jones recounts three fainting attacks of Freud's interpreted in terms of the death of his younger brother when he, Sigmund, was one year and seven months old – in other words, the defeat of an opponent,[14] which is no doubt guilt-provoking; fainting is thus a way of opting out.

Jung had seen Rome only from a distance and had been struck with awe. 'If you are affected to the depth of your being at every step by the spirit that broods here,' as he put it, 'you cannot just visit it like a tourist.'[11] In old age he tried to repair this omission, and finally bought railway tickets to see the eternal city. But he fainted at the station and therefore decided that he had to abandon the attempt for good.

The essential requirement then for those who live in two worlds (my term for the reborn) is that they must know what *their* limits of a successful synthesis are. As long as success is unconsciously equated with being stifled by an outer shape or form constricting the inner source of new life, avoidance of success must appear preferable to sterility.

VI. Syntheses: renaissance today

The tendency towards syntheses of various kinds, which seems to me a character trait of the twice-born, became, if anything, more powerful as Jung grew older. I think that it exerts an influence on divided minds and can be beneficial. It can also lead to undiscriminating nonsense.

When during the Renaissance new discoveries were made on a vast scale with the help of rediscovered Greek mathematics and the experimental method, an era during which scholasticism and magic had held undisputed sway came to an end. This coincided with questioning the authority of God and instead giving man 'in his mightiness, intellectual power and beauty a visible place beside God'.[15] We know of Jung's strong attraction to the great figures of that age, like Angelus Silesius, Paracelsus, Agrippa of Nettesheim and others who tackled the task of remaining whole persons in an age when the specialization of science, separating it from magic as well as religiously conceived dogma, were threatening a former unity of knowledge – and ignorance. But remember: Kepler still cast horoscopes, Isaac Newton still had unpublicized interests in alchemy. The development of specialization of knowledge has continued to our day and this in combination with the population explosion may well be said to have estranged man from a necessary sense of harmony with the world and an awareness of its meaning, thereby threatening him with chaos. During the Renaissance, which took at least four hundred years, many attempts were made to unify man's expanding knowledge with God and his creation. A new social order, a new cosmos and harmony were the aim. It has remained an ideal which confronts and challenges us again today, after the age of reason has left us not a little disillusioned.

But what in practical, rather than ideological, terms could remedy the estrangements between man and his nature, on the one hand, and his technological achievements, the machine of which he has become a kind of 'sorcerer's apprentice' on the other? We can hardly expect that one man in our day and age can become master of many scientific disciplines and write moral essays as was still possible in Francis Bacon's time. But could not education of young and not-so-young persons take note of the rôle which the artisans played during the Renaissance? Their accomplishments were required to bring together technical and scientific knowledge. On a humble level of achievement – one thinks of Churchill as a bricklayer and painter and Jung as a stonemason and builder – it would surely be possible for people from all walks of life to get some real understanding about the fundamentals of each other's work. Even so we can no longer hope to combine in one person the accomplishments of a physician, navigator, mathematician, alchemist, astronomer, philosopher etc. as was possible during the Renaissance. But by getting to know each other's work on an elementary level, in a way which is free from vested interests, like party politics, we might be able to be therapeutic in a social as well as psychological sense. At all events it seems possible to me that there exists an unexplored area of collaboration and potential synthesis of knowledge more in the sense of 'how the other half lives' than in specialized detail.

I cannot end this section on syntheses resulting in rebirth without at least mentioning the powerful and unforeseeable effect which approaching death can have – be it one's own or that of somebody close to the dying person. Regeneration of oneself in these circumstances can be so marked, if mysterious, that the thought of another person dying *for one* comes easily to mind. Jung himself thought so about his own doctor who actually died when he nearly did.

VII. Reconciliation and symbolic incest

In her book *Shakespeare's last plays* (of which *The tempest* is of course the best known), Frances Yates shows how, by the device of the double-plot, one concerned with the older, the other with the younger, generations, old unhappinesses and feuds are healed through the action of a younger generation.[16] Now I am not so starry-eyed as to believe that all the old differences between psychologists, as for example between Freud and Jung, can be done away with. But it is encouraging to see that younger, or, at least later, generations have been able to meet in a harmonious atmosphere which is an essential first step towards reconciliation and possible later syntheses of theory and further discoveries in the art of psychological healing.

Why has this not happened earlier – why has the older generation tried to enlist the loyal support of the cause or ideology *they* espoused, rather than let the young contribute to understanding with the help of *eros*?

The answer, I believe, is that much potential rejuvenation has been spoilt by fear of incest. In order to support my view let us have a brief look at the significance of incest in Jung's writings. To anticipate the main point and major difference from physical incest, Jung's attitude is, as usual, forward-looking.

In the psychology of transference incest is regarded by Jung as 'a genuine instinct' (as well as archetype). Why else, if it were not universally liked and desired, would it require prohibition? He sees it as *the* emotional complication, both in the therapeutic situation as well as between parents and children. As for the regressive tendency of incest Jung postulates that the patient is seeking *himself*, more particularly the left out neglected parts of himself. Ultimately, therefore, incest symbolises union with one's own being, bringing about individuation. The unholy fascination is, therefore, due to the vital need of becoming oneself.

I wonder whether, looked at in this light, the fear of incest may not be comparable to the fear of success, of more synthesis, i.e. resolution of conflicts, than we can bear, as mentioned earlier on. Success would correspond to self-discovery and unification, which we seem to desire as well as dread more than almost anything else, hence the refuge we take into endless projections with destructive consequences. And self-discovery would, in turn, be a rebirth including, most importantly, one's bisexuality, indicated in alchemical pictures and concepts by the hermaphrodite, the ultimate symbolic synthesis which takes place after incest has led to death and resurrection. But whatever explanation of incest-fear we subscribe to, the taboo against incestuous union demands strong lines of demarcation between generations. Therefore, the roles of the elders of the tribe, say the parent generation of analysts *vis à vis* their pupils, have been laid down hierarchically. The resultant mixture of incestuous identification and Oedipal rivalry might have led to stagnation. That this has not happened is, I think, largely due to that indefinable yet very effective 'thought or feeling peculiar to a generation or period', the *Standard Oxford English Dictionary*'s definition of *Zeitgeist* which according to Jung 'compensates our conscious attitude and anticipates changes to come'.[17] I need only add, as one belonging to a parent generation, that their job is not to abdicate nor to be 'with it' nor to adopt an authoritarian stance, but to enter into a partnership with the younger generation. This requires, in the first place, an acknowledgement of our and their incestuous longing and the defence both parties have developed. Here, as in all other symbolic realizations, the question of how close we must and dare come to the symbolic realization of these wishes is one which must be left to our individual consciences.

On a more down-to-earth level, I want to emphasize how much parents can learn about themselves through their children. It is true that, to begin with, the parents are the carriers of culture and tradition, but when the children grow up and into adolescence, the opportunity to develop and learn about themselves, and to keep in touch with the *Zeitgeist*, is on the side of the parents. But now the invitation to participate must be issued by the younger generation. We, the elders, have to wait for it, the reason being that the young have to be sure enough of their identity not to experience us as gate-crashers. If accepted without incest fear, it is rejuvenating to work side by side with the young, although it cannot be painless either: they have home-truths to tell and the biological clock inside ourselves will tell us what the hour has struck.

VIII. Rebirth: from superego to self

If, as Jung says, religions were the great psychotherapeutic systems in the past, they functioned as such largely because they laid down guidelines of moral conduct. It follows that every form of psychotherapy contains either overt or implicit moral values. Analysis is no exception to this. If one were to state the situation in polarised terms, behaviour therapy and psychopharmacology could be put at the collective, society-conforming end of the spectrum, while analysis and allied forms of psychotherapy could be said to subscribe to the cult of the individual.

Now, I am well aware that Jung borrowed the term superego from psychoanalysis, ignoring, however, that it remained a hotly contested area which is still unresolved within psychoanalytic theory. Both in the 'Transformation symbolism in the mass'[18] and in 'A psychological view of conscience'[19] Jung equates the Freudian superego with a collective moral conscience or code. No doubt this oversimplification suits Jung because the resultant contrast with the self as an inner authority – assumed to be free from conventional morality and, in fact, ready to do battle with it, because 'no longer identical with public opinion' – is a victory over the dreaded conformity which indicates that one is only the child of one's parents, the No. 1 personality, in fact, a mass product. The true conscience thus becomes for Jung an ethical issue in contrast to the morality which conforms with public opinion.

But the matter is not so straightforward. When I visited Switzerland I saw a monument describing an illustrious citizen as 'this independent man'. A friend told me that this was the highest praise which could be bestowed on a Swiss (cf. also William Tell). If independence becomes an ego ideal, and thereby part of the superego in keeping with a national ideal the contrast with that inner authority, the self, becomes difficult to determine. And again: if the *Zeitgeist* moves from a time and place in which public opinion does not tolerate a respectable man to have a mistress, to another where it does not matter much one way or another, a public acknowledgement of such an affair would be no great sacrifice nor defiance, and therefore another criterion as to whether superego or self were informing a person's conduct would have become void.

As this may sound rather theoretical, let me offer the example of a man who comes from a culture where the choice of a wife is determined by the parents. There are degrees by which he could deviate from his tradition. He could marry a girl of his own choice, but still from the same racial and religious background. On the other hand, he could choose a girl with all the extremely opposite attributes, or again he could stay single, which would cast a different kind of reflection on his parents and himself.

The question arising out of the various courses of action which are, in theory, open to him is whether they originate from within himself as an individual or as a member of a group, and what is more, of a strongly knit family group who live now as a minority under the external pressures brought to bear by a foreign culture. These pressures are balanced by strong early imprints of mother-worship. Not the least weighty factor among those which could influence him now is that of the authority which he has vested in me. Obviously, if he were not in doubt, he would not have come to me. So he assumes that I know what is good for him. But I have to be mindful of my own orientation which assumes that a process of psychic development towards his becoming himself (his own inner authority) is possible and, if so, desirable. Therefore we wait and watch what looks like labour pains which come and go: sometimes it seems as if he were ready to leave the bosom of his family and as if sexual attraction to a girl alien to his culture would win the day. Then the tide recedes again, a religious festival comes along and he feels warm and safe within the traditions and under the protection of the goddess he and the family worship fervently. But for how long do we wait and watch, dreams included? Sometimes they seem to speak out of his sexual drive in the foreign direction, but by the same token they also show his incest fear. To use the *I Ching* in these circumstances would not only be likely to result in an answer which could be read in one way or another, but it would also strengthen and add to the many superstitions which he is already subject to. In short, I am saying that before we can speak of rebirth we must have a birth, before we can speak of a struggle between the superego – according to Jung, the moral code – and the self there must be an ego, capable of separation. Without this ego, consciousness will only function according to the meaning that conscience has in Shakespeare's *Hamlet*; making cowards of us all by means of reflection, taking all pros and cons into consideration, but never arriving at that clarity of judgement, which enables a person to act with conviction. Alternatively, if my patient could at least come to a decision based on an ideal shared with the rest of the family (used as ego-ideal), he would then be ready for disillusionments and hence further developments involving separation and becoming an individual.

I want to say that Jung's distinction between what is moral because according to the mores and the genuine conscience, which he calls 'ethical' because it results from the collision of consciousness with a numinous archetype,[19] is clearer in theory than in practice. But I think that it is in the nature of the magic surrounding words, especially technical terms in that they raise our expectations. In the long run, in or out of analysis, the question is whether our actions are based on faith – faith that man's constructive potential is just a little greater than his power to destroy. It is this faith which is in constant need of renewal. Jung's formulations have to be reviewed, since they were made in a relatively stable social environment. Cases like the patient I mentioned are becoming far from exceptional. The confusing thing is that under the guise of uniformity of outer circumstances in various centres of civilization – same food, same clothes, same mores or lack thereof – men are still conditioned by very different traditional influences.

IX. Minor rebirths

Of course it could be said that faith is an even larger cover word than any of the others, but if I were to show how quite small, easily overlooked daily events might contribute to the renewal of it, I could still be justified. I have spoken also about the need for ideals. Even if they lead to dangerous enthusiasms they do spur us into life and activity, followed by the realization of how little can be achieved in terms of fundamental changes: try as we may, we can only become what we are. It may take more than one generation before an ideal changes or is re-discovered and reborn.

There is then a great need to review all these global concepts not only in terms of phases of life, to which Jung drew attention; not only in terms of a concentric in preference to a linear idea of development, but in terms of cycles of much shorter duration. A neglected area is the one which Jung touched on when, as a case of 'hunger afflux', he mentioned a woman whom he had pretty well freed from symptoms until she turned up one day with what looked like a complete relapse. He discovered that she had been so engrossed in a phantasy that she had forgotten to eat her lunch. A glass of milk and a slice of bread successfully restored her.[20] I quote this in order to draw attention to the different ego-states we find ourselves in during a twenty-four-hour cycle. Sleep and hunger are obvious examples but I feel pretty certain that if we were to pay more attention to these individually different cycles and the natural influence they have on our psychology and physiology we could adjust the functioning and feelings of our bodies and minds more harmoniously. Big phrases like 'holding the opposites together' or 'good inner object' may consist of no more than observing these rapidly fluctuating phases. I think that Jung was predisposed by a whole philosophical tradition – as indeed was Freud – to see energy potentials in terms of polarities or 'the opposites'. The duality of his own personality referred to as No. 1 and No. 2 may have increased this tendency, starting with such biological opposites as male and female, birth and death and continuing with concepts of body and soul, conscious-unconscious, *eros-logos*, instinct and spirit, good and evil and many others, all forcing the issue of the third, the reconciling states and symbols. Valid and useful as these concepts are, it seems to me that this emphasis on the Faustian dual personality makes us underestimate the multiplicity of personalities and potential states of existence which can also be experienced. I got that far with my own thoughts when I read in Hermann Hesse's *Steppenwolf*, 'Harry' – the hero's name – 'consists of a hundred or a thousand selves, not of two. His life oscillates, as everyone's does not merely between two poles, such as the body and the spirit, the saint and the sinner, but between thousands, between innumerable poles'. And further:

And if ever the suspicion of their manifold being dawns upon men of unusual powers, so that, as all genius must, they break through the illusion of the unity of their personality and perceive that the self is made up of a bundle of selves, they have only to say so and at once the majority puts them under lock and key, calls science to aid, establishes schizophrenia and protects humanity from the necessity of hearing the cry of truth from the lips of these unfortunate persons.[21]

I do not agree with Hesse's conclusion about schizophrenia and the truth. But when he writes about Yoga as a technique for unmasking the illusion of personality I feel that there may be something in these multiplicities of our states of being which could be proved physiologically and be put to use in psychotherapy. If coming or being together, whole-individual making, is as important as Jung states, then it seems to me essential to start from the true position of one's multiplicities.

I am not yet thinking of adding to the many supposedly health-promoting techniques. Let each person discover what suits him best. The only thing that matters is that these daily minor renewals should be totally free and yet appreciated. Free from utilitarian purposes, leading nowhere in particular and not costing any money. Whether you receive such a minor renewal by talking to a stranger or from observing your breathing is a matter of temperament and opportunity. But don't let us overlook the small, obvious yet unobtrusive daily opportunities for experiencing life afresh. The difficulty in allowing this to happen is our inertia: we want to make sure that anything that is good should last. We think in terms of getting more of it and forget, time and again, that both physiologically and psychologically we are best able to appreciate life in terms of contrasts. The glass of water when thirsty, a bed after not having slept all night, no newspaper or television when there is a strike, a letter from a friend when we feel forgotten – these are the small coinage of daily renewals of which our big conceptual words consist, the doors through which richness can enter when we are low in spirit and lacking in faith.

Now I know very well that in a depressed state of mind these minor rebirths are the last thing we can appreciate. We only want to know how to get out of blackness without having to work through the small steps which make up the day. But could it not also be relevant that the contrasting shades of minor events, if carefully and regularly observed, could act prophylactically? In any case, such observations could promote the discovery of the self in the most practical description which Jung gave of it: 'the greatest *limitation* (italics mine) for man is the self'; it is manifested in the experience: 'I am *only* that!' And further: 'In knowing ourselves to be unique in our personal combination – that is ultimately *limited*, we possess also the capacity for becoming conscious of the infinite. But only then!'[11]

Salient points summarised

Rebirth is one of the leitmotifs in Jung's life and work. As such it is connected with the losing and finding of himself, with the divisions in his personality and the vital need for syntheses. He lived so close to the unconscious forces, which were both a threat to his survival as well as the mainspring of his creative work, that syntheses of various kinds had to be attempted and complete success, the sterilising effect of wholeness or of public acclaim, had to be avoided.

While some syntheses, like the *unus mundus* ideas, are less convincing than others, the following points of what in Jung's work could currently lead to rejuvenation, are stressed:

1. Combining higher education with the artisan's skills.
2. To further partnership between generations by overcoming incest fears and defences.

3. To update Jung's view on conscience by reviewing the apparent distinction between mores and ethos in the light of social changes.

4. To pay attention to minor (daily) rebirths and thereby getting renewed insights into the workings of the self.

CHAPTER 2

The Favourite Fairy-tale
of Childhood

BY HANS DIECKMANN

It is often asked nowadays whether the old-fashioned fairy-tale still has any value or interest for our children. Some people say that it is too magical, too cruel, and that it is not appropriate for our modern technical world. On the other hand many people, in Europe more than in America, passionately defend fairy-tales from their enemies, often because of their own sentimental memories, romantic ideas and devotion to the past.

Meanwhile, quite apart from the controversy, fairy-tales are told by mothers all over the world to their children, and children also hear and read them on other occasions. Most children are fascinated by this magic world of witches, flying carpets, giants, and fairies. Fairy-tales comply in a very special way with the young child's way of experiencing the world. So the fairy-tale still has a certain independence in this struggle between grown-ups for and against its survival.

I have no idea as to what degree fairy-tales are still alive in American nurseries. I have often heard from American friends that stories about Mickey Mouse, Superman or other modern narratives have displaced the old fairy-tale. And I wonder at the great success of such films as Walt Disney's *Snow White*, which comes from the U.S.A. Scientific experiments similar to my own[4-6] have been made in U.S.A. by Karpman on the subject of fairy-tales and script drama analysis.[19] Perhaps one could say that the fairy-tale is surviving but has been driven underground.

Incidentally, one finds that this problem is a very old one. More than 70 years ago the German poet Wilhelm Hauff, who wrote many well-known fairy-tales himself, introduced his book about fairy-tales with the story 'Märchen als Almanach'.[14] In those days of the late 19th century the Almanach played nearly the same role as do the illustrated papers or the popular scientific magazines of today.

In this story Hauff describes how the poor little fairy-tale is displaced from the rationalistic community of mankind and returns crying to her mother, Fantasy. Her mother is very upset about this and also that the people of the world are employing very rationalistic thinking defences to prevent the return of her beloved eldest daughter, the fairy-tale.

She suspects rightly, that the bad aunt, Fashion, has defamed her child. Because she is a creative and imaginative woman she makes for Fairy-Tale a dress, which looks like an Almanach, and in this dress Fairy-Tale is able to return. The guards recognize Fairy-Tale in this dress and laugh at her, but she places all the curious pictures of her stories before the eyes of these guards so that they are bewitched and fall asleep. After that a friendly man takes Fairy-Tale by the hand and leads her to the waiting children.

We know there is a close connection between fairy-tales and dreams. In 1901, one year after Freud's dream-book[11] was published, F. von Leyen wrote a paper entitled 'Dreams and fairy-tales' in which he postulates that the origins of the fairy-tale lie in the narratives of strange dreams, which are told by one generation to the other until at last they become fixed stories.[21]

This process of creating a fairy-tale out of dreams had already been investigated by Paul Heyse in 1889 before the beginning of psychoanalysis.[15] It is natural that psychoanalytical research has always been interested in the identity of motives in dreams and fairy-tales. In 1913 Freud himself published his study 'Märchenstoffe in Träumen', and from his school emerged the work of Abraham,[1] Rank,[25] Fromm[13] and others.

A special interest in these formations of collective human fantasies was stimulated by the work of C.G. Jung and his co-workers, such as v. Franz, v. Beit,[2] Jaffé,[17] Bilz,[3] Laiblin[20] and others. The main subject of these investigations was the existence of striking analogies between the archetypal collective images in fairy-tales and those that were found in the unconscious during analytical therapy. In both cases one finds the symbolization of psychic processes concerning individuation, maturity and development.

There are two possibilities as to how these pictures may arise out of the human soul, so that they are often found in the analysis of grown-up patients. One is that they have been heard or read during childhood and remained alive in the unconscious of the person. The other is that they are created in a particular situation by the autonomy of the unconscious psyche, because they are the best expression of the inner psychic situation at the moment concerned. There are many typical human situations and conflicts and equally typical psychic ways of resolving those situations and conflicts. So it is natural that similar pictures are built up by unconscious fantasy whenever people have to deal with similar human problems.

The same two possibilities also arise in the investigation of fairy-tales themselves. As is well-known, fairy-tales of all cultures, whether they come from India, China, the South Seas, Europe or Africa, will have many almost identical themes. To explain these facts the first theory which was developed was the migration theory; namely, that the fairy-tale originated in one place and migrated afterwards through different peoples and countries. Such migrations are well-known, for example in the great Oriental collections of fairy-tales such as the 1001 Nights, the Pantscha Tantra, the Tuti-Nameh, and so on. Because it was not possible to explain all phenomena by this theory, Taylor and Rank among others later developed the theory of the polygenesis of identical motifs, which is in some respects identical with our own theory of the autogenesis of the same archetypal images.

My interest in the motifs of fairy-tales in dreams was strongly awakened by a particular analytical situation nearly 10 years ago. One of my patients, a 22-year-old girl, suffered from an abasia-astasia syndrome. She could hardly walk and was brought for the first treatment by her mother to my house in a taxi-cab. After sixty analytic sessions the symptom took a slight turn for the better. She told me that now she always had pains in her feet when attempting to walk. We considered that this might be a sign that her legs were beginning to regain normal muscular capacity. Then came a session in which she told me the following dream:

I was standing on a platform with many other people, who were unknown to me. A storm was raging and the platform was in the middle of the sea. An enormous and dangerous wave went over us on the platform, but nobody was injured. Shortly afterwards I was in our kitchen. Outside there was a violent storm and the sea was raging. In our court-yard I saw a red fishing-boat, which was wrecked.

According to the associations of the patient we can understand this dream as a deep emotional movement starting from her unconscious, which goes on to overwhelm the ego-complex and other contents of her conscious mind. This dangerous storm of emotions is coming out of the sea, the symbol of the great mother and the collective unconscious, but in spite of all anxieties the patient is able to withstand this event and to let the emotion flood over her conscious mind without destroying the ego-complex.

Afterwards she is in the kitchen looking from inside on to this stormy scene. The kitchen is a room of transformation, in which the world of nutritional food is transformed from its natural state into edible form. Translated into the categories of the soul the analytical process is doing the same. In this work the archaic contents of the unconscious are transformed into bearable and useful energies.

Finally we have to ask what might be the matter with the red fishing-boat in the court-yard. Obviously this is a content brought out from the unconscious into the view of the ego. This red boat reminded my patient of the favourite fairy-tale of her childhood. It was the mermaid of Hans Andersen, the Danish poet. At a certain period in her life she was deeply impressed by this story and had a lot of fantasies in which she herself was the mermaid. This story and the fantasies had been suppressed later. During this session she could not remember the contents of the fairy-tale, only that there was something about a ship-wrecked prince who was saved by a mermaid. So I told her to read the story again.

In this fairy-tale, right on the bottom of the sea stands the castle of the sea king, in which he lives with his six daughters. They are educated by their grandmother, because their own mother died a long time before. In their fifteenth year the princesses are allowed to rise up to the surface of the sea and to look at the world of human beings and their ships. Mermaids are different from humans in that they are able to remain young for 300 years, but they do not possess an immortal soul. After their death they vanish in the foam of the sea. There is only one possible way for them to obtain an immortal soul: if a man falls in love with one of them so deeply that he will marry her, his soul goes over partly into her body and will give her immortality.

Our heroine is the youngest of the six sisters and has to wait impatiently for the great day of her fifteenth birthday. At last it comes and she rises to the surface decorated with the royal jewellery of six oysters fixed into her tail. There she sees a fine ship in which a young prince is having his own birthday party. During the night a storm comes up and the ship runs aground. The mermaid saves the prince, brings him to the beach and hidden behind high waves she sees him found by a young girl.

From this moment on she loves the prince and every day she swims near his castle. At last she decides to go to the sea-witch, hoping that she will help her to get human legs instead of a tail. After a dangerous journey through a bewitched forest on the sea-bed, she stands before the sea-witch. The price for getting human legs is very high. She has to give up her tongue, and furthermore every step with her new legs will cause her great pain, like going barefoot over sharp knives.

The mermaid does everything the witch demands and after being given her human legs she goes to the castle of her prince. She is not able to speak, but her capacity to dance in spite of her pain enchants everyone including the prince. A short time later the prince has to marry the princess of a neighbouring country, who is the same girl who found him on the beach. He falls in love with her, and the marriage takes place. So all the mermaid's pains have been in vain.

On the way back to the prince's country the mermaid is on board the ship together with the prince and his young wife. During the night her sisters appear swimming around the ship, and they offer her a knife, given to them by the witch. If she were to stab the prince and his blood ran over her feet, she would get her fishtail back again and live for 300 years. She cannot decide for a long time whether or not to kill the sleeping prince, but at last her love wins. She flings the knife into the sea and at sunrise she throws herself overboard. But like most other fairy-tales, this one also has a happy ending. Our mermaid does not turn into sea-foam, but is transformed into a daughter of the air. These fairies are able to acquire immortal souls by doing good things over a period of 300 years.

Coming to the next session my patient (and I also) had re-read this fairy-tale and re-experienced a lot of the old fantasies she had had around the story. She was very excited and fascinated by this experience because she herself had also recognized some analogies with her way of life and her illness. In her illness she, like the mermaid, was not able to walk on earth and now, when she made her first steps again, she had the same pains.

A very important point was also that her symptoms had begun in a situation very similar to the one in Andersen's fairy-tale. At that time she loved a young man, who lived in a small town far away. She had made his acquaintance during a holiday she had spent there. It was only a short romance, and as she was very shy she could hardly speak to him during this time. This was not the least important reason that the young man did not wish to marry her and he broke with her after some time. It was then she got her symptoms. One could say that she was already during her friendship with this man a little like the nymph of the fairy-tale, in that she could not speak, but after he left her she changed even more completely into this figure.

There were also many analogies with the fairy-tale concerning her patterns of behaviour and the genetic aspects of her childhood. For example, she too was educated only by women (mother and grandmother) because there had been deep quarrels between her parents, who had separated during her early years. However, I do not intend to go deeper into this single case report, but only wish to draw attention to another aspect.

As I have already stated, the patient was very excited and fascinated in seeing by herself the profound connection between this fairy-tale, her fate, and her neurosis. So during the following analytical sessions we worked through this material with excellent effect. The symptom of abasia–astasia nearly disappeared and further analysis resulted in favourable progress. The growing consciousness of her old favourite fairy-tale and the connections between this story, her childhood, her later fate, her patterns of behaviour and her patterns of inner experience were obviously very strong therapeutic factors.

After this experience my own interest was naturally concentrated on ascertaining whether such favourite fairy-tales could be found in other patients and what form of relationship existed between these old stories, the symptoms of a later neurosis, the structure of the personality and the patterns of behaviour. I was also interested in the therapeutic factor, the phenomena of synchronicity between fate and fairy-tale and the connection with the genetic factor.

The material I was able to collect during the next few years is based on about 50 long-term analyses. Such a favourite fairy-tale could be found in the unconscious of most of the patients I treated over a long period. Not all of them have been common fairy-tales. There were a lot of not so well-known ones from Andersen, Hauff, Brentano and others, and also, though seldom, stories from modern children's books like *Winnie-the-Pooh*, *Alice in Wonderland*, and so on. In most cases this material was more or less repressed in the unconscious.

If you ask the patient during the first session you usually get one of the common traditional fairy-tales remembered at that moment, such as Cinderella, Snow-White and the Seven Dwarfs, or Little Red Riding Hood, as the investigations of Wittgenstein have shown.[26] The really individual favourite fairy-tale will emerge from the unconscious for the first time after some regression into the early childhood has taken place. Sometimes a dream symbol will give the first hint of it, sometimes the associations of the patient during a certain period of childhood. To my own astonishment this material was very individualistic. Among the 50 patients the same tales have been found only two or three times.

It is hardly surprising that one should find, at least in most European patients, a favourite fairy-tale from childhood. As a rule, such tales are among the earliest cultural products taken up by the human soul. In this way the typical imaginings of the culture can be assimilated and the structures of the archetype *per se* filled out with forms and pictures. On the other hand the main fairy-tale period of childhood is also the time when fundamental neurotic patterns are formed and the first neurotic symptoms come into existence. So we may have here a very important point: that the fairy-tale can tell us something about the basic structure and dynamics of the individual neurosis. It may also show us the organization of ideas and experiences of archetypal forms.[7] The partial or total identification of the ego with an archetypal image as the nuclear charge of a complex is one of the principal criteria of neurosis.

On the other hand the healthy ego-complex will only have such identifications in a passing way.[16] So it is reasonable that we should also find such fixed identifications if the favourite fairy-tales of childhood return to consciousness during the course of analytical treatment. In practice one finds in this way many comparisons between the themes or symbols of the fairy-tale and the symptoms of neurosis. I should like now to give further examples of this process.

Two other women patients who also had the mermaid story as their favourite fairy-tale had frigidity as the principal symptom of their neurosis. A ten-year-old boy with a compulsive neurosis had the symptom of breaking through closed windows with his hands. His favourite fairy-tale was the Bremer Stadtmusikanten, in which a couple of beasts overwhelm a house of robbers in the woods by breaking in through the window.

A female patient told me that she had suffered all her childhood from sleep-walking. When I asked her what her favourite fairy-tale had been she did not remember, but she asked her mother. A short time later she told me, half-laughing and half-thoughtfully, that it was Peterchen's Journey to the Moon.

A patient with a phobia against frogs, so severe that she could not even touch the toy frog of her little daughter, was most of all fascinated by the story of the Frog-King. Sometimes the connection between the figure of a fairy-tale and the neurotic symptom is very curious: a patient with the favourite tale of 'Red Riding Hood' had an erythrophobia.

The relationships between the symptom and the hero of the fairy-tale lead to the conclusion that unconscious parts of the ego with its patterns of behaviour and the structure of the patient's character are fixed in the specific pattern of the fairy-tale. This fixation can go on until it penetrates to very deep similarities in the experiences of life, the 'Welterleben', and the fate of the person. In longer case reports, which I have published previously, these similarities may be studied more exactly. Here I can only give a brief instance.

A 29-year-old woman patient came for analytical treatment because she suffered from such strong fears that she had to run away in the face of all difficulties and problems, as she said herself.

She had lost all contacts with other people and suffered from schizoid experiences like being behind a glass wall. Her nervousness and tension had been so severe that she had been unable to sleep for four years without sleeping pills. Her favourite fairy-tale, which she told me after three months of treatment, was 'The Red Shoes' of Hans Andersen:

Once upon a time there was a little girl called Karen, who was so poor that she always had to go barefoot. When her mother died, a good-hearted shoemaker gave her a pair of old red shoes. A little later a rich old widow in a noble carriage visited the village. She adopted the girl but she did not like the red shoes and threw them into the fire.

Karen grew up and became a beauty and one day the king was in the town in which she now lived: his daughter, the princess, had a pair of wonderful red shoes. Now came the day of Karen's confirmation and she was to be given a new dress and new shoes. The shoemaker had one pair of red shoes which Karen desired and because the stepmother was too old to see properly she got hold of these. But when Karen came into the church all the people looked at her shining red shoes and whispered about them, and so the old lady noticed them and forbade Karen to wear them.

Next Sunday was Lord's Supper and Karen after some indecision at last chose to wear the red shoes again in spite of the old lady. An old soldier was sitting in front of the church that day. When he saw the red shoes, he said: 'What a beautiful pair of dancing shoes. They shall be fastened on your feet and you shall dance with them forever'. Karen went into the church. She could not think of anything other than her red shoes and about dancing and she forgot to say the Lord's prayer.

After leaving the church she could not help trying some dancing steps and from that moment on the shoes began to dance on their own. They danced with Karen through the streets, out of the town, into the woods, over the fields and meadows. She could not get rid of her shoes, and she danced day and night.

While she danced in a churchyard an angel told her: 'You shall dance and dance in your red shoes till you become pale and old, and all arrogant and vain children shall hear about you and have fear'. So Karen danced away for more days and nights. One night she came to a house, where the public executioner was living, and begged him to cut off her feet with the red shoes. The shoes with her feet in them danced away, and the executioner made a pair of crutches for Karen. She went to a parsonage and became a maid there and worked in silence, modesty and diligence. But she could never go into the church again because if she tried to do so she found her red shoes dancing before the door of the church.

After many years the angel returned while she was reading a holy book. He touched the walls and the ceiling with a branch of roses and suddenly she was watching the church, the priest and his congregation. When she heard the organ and the clear voices of the children, her soul flew upwards to God.

You see already that we find again in this fairy-tale the symptoms of our patient mentioned earlier. She always has to run away, she is not able to sleep during the night and she is deeply depressed because she is cut off from an important side of her life. But here I must give a brief report of the life history of this patient.

She was born in 1939 in Berlin as the second of three sisters. Shortly after her birth the father, a bank clerk, was drafted and did not return from a Russian prison camp until 1948. To my patient he was a complete stranger, who broke into the family and took over all the power which her mother had before. She hated him, because he was a hard man, who often beat the children. We may have here the first analogy to the fairy-tale, in which the little girl is living with her poor mother only, and as in the fairy-tale the family of my patient was very poor.

During the time her father was a prisoner-of-war, her mother had to do menial work to earn a living: she had to make mail bags as though she were a prisoner herself. When the father came home, he was not allowed to work in his old profession, because he had been a member of the Nazi party. He had to take a job as a labourer. A little later he became an alcoholic, his strength was broken, and he never managed to get back to his old profession. One can probably see a symbolic death of the mother, when the father came back and ruled the family. At least that was in some way the inner experience of my patient.

About two years later, when my patient was 12 years old, a sister of the father, who was married in West Germany and well-to-do, came to Berlin. She had lost her two sons during the war, and asked her brother to give her one of his children. Because they were very poor, and had no hope for the future, the father was rather glad about this offer, and my patient became the child of 'the old lady, who came in the noble carriage'. This is a very striking analogy, because the girl in the fairy-tale was also 12 years old. I will return to this point later.

In the following years my patient lived with her aunt in a very small German town in a puritanical atmosphere. At 16 she was allowed to learn dancing, and during this time she met her first boy-friend. Nobody was allowed to know this, and she always had to tell a lot of lies to meet him. In her inner experience, dancing and erotic and sexual feelings had been closely linked. The last-mentioned were certainly strictly forbidden. If she had such sexual feelings she felt waves of fear. So she told me: 'I always had dreadful fears and feelings of guilt if I heard or felt something of this drive. It seems to me so absolute and so dominant in this situation that I'm not able to do the things I want to do.' We may add here: like the red shoes, dancing away with the girl.

Later, she told me: 'I have cut off all sexual pleasure, and I always try to avoid emotions because in every case it brought complications and made me very unhappy.' Because this area of her life was always suppressed, it never could be ruled or governed by the ego-complex and remained in the state of a wild horse. If she came into a specific situation in which she could not preserve her equilibrium, she had to break away and could not stop dancing and dancing whether it was with men, with alcohol, with sleeping pills, or similar things. She had to love, drink, and eat until she exhausted herself.

When she began analytical treatment, she had cut off all expansion in her life, doing only her work and living the rest of her time like a prisoner in a dark and narrow room. She lived like the girl at the end of the fairy-tale, only for her work and always sitting alone in her room. There is one further striking analogy with the end of the fairy-tale. As the reader will probably know, many of the fairy-tales of Hans Christian Andersen have a mystic, spiritual end like this one. For example, in the story about the mermaid the nymph finally joins the daughters of the air and lives as a sylph for 300 years, finally to be given a human soul.

I would say that we find in these images a problem of Andersen himself: he also suffered from serious depressions and found an outlet in his creative faculty. He also became to some extent a spirit of the air by working his fantasies and depressions into his famous fairy-tales. My patient tried to find the same outlet. She wrote stories and poems, very good ones, which were also printed, but nevertheless they were not sufficient to compensate for her suffering. She also tried to reach the real and not only the symbolic end of the fairy-tale, always wanting to die and trying to commit suicide.

On the other hand she sometimes had the aforementioned breakdowns. Then, as she said, she was not herself, but her cellar-child in the red shoes came out of the depth of her unconscious and danced with her.

I would like now to come back to the point that my patient was exactly 12 years old, like the girl in the fairy-tale, when she had to leave her parents and was given away to the aunt. The patient knew for certain that the story of the girl with the red shoes was her favourite fairy-tale before she was 12 years old and before she knew anything of her future fate. Her mother told her this fairy-tale when she was 6 to 8 years old. After she joined her aunt, she was never interested in, nor read, any fairy-tales. It seems that her soul had in some way a presentiment of her future life.

I found nearly the same in other cases. There was a woman patient whose favourite fairy-tale was Rapunzel of the Grimm brothers. In this fairy-tale the girl Rapunzel was shut up in a tower by a witch when she was twelve, and held there as a captive. When my patient was 12 years old, her beloved father died. He was an extroverted man with a good sense of reality. Her mother, on the contrary, was an introverted type, with pathological anxiety, deeply involved with a compulsive neurosis. When her father died the patient came completely under the influence of this anxious mother and was cut off from all possibilities of expansion. One may really say that she was incarcerated in a tower of fears and anxieties. In this case too the favourite fairy-tale was familiar to the patient long before the twelfth year of life.[9]

It could be argued that these analogies arise only by mere accident, and that by identification and projection a situation is created in the *Umwelt*, which complies with the structure of the myth. The soul of the patient reacts to it again with corresponding archetypal inner experiences.[7] But that is not entirely satisfactory. We are only able to understand these phenomena according to the conception of the *Unus mundus*[18] or the *Einheitswirklichkeit* of Erich Neumann[23] in which the archetype is just as much psychic image as part of reality in the world, and the two together may in certain situations bring about a synchronization. Psychic and extra-psychic belong here together like key and lock, and the unity of psychic man and cosmos comes to light. The experience of these phenomena of synchronization in connection with the particular favourite fairy-tale is of great therapeutic value. It can give the patient a deep inner feeling of the order of this world, and is able to open the way to an experience of the self and the sense of life.

I will now finally make some comments on the therapeutic value of all these fairy-tales in analysis. The process has already begun with the first emergence of these motifs out of the unconscious. This may be in a dream or in associations. In this state the forgotten or wrongly recalled motifs are often more important than those remembered. A typical example of this was a patient who was at the age of 10 fascinated by the 'Snow Queen', also by Andersen.

She believed at first that it was a boy in this fairy-tale who went out to liberate his sister. She was very astonished when she re-read the story and found out that the contrary was true: it was a *girl* who went out to search for her brother. In her mistake there was on the one hand the wish not to be a woman but a man, which came to consciousness in her subsequent dreams; on the other hand there was the problem of her brother-animus (she also had a younger brother in reality) which had suppressed her female independence.

Most of my patients have been fascinated by this spontaneously obtained material and have begun to work it through during the sessions which followed the emergence. From the analyst's side it is, naturally, treated like an archetypal dream. The figures and motifs have to be amplified by analogies, which give to the patient an insight into the hidden or secret meaning of his fairy-tale in his life and his fate. It is not only necessary to make the patient realize that he has identified himself with the hero of a fairy-tale, but it is also not less important that he understands something of the meaning of his figure and its different manifestations in myth and history. Here the favourite fairy-tale is at an advantage over an archetypal dream because it is nearer to consciousness and has a stronger personal meaning. So there is less danger that in the process of amplification a lack of reality is brought about.

It is important that not only the ego-complex should be resolved out of the identification with male or female hero of the fairy-tale, but also all of the other figures and motifs should be understood on the subjective level as personifications of a patient's own unconscious complexes. In the overwhelming majority of analytical treatments the fairy-tale disappeared after a few hours of intensive analytical work. On the other hand patient and analyst in most cases come back to this material in specific situations until the end of treatment and this constant 'working-through' at last leads the patient to see the figures as a part of the non-ego, and the patient becomes able to differentiate his ego from the pathologically fixed identifications. During this process the method of active imagination can be very helpful. Many patients draw pictures or model their problems in clay.

It seems to me that a real understanding on the symbolic level of the solution of the problem in the fairy-tale is of great importance also for the analyst. All fairy-tales include individuation processes as is shown by many authors (v. Franz,[10] v. Beit,[2] Jaffé,[17] Laiblin[20] and others) and they show in a symbolic form different ways of psychic growth and progress. So it may be possible to translate the tales in a behaviouristic way and to understand them on the objective level. This will lead to complications, because in this case the analyst will unconsciously accept the identification of the patient's ego with the image of the archetype.

I will give an example. A female analyst, who was still in training, was treating a 10-year-old boy with enuresis nocturna. His favourite fairy-tale was 'The ugly duckling'. In this tale a swan grows up in a family of ducks. The patient was a very nice and intelligent boy with a lot of interesting fantasies. On the other hand his father and mother had many neurotic features in their characters. So the analyst began to understand her patient as a swan, who was not understood by narrow-minded parents, the small-minded duck family. And at this point further progress in treatment stopped, because the problem of this lonely and anxious boy was to find some possibility of contact and understanding either with his mother or his father and not to separate even more from them, by seeing his parents as poorly qualified ducks and himself as a swan. The problem could be solved only by understanding the fairy-tale figures on the subjective level. Thus the swan is here the ego growing out of its formerly too narrow position and obtaining another view of the world. In my experience the main problem has always been the taking back of projections and their understanding as a part of the patient's personality.

In this chapter I have been able to give only a short review of the problems and possibilities one may find in the favourite fairy-tales from childhood. There may also be much wisdom in these old stories which we do not understand even today, and the words of Scheherazade in 1001 Nights are surely true, when she says: 'Oh King, these stories are full of secret meanings which will be understood only by the wise and initiated man.'

CHAPTER 3

Jung as Dialectician and Teleologist

BY JOSEPH F. RYCHLAK

When a truly great thinker comes on the historical scene it is likely that those of us who study him will be moved by what he has to say, and instructed in some basic way to think otherwise than we did before reading his works. We may not agree with all that he says and our understanding of what he has communicated is not necessarily complete. But he will have an effect on us in some way. Carl Gustav Jung has had such an impact on my own development as theoretician, in that he has given me the support and assurance to see human nature in ways that are not widely accepted in current academic circles. We American psychologists are brought up to think of Jung as a mystic, as someone who had so enmeshed himself in esoteric writings that no one but a classical scholar could really understand him, much less hope to apply his image of humanity to the everyday world of affairs.

My own studies of Jung failed to support this erroneous view, drawn no doubt by psychologists who had either not read Jung, or misunderstood what little they did read of him. My fascination with Jung did not stem from his more widely cited theoretical constructs, such as the collective unconscious or the archetypes. I was not even converted to the specifics of his personality theory (i.e. I would not call myself 'a' Jungian). Coming to Jung with my own thinking already underway on the nature of personality, I was struck how, here and there, betwixt and between his other topics Jung was portraying exactly the image of humanity which I had felt for some time was being entirely missed by modern psychology. Freud and Adler were capturing aspects of this image in other terminology as well, but they were not so aware of what they contended as was Jung. He seems clearly to have been the most sophisticated of the classical analysts when it came to issues of theory-construction, to an understanding of how his ideas related to the broader issues of theorizing in philosophy and the sciences.

The essentials of the human image which Jung was capturing relate to what has for centuries been termed dialectics, dialectical logic, dialectical reasoning, or simply as 'the' dialectic in the descent of knowledge.[1] Furthermore, and most importantly, Jung captured the vital link which dialectics has with the problem of how we can – and I feel, must – conceptualize human behavior in telic or teleological descriptions. There are some technical problems which we must work out, particularly in the realm of unconscious behaviors of a telic nature, but for those psychologists who have been searching for a humanistic (i.e. non-mechanistic) approach to the description of behavior, Jung provides all the necessary ingredients. Before we can trace his contribution to the proper and correct image of human behavior we must first get clearly in mind what teleological description and the dialectic refer to. We turn first of all to a consideration of how teleology relates to the choice of causal description which the theorist employs in his or her explanations.

Causation and Telic Description

The first accounts of nature made by ancient theoreticians were quaintly anthropomorphic descriptions. Nature was made up of human-like gods and demi-gods having intentions, moods of vengeance or lust, hopeful aspirations, and so forth. Philosophy and thereby science is often said to have begun when Thales of Miletus and his student, Anaximander, began giving accounts of nature in terms of the basic 'stuff' which presumably made it up – water or the 'boundless' as their respective views expressed it. Heraclitus and Parmenides raised the issue of change, of whether anything really happened in this world of days and nights, and thus brought forward a concern with the flow of events, the impetus or thrust of something occurring first making something second 'happen'. Heraclitus was also instrumental in bringing another notion to the fore, dealing with the *logos* or *Rationale* by which events flowed. The movement of events over time was patterned into a rational order which was not happenstance. Based on this precedent belief Democritus was later to say that there was no such thing as 'chance' in the universe for everything is subject to patterned laws. Lastly, Socrates had in his discussion of ethics referred to the fact that human beings behaved 'for the sake of' an end (*telos*) which they intentionally tried to bring about (arrive at, create, achieve, and so on) because it was desirable to do so.

Aristotle was to take these conceptual models of substance, impetus, pattern, and intention and combine them into his profoundly influential theory of knowledge known as the 'four causes'. Aristotle's preferred word for cause was *aitiá*, which has the meaning of 'responsibility for' that which exists or is taking place. In describing the nature of anything Aristotle thus believed that we would be trying to capture what is responsible for its existence or occurrence. We might even say that the causes are four descriptive models which thinkers in all types of intellectual endeavor have used to make sense of their areas of interest (see Rychlak[2] for a table listing constructs from over a hundred great Western thinkers, broken down according to the causal meanings).

What are these 'four causes'? The first Aristotle called the *material* cause, which is tantamount to Thales' and Anaximander's attribution of a pervasive substance to the world. We characterize 'things' made of flesh differently from things made of stone or snow. Another cause of anything is how it came to be through assembly or creation. Human beings develop physiologically through an expenditure of physical energy in chemico-biological terms. They grow. Houses and the furniture which they contain are assembled by skilful hands, either directly or through the mediation of machines which have themselves been assembled and made to 'run.' This motile assembly and moving of events Aristotle termed the *efficient* cause, and we can see here the matter of flux and change which so fascinated Parmenides and Heraclitus. Events change, things get done, some form of energic propulsion seems evident in the flow of events. People, houses, and furniture also take on patterned hence recognizable patterns. We know a human being by his or her shape, which differs from that of an ostrich or antelope. Indeed, we distinguish man from woman on similar grounds. Chairs look more like chairs than they look like kitchen tables or television sets. This usage, drawn from the *logos* or *Rationale* conceptions of Heraclitus and Democritus, Aristotle termed the *formal* cause.

It is important to appreciate that Aristotle did not think it advisable to limit the number of causes one might use in describing the nature of anything. It is possible to have formless substances, as in a 'blob' of mud, and we can even think of formless movements, such as the impact of a breeze which wafts against our face. But mud can be shaped and baked into statues or dinnerware, and breezes can be elevated and patterned into an easily recognizable tornado cloud. In like fashion, Aristotle believed, the enlightened physicist can bring to bear more and more causes to enrich his account of natural events. Indeed, Aristotle would not have believed a complete rendering of something in nature had been achieved until we had captured the purpose of that which was under descriptive analysis. What is the purpose of flesh, snow, different life forms, the construction of a house, and so on? This notion of a purpose or an intentional side to description and explanation was called the *final* cause by Aristotle. Taking the phraseology of Socrates-Plato, Aristotle defined the final cause as 'that for the sake of which' something exists, is happening, or is about to take place. We can think of it as the reason for such circumstances. The 'sake' for which a house is constructed – its reason for existing – might be termed 'human comfort and protection' or some such.

Of course, the house does not *itself* decide to 'come about' or 'to be'. It is the human being who obtained the wood (material cause) and built it (efficient cause) according to a blueprint (formal cause) organized to meet his aspirations for a shelter (final cause) who may be said to have a purpose or intention in his behavior. Aristotle was not above adding-in such final-cause terms to his description of what today we call 'inanimate nature'. For example, in his *Physics*, Aristotle theorized that leaves exist for the purpose of providing shade for the fruit on trees, and he concluded thereby 'that nature is a cause, a cause that operates for a purpose'.[3] Though mythological thinking had been dropped, the use of the final cause gave Aristotelian explanations a certain coloring – a coloring known as *telic* or *teleological* description (from the Greek word *telos* which means 'goal' or the 'end' for the sake of which it is assumed events are aiming). In this instance of leaves and fruit Aristotle was proposing a natural teleology, but of course it was a short step to the deity teleology for if there is a purpose (design) in nature then it is easy to believe that there is a designer, an intender who is aiming to bring these ends about. Strictly human teleologies need not be predicated on either a natural or a deity teleology. That is, it would be possible for human beings to be telic in a world which is not designed and put under way by a deity, or, in which there is no built-in purpose of a natural variety.

The historical fact, however, is that the early philosophers, many of whom were theologians, mixed in a deity teleology with their image of human behavior as also telic. It was the mixing of teleology with explanations of the origin and nature of the universe which was to bring down the wrath of natural science on this style of explanation. That is, the churchmen on through the Middle Ages continued to reason teleologically, which resulted in a deity teleology rather than simply a natural or human teleology. A common tactic used was the 'argument from definition', in which the theologian asked 'What did God intend when He . . . ' or 'What is the intention of this natural act, as created by God?' This emphasis on formal causality (God's plan) and final causality ('that for the sake of which' He intentionally created) was to place restraints on the empiricists who might dare to contradict the assumptive understandings of nature which the theologians had arrived at. Granting that humanity could surmise God's intention (Divine Plan) it followed 'by definition' that what Scriptures taught us was true. Hence, the geocentric theory of the universe became a God-inspired dogma, which, when contradicted by the empirical studies and proofs of the heliocentric theory resulted in a clash of science and religion from which we have yet to recover in Western history. The unfortunate house arrest and recantation of Galileo has since been a symbol of the evils which teleology fosters in scientific accounts.

   Thanks to the subsequent rise of British Empiricistic Philosophy, with special assistance from the writings of Sir Francis Bacon,[4] it was not long as history is measured before the suitability of final-cause description in science was challenged and then dropped – or, more properly, moved over to the realm of metaphysics. As 'natural' scientists, Bacon argued, we are not at liberty to speak of a rationality 'for the sake of which' leaves shaded the fruit on trees or bones held up the muscles of bodies. Though we can speak of such planful ends in metaphysical discourses, as rigorous empiricists we must explain things in *only* material and/or efficient cause terms – even if this means reducing our descriptive concepts below what they seem to be like in the natural form seen by the eye. In other words, even the formal-cause factor in understanding can be brought down to the underlying substances and energic forces which go to make up these recognizable patterns.

   The mechanistic account of nature begins right here, in the unwillingness which the emerging scientists of the seventeenth century had to explain their observed regularities in anything but material-cause and efficient-cause terms. This works well enough for inanimate nature. The universe may well be an intricate system of interlocking mechanical laws without aim, fortuitously balanced into a viable combination 'by chance'. But does this ideology hold equally well for human behavior? Bacon and most of the budding natural scientists of the seventeenth and eighteenth centuries did not consider themselves to be framing rules for a *human* science. They in general retained a theological faith encompassing final causation in regard to their own natures. But when psychology came on the scene in the nineteenth and early twentieth centuries a new development took place, for now a claim was being made that science was indeed describing the behavior not simply of stars and tides and digestive juices or circulating blood, but of the mind as well. Freud, Adler, and Jung as well as the other psychoanalysts participated in this claim. They thought of themselves as more than simply healers. Psychoanalysis and its offshoots was presented as a *science* of mind. If this was so, where did the analysts stand on causation and the telic form of description? Before taking this matter up we must consider another important aspect of the rise of natural science.

Dialectical versus Demonstrative Conceptions

There is another pair of terms which we can credit Aristotle with having first clearly opposed, although the concepts themselves are just as ancient as the causal meanings. There are two ways in which we can draw this distinction, each of which comes at the central contrast from slightly different angles. First of all, we can come at the issue from the point of view of human reasoning. It was Aristotle who first framed the well-known steps of logical reasoning known as the syllogism, which begins in the major premise (e.g. all men are mortal), continues through an affirmation in the minor premise (this is a man), and ends sequaciously in the conclusion (therefore, this is a mortal). It seemed obvious to Aristotle that the crucial factor in this logical ordering of meanings was the accuracy or inaccuracy of the original (major) premise. That is, although we might make logical mis-steps in our chain of reasoning from initial premise to conclusion, this kind of error could be cleared up through a proper re-analysis. But if our major premise contains erroneous meaning relations (e.g. all men are hostile) then even if from there on we reason soundly ('logically') we can nevertheless arrive at an incorrect conclusion.

Aristotle's immediate philosophical forefathers – Socrates and Plato – had embraced a style of coming to know truth termed the dialectic or the dialectical method. In the Dialogues, for example, we see Socrates posing questions for students to answer. If a student chose position A, Socrates defended not-A; if the student chose not-A, Socrates defended A: for it was he believed *all the same*. Truth and error interlaced oppositionally (dialectically), so that no matter where the participants in a dialogue positioned themselves, in time through dialectical discourse they could weed-out the error and come to know its opposite – i.e. truth! Socrates did not feel that he was skilfully and deviously manipulating (or controlling) the flow of a student's thought in asking his questions. He would have considered this sophistry. We erroneously interpret him as sophistical today because Plato's written account of the dialectical method in the Dialogues makes it appear that we are reading a cybernetic program. Socrates never wrote a book precisely because he did not believe that knowledge could be recorded 'univocally' in this fashion. Two men, each of whom had 'potential knowledge' within their capabilities, had to bring reason to bear in discussion in order to create knowledge dialectically.

Aristotle believed that dialecticians were more likely to fall into the trap of beginning in major premises which were erroneous than a thinker who started on firmer ground. He proposed a distinction in reasoning be drawn as follows:

Now reasoning is an argument in which, certain things being laid down, something other than these necessarily comes about through them. (a) It is a 'demonstration', when the premises from which the reasoning starts are true and primary, or are such that our knowledge of them has originally come through premises which are primary and true: (b) reasoning, on the other hand, is 'dialectical', if it reasons from opinions that are generally accepted.[3]

Thus, in the first approach to the question of what we now appreciate is the 'dialectical versus demonstrative' distinction in reasoning, we have a question relating to how basic or major premises, predications, groundings, assumptions, and so on are arrived at by the reasoner. Are they accepted based upon the *opinion* of a fellow participant in discourse, or are they based more certainly on *primary and true* considerations? By 'primary and true' Aristotle meant either a tautological premise which one uses in defining terms, such as 'all bachelors are unmarried males', or a statement which has been empirically established as fact, such as 'it is raining outside'. The dialectical course of reasoning is not tied down by such 'reality' considerations, particularly since it is usually employed when our most basic assumptions are brought into question, and there is no way possible in which to settle things empirically. Even Aristotle agreed that in such instances, when empirical evidence cannot resolve the issue, we all become dialectical reasoners and defend our position to the verge of sophistry and beyond if necessary.

The second way in which to approach the dialectical versus demonstrative distinction is to focus on the 'meaning of meaning'. To reason is to interrelate meaningful ties in some patterned fashion, captured for us by Aristotle's syllogism or more generally in the concept of 'association of ideas'. It is possible to look at the nature of the relational tie between items of experience known as meaning in two contrasting ways. We can view this as an associative bonding of independent, unipolar units or we can see in certain meanings a bipolar designation from the outset – i.e. even before anything 'gets associated' together. Nouns carry the unipolar designations well, because we can relate definite attributes to the definitions of things like trees or houses. The word tree can be viewed as a compendium of unipolar 'givens' such as leaves, bark, roots, and so on. None of these items in the definition necessarily implies the others. But our more evaluative and orienting language terms are likely to be bipolar in intonation so that, for example, one cannot really define 'up' without necessarily defining 'down' in the process, 'good' defines 'evil', and 'dominance' necessarily defines 'submissive' – and *vice versa*! Each of these latter meanings intend their opposite and really *cannot* be thought of singularly unless we change the core meaning intended. As dialectical conceptions they bear more on the relational than on the solitary features of language.

We now appreciate that the demonstrative interpretation of meaning places emphasis on the association of unipolar designations which stand basically clear of each other, but which can be tied together associatively. As such singular 'units' (items, terms, words, concepts, and so on) combine into richer associative ties they take on a hierarchical arrangement. Contradictory meaning relations do not intend each other 'by definition' but are rather brought together in an 'unnatural' pattern because of the functioning of a supposed 'law of contradiction'. This law holds that 'A is not not-A'. Opposites are separate and distinct. On the other side of the ledger, the dialectical interpretation of meaning holds that at least certain associative ties in language and reason have been bipolar from the outset of understanding. Rather than a law of contradiction the dialectical interpretation perceives meanings as naturally interlacing into an over-all pattern of 'one and many' or 'many in one' without regard for contradiction. This thesis provided the rationale for the Socratic dialogue, because rather than empty 'opinion' Socrates took the beginning views of a fellow-discussant as a starting point to truth. Even if the discussion began in this discussant's error it could end in truth via oppositional, dialectical analysis (refer above). Rather than hierarchical, the dialectical conception of a 'body' of knowledge is as a complex pattern. The demonstrative pattern of meaning 'emerges' from the elemental factors making it up hierarchically 'from below' in constitutive fashion. The dialectical pattern of meaning is conceptually 'there' (or given) from the outset of meaning-extension in knowledge creation, lending its order 'from above' rather than being constituted from below.

In British philosophy we have the Lockean, constitutive model of mind being propounded in which it was assumed that simple ideas which have been ordered in reality and thence etched upon the *tabula-rasa* mentality 'total up' to increasingly complex ideas depending on the frequency and contiguity of past associations over the person's life span. There is no clear role for intention on this model, since decisions occur based on the resultant probabilities of such past 'input' influences.[5] On the European mainland, Kantian interpretations of mind held that the reasoning intelligence – thanks to certain *pro-forma* conceptions native to the understanding – brought order to experience rather than taking it in 'ready made' from experience. The Heraclitian logos was not 'out there' but 'in here'. Moreover, the bi-polarity of meaning was retained in the Kantian model of mind thanks to the operation of what was called the transcendental dialectic.[6] That is, in the very act of affirming premises (major, minor, and so on) the individual is always cognizant of being able in principle to 'turn the tables', rise above the arguments and even dictates of reality and question, challenge, or defend the opposite of any or all meanings under affirmation – going against 'reason' or 'logic' itself, if so inclined!

It is this distinctive contrast between a Lockean and Kantian image of human mentation which was to divide – and continues to divide – descriptions of behavior in psychology.[2] Though experimental psychology was founded in continental Europe, the British Lockean model was embraced initially and forcefully by the founding fathers of experimental psychology, namely Helmholtz and Wundt (the former embracing more zealously than the latter). In America, the functionalist and then behaviouristic schools which are still dominant today were adamantly Lockean in outlook. By taking over the 'natural science' approach and applying it to descriptions of human behaviour American academic psychology has consistently painted human behavior as fundamentally an efficient-cause succession of demonstrative events, which become through frequency and contiguity of past associations or inputs organized into hierarchies of response, mediated into complexities without the benefits of telic direction. Modern 'cognitive' psychology gives increasing weight to the formal-cause and even employs terms like 'construction of input stimuli', which lead many today to believe it has solved the problems of teleology by such pseudo-Kantian expressions. However, as I have shown in detail elsewhere, because it lacks a final-cause meaning modern cognitive psychology like its behaviouristic progenitor simply fails to capture the fundamental meanings of telic description[1,2].

Looking back at my formal education, steeped as my coursework was in the traditions of behaviourism, I do not know how I could ever have arrived at an understanding of what it might mean to say that human beings are psychologically free – have what we are taught from childhood is our 'free will' – to behave in a self-initiated, responsible fashion. So far as my undergraduate classroom instructors were concerned, this was either an impossibility or something which only philosophers could touch upon. In graduate school I had the good fortune of meeting a few instructors who were at least open to the examination of something besides stimulus–response, behaviouristic psychology. It was in one such course that I for the first time read Jung's original writings. I was at first somewhat hesitant, having heard that Jung was going to be 'mystical' in his theories, but before long I became excited over his use of terms and the image of behavior which they suggested. I do not refer here so much to his premiere concepts but rather to the supporting terminology and the conceptualization of behavior they made possible. Unlike Freud, whom I found to be easily intimidated by the charge of being a teleologist[7] or who seemed inordinately puzzled by the dialectical construct,[8] Jung was secure in his telic formulations of mind and marvelously clear on the importance of dialectical conceptions in the understanding of human nature.

As I traced Jung's developing ideas on the psyche I was – at first unknowingly – being educated in the essentials of what I now believe to be the correct image of humanity. I do not say that all of Jungian theory is correct. I do not even mean that Jung would be fully cognizant of or in accord with the case I will now make, based on his developing writings. I mean only that his fundamental image of human nature is one hundred percent correct, and that, although other psychoanalytical theories rely on this same image, no one has been as terminologically clear on the matter as Jung. In the remaining pages of this chapter I would like to draw out this terminological clarity, tracing for the reader my reasons for considering Jung to be a conscious, knowing dialectician, and why this in turn makes it possible for him to frame a clear *human* teleology.

Jung as Dialectician

It is fascinating to trace a continuing reliance on the dialectical conception in Jung's writings. From the very first, in his 1902 inaugural dissertation having to do with 'so-called occult phenomena', Jung is seen to use a kind of internal dialectic to explain how it is that a medium calls into existence a 'personality within a personality' – i.e. the feeling-toned complex: 'The question "Who is doing this?" "Who is speaking?" acts as a suggestion for synthesizing the unconscious personality, which as a rule is not long in coming. Some name or other presents itself, usually one charged with emotion, and the automatic splitting of the personality is accomplished'.[9] This is not unlike the Socratic prompt, the asking of a question intrapersonally rather than interpersonally, but which nevertheless can stimulate a dialogue and a counter-position within the psyche of an individual, bringing about a 'voice from the beyond' which is in fact a 'complex from within'.

In 1907, writing on the psychology of dementia praecox, Jung took up Bleuler's concept of 'negative suggestibility' in both normals and abnormals.[10] Bleuler had noted this compulsion to produce contrary associations in human behavior, interpreting it as a natural check on the propensity to be easily susceptible to suggestion. Jung defined suggestibility as the capacity to accept and put into effect feeling-toned ideas. Negative suggestibility enabled the person to weigh the 'pros and cons' of such impulsive belief formations before putting them into overt behavior. Having noted this oppositional quality in his own researches on word associations, Jung comments on the frequency with which language terms take on this dual relationship, adding: 'In primitive languages there is sometimes a single word for contrary ideas'.

By 1909 Jung had embarked on his study of ancient myths and symbols. He writes to Freud just after their return from the trip to Clark University that 'archaeology or rather mythology has got me in its grip'.[11] He is to find these studies a rich storehouse of the dialectical manifestations of human reason. Thus, by 1912 we find him saying: 'Every psychological extreme secretly contains its own opposite or stands in some sort of intimate and essential relation to it . . . Indeed, it is from this tension that it derives its peculiar dynamism. There is no hallowed custom that cannot on occasion turn into its opposite, and the more extreme a position is, the more easily may we expect an enantiodromia, a conversion of something into its opposite'.[12] It is not a stretch of imagination to see in this developing line of thought Jung's budding conception of libido as an *élan vital* which is generated through the disbalance and splitting-up of psychic contents which are naturally tied together by dialectical oppositionality. Jung's dissatisfaction with Freud's conception of libido has been widely commented on and is easily documented in the *Freud/Jung letters*.[11] Thus, in December of 1909 Jung asks Freud for a clearer definition of libido and a few weeks later Freud responds by quoting a sentence from his writings on sexuality in which he states: 'The analagon to hunger, for which, in the sexual context, the German language has no word except the ambiguous *Lust*'. Within a week Jung responds that he has still not adjusted to Freud's attitude on the libido question.

I have argued in other contexts that though Freud too relied upon dialectical theoretical formulations he was – as noted above – more concerned about appearing traditionally 'scientific' than was Jung (see Rychlak[13-15]). What this position comes down to is that Freud was still identified with the older, Newtonian approach to science, which drew from the Lockean, reductive form of explanation. A more Kantian approach to modern physics was on the rise as psychoanalysis was being framed, and it is now clear that Jung was more in tune with this development than Freud. One of the major thinkers influencing the rise of modern physics was Ernst Mach, who called his approach *phenomenological* in opposition to the reigning atomic (i.e. Lockean) models at the turn of the nineteenth century.[16] We know that Freud avoided the social philosopher Josef Popper-Lynkeus, a man he admired, because the latter had Mach as a friend and frequent visitor.[17] It seems that Freud simply could not brook the seeming intellectual nihilism of a theoretical scientist like Mach who found it possible to accept more than one 'factual' account of reality as valid *at the same time*.[18]

Though a phenomenological interpretation of science would have greatly benefited psychoanalysis, Freud never saw the possibilities of the 'new science' then emerging. Freud was a transitional figure in the history of science, and though he did not need a libido construct in the mid-1890s when he was framing the basic outlines of his style of thought, after 1900 we find him relying upon this pseudo-energy as the supposed reductive force which impelled behavior along in ways analogical to the efficient causes of physical energy. But libido, a psychic energy unamenable to measurement even in principle, was never a satisfactory theoretical conception. The Freud-Jung correspondence shows that Jung was aware of its limitations, and that he may also have objected to its one-sidedness in the final Freudian treatment. It is common to hear that Freud and Jung disagreed over the sexual 'nature' of libido. Though true enough, this simplistic version of the disagreement between the participants masks an important though subtle issue at the heart of the debate having to do with where dialectical oppositionality is best brought into the explanations of behavior.

To demonstrate this point we begin a review of the correspondence in the December of 1910, where we find Jung bravely aligning himself with Freud's use of libido, a concept already under attack in the writings of Alfred Adler.[11] Jung tries, over the next several months, to bring libido into his studies of the zodiac and other mythological motifs. The explanations of these conceptions continue to reflect Jung's basic commitment to dialectical oppositionality, and libido has to fit in here in some way. However, in November 1911 Freud makes it clear that libido is one of two basic life drives; i.e. it is the 'power behind the sexual drive'. Though Freud has a dialectical opposition taking place between what he will someday call the life and death instincts, he is of necessity in this treatment assigning libido a singular function in the personality structure. Though Freud had begun in a style of explanation remarkably similar to Jung, accounting for neurosis based on the operation of a counter-will in mind with antithetic ideas,[19] his subsequent theorizing had resulted in making libido an active force at merely one end of a bipolar process. As we know, Freud never named the 'other' energy of the mind (called 'mortido' today by some people), and he was pointedly lax in working out the full picture of how these dual or multiple energies added explanatory power to psychoanalytical explanations that did not use them.

Reframing Freud's theoretical task, we can suggest that he had borrowed his psychic energy concept (analogically) from the demonstrative tradition of physical science. Since there are no dialectical formulations in this tradition, the dynamic 'clash' in

Freudian theory had to emanate from the contrasting instincts *per se*, or between the counter-ploys and compromises worked out by the identities of the personality known as id, ego, and super-ego. Libido was not germane to such dialectical antitheses and syntheses, though it was – so to speak – being passed back and forth or used against itself by the personality identities. Jung seems to have wanted to keep libido tied directly to dialectical clashes of all sorts in the personality structure without postulating any 'other' energy in what then becomes a kind of demonstrative apposing rather than a dialectical opposing. In the former case we have two different 'essences' brought together whereas in the latter we have the same 'essence' in contradiction with itself! Thus, Jung can be seen struggling to find some way of describing the many sides of the psyche as all tied into one manifestation of psychic energy. In December 1911 he tells Freud that he is trying to replace the descriptive concept of libido by a genetic one, which to him means a global source (one) from which all life activities (which are many) spring: 'Such a concept covers not only the recent-sexual libido but all those forms of it which have long since split off into organized activities. A wee bit of biology was unavoidable here'.[19]

Freud and Jung's relationship is very strained at this point, and the disagreement over libido is wound into the supposed motives which each man has for agreeing or not agreeing. This side of the dispute constitutes another chapter in the history of psychoanalysis and we cannot go into the matter here for it would take us back to Freud's earlier relations with Wilhelm Fliess. Though Freud considered it an opportunistic move to curry favor with the detractors of psychoanalysis, Jung's so-called desexualization of libido as a theoretical construct was actually an elevation of the construct in the over-all theory. Jung considered libido a magnificent, over-arching 'one' rather than a unipolar portion of the 'many' energies in mind.

Furthermore, and much to the point of the present analysis, libido's analogy to physical energy is strained at Jung's hands beyond recognizability. Libido becomes the desired value of a behavioural intention, the worth of a goal for the sake of which the person behaves[20]. The determining power of behavior is no longer analogized to a material-cause and/or efficient-cause thrust, but is clearly telic in conceptualization: 'Libido is intended simply as a name for the energy which manifests itself in the life-process and is perceived subjectively as conation and desire'.[20a] Jung readily equated libido with Schopenhauer's concept of will.[21] And *always* he has libido bound into a dialectical psychic ploy of some sort. Oppositionality and libido-creation were really two ways of discussing the same thing in the psychic sphere. Thus, by 1929 we find Jung saying: 'I see in all that happens the play of opposites, and derive from this conception my idea of psychic energy'.[20]

From this time forward we find Jung's commitment to dialectical formulations complete. In 1933 he speaks of a 'fundamental axiom' which is that anything psychic has at least two sides and should never be looked at one-sidedly.[21] A year later he is referring to the 'dialectical procedure' employed by the alchemist, who comes to terms with numinous inner contents of mind through dialogue or an 'inner colloquy'.[22] This becomes a major facet of his theory of cure in psychotherapy, where in the last phases an individuation is achieved through an inner confrontation with the unconscious. By 1935 Jung is using the proper terminology quite openly:

. . . psychotherapy is not the simple, straight-forward method people at first believed it to be, but, as has gradually become clear, a kind of dialectical process, a dialogue or discussion between two persons. Dialectic was originally the art of conversation among the ancient philosophers, but very early became the term for the process of creating new syntheses. A person is a psychic system which, when it affects another person, enters into reciprocal reactions with another psychic system.[23]

Jung drew two further implications from his dialectical conception of the psychotherapy process, i.e. that the doctor was in this dynamic process along with the patient, and, that the therapist was not 'special' but had to recognize the individuality of the patient as an equal partner in the relationship. In the Socratic spirit of complete openness, Jung found a rationale for reducing the authoritarian stance which he felt Freudian psychoanalysis had taken in relation to the patient. By 1936 Jung was convinced that 'the problem of opposites . . . should be made the basis for a critical psychology'.[24] He could see the manifestations of dialectic in all systems of thought. There is no meaningful position expressible which lacks its negation. In the East we see this truth manifested in the ying-yang principle.[22] In 1939 we see a kind of transcendental theme in his formulations of psychotherapy, where he notes that the dialectical procedures of individuation *transform* the personality as the ego is set back in favor of self emergence.[25]

In the 1940s, through the years of World War II and shortly thereafter, Jung seems to have refined his thinking on the transcendental function and self emergence. Even though the self acts as a unifying balance of the opposing sides of the personality, Jung does not permit this construct to lose its dialectical features. He observes in 1950 that: ' . . . the self is a *complexio oppositorum* precisely because there can be no reality without polarity'.[26] He is now referring directly to the *principle of opposition* on which he bases his psychology. I can only wish that he had called this a *principle of dialectic*. My studies of

Jung began in the 1950s, and I was greatly helped by his interpretation of the dialectic. Specifically, he helped me clarify where this dialectical process stems from. Is it part of the 'material reality' as communistic theories imply, or are there such forces as 'laws' in the social structure *per se*? Or, do we find the dialectic emanating from the psyche, reflecting the nature of mentation rather than some independent 'reality'? Jung's view comes down on the side of the psyche, the cognitive processes which we generate mentally to order and make sense of what we then know as reality in terms of such oppositionality. Thus, in 1950 he observes: 'It is not . . . probable that anything so intrinsically bound up with the act of cognition should be at the same time a property of the object [of that cognitive process; i.e. of non-psychic experience]. It is far easier to suppose that it is primarily our consciousness which names and evaluates the differences between things, and perhaps even creates distinctions where no differences are discernible'.[26]

Over the next two or three years Jung stresses the importance of his principle of opposition for a satisfactory psychological theory. The psyche is described as a self-regulating system which gains its motive force (libido) and its harmony via this play of opposition and occasional syntheses into what is still and always must be a duality.[27] Meaning itself must always have this quality of more than one conceptual stance: 'We name a thing *from a certain point of view*, good or bad, high or low, right or left, light or dark, and so forth. Here the antithesis is just as factual and real as the thesis'.[25] In 1959, I wrote a letter to Jung, asking him about his education and pointing up a few direct parallels between Hegelian writings on the dialectic and his own writings (see Adler and Jaffé[28]). Jung was gracious enough to respond, and to observe that although he was influenced by Plato, Kant, Schopenhauer, von Hartmann, and Nietzsche, he was most surely not influenced by Hegel, whom he considered a 'misfired psychologist' who had essentially projected his own unconscious processes into his philosophy.

As for the dialectic, Jung emphasized that he did not view this as merely an 'intellectual procedure', but rather as a practical method of dealing with the meaningful propositions presented to us by the unconscious: 'Since neurosis consists in a dissociation of personality, one is always confronted with an opposite or a *vis-à-vis* you have to reckon with; a fact which is unknown only to people who know of nothing else but the contents of their consciousness'.[28] Note the relational quality which Jung gives mentation at this point. He teaches us that the human being can only create a meaningful understanding of the 'given' by relating it in contrasting fashion with the 'not-given'. I took this as support for a view of the mind as a logical process in which human beings must ever 'take a position on' that which confronts them. The *vis-à-vis* quality of mentation is not merely 'consciousness confronting unconsciousness' but is far more general in that we can only speak of the 'known' by relating it to the predications which are affirmed after dialectical examination of what is taken as the 'not-known'. Jung teaches us that this not-known, incorrect, improper, wrong, 'bad' and so on side to knowledge never really disappears from mind. The not-known of unconsciousness ever remains as a possibility for future counter-influence as life unfolds. Jung gives us an example of this very human propensity in his 1963 autobiography where, speaking of his life as a whole, he observes: 'I had to obey an inner law which was imposed on me and left me no freedom of choice. Of course I did not always obey it. How can anyone live without inconsistency'.[29] This marvelous self-observation takes us into the next section of this chapter.

Jung as Teleologist

As noted in the introduction (refer above), I believe that Jung's developing commitment to the dialectic enabled him to be a teleologist and to instruct us thereby in the *correct* image of human nature. There is just something about the dialectical conception which demands that we consider the person to be an agent in his or her behavior, a selector (affirmer, decider, chooser, and so on) of the one premise on which to behave from among the many possibilities open to behavior.[1] Thus, Jung is able to frame his theoretical commentaries teleologically. As early as 1916 he asserts that: ' . . . in my opinion the nature of the human mind compels us to take the finalistic view. It cannot be disputed that, psychologically speaking, we are living and working day by day according to the principle of directed aim or purpose as well as that of causality'.[20] By 'causality' here Jung means efficient causality. His sophistication concerning science is revealed in the following, where Jung clarifies that though science may trace functional relationships between variables in empirical study this does *not* mean that a final cause is necessarily excluded from the theoretical description of that which is being tracked empirically: ' . . . "function" as conceived by modern science is by no means exclusively a causal concept; it is especially a final or "teleological" one. For it is impossible to consider the psyche from the causal standpoint only; we are obliged to consider it also from the final [-cause] point of view'.

The picture we have emerging here is that of a mind under dialectical or oppositional tension in the manufacturing of meaning, with all of the balancing, one-sidedness, and re-balancing that this can suggest. Though the person is limited by reality considerations in the choices he or she can make, there *is* a contribution being made to each lived reality by the psychological identity 'coming at' life to order it in the sense of the Kantian model.[24] If we look at the psyche as fraught with the possibilities of opposition then we must necessarily appreciate a sense of the freedom which the person has to predicate behavior 'this' way rather than 'that [i.e. not-this]' way or *vice versa*. The person's psychic identity – or identities (ego, self) – are also limited internally by subjective evaluations.[26] It is only when the internal duality of the psyche is wrent apart in one-sidedness that free-will potentials are completely checkmated as the person now falls under the sway of a numinous mental content. The essence of Jungian mental health is to see both sides of knowledge, and to guide one's behavior in light of oppositional and even contradictory understandings of that which 'is' in reality.

Jung knew perfectly well that a free-will conception was unamenable to what he liked to call the causal-mechanistic (reductive) explanations of 'natural' science. He championed a special branch of science relating solely to the psyche, where its oppositional features could be studied and dialectical principles of learning such as paradox could be appreciated instead of being dismissed as illogical – as is so often done in the demonstratively framed natural sciences. Thus, he said: 'The will . . . is a phenomenon, though "free will" is not a natural phenomenon because it is not observable in itself, but only in the form of concepts, views, convictions, or beliefs. It is therefore a problem which belongs to pure "science of the mind".' Psychology has to confine itself to natural phenomenology if it is not to go poaching on other preserves'.[12] Free will, the capacity to rise above what 'is' in nature to see what 'is not' and thence bring it about – for good or evil! – is most certainly *not* something natural or 'of nature'. The human being is surely that contradiction in terms – born of nature yet so often enemy to nature – which the dialectic permits us to understand. Thus, the human being can transcend natural promptings ('do this') and find in this very prompting an alternative to affirm ('no, I'll do that') without requiring any of that additional 'input information' which the mechanistic accounts require. Once affirmed, the predication taken becomes a willful course of action which the person creatively brings into existence quite by *intention*.

Jung teaches us that we can see what is not there. Those who call him mystical doubtless take this negation of the law of contradiction as grounds for this charge. Jung teaches us that we are psychologically free to behave as we *will* alternatively thanks to our dialectical understanding of events. Those who call him an apologist for religion doubtless take his acceptance of free will as grounds for this charge. All such critics are either uninformed on or misunderstand what Jung's theory of humanity is driving at. There is nothing mystical or simply 'religious' about his views – although both mysticism and religion are brought within the purview of Analytical Psychology, as indeed they should if this psychology is to be a comprehensive explanation of what we observe human beings doing in life.

The Jungian Lesson

I noted at the outset of this chapter that Jung has given me the confidence to view human nature in ways not now accepted by the 'science' of psychology, which is still under the sway of a kind of Lockean numinosity. Though my training is as a psychological psychotherapist, in recent years I have been trying to confront mechanistic psychology in the laboratory context with a humanistic explanation of behavior. This was a conscious decision on my part, after realizing that virtually all of the 'lab psychologists' were mechanists and hence even when telic findings emerged in experiments they were likely to be dismissed as error or explained away through reductive explanations. Though I noted considerable support for telic behavior in psychological experimentation, I found it impossible to express these results in what Jung would term the 'final energic' sense.[24] He was asking for a [final-] *cause* phrasing, and yet in psychology the concept of behavior as response(s) or output(s) places it on the *effect* side of things. As we saw above, final causes are brought to bear on the initiating, getting-started side of things. They are the reasons why we do things, the goals toward which our behavior is to be pointed.

After a few years of trying to capture final-cause meanings in the language of responsivity, I realized that this was impossible and that another term was called for to oppose the meaning of 'response' in descriptions of behavior. It was several more years before I got up the courage to begin talking about what I now call a *telosponse*.[2,15] Though it mixes Greek (*telos*) and Latin (*spondre*) roots in a most 'unscholarly' fashion, I think it succinctly captures the meaning needed at the proper level of abstraction in opposition to the 'response' construct. Thus, a telosponse is a mental act in which the person takes on (predicates, premises) a meaningful item (image, language term, a judgment, and so on) relating to a referent acting as a purpose for the sake of which behavior is then intended. Telosponsive behavior is therefore done 'for the sake of' grounds (purposes, reasons, and so on) rather than 'in response to' stimulation or input promptings. Telosponsivity is what occurs if, as the Kantian model suggests, human beings have a pro-forma intellect. Telosponses are *not* former inputs being mediated along today as feedback mechanisms. I assume that from birth the individual has this capacity to telospond, beginning as Kant said in the ordering and arraying of perceptual processes rather than responding to the order which is 'there', in reality, according to the *tabula-rasa* assumptions of the Lockean model.

In my *logical learning theory*, which frames the essentials of telosponsivity as a process of predication or the affirming of premises at a proto-point, the claim is made that due to the human's fundamentally dialectical intelligence a selection must always be made from among the various possibilities open for predication. In other words, the world of experience which confronts us from moment-to-moment is never unidirectionally *certain* as regards the course of action which we must *necessarily* enact. Indeed, its very openness to alternative possibilities is what prompts us to seek an iron-clad predication to 'believe in' before acting. That is, we seek the certainty of the 'right, true, scientific, moral, Godly, modern' or whatever premise in our approach to life because we can appreciate that since there are so many different ways to predicate things there *must* be some one way which is best – i.e. a way which ensures the greatest advantages in life. Fixing 'the' premise is one of the ways we can describe demonstrative reasoning, for the judgment of 'primary and true' is not as easily done as Aristotle made it appear. Once taken as 'the' truth, however, we have a course of reasoning which is surely demonstrative taking shape. Logical learning theory suggests that there is always some degree of dialectical reasoning taking place preliminary to demonstrative reasoning.

It is this capacity to alter grounds – even 'primary and true' grounds – which makes free will possible. Based on their transcendent dialectical reasoning capacities human beings can turn back on what 'is' to see any of a number of opposites ('is nots') through which they can rearrange and reframe what are then alternative grounds for the sake of which they are determined. Freedom of the will and psychic determinism are thus simply different perspectives on the same telosponsive process. Before affirmation we can speak of freedom, and, after a precedent premise is affirmed the meanings which are put down and extended sequaciously constitute psychic determination, which ever flows from the given, presumed, 'known' to the implications, possibilities, and the 'knowable'. Symbolical expressions in the Jungian vein are considered entirely possible on this view, as they are merely another manifestation of the intentional nature of mentation.

Logical learning theory has many empirical findings in its support (see Rychlak, 1977).[2] It has taken the spirit of Jungian, dialectical psychological theory and applied this style of explanation fruitfully. Experimental subjects have been shown to evaluate and direct their course of behavior willfully – i.e., telosponsively – precisely as Jung claimed. The concepts of dialectical logic and bipolarity in meaning have been shown to relate to human learning in a most basic sense. Though we have not provided a direct translation of Jungian psychology into the tenets of logical learning theory, we have some interesting beginnings and the future promise of a rapprochement between the insights of the consulting room and the empirical demonstrations of the laboratory. In the years ahead advocates of logical learning theory (and other teleologies) will doubtless continue to take strength from the wisdom of that great, great psychologist whom this volume honors.

CHAPTER 4

Jung and the Concept of the Other

BY RENOS K. PAPADOPOULOS

This chapter is an attempt at a new approach to the psychology of C.G. Jung from a metatheoretical point of view, exposing a central problematic in the Jungian opus. (Theoretical studies investigate the internal consistency of a particular theory i.e. how certain parts relate to others *within* the same framework. *Metatheoretical* approaches discuss the theory from a viewpoint which does not incorporate the basic premises of that theory.) This is the problematic of the 'Other', the pivotal phenomenon of the composition and dissociability of the psyche.

The great majority of studies dealing with the work of C.G. Jung come from 'within' the Jungian system. Even the recent trend of revived interest in Jung has not significantly altered this state of affairs (cf. Brome[10]; Cohen[13]; Fordham[18]; Hannah[34] Jaffé[39]; Odajnuk[76]; Van der Post[96]; Von Franz[97]). It is rather unfortunate that after a great man's death his followers tend to stare in adoration at his pointing finger, rather than trace the implications of the pointed direction – to paraphrase Alan Watts' expression. Notable examples of the few metatheoretical studies in this field however are the works of Drs. Rauhala[80-2] and Rychlak[85-7] as well as the remarkable monograph by Christou.[12] The first of these points out that the 'source and point of departure' of a metatheoretical approach (his own particular one is Hermeneutic Metascience) is ' . . . the realization that not only is the matter to be investigated a problem, [but] the investigation itself is also problematic'.[81]

The present paper similarly attempts an inquiry primarily into Jung's investigations. In other words, Jung's writings are examined with a view to illuminating his choice of the particular areas which he decided to study, the meaning of his interpretations, and their implications for the development of his subsequent direction. Thus this study represents a *re-reading* of Jung, in that it endeavours to re-construct the meaning of Jung's problematic, that is, the manner in which he posed questions and the routes he followed in answering them. The terms *reading* and *re-reading* come from the French structuralist tradition which emphasizes the active reconstruction of the meaning of a given text (Lacan[67-9]). A metatheoretical structure will here be sought which enables the Jungian contribution to be meaningfully located within it. The problematic of the Other has emerged as such a structure with particularly promising heuristic value.

The Other

The term 'Other' does not have a self-evident connotation. Its meaning depends upon the specific theoretical territory within which it is defined. It falls into the category of words which Gilbert Ryle calls 'index words': ' . . . they indicate to the hearer or reader the particular thing, episode, person, place, or moment referred to'.[88] Other words classed in this category by Ryle include: today; now; I; you. All of these depend upon the context referred to.

However, the word 'other', by virtue of its dependency on a 'this', may be understood as an index word of a higher order, because it refers to something *other* than what is referred to by the index word. It is therefore tempting to call the 'other' a 'counter-index word', but this would inevitably force a meaning according to which the 'other's' relation to the 'this' would always be that of *opposition*. Linguistically, such a meaning would be unjustifiably restrictive, as the 'other' may also be *complementary* to 'this'.

In Greek there are two words for the 'Other': '*allos*' and '*heteros*'. Liddell and Scott[71] regard 'heteros' as 'better Greek', whereas Barber[5] as well as Chantraine[11] maintain that 'heteros' is the Attic form of 'allos'. Both of these words are to be found in modern English, for example in *allo*theism – the worship of strange gods; and *hetero*genous – composed of diverse elements[19]. Strauss, in his phenomenological analysis of the 'Other', prefers using 'allon' (the neuter form of the male 'allos') in order to 'avoid confusion'[93] which surrounds the meaning of the English word 'other'. Allos is related to the Latin *alter*, *alienus*[71]; and the latter is of course the root of *alienation* – otherness, estrangement. Allos belongs to the same family as the Sanskrit *ant-aras* – other, 'of many with a sense of difference'.[7] Additional meanings of antaras include 'interior, the main substance' as well, as 'difference'. Benfey, in his Sanskrit-English Dictionary relates, in turn, antaras to the Latin interior, alter, ulterior, ultra. Chantraine[11] finds that heteros relates to the Sanskrit *eka-tara* – one of two – which has the following, related relevant meanings: on one side, harmony, conjunction, solitarity, same, unanimity; and finally, Benfey connects the Sanskrit root *eka* to the Latin *aequus* – equal.

Thus, although in colloquial English the 'Other' usually suggests a separation or an opposition, this brief excursion indicates that in the linguistic family of the 'other' some seemingly contradictory meanings are included: a) difference, separation; b) sameness; c) interior, main substance, harmony. A phrase from Plato may combine these meanings in a coherent framework. In *Meno* he writes about 'alle psyche' (88d) which could be translated as 'the other psyche'. Barber however, correctly renders it as 'the *rest* of the soul'.[5] This neutral translation implies that there is still some *other* part of the psyche which constitutes the *rest* of the one already mentioned. Therefore the inherent duality of meaning in the 'other' may be comprehended as follows: If the rest is added to the existing part, a wholeness, a totality may be achieved; but if the rest is left apart, then a separation, a division will result.

The central theme of the Other is an important issue in philosophy and has been studied in its various forms and formulations by a great number of philosophers (e.g. De Greef[15], Macmurray[73], Ramfos[77], Sartre[89], Szczepanski[95]) in addition, of course, to the whole dialectical tradition from Heraclitus and Plato to Hegel and Marx, where a concept of the Other constitutes an essential element in any dialectical construction. In psychology this concept has received relatively little attention. It has however recently been revived by the interest shown in the work of Jacques Lacan, where its place is prominent. This controversial French psychoanalyst examines the Other within the framework of his own structuralist approach to language and the psychological subject (e.g. Lacan[67], Lemaire[70], Wilden[98]). A handful of other psychologists investigated related themes such as the double (Rank[78-9]), the other in society (Mead[75]), the 'not I' (Harding[35]), human duality (Bakan[4]), splitting (Lustman[72]), and opposition (Jarrett[40]).

Jung never presented an explicit and systematic theory of the Other as such, although it will be here argued that not only was it implicit in his entire opus, but the constant quest for formulating such an adequate theory of the Other (here referred to as his problematic) was one of his central motivating forces throughout. Nevertheless Jung did use the term 'other' in his writings, and referred to it in all his theoretical formulations.

Appreciating that which Fordham noted as the 'remarkable inner coherence' throughout Jung's researches, and accepting that 'the only way to understand Jung is to take his researches as a whole, perceiving how one stage grows out of that preceeding it'[17] this article will venture into an exploration of Jung's life and work starting from the experiences of his early childhood and allowing its developmental course to unfold. In this fashion a series of reformulations of his problematic of the Other will emerge. This course will be punctuated by a number of periods which represent more or less coherent formulations of the Other.

Childhood period

Jung made his first reference to the Other in connection with his childhood 'second personality' which he named 'No. 2 personality'. In his autobiographical work *Memories, Dreams, Reflections* Jung emphasised that 'the play and counterplay between personalities No. 1 and No. 2 . . . run through my whole life' and that their interrelation and dialogue offered him his 'profoundest experiences: on the one hand a bloody struggle, on the other supreme ecstasy'. He had thus early established a second, an 'other' personality within himself whose contribution he valued very sincerely. But before discussing the differences between the two personalities and their significance, it will be useful to examine the precursors of No. 2, especially since no mention was ever made of them within this context in the relevant literature.

We read in *Memories, Dreams, Reflections* that as a child Jung often experienced 'disunion' with (p. 36) and 'alienation' from himself (p. 34). These states were due to

the influence of my schoolfellows, who somehow misled me or compelled me to be different from what I thought I was. The influence of this wider world, this world which contained others besides my parents, seemed to me dubious if not altogether suspect and, in some obscure way, hostile.

To alleviate the fear and insecurity which these states produced Jung, in his childhood world of imagination, found three ways of healing that 'split' and reestablishing his 'inner security' which was 'threatened' (p. 35). First, through a game of making a fire at a particular spot in his garden, he developed a particular 'relationship' with 'his' fire. Other children had their own fires too ' . . . but these fires were profane and did not concern me. My fire alone was living and had an unmistakable aura of sanctity'.

Another game which seems to have been of still greater importance to Jung was to sit on a stone in his garden and wonder 'am I the one who is sitting on the stone, or am I the stone on which *he* is sitting?' (p. 35). This imaginary game offered him much security and he could sit on the stone 'for hours' cherishing their 'secret relationship'.

Perhaps the most significant of all of Jung's childhood 'imaginary games', and which at the same time represented a 'climax and conclusion' of his childhood (p. 38), was with a carved manikin and a pebble from the Rhine. He had carved the manikin at the end of his school ruler, sawed him off and then placed him in a pencil-case along with the 'oblong blackish stone' from the Rhine, and hid them together in the attic of his house. He visited them whenever he felt unhappy and in any way 'unsafe'. The entire ritual, which was carefully kept secret from his family, had a profoundly soothing effect on Jung. Every time he used to go up to the attic to be with his precious inanimate companions he

. . . placed in the case a little scroll of paper in which I had previously written something during school hours in a *secret language of my own invention*. The addition of a new scroll always had the character of a ceremonial act (p.37, my italics).

There is an implicit similarity in all of the three games. They all involved a fascinating 'secret relationship' with an 'object' (fire, stone, manikin and pebble) which somehow represented an Other in Jung's own personality. It is evident from his descriptions that these Others were in such a close relationship to himself that at times there was confusion of the actual boundaries of his own personality and to the extent that he was totally absorbed in the Other. It is significant that Jung related these games to a state of inner split. The function and purpose of the Others was to restore the threatened unity of his being. In their presence Jung 'felt safe, and the tormenting sense of being at odds with myself was gone' (p.37). The sequence of the fire, the stone, and the manikin and pebble could be considered as a progression in the development of a clearer articulation of the Other: Fire, the 'archetypal substance'[66] of an elusive and intangible form of nature yet with very tangible effects, may be seen as the most primitive form of the Other which then takes the form of a stone (solid material substance) in order to culminate in the pebble and manikin (a more personalized form of the natural stone, along with an actual model of human figure).

A noteworthy aspect of this period is also the appearance of a 'secret language' of Jung's 'own invention'. This childish game reflected perhaps Jung's need to express vitally important issues concerning his existential security in a language that was *adequate*. Common everyday language was apparently inadequate for him to formulate those secret messages as it was inextricably part of the alienating verbiage of home and school situations where what was said and what was actually meant were obviously not congruent. It may thus be suggested, in anticipation, that the language of the little scrolls represented Jung's first attempt to develop a language of the Unconscious, after he had experienced the inadequacies of ordinary conceptual language.

The appearance of No. 1 and No. 2 personalities was immediately preceded by a dramatic awareness of what could be identified as his differentiated Ego when, while returning from school one day:

. . . suddenly for a single moment I had the overwhelming impression of having just emerged from a dense cloud. I knew all at once: now I am *myself*! It was as if a wall of mist were at my back, and behind that wall there was not yet an 'I'. But at this moment I *came upon myself* (p.49).

It was then that it 'occurred' to him that he 'was actually two different persons' (p.50).

Jung understood his 'No. 1 personality' as more or less coinciding with his ordinary, everyday identity. No. 1 was thus 'the son of my parents who went to school' (p.61), whereas 'No. 2', the 'other' or 'second' personality, was a ' . . . grown up – old, in fact – . . . remote from the world of men but close to nature, . . . above all close to the night, to dreams . . .' (p.62).

No. 2 personality had all the qualities of the previous Others: while in touch with him it felt

like a temple in which anyone who entered was transformed and suddenly overpowered by a vision of the whole cosmos, so that he could only marvel and admire, forgetful of himself (p. 62).

The 'timelessness' (p.110) of No. 2 along with his other reassuring effects, produced in Jung feelings of 'peace and solitude' (p.62), much the same as he experienced in the company of his fire, stone, pebble and manikin. Moreover, this time he did not have to go to them. No. 2 was in Jung himself. Thus, he now acknowledged a division within himself which was a source not just of suffering but also of potential unity. Since that Other was now located within, Jung was no longer a lonely, frightened boy, but had the resources to heal his condition of 'disunity' and 'alienation'. In addition, he began observing similar divisions in other people. This made him aware of the complexities of human personality and he ceased to see people in terms of unidimensional, childish divisions of good and bad. As a first step, he distinguished his own mother's No. 2 personality. It also gradually dawned on him that insofar as No. 2 was of an impersonal, timeless, cosmic nature, and all people had a No. 2, by implication, then all people were in a sense connected through this transpersonal eternal realm. Such an understanding of human nature enabled Jung to go on to apprehend a very profound unity within the entire cosmos. This insight

. . . was not only comforting to me, it also gave me an increased feeling of inner security, and a sense of belonging to the human community. I was no longer isolated and a mere curiosity, a sport of cruel nature (p. 107).

Despite his great virtues, the internalized Other, No. 2 personality, led to severe conflicts with the immediate interests of No. 1

personality, which were of a pragmatic and social nature. The
passivity of No. 2 contrasted sharply with the zest for activity of No.
1. Gradually each one developed into a more articulate personality
with its own separate characteristics and interests, so much so that
when later Jung came to decide about his future career the conflict
between No. 1 and No. 2 was again enacted. The dilemma then
manifested itself between science (which was associated with No. 1)
and the humanities and religion (which were closely connected with
No. 2).

During the period before entering university Jung's No. 1 was
absorbed in the scientific materialism which was predominant at the
time, whereas his No. 2, with its idiosyncratic tendencies, was for
Jung a source of embarrassment. It is indeed rather curious that Jung
did not perceive his 'sudden inspiration' to opt for medicine as a
compromise between No. 1 and No. 2, but as a relative triumph of the
former: 'I had definitely opted for science' (p.105). Yet, a few years
later when faced with another decision (this time about his medical
specialization) his final choice of psychiatry was a product of a
deliberate effort to bring together the antagonistic realms of No. 1 and
No. 2. Jung realized with great excitement that psychiatry represented
' . . . the *empirical* field *common* to *biological* and *spiritual* facts, which I
had everywhere sought and nowhere found' (p. 130, my italics).

Psychiatric period

By launching into a psychiatric career Jung had embarked on a life-
long exploration of the complementary and yet opposing worlds of
No. 1 and No. 2. A formidable odyssey indeed, which he undertook
perhaps out of some sense of inevitability, as the attraction and
experienced beneficial effects from both realms were irresistible.

Jung's problematic of the Other, having been instrumental in his
opting for psychiatry as a specialization, was also central in his
inaugural dissertation for his medical degree, which was entitled *On
the psychology and pathology of so-called occult phenomena.*[41] In this work
Jung recorded, analysed and discussed his observations of a spiritual
medium to whom he gave the initials S.W. Behind these initials Jung
concealed the identity of Helene Preiswerk, a cousin on his mother's
side. Over a period of years Jung monitored her behaviour as a
participant observer in her spiritualistic seances and documented her
progression from an insecure little girl to an assertive personality
which had striking similarities to his own No. 2 personality. S.W.
impersonated the 'control spirits' which were talking through her and
gradually assumed their personality.

In seeking to explain these phenomena Jung rejected the notion of 'double consciousness', which was fairly popular at the time, as he had noted that S.W.'s 'personalities' shared the same memory. He concluded that this was a case of 'semi-somnambulism'. However, his analysis did not stop there. He meticulously discussed the various 'other personalities' which S.W. assumed. First was an old man who was her 'protector and guide', full of paternalistic and moralistic sayings, then came a young, childish and frivolous man, while gradually a more coherent 'somnambulistic ego' emerged, indeed an 'other' personality whom S.W. herself gave the name Ivenes. Unlike the first two, Ivenes was a 'serious, mature person, devout and rightminded' and Jung emphasized her *teleological* function:

S.W. *anticipates* her own future and embodies in Ivenes what she wishes to be in twenty years time – the assured influential, wise, gracious, pious lady . . . builds up a personality beyond herself (p.66, my italics).

Moreover, Jung commented on the progression of the other personalities:

The patient is obviously seeking a middle way between two extremes; she endeavours to repress them and strives for a more ideal state. These strivings lead to the adolescent dream of the ideal Ivenes (p.77).

Placed in the context of his problematic of the Other, Jung's theory about the 'two extreme' and 'ideal middle' personalities may be accepted as a more advanced formulation of the No.1 and No.2 model. Insofar as the two extreme personalities represented existing unconscious tendencies within the individual, and the 'ideal middle' was an anticipated projection into the future of a mature personality, Jung's analysis implies the two following steps in the development of personality: a) Undesirable strong unconscious tendencies are repressed before appearing in an individualized and personified form within the personality; b) These 'split off egos', by acting independently, somehow activate a teleological function which produces a reconciliatory figure which at the same time i) reduces the tension between the two existing opposing tendencies by representing the 'ideal middle' and ii) paves the way towards the natural progression and development of the personality by anticipating a state of wholeness where the opposite aspects harmoniously coexist.

Our reformulation here differentiates two types of 'others': (1) the Other as exemplified by Ivenes (and earlier by No.2 personality) and which may now be called *Anticipated Whole Other* and (2) the Other which is the personification of the extreme unconscious tendencies, and which may be termed *Fragment Other*: this type of Other does not correspond to any previous descriptions offered by Jung.

Two observations can now be made. First, Jung advances here the 'explanatory hypothesis' that there are layers in the unconscious which are not affected by the split in the personality and which are instrumental in anticipating the 'ideal middle'. These layers moreover might account for the qualities of the Anticipated Whole Other which do not come from the personal repertoire of the personality (unlike the Fragment Other personalities which consist entirely of existing personal tendencies). Thus in this reformulation of the Other Jung again reiterates the transpersonal realm of the Other. Second, Ivenes too (like Jung as a child) had a 'secret language' of her own, which, although it bore some superficial similarities to Latin, was in fact nonsensical gibberish. Ivenes used this 'mystical language' to comprehend her broader cosmic connections. It may therefore be inferred that here is yet another attempt by an individual to forge an adequate language of and for the unconscious.

Jung's dissertation is indeed a milestone in his theoretical development in that, being his first scientific work, it recapitulated his previous understanding of the Other, formulated it in objective psychological language and also included some new insights. Moreover, here are to be found seeds of some later theories. It was here that Jung first introduced the term *complex*. He called the 'extreme personalities', the 'split off egos', *complexes*, and understood Ivenes as constituting an *ego-complex*. Right from the beginning he attributed to complexes functional autonomy. As clusters of more or less organised psychological tendencies, complexes formed in a sense minature personalities. Following the same rationale Jung recognised that the ego, the 'I', itself was a complex; and indeed the main and dominant complex of the whole personality by which the person is usually identified.

By conceptualising the Other in terms of complexes Jung opened up new vistas in his problematic. His entire pioneering research into *word association* may thus be located within this perspective. The initial aim of the word association experiments was to reveal clusters or complexes of associated ideas. Sudden embarrassment, lengthened reaction time, unusual responses to the cue list and so on were accepted as indications of a complex existent within the patient/subject. Such complexes were formed by means of splitting off or dissociation of 'emotionally charged ideas'. A person may possess (or more accurately be possessed by) one or many more complexes. Jung's approach to complexes emphasized not only their affective dimensions (in addition to the cognitive ones – after Galton and Wundt) but also their antagonistic and conflicting relationship to the main body of the personality. He called them 'independent beings', 'split off egos', and even 'separate personalities'. Jung's entire psychological system at the time revolved around complexes, so much so that he maintained that the aim of psychotherapy should be to resolve the patient's 'possession by complexes'.[42]

Once the power and meaning of Jung's early problematic of the Other has been judiciously understood and appreciated, the metatheory as well as the content of his first theoretical framework (which he systematized during the period under examination) should come as no surprise: Jung's personal quest for exploring the realm of the Other found suitable expression in the theory of complexes. The Other, no longer a global and undifferentiated other personality (as in No. 2 personality), was now defined in terms of more differentiated psychological processes and tendencies, that is, complexes. In conceptualizing his old problematic during this period, Jung obviously and inevitably utilized the psychological paradigm and language of the time, so that his theory of complexes represents a unique dialectical interrelationship between his scientific investigations and his own personal search for meaning.

Psychoanalytic Period

Jung's name is so commonly associated with Freud's that he is often thought of as nothing but one of Freud's disciples. He may be remembered as a rebellious disciple or even as the very archetypal example of a rebellious disciple. Yet in all these casual assessments two facts are ignored: that Jung entered psychoanalysis with an already formulated problematic of his own which he was pursuing, and that his personal contribution to psychoanalysis was considerable.

Right at the outset of their personal friendship and professional association Jung was aware of the respective differences between himself and Freud and felt the need to communicate them. As if he wished to reserve the right to his autonomy, Jung, in a letter to Freud (19 December 1906) remarked that their differences were not limited only to the factual and circumstantial (i.e. to different clientele and working conditions, as well as imbalance with respect to psychoanalytic experience). 'My upbringing, my milieu, and my scientific premises are in any case utterly different from your own'.[74] Freud, far from being oblivious of these differences, actually welcomed them as beneficial to the budding psychoanalytic movement. He particularly valued Jung's 'hard-nosed scientific' work and hailed the association experiment as 'the first bridge linking experimental psychology and psychoanalysis'.[29] Freud appreciated Jung's experimental and scientific approach for increasing the respectability of psychoanalysis especially in the German speaking world of the time (cf. Decker[14]). Yet, the irony is that Jung was to be subsequently accused by Freudians, as well as by Freud himself of precisely the opposite, that his theories were unscientific, a product of his allegedly speculative and mystical inclinations and thus ultimately 'scientifically sterile'.[33]

Jung's list of contributions to psychoanalysis is however impressive. Freud acknowledged explicitly at least five major contributions by Jung:

a) the tradition of experimentally investigating psychoanalytic concepts[28,30]

b) the notion of the *complex*[21,23,29]

c) the institution of *training analysis* as an essential part of the education of new analysts[27]

d) the use of anthropological and mythological material in psychoanalysis[26,28,29]

e) the application of psychoanalytic theory in the understanding of psychotic conditions[25,29]

To further clarify Jung's relation to psychoanalysis, careful examination of his initial contact with it and its originator is warranted.

Theoretically, Jung's own findings in the field of the association experiment, particularly his theory of *complexes*, bore striking resemblance to Freud's discoveries in treating hysteric and neurotic patients. Both had tapped an area of psychological functioning which did not obey the rules of the conscious, everyday ego. Freud however referred to this area as the *unconscious* whereas Jung understood it in terms of automatism and independently functioning complexes.

Eager to find a theoretical home of wider acceptance and, applicability for his own problematic, Jung saw in psychoanalysis a potential for the best possible of such arrangements. He received psychoanalysis with enthusiasm and very early on tried to include Freudian theories in his own writings. The first such example occurred already in his dissertation. There, although these were not central to either his theme or basic interpretations, Jung attempted to incorporate the then most modern and controversial psychological theories, namely Freud's. A typical passage is the following:

. . . We shall not be wrong if we seek the *main cause* of this curious clinical picture of her *budding sexuality*. From this point of view the *whole essence* of Ivenes and her enormous family is *nothing but* a dream of *sexual wish-fulfillment*, which differs from the dream of a night only in that it is spread over months and years . . . [41] (my italics).

There are two curious features about this quotation – its content and style. In no other place in his dissertation did Jung mention seriously the theory of sexual wish-fulfillment and in fact it does not tie in with the *teleological function* and other characteristics which he ascribed to Ivenes. Jung does not even pretend to reconcile these two theories. Moreover, it becomes rather ludicrous to claim that such an explanation provides 'the main cause' and 'the whole essence' of the subject matter, and yet not give it any more prominence in the text. From the point of view of style, dogmatic phrases such as 'the whole essence . . . is nothing but' are not to be found in the rest of that work, and neither in any other writings by Jung, for that matter. On the contrary, Jung was later extremely critical of Freud's frequent use of 'nothing but' as an inflexible manner of theorising. With evident contempt he even grouped all such theories into a '"nothing but" psychology'.[51]

These considerations lead one to assume that the above quoted paragraph is an attempt to include theoretical trends, nevertheless without giving them the weight that the strong language of their formulation implies. This incident is by no means an isolated one. The careful reader will find more examples in Jung's early writings.[43] This practice suggests that at least at this stage Freudian ideas did not form an integral part of Jung's theoretical system, and his introduction of them was, perhaps, for other than purely theoretical reasons.

Looking at Jung's personal position during this period, it should be appreciated that he was young and at the beginning of his career. His great dynamism and creativity could not have been contained within the theoretical framework of association experiments and complexes, however original these were. In addition to being an expression of his own personal problematic, the theory of complexes was also firmly established within the Burghölzli tradition of investigating the dissociability of the psyche: from Forel's 'dissociation', to Blueler's understanding of 'schizophrenia' as a 'loosening of associations' and a 'disharmony among affects'.[9] Jung trained and worked at the Burghölzli hospital between 1900 and 1909 under the directorship of Eugen Bleuler. This was a particularly fertile time for him with an eminent team of researchers – psychiatrists from Europe and the United States. There was much encouragement to new ideas and trends. Thus, Jung's great interest in the novel and controversial methods of psychoanalysis of the Viennese rebel fitted well with the spirit of Burghölzli. Moreover, Jung's immense attraction to and respect for Freud should be placed against the background of his ambivalent relationship with Bleuler. Ellenberger reminds us of the oddity that Jung made no reference whatsoever in his autobiography to his teacher, supervisor and chief![16] Jung, for whatever reasons, was not inspired sufficiently by Bleuler as a model and leader. But with Freud it was different. The relationship between these two men has since assumed almost legendary dimensions and has created a controversy which even today does not seem to have uttered its last formulation (cf. Redfearn[83]). This controversy spreads well over the boundaries of their technical differences, and includes many myths about their personal temperaments and life styles.

To return to Jung's theoretical development, during this period he understood 'the elements of psychic life' as forming 'functional units' with three components: 'sense-perception, intellectual components (ideas, memory-images, judgements, etc), and feeling tone'.[44] These were interlinked, so that when one was focused upon, all the others were also activated. Now Jung's experience with the word association experiments and his reading of Freud gave rise to a new understanding of complexes which incorporated the theory of repression.

At a given moment, when any component/s of the complex (sense-perception, intellectual or affective elements) comes to the individual's attention, it inevitably 'irritates' all the other components as well as producing

bodily changes . . . which in turn alter most of the sensations on which the normal ego is based. Consequently the normal ego loses its attention-tone (or its clarity, or its stimulating and inhibiting influence on other associations). It is compelled to give way to the other, stronger sensations connected with the new complex . . . [44]

The ego, therefore, tries to avoid being overwhelmed by the 'stronger sensation' of individual complexes and attempts to 'silence' aspects or components of the threatening complex. The stronger the feeling-tone accompanying a complex, the more undesirable it will be for the ego. Following this approach, Jung had no difficulty in accepting the limited importance of *sexuality* in the formation of psychopathological conditions because, undeniably, sexual complexes have 'the strongest and most lasting effects . . . where their feeling-tone is constantly maintained, for instance by unsatisfied sexual desire'.[44] Thus it was in the context of this framework that Jung utilized the concepts of repression and sexuality, two of the main tools of the Freudian theoretical arsenal. Starting from different premises, both men arrived at a similar understanding of repression as a partial process of interlinked mechanisms of sensory, perceptual, and intellectual as well as affective elements, necessary in maintaining the supremacy of the ego over the potential thread of disrupting impulses. In addition, both underlined the important role of the affective components (Freud: 'unpleasure'; Jung: strong feeling-tone).

Thus, Jung kept developing his own theory of complexes along the lines he had established during his earlier researches while incorporating those psychoanalytic ideas and terms which he found compatible with his own views. Continuing along this way Jung understood symbols once again in terms of his theory of complexes: Normal functioning requires a certain inhibition of the various complexes:

The effects of the complex must normally be feeble and indistinct because they lack the full cathexis of attention which is taken up by the ego-complex . . . For this reason the autonomous complex can only 'think' superficially and unclearly, i.e. *symbolically*, and the end–results . . . which filter through into the activity of the ego-complex and into consciousness will be similarly constituted (my italics).[44]

Jung, therefore, in this period understood symbols as precisely those complex components which, burdened with the task of expressing the 'whole system behind them', i.e. the autonomous complex in its entirety, inevitably have to convey meaning that exceeds their 'normal capacity'. Following the essence of this analysis Jung was able to write that ' . . . dreams, too, are constructed along similar lines; they are symbolic expressions of the repressed complex'.

Jung always remained faithful to his own problematic and in a sense never identified completely with the Freudian theories, although he used great parts of them. Yet, again, this usage was in line with his own terms. Even during the peak of their relationship, in 1909, Jung kept the association experiments so central to his psychological understanding that he wrote that 'everyday life is at bottom an entensive and greatly varied association experiment'.[47] However, at no time did Jung feel disloyal to what he considered to be the fundamentals of psychoanalysis. He identified with it completely (being the first president of the International Psychoanalytic Association, and editor of its official publication) and defended both the cause of psychoanalysis and the person of Freud in international forums. He saw no contradiction in that, as he accepted psychoanalysis not as a set of dogmatic and irrevocable principles, but as a revolutionary new theory in its early stages, flexible and receptive to innovations.

As early as 1906 Jung made his position very clear to Freud regarding psychoanalytic theories by making an important distinction. In a letter to Freud, referring to a critic of psychoanalysis, Professor Aschaffenburg, Jung wrote:

What I can appreciate . . . are your psychological views, whereas I am still pretty far from understanding . . . the genesis of hysteria . . . It seems to me that though the genesis of hysteria is predominantly, it is not exclusively, sexual. I take the same view of your *sexual theory*. Harping exclusively on these *delicate theoretical questions*, Aschaffenburg forgets *the essential thing*, your *psychology*, from which psychiatry will one day be sure to reap inexhaustive rewards (my italics).[74]

Two days later Freud replied: 'Your writings have long led me to suspect that your appreciation of my psychology does not extend to all my views of hysteria and the problem of sexuality, but I venture to hope that in the course of the years you will come much closer to me than you now think possible'.[74]

Thus Jung differentiated between

a) Freud's 'psychology' which he understood as the main innovation, as 'the essential thing' and

b) the whole body of those 'delicate theoretical questions' connected with hysteria and, mainly, sexuality, which he considered peripheral and unpalatable – Freud knew of this throughout but preferred to hope that Jung one day would 'come much closer' to him.

Jung sincerely believed the inconclusiveness of those 'delicate theoretical questions'. (cf Stepansky[92]). 'Freud had never propounded a cut-and-dried theory of hysteria . . . his theoretical formulations can claim the status of working hypothesis' Jung wrote in 1908[45] at a time when Freud had already produced a number of major works on the subject. Having, though, later placed the theory of sexuality within the framework of his own theories (i.e. accepting it as a legitimate form of a particularly powerful complex), Jung had no difficulty at all in actually defending (his own reading of) it. A characteristic example of such defence is the following passage:

. . . The public can forgive Freud least of all for his sexual symbolism. In my view he is really easiest to follow here, because this is just where mythology, expressing the fantasy-thinking of all races, has prepared the ground in the most instructive way . . . there are uncommonly far-fetching and significant analogies between the Freudian symbolisms and the symbols of poetic fantasy in individuals and in whole nations. The Freudian symbol and its interpretation is therefore nothing unheard of . . . [46]

It may thus be noticed that once Jung *read* Freud according to his own problematic it was possible to extend his own earlier system of the Other-as-complex. Gradually Jung adopted *symbol* as an equivalent of *complex* (Jacobi[38]). However, this exchange of terms should not be seen as a static and meaningless exercise. Jung soon moved on, referring to symbols more as carriers of the meaning of complexes. One of the most significant implications of this development was the broadening of the meaning and application of the Other (as complex) by including more 'shared' or 'collective' forms of the Other. Jung had earlier noted 'shared' complexes in his studies of patterns of complexes within families.[47-8] In his paper on the psychology of rumour he discussed the case of a girl's dream with sexual overtones toward her teacher and how that sparked off a rumour about some alleged actual sexual involvement with that teacher.[49] Jung interpreted that phenomenon in terms of a general sexual complex that all girl students 'shared'. It is worth observing that no more reference to the 'shared' complex is to be found in Jung's work and it may be assumed, with not undue justification, that he found it extremely difficult to relate this type of complex within the framework of his existing system of the Other-as-complex. In order to expound on this 'shared' and 'collective' Other he had to move on to a new conceptual framework, i.e. the Other-as-symbol. The latter offered him a better opportunity for investigating the ramifications and consequences of this phenomenon. Hence the Other-as-symbol enabled Jung to explicitly associate the Other with mythology, history of language, and artistic creativity, as well as with the national, racial and collective network of symbolism.

Thus in this period, by marrying the complex to psychoanalysis, Jung was able to establish contact with a whole new world of rich relatives. Freud's theory of the unconscious provided the much wanted fruitful theoretical context for Jung's own investigations and problematic. However, it should be borne in mind that the 'Psychoanalytic Period' should more accurately refer to the time when Jung utilized Freudian theories to express his own problematic rather than a period of theoretical coincidence between the two men under the banner of psychoanalysis.

Period of Transition

In this section the examination of Jung's life and work in the light of his problematic of the Other will cover approximately the period between the years 1912-16. The most widely discussed event of this time is, of course, his parting with Freud and his subsequent struggle to find his own way. In order to deal with the complexities which this period presents the researcher the material is divided into three subsections entitled: 'The Break', 'The Breakdown', and 'The Breakthrough'.

THE BREAK

The logical question arises as to what kind of 'break' one is referring to if, as it was shown above, Jung never actually identified totally with the Freudian theories in the first place but always remained true to his own problematic. On a purely pragmatic level the 'break' should refer to the termination of the externally manifested forms of personal friendship and professional association between the two men. The qualification 'externally manifested forms' is necessary as it is difficult if not impossible to ascertain when and if at all their friendship ended.

At least on Jung's part there was always a sense of loyalty and respect for his master despite their differences. An example of this was 'the warmest of telegrams of welcome' (van der Post[96]) which Jung sent Freud when he heard the good news of Freud's safe arrival in Britain after leaving Nazi-occupied Vienna in 1938.

Much has been written about the legendary relationship of these two men and its tragic end when the brilliant 'Crown Prince' broke away from his mentor, and many theories have been advanced as to the cause of this unlooked for termination. It might thus be useful to group the contributing factors for the break into the political, psychological, and theoretical.

Understandably, Freud was very sensitive about the survival of his revolutionary theories. Szasz goes as far as to liken the institution of psychoanalysis to industrial corporations which have to protect their patent products.[94] In Jung Freud saw not only a capable successor with an impeccable scientific background but also a non-Jew who could add credibility to the early psychoanalytic movement, which consisted mainly of Viennese Jews. Freud did not hide his fears 'that people would think of psychoanalysis as a Jewish movement' (Blanton[8]) and insisted that 'a gentile [Jung] must be the leader of the movement' (Stekel[91]). This did not please the old faithfuls however, who viewed Freud's fervent favouritism of Jung with suspicion and bitterness. They frequently exerted considerable pressure on Freud to abandon his preferential treatment of Jung, whom they called 'Blond Siegfried'. Stekel, a characteristic example of the objectors, left the psychoanalytic movement accusing his 'adorable master' of 'sacrificing' him, his 'most faithful collaborator, for an ungrateful one'.[91]

An overemphasis of the political factors in the relationship between Freud and Jung could lead to a hypothesis that the break was due to changes in these political considerations, that is, either Freud could not withstand the excessive pressure on him by his Jewish Viennese colleagues, or that there was later a time when he saw more profit for the 'organisation' in the removal of Jung. Yet neither of these views have sufficient support. Another use of political factors in interpreting the break is advanced by Stepansky. Also aware of the existence of theoretical differences right from the beginning of the Freud-Jung relationship, Stepansky suggests that the break did not occur earlier because Freud needed Jung for the political survival of psychoanalysis.[92]

Although there was some validity in Freud's fears of growing anti-Semitism against psychoanalysis, most commentators agree that his misgivings were exaggerated and bordering on obsession. Allowing for the justifiable overprotectiveness pioneers usually have for their new discoveries, Freud's reaction in this respect does seem out of proportion. In order to comprehend these phenomena therefore a psychological approach should also be considered. For one, Freud's ambivalence toward his own Jewishness should not be forgotten (cf. Bakan[4], E. Freud[20], Robert[84]). His emphasis, time and again, of Jung's non-Jewishness might be more indicative of his own inner struggle for identity rather than of an objective assessment of Jung's positive political role as a gentile. The most important psychological consideration, however, is Freud's personal attachment to Jung. He called him 'Crown Prince', likened him to Alexander the Great who expanded his father's empire, and in general attributed almost messianic qualities to him. But the feelings were reciprocal. Jung had an immense admiration and respect for Freud which he did not hide. Both men valued tremendously their relationship as it came at a very opportune moment for each. It should therefore not be surprising if both, consciously or unconsciously at first underestimated existing theoretical differences for the sake of their relationship.

The majority of authors dealing with the break, however, seem to ignore or underemphasize the political and psychological factors involved and prefer to concentrate almost exclusively on the theoretical differences as the only or main cause. This position is not without justification, as the two protagonists themselves seem to have strongly supported if not actually originated this interpretation. A typical instance is Jung's remark in 1935 in his Tavistock lectures: ' . . . I started out entirely on Freud's lines. I was even considered to be his best disciple. I was on excellent terms with him until I had the idea that certain things are symbolical. Freud would not agree to this . . . '.[59] Even the first claim in this statement is incorrect; Jung did not start out *entirely* on Freud's lines. Freud, too, repeatedly emphasized the theoretical nature of their disagreement. He, in fact, never mentioned any other reasons for the break. At the end of his history of the psychoanalytic movement he succinctly summarized his views when he wrote: (Jung's) 'new teaching which aims at replacing psychoanalysis signifies an abandonment of analysis and a secession from it'.[29] Jung at least mentioned in his autobiography some additional reasons of psychological nature, such as Freud's dogmatic and authoritarian personality, as well as his own inner turmoil.

The overall insistence, however, on both men's behalf in excluding non–theoretical reasons to account for their break could be understood in terms of the following: first, no self-respecting serious theorist wishes to mix his personal feelings in his scientific work; and second, it is possible that they themselves were not aware of the exact reasons.

According to the argument of the present chapter, the question to be asked is not 'what are the theoretical differences which led to the break?' but rather 'why at *this* time did the existing theoretical differences assume such importance as to contribute to a break?'

Jung's book *The Symbols of Transformation* (or *Wandlungen*, the abbreviated German title) is often cited as *the* cause of the break. Yet in it Jung very clearly explains that since the appearance of Freud's book *Three Essays on Sexuality* in 1905 'a change has taken place in the libido conception; its field of application has been widened. An extremely clear example of this amplification is this present work. However, I must state that Freud, as well as myself, saw the need of widening the conception of libido . . . ' In other words what Jung was doing was not an act of defiance but simply following common direction with Freud. It should be noted that this passage (p.77) has been removed from the subsequent editions of the book and it is therefore not included in Jung's *Collected Works* (which takes the 1952 edition)!

A significant development took place when the two men 'saw the need of widening the concept of libido': a common joint expedition into the realms of archeology, mythology and anthropology. It is rather difficult to establish which of the two first ventured into those virgin lands and Selesnick's words seem to capture the essence of this issue: 'Jung's application of psychoanalytic theory to the understanding of myths and their relationship to dreams and neuroses, rekindled Freud's interest in anthropology'.[90] These researches created an almost frantic atmosphere of excitement which is clearly reflected in their correspondence.

On 14 October 1909 Jung communicates to his older friend his 'obsession' to 'cast the net wide' and that their researches should include 'archeology or rather mythology', fields which Jung described as 'a mine of marvelous material'. Freud replied 'I am glad you share my belief that we must conquer the whole field of mythology'. A few weeks later Jung wrote how he 'was immersed every evening in the history of symbols, i.e., in mythology and archeology', and Freud welcomes that with 'delight', as he would feel 'a little less loneliness' with Jung also involved in the same work. Further in the same letter, referring to a certain student of mythology he wrote that his ideas are similar to '*ours*'. And again, 'your letters delight me because they suggest a frenzy of satisfying work'.

The euphoria of this period is overwhelming. The correspondence is full of superlatives. Jung writes 'I often wish I had you near me' and Freud says how 'desperately sorry' he is that he is not. Freud writes 'your deepened view of symbolism has all my sympathy' and later he is 'overjoyed' that Jung shows such enormous interest in his essay on Leonardo 'and at your saying that you were coming closer to my way of thinking'. Jung talks of the 'rich booty for our knowledge of the human psyche' which he will bring from his 'wanderings' and Freud replies that 'it is always right to go where your impulses lead'. Jung gradually feels that they 'are on the threshold of something really sensational'.

Such is the general feel of their correspondence, until Jung starts writing about the emotional strain that his work has on him while at the same time shows signs of procrastination in his correspondence. He had actually mentioned earlier how he 'was plagued by complexes' and about 'the Walpurgis Nights' of his unconscious but somehow because his work and correspondence were not affected the issue does not seem to have been given much significance. By February 1912 Jung writes about 'having grisly fights with the hydra of mythological phantasy' and 'feeling intellectually drained'. Freud appears to have failed to appreciate the extent of his younger friend's psychological turmoil or to understand its meaning. Responding more to Jung's remissness in his correspondence, Freud interpreted it as a manifestation of Jung's 'father-complex', i.e. as an expression of Jung's ambivalence toward his 'father', Freud. Jung does not seem to have been seriously drawn into this interpretation although he did entertain it for a while. One gets the impression that he was so involved with his own internal upheaval that he could not afford to put much energy in trying to clarify further his position to Freud. The gap began to widen. Freud attempted to pacify Jung, admitting to have been 'a demanding correspondent' and how he had since 'become undemanding and not to be feared'. The situation, however, began to deteriorate rather rapidly and within about a year the correspondence and the relationship came to an end.

In trying to further understand the meaning of the 'break' within the broader perspective of Jung's life and work four interrelated hypotheses will now be advanced.

First hypothesis: Jung's reference to his interest in archeology and mythology at this time, which he admitted was a revival of an old similar interest, is to be understood as referring to a revival of his old interest in the No.2 personality and, broadly speaking, to the whole problematic of the Other.

In Jung's letters to Freud one finds the following relevant passages:

. . . all my delight in archeology (buried for years) has sprung into life again . . . (10 November 1909)

. . . mythology certainly has me in its grip. I bring to it a good deal of archeological interest from my early days . . . (10 January 1910)

. . . I have read *Leonardo* straight through and shall soon come back to it again. The transition to mythology grows out of this essay from inner necessity, actually it is the first essay of yours with whose inner development I felt perfectly in tune from the start . . . (17 June 1910)

Jung spoke about previous interests in archeology and mythology when, in his memoirs, he discussed his dilemma of what to study at the University. He then wrote of two opposing directions: on the one hand, history, philosophy and particularly archeology ('. . . I was intensely interested in everything Egyptian and Babylonian, and would have liked best to be an archeologist . . . '[65]), and on the other hand, science. On the very same page Jung describes this dilemma as '. . . No.1 and No.2 . . . wrestling for a decision . . . ' This is not the only connection Jung made between No.2, the Other, and archeology. In the chapter on his school years of the same book, *Memories, Dreams, Reflections*, he explicitly noted that ' . . . Science met . . . the needs of No.1 personality, whereas the humane or historical studies [Graeco-Roman, Egyptian, and prehistoric archeology] provided beneficial instruction for No.2 . . . '. In his letter to Freud 17 June 1910, Jung stresses the *inner development* and *inner necessity* of the transition to mythology, with which he feels 'perfectly in tune from the start'. The strong wording of this passage merits further examination. After such intense collaboration and friendship, Jung admits that Freud's *Leonardo* was the *first* work of his master with which he felt 'perfectly in tune'. *Leonardo* was indeed Freud's first essay where he introduced mythology in a serious manner, so if the close link between mythology and the Other is accepted, then Jung's excitement is understandable – it must have been the first indication to him that Freud perhaps shared his problematic of the Other. This inference is further substantiated if the actual theme of *Leonardo* is considered. In that essay Freud discusses da Vinci's 'double nature' ('as an artist and as a scientific investigator')![24] It is thus highly probable that Jung's enthusiasm for this work was directly related to his problematic of the Other.

Second hypothesis: Jung's reference to himself being gripped by mythology and archeology is to be understood as suggesting that at this particular period he was gripped by the problematic of the Other in an especially forceful manner.

In addition to the points already made and according to the general development of Jung's problematic of the Other, one would expect that Jung would now have arrived at a decisive turning point in his own relationship with his problematic. Jung, at the end of his previous period, had started seemingly to return to the globality and generality of the Other, although this time not in the primitive manner of his early childhood formulations, but within an appreciation of the Other in terms of *differentiated functions* (more precisely, differentiated structuring principles) of collective application (= the Other-as-symbol). This return to the original problematic with the enrichment of the meticulously and painfully traversed routes of clinical and experimental psychiatry, as well as Freudian psychoanalysis, coupled with the timely revived interest in archeology and mythology (in short, the modes of No. 2 personality) must have created a climate in him which would make intelligible to any researcher Jung's strong wording in describing the 'grip' that his work had on him during this period. Additional support for this hypothesis is offered in the letters where Jung insisted that nothing in his work was 'drawn out of a hat', but was a 'natural development' which could 'not be halted' and claimed that a great amount of libido had 'disappeared into' his work, leaving him 'intellectually drained'.

Third hypothesis: Jung's reference to the 'something really sensational' that he and Freud were on 'the threshold' of discovering is to be understood as an expression of Jung's genuine belief that despite their original differences they were now marching together with a common purpose, approaching the territory of the problematic of the Other; and that this belief created in him great expectations of Freud.

Even the casual reader of the Freud–Jung correspondence of this period would arrive at the conclusion that both men *believed* that they shared a common theoretical platform. The references to 'our' theory as well as to the common investment in the fields of mythology abound. If this is added to our previous two hypotheses one would accept that Jung believed that Freud shared his own problematic. This view can be further supported by Jung's special exhilaration at reading Freud's *Leonardo*. It is very likely that Jung thought that the theme of the Other (which was the motif in *Leonardo*) had the same 'inner' meaning for Freud as it had for himself. This special shiver of hope must have activated hoards of expectations in Jung that Freud would assist him in solving their 'common' problematic. Moreover, Jung received repeated encouragements from Freud to follow his own 'impulse'. Freud not only allowed him to criticize the 'libido question' but also 'expecting much light' from him, hoped that he would 'clarify certain vague ideas' of his (Freud's) own. One therefore wonders what Jung was thinking of while reading Freud's blessings to 'conquer more than he himself had managed', and also of what he meant when he wrote to Freud about 'something really sensational' which they were on the threshold of discovering.

Fourth hypothesis: Jung's reference to his 'conflicts' and difficulties during this period is to be understood as suggesting: a) a primary *inner conflict* created by the critical stage of the problematic of the Other; and b) a secondary conflict between Freud and himself which developed after realizing that Freud could not meet his expectations, as he did not, after all, share Jung's problematic.

Jung repeatedly wrote about the 'grisly fights with the hydra of mythological phantasy' (read: inner conflicts with the problematic of the Other) and how they occupied all his libido, and as a separate issue from his 'father-complex' which he felt was responsible for his difficulties with Freud. In other words there were initially two sources or types of conflict: the one in connection with his newly launched expedition (read: his old problematic); and the other, in connection with Freud. The second conflict does not appear to have had much power. It was to this conflict, however, that Freud attributed Jung's procrastination in writing and it was Freud who time and again went back to this. Jung, on the other hand, was not that concerned about his correspondence, and after all, his delays in replying were not that protracted.

The problem with Freud, however, became more serious when Jung saw his own expectations not being fulfilled. Each of the two men was expecting clarification of his views from the other, believing meanwhile that their theoretical positions were identical. And it was at this particular time that they both became victims of their blind excitement, when each one hoped that a) previous differences would be eradicated and b) that they would soon together make the 'sensational' discovery which would prove the correctness of each one's previous (separate) direction. Their common excitement, alas, was as it turned out not about the same thing. Gradually, and despite his earlier impressions, it started dawning on Jung that Freud in fact did not even share his problematic. It was only then that his original and primary conflict with the Other flared up in painful dimensions. This conflict assumed even greater proportions when he experienced the withdrawal of Freud's friendly and moral support. Jung was now left alone to cope with the soul-breaking disappointment that the 'sensational' solution to the problematic of the Other was no longer in sight, and with the 'grisly' fights with the Other which were now becoming fiercer, as well as with Freud's increasing suspicion and hostility because he (Jung) was likewise not living up to Freud's expectations.

THE BREAKDOWN

After breaking away from Freud, Jung plunged into a period of intense 'inner uncertainty', 'disorientation' and suffering which he has vividly described in his autobiography under the title 'Confrontation with the Unconscious'. By leaving Freud, Jung did not only leave the security of a friendship; he also let loose his hopeful grip on the psychoanalytic framework. Without now any framework within which to render comprehensible even his own drifting away Jung found himself alone and unprotected on the seas of his unconscious. His last attempt to make a meaningful use of the psychoanalytic language by expressing his personal problematic was in t'ie *Wandlungen*, and it failed. (see below). The findings of his ventures into the enchanting lands of mythology, archeology and history, undigested as they were, had no significant impact on him. Moreover, his sense of unfulfillment became more acute as he painfully experienced the gap between the meaning of his findings and the psychoanalytic language that was used to account for them. Thus, with the gradual realization that the Freudian 'terminology and theory' were 'concretistic' and 'too narrow'[65] and his own framework so hopelessly inadequate that amounted to 'a few theoretical prejudices of dubious value' Jung had understandably arrived at a deadlock. Further self-exploration proved equally futile at this stage: ' . . . the dialogue with myself became uncomfortable and I stopped thinking. I had reached a dead end'.

The only way out left for Jung was to stop attempting to understand his inner experiences and allow them to follow their own course without much interference from the conscious. He thus allowed a series of powerful dreams progressively to 'activate' his unconscious. This method led him to a yearning for the security of his childhood and he began to play old favourite games by 'gathering suitable stones'. This activity in turn re-evoked forgotten memories and experiences, and Jung felt that he was then 'on the way to discovering my own myth'[65]. The force and complexity of his rich unconscious fantasies soon impressed upon Jung that if their 'meaning' was not grasped their disruptive and destructive potential could come to the fore. Finding himself under this pressure and without an adequate theoretical structure to account for the meaning of that inner turmoil, Jung resorted to a new method by *translating his emotions into images*. A number of such images gradually emerged from Jung's psyche which he experienced as 'not me', as Other personalities. He accepted them as 'mediators' communicating meaning from the unconscious. His experience taught him that 'the essential thing [was] to differentiate oneself from these unconscious contents by personifying them, and at the same time to bring them into relationship with consciousness . . . '.

Jung made several attempts to bring these images into relationship with his consciousness but always became more aware that he had not yet found the 'right language' to do so in a satisfactory manner. He had tried to write down the fantasies (in the Black Book) and later even to pictorially represent them in drawings and paintings (in the Red Book) only to painfully feel the inadequacy of these attempts. He was desperately seeking a firm and real understanding of the situation and for him 'reality meant scientific comprehension'. Yet the reality of those fantasies was as convincing and gripping (if not even more so) than any rigorous theoretical formulation. Jung's confusion was thus increased and his suffering became almost unbearable.

These phenomena stirred the imagination of many authors who offered a variety of interpretations of them ranging from insane and psychotic to visionary and occult. Remaining, however, within the contours of the present *reading* of Jung, the breakdown should not refer to a psychological, emotional, psychotic, or similar event but to an *epistemological* one. It is noteworthy that Gregory Bateson, admittedly from a different approach, also characterised Jung's predicament of this period as an 'epistemological crisis'.[6] In the face of the events and experiences Jung's system/language which he used to account for his reality and problematic broke down. In other words, the theoretical formulation of the problematic of the Other that time became inadequate to account for the actual manifestations and very experience of the Other!

At closer examination, the steps Jung followed in his attempt to remedy his critical situation bear a striking resemblance to what he did in his childhood. They are also similar to the steps Jung discerned in his analysis of S. W.'s stages of development. As in his childhood games, Jung again during this period played with stones. This time, however, he was aware of the emotions that such activities released and, of course, the 'conversation' he now had with 'his' stones was much richer than the ones little Jung had with 'his stone'. Having thus successfully recapitulated his childhood process of encountering the Other, Jung proceeded with new forms of this encounter. This was hardly his free choice. It was as if Jung's unconscious, having gathered momentum from the successful recapitulation, was now forcing a full confrontation with his conscious part in a struggle for recognition. The most important image that emerged during this period was that of an ageless wise man whom Jung named Philemon. Jung had the highest respect for this inner image whom he considered as his 'psychagogue', 'inner guru' and who 'psychologically . . . represented superior insight'.[65] Philemon as Judith Hubback correctly noted, represented 'the other within'.[37] He was in many ways similar to S.W.'s Ivenes. However, it should be remembered that although Ivenes (as an Other) constituted a significant step in Jung's understanding of the Other she was actually no part of his own inner world. She was part of his theory, not of his own experience. After the No.2 personality of his childhood Jung did not have any direct experience of a personified form of the Other. It may thus be postulated that Jung's experience had to 'catch up' with his theoretical understanding of the Other. In this sense, Philemon was Jung's own Ivenes. Both internal images were similar insofar as they represented some inner wisdom but they were also different in at least one important aspect: whereas Ivenes took over completely S. W.'s personality, Jung had the great advantage of being in actual relationship with Philemon. This meant that he interacted with his inner image in a manner that allowed him to subject Philemon (and all other inner images of this period) to the ethical scrutiny of his consciousness.

Philemon had all the characteristics of what was earlier termed Anticipated Whole Other: he emerged at a time when Jung's personality was fragmented, in the sense that his language could not adequately account for his experiences, and represented an anticipated state of wholeness. Moreover, Philemon, unlike Fragment Others, possessed qualities and wisdom that transcended the personal repertoire of Jung's own conscious personality. Yet it is puzzling to observe that Jung during this period had experienced another inner figure which was in opposition to Philemon. According to Jung this other figure represented 'a kind of earth demon or metal demon' and was 'the spirit of nature', as opposed to Philemon whom Jung experienced as representing 'the spiritual aspect, or "meaning"'. His name was Ka and he was, in essence the earthy counterpart of Philemon. Should then Philemon (and Ka for that matter) be accepted as Fragment Other personalities and not, after all, as Anticipated Whole Others? From the above discussion there would be no justification in relegating Philemon to the status of a Fragment Other personality, especially when it is remembered that such Others were personifications of undesirable strong unconscious tendencies and had rather detrimental effects; Philemon was obviously not that. If, however, this puzzle is examined within the context of what was to follow, a new formulation of the problematic of the Other emerges.

Jung wrote that two events contributed to his emergence out of the darkness of this period. The first was his successful confrontation with the negative influences of anima and the second and 'principal event' was his understanding of mandala drawings. It was about the same time when Jung experienced Ka that he also felt the presence of 'a woman within himself' whom he named anima. Ka's feminine qualities are not difficult to recognize. Contrasting him to Philemon Jung accepted him as the one 'who made everything real, but also obscured the halcyon spirit, meaning, or replace it by beauty'.[65] Later in his researches Jung confirmed that the ancient Egyptian Ka-soul corresponded to the Western anima and that both were of the same complex which 'is invariably of the feminine gender'.[56] Jung first experienced the negative aspects of the anima when he felt her seductive power, in trying to make him believe that his drawings and other pictorial representations of his unconscious which he was producing at the time were of great artistic value. He felt pressurised by the anima to see himself as a 'misunderstood artist'. Jung dealt successfully with those urges by relating consciously to them, thus subjecting them to his conscious and ethical scrutiny. It was then that his mandala drawings, which he had begun painting earlier, started becoming intelligible to him. In them he saw the *self*, the 'wholeness of the personality'.[65] He wrote that through them he 'acquired a living conception of the self. The self, I thought, was like the monad which I am.' Thus the mandalas with their clear centre and peripheral parts all arranged as ornamented wheels represented the transcendental totality of the personality, the unity of all Others. Jung unmistakably felt the profundity of his new discovery and realized that he had reached the end of the period of dark disorientation. His problematic was yet again enriched by new insights which led to another reformulation.

Jung found experientially that there was an Anticipated Whole Other of a higher order than the ones he knew of before. Philemon, indeed an Anticipated Whole Other, had a counterpart, Ka. Only when these two were dialectically superseded the higher Other emerged, the Self. The Self, therefore, could be understood as the ultimate form of the Other, the highest Anticipated Whole Other, which at the same time also paradoxically represents the most inner core, indeed the centre of personality. Having achieved a direct contact with the Self, Jung had experientially completed his search for the Other. However, he immediately realized that these experiences were too personal to have had any theoretical value that could be communicated to others, and so set himself a task to translate them into scientific language. They provided the *prima materia* of all his future work.

THE BREAKTHROUGH

Jung's life and work stand as one of the clearest examples of the dialectical interrelationship between experience and theoretical language in psychology. Furthermore, it is here argued that Jung forged the bonds of this relationship in terms of his problematic of the Other. His theoretical development and understanding of this issue had outpaced his actual experience of the Other, after his No. 2 childhood personality, culminating in an alienating discrepancy when he adopted Freud's psychoanalytic language. However much he tried to mould psychoanalysis to suit his own problematic the point came when he could do that no longer and had to abandon his efforts. Philemon, Ka and the mandala-Self (among other images and figures) however not only brought forward Jung's experiential understanding of the Other, but even outpaced all theoretical formulations of his problematic. What remained now for Jung was as he put it, 'to distill within the vessel' of his 'scientific work' all his newly acquired experiences, i.e. by developing a new theoretical formulation which would account for the Self as the ultimate Other. In order to gradually

follow this new development it will be helpful to consider briefly the
roots of this conceptualization in two significant works of this period:
The Symbols of Transformation and *The Seven Sermons to the Dead*.

In his book *Symbols of Transformation*:*[50] Jung undertook an
extensive analysis of a series of fantasies of Miss Miller, an American
patient of a respected colleague of his. Working on somebody else's
fantasies offered Jung the opportunity to examine his problematic
from a safe distance while actually dealing with real experiences and
not abstract theories. He admitted that they were the perfect catalyst
while his wife Emma went a little further when she wrote to Freud that
this work in fact meant for her husband 'self-analysis'.[74]

In the theoretical introduction to the book Jung examined a number
of themes of the *double* (or, according to the terminology of the present
study, the Other) including the double role of Faust: creator –
destroyer, the Sun-hero: creative – destructive, Byron's Heaven and
Earth. The most important of all was his thesis on two kinds of
thinking. He called them 'directed' (relating it to science and 'thinking
in words') and 'non directed' (related to 'dream phantasy' and
'thinking in images') respectively. Insofar as non directed thinking
was producing an 'overwhelmingly subjectively distorted idea of the
world' Jung regarded that 'state of mind as infantile'. It lies, he said, 'in
our individual past, and in the past of mankind'. He understood non –
directed thinking as not only the characteristic mode of thought in
children but also of earlier historical times and accepted that
'ontogenesis corresponds in psychology to phylogenesis'. This central
distinction unmistakably corresponds to Jung's original dichotomy
between the No.1 and No.2 personalities and we can now understand
it to be his first serious attempt to conceptualize his problematic in a
broad system elevated to an almost universal principle of
psychological functioning.

Against this background Jung analysed Miss Miller's fantasies and
found similar dichotomies. For example in her first poem he identified
'a creative god' with 'dual nature, moral and physical' and in another
discerned two tendencies. The first he called 'renunciation of the
world' which meant a movement of the libido inwards, an
'introversion' offering one the opportunity to deal with inner conflicts
and tune in with nature, whereas the second, 'acceptance of the
world', referred to an outward movement of the libido with
'adaptation' as the aim. From these two tendencies Jung proceeded to
reconstruct a theory of the libido. Postulating the same fundamental
duality in libido itself, Jung replaced his own expression 'psychic
energy' with the term libido. Calling upon the Freudian terms of
sublimation and repression he argued that the 'primal' sexual libido

*The first edition of this book was titled *The Psychology of the Unconscious*.

can be *transformed* into 'secondary impulses' of 'associated functions' thus becoming 'desexualized' and/or 'spiritualized'. Focusing, in particular, on the issue of incest Jung saw it as a *symbolic* representation of the critical conflict of libido in either returning to its source (mother) or branching 'outside into human contact'. Without a suitable, coherent theory of his own Jung had to borrow Freudian notions in order to clothe his new insights. A characteristic example of this borrowing was his use of the term *wish*. Jung proposed that the non-directed or 'phantastic thinking tells us of mythical or other material of undeveloped and no longer recognized wish tendencies of the soul'. Wish in Freudian psychoanalysis is unequivocally connected to sexual libido and is a product of repression, in short, it is an integral part of Freud's language or system. Jung's new usage of the term overstretches it to cover non-personal (collective or transpersonal) unconscious tendencies, thus extracting it from its own native structure and creating a contextual vacuum. Although it is easy for us now to understand what Jung was referring to, one has to appreciate that before the theories of collective unconscious and archetypes were introduced, phrases such as 'wish tendencies of the soul' meant very little. Yet Jung went further and postulated 'typical' images which expressed symbolically 'typical' wish tendencies of the soul. Examples were the 'hero' and the 'mother' which Jung termed *primordial images*. Jung subsequently wrote that these were the first formulation of what he later called 'archetypes'.[2]

Jung's dissatisfaction with his work at this point is therefore understandable, as it included seminal insights which, by the virtue of having been planted in a foreign theoretical territory, could not grow and come to any fruition. A development of his own theoretical ground was needed, rich in its own experiential substratum.

Four years after *The Symbols of Transformation* Jung, deep in his period of disorientation, wrote *The Seven Sermons to the Dead*[52] as one of his many attempts to formulate the 'right language' and adequately account for his own experiences. He did not claim authorship of it as he felt that 'it fell quite unexpectedly into my lap like a ripe fruit'[1] and attributed it to a Basilides from Alexandria. Although it is not included in his psychological writings (it is not part of his *Collected Works*) this short poetical piece occupies an important position in Jung's development of his problematic. It consists of seven sermons that the author gave to the dead who 'came back from Jerusalem where they found not what they sought'.

In the first and longest sermon Basilides/Jung presents a universal dichotomy: the realms of Pleroma and Creatura. The first is 'infinite and eternal, hath no qualities, since it hath all qualities' whereas the second, the realm of created beings 'is confined within time and space' and it has 'qualities'. It was to represent these two realms with their various qualities and subdivisions that Jung drew his first mandala. Anything beyond the outer circle belonged exclusively to Pleroma and everything within that circle belonged to both Pleroma and Creatura. Human beings insofar as 'we are parts of the pleroma, the pleroma is also in us'. If however, 'we fall into the pleroma itself' we 'cease to be creatures. We are given over to dissolution in the nothingness. This is the death of the creature . . . '. We therefore have to remain in the differentiated realm of creatura while at the same time retain our pleromatic nature. This delicate pursuit was called 'Principium Individuationis' and it was the first reference to the 'process of individuation' that Jung was to later develop. The author further reminds the dead of the 'pairs of opposites' which in the pleroma are perfectly balanced producing no overall 'effect', which is not the case with us. By the same token, since the pleroma has no qualities 'we create them through thinking. If therefore ye strive after . . . any qualities . . . ye pursue thoughts which flow to you and out of the pleroma'. This is yet another hint at the collective unconscious. Thus the 'principium individuationis' does not refer to any intellectual, theoretical pursuit; 'not your thinking, but your being, is distinctiveness. Therefore not after difference, as ye think it, ye strive; but after YOUR OWN BEING.[9]

Having established these basic principles the author continues in the later sermons to develop the various subdivisions of creatura as progressively smaller, concentric circles and to interrelate their various characteristics and symbolic representations. Since the Creatura presupposes differentiation and includes pairs of opposites, all subsequently mentioned entities and symbols are arranged in such pairs. Not unexpectedly, one of these dichotomies is that of spirituality-sexuality, which appeared in the *Wandlungen*, and again their transpersonal nature is emphasised: 'Spirituality and sexuality are not your qualities, not things which ye possess and contain. But they possess and contain you'. They are 'things which reach beyond you, existing in themselves'. For these the author advises that they are both desirable but should be pursued only in the 'right measure'. In the last sermon the dead ask to be taught about man and Basilides/Jung likens him to a 'gateway through which from the outer world of gods, demons, and souls ye pass into the inner world'. Although man is not the centre of the universe but a 'small and transitory' speck in it, he is also of the pleroma and he has the potential of actualizing his pleromatic nature. The symbol of this potentiality when it becomes an actuality was that of one *star* lying at the very centre of the mandala, which the author urged the dead to see as man's ultimate goal, as his 'guiding god' and the final aim of life's journey. In his own Star man finds full fulfillment. 'This is his world, his pleroma, his divinity'. The centre of the mandala 'is a microcosm' which mirrors the macrocosm, as Heisig aptly noted,[36] and the Star cannot be anything else but the first symbol of the Self that Jung had experienced.

The *Seven Sermons*, written in poetic form, gave Jung the freedom to weed out all theoretical parasites unnecessary and alien to his own experience. He had already struggled with these in the *Wandlungen*, which had indeed constituted the spadework for establishing his own theoretical ground enriched with his own experiences. Moreover there were no demands on him to develop in an edifying poem a systematic and new theoretical language. The symbolic language of poetry enabled him to delve deep into his own psyche and record faithfully his new impulses in their embryonic form. The artificiality of theoretical formulations of the *Wandlungen* here gave place to genuine expressions of his lived experience which in turn paved the way for the clearer and more articulate experiences of the inner images such as Philemon and Ka. The two works in question, therefore, provide the actual link between on one hand Jung's psychoanalytic period, and on the other hand his ensuing epistemological breakdown, his dark disorientation with the emergence of the inner images (described in the Breakdown) and his later work.

The culmination of this whole period (of the Break trilogy) was the emergence of the Self as the ultimate Other, as an Anticipated Whole Other of a higher order capable, like the Star in the *Seven Sermons*, to transcend all existing oppositions. The Self was first alluded to in the *Seven Sermons* and was later experienced in the form of mandalas. What still remained was to formulate an adequate theoretical language and to render it intelligible within an objective psychological framework. As with the Homeric hero, the task was not completed by arriving (incognito) at the shores of Ithaka. Jung still had to conquer the inner palace and receive the crown . . .

The Years of Individuation

Having survived the treacherous traps in their varied forms Jung could now afford to concentrate on the final elaboration of his problematic. All the 'prima materia' of his later work was now ready. He had externalized his unconscious images, interacted with them and thus arrived at a clearer understanding of the Other, having even experienced glimpses of the Self. With the spade–work completed, it is not surprising that almost immediately the first seeds started growing. The same year he wrote the *Seven Sermons* he gave a lecture in Paris in which he began laying the foundations of his new theoretical language. In this significant work, entitled *The structure of the unconscious* Jung introduced the distinction between the personal and collective unconscious, the concepts of persona, anima and animus, as well as the principle of individuation (in a psychological context).[53]

In an attempt to rectify previous theoretical inconsistencies Jung now proposed that the contents of the unconscious do not only consist of the repressed 'infantile-sexual wish-fantasies' but also of 'all the psychic material that lies below the threshold of consciousness'. Moreover, 'the seeds of future conscious contents' are to be found in the 'material that has not yet reached' that threshold. It was to refer to the source of this material that Jung introduced the 'collective psyche'. He based his claim on his observations of the 'quite remarkable correspondence' of unconscious processes 'of the most widely separated peoples and races' which 'displays itself . . . in the extraordinary but well-authenticated analogies between the forms and motifs of autochthonous myths'. No longer the need for the distorted use of the 'wish tendencies of the soul' of the *Wandlungen*. The ground and matrix was now named and theoretically identified. The next step was to investigate its relation to the individual psyche with all its possible implications. Along similar lines which he followed in the *Seven Sermons*, Jung appreciated the dangers of a fusion between the individual and collective psyche and advanced the concept of 'individuation' (which at this time he used interchangeably with 'individuality') as 'the principle which makes possible, and if need be compels, a progressive differentiation from the collective psyche'. Discussing further these implications Jung understood 'persona' as the 'mask that feigns individuality, making others and oneself believe that one is individual, whereas one is simply acting a role through which the collective psyche speaks'). Anima and animus were 'kinds' of personae and represented the 'feminine being in man' and its counterpart, the male being in woman, respectively. All three of these 'typical' aspects of the human psyche (persona, anima, animus) constitute, in a sense, channels between the personal and collective, and as such they are mediating agencies between these two realms.

Three years later in a lecture at a joint meeting of the Aristotelian Society, the Mind Association and the British Psychological Society, at London University, Jung coined the term 'archetype': 'Wherever we meet with uniform and regularly recurring modes of apprehension we are dealing with an archetype, no matter whether its mythological character is recognized or not'.[54] Jung also maintained here that archetypes 'are the necessary *a priori* determinants of all psychic processes', thus creating a new category which included not only the above three 'typical' aspects of the psyche but also all other such 'typical' determinants.

Pondering on the fact that Jung introduced such significant key terms of his new theoretical language not actually in German but in French and English, one wonders whether he needed the distance of a complete break from his previous theoretical structure including even from the very language in which it was formulated. Moreover, these innovations were introduced neither in Zurich nor in Vienna but in Paris and London.

It was not until 1921 that Jung felt confident enough to systematize his new theoretical language into a coherent whole. He did this in his book *Psychological Types*,[55] where he also used the term *Self* for the first time. Essentially this book is a discussion of two main kinds of human nature, two psychological types (the introvert and the extravert) and of the Self as a uniting totality of the whole personality, which however, in unifying does not obliterate the underlying psychological types. The types undivided represent two natural and complimentary movements of the libido, i.e. inwardly towards the subject and outwardly towards the object. Once *one* such movement becomes 'habitual' and characteristic of a person, then one speaks of either an introverted *type* or an extraverted *type*. Jung further distinguished four 'psychological functions': thinking, feeling, sensation, and intuition; these he understood as the four primary 'phenomenal forms of libido'. The first two were 'rational' and the second pair 'irrational'. Jung argued that the selection of these categories was based on his own experience and not on any *a priori* theory. One can easily accept that claim as these divisions and subdivisions could be traced back to both the *Wandlungen* and the *Seven Sermons*. It was the appearance of the term *Self*, however, that threw into relief all other crucial terms, thus adding the last corner-stone to the ultimate structure of Jung's psychological language.

Jung defined the Self as 'the subject of my totality' which 'includes the unconscious psyche' in addition to the conscious Ego. He maintained that 'the individual Self is a portion, or excerpt or representative, of something universally present in all living creatures, and, therefore a correspondingly graduated kind of psychological process, which is born anew in every creature'.[55] One cannot help but be reminded of earlier insights into the No.2 personality and the Anticipated Whole Other. Jung actually stated that 'in unconscious phantasy the Self often appears as a super-ordinated or ideal personality'. Thus No.2, Ivenes, and Philemon might be accepted as *Self images*.

In the following forty years until his death in 1961 Jung went on elaborating on the interrelationships among these same main elements of his new structure, as well as broadening the scope of their applicability. There were no further large 'paradigmatic' changes. The rest of Jung's work may thus be accepted as a constant refinement of the last two complimentary formulations of his problematic, viz. The Other-as-archetype and the Other-as-Self.

Insofar as the Self is a typical and collective structure of psychological determinants or a typical quality of psychic phenomena, Jung understood it to be an archetype, indeed the archetype par excellence.[62] Archetypes are autonomous fragments of the collective unconscious which, piercing the surface of the conscious part of the personality, bring forth the inarticulate messages from the depths of the objective psyche. It is then up to the conscious personality whether to take such signals seriously and try to decipher them or ignore and suppress them. Jung's notion of *objective psyche* represents 'the psychic substratum upon which the individual consciousness is based'[58] and therefore 'stands for the collective unconscious'.[60] Neurosis, according to Jung, is the 'defence against the objective, inner activity of the psyche',[58] the rejection of the archetypal Other. Psychotherapy facilitates the otherwise natural and 'dialectic process of individuation' by establishing adequate channels of communication between the 'subjective ego' and the 'autonomous contents of the collective unconscious', the archetypes.[64] When activated archetypes convey in an experiential manner the corrective objectivity of the unconscious and thus force the individual to differentiate himself from the collective Other. The goal of individuation is the achievement of Selfhood. The Self, the ultimate form of one's own individuality is at the same time a collective form, an archetype. Although it represents the highest form of inner reality it also represents the individualized form of the outer, objective reality. Despite being the definitive Other, the Self also remains the innermost non-other. These seemingly paradoxical observations can only be appreciated as dialectical interrelationships. This is a reality that Jung was well aware of and hence he repeatedly emphasized the dialectical nature of his most recent formulation of his problematic.[61, 63] Jung defined *dialectic* as 'the term for the process of creating new syntheses'.[59] Psychotherapy was not 'a method which anybody could apply in stereotyped fashion in order to reach the desired result'[59], nor a technique 'based on premises held to be generally valid', but a highly individualized relationship in which the 'psychic systems' of both therapist and patient entered 'into reciprocal reaction'.[63] Jung wrote: 'If I wish to treat another individual psychologically at all, I must for better or worse give up all pretensions to superior knowledge, all authority and desire to influence. I must perforce adopt a dialectical procedure consisting in a comparison of our mutual findings . . . '[59] Thus, in order to deal with one's own Others and arrive at the dialectical synthesis of the Self, the individual needs an external Other, the analyst/therapist, who could facilitate this synthesis.

The analysis of Jung's life and work adopted in this chapter revealed a progression of reformulations of the problematic of the Other. The initial fire, stone, pebble and manikin were global, undifferentiated, primitive forms of animistic Others, whereas the No.2 personality, although retaining the global quality of its predecessors, was nevertheless of a human form. The Fragment Other was a further personalized and differentiated Other to such a degree that it almost constituted a mini-personality in its own right. The Anticipated Whole Other had more unifying qualities and anticipated the extension of the personality. Next Jung proceeded to define the Other in terms of more specific functions and the Other-as-Complex of his psychiatric period which was understood within the context of association experiments was replaced with the Other-as-Complex of his psychoanalytic period which was defined in terms of the unconscious. The further he investigated *analytically* the differentiated functions of the Other, the more in fact he worked *synthetically* in unifying antithetical individual tendencies by placing them in their collective and yet at the same time human and individual contexts. The concept Other-as-Symbol began indicating this direction when it was conceived as an apparent return to the globality of the Other while yet still retaining its differentiated specificity. The Other-as-Symbol essentially referred to *specific structuring principles* rather than individual functions. This process culminated in the formulation the Other-as-Archetype where the structuring principles are appreciated in their broader cultural and human perspectives. Moreover, this formulation also accounts for the developmental process of individuation. Therefore the problematic of the Other which Jung embarked on in an attempt to isolate and identify the Other gradually grew to reveal the whole dialectical process of the individual's arriving at the Self. Like the Wittgensteinian ladder, this problematic provides the necessary steps of the earlier formulations. However, once having climbed the problematic of the Other, the centre shifts from the Ego to the Self (cf. Jung[57]). Then the ladder should be dropped, for at the new centre is the Self, and being the ultimate unity and wholeness of the total personality, no problematic any longer exists, nor any 'Other'.

Wittgenstein aptly expresses this twist at the end of his *Tractatus*:

My propositions serve as elucidations in the following way: anyone who understands me eventually recognizes them as nonsensical, when he has used them – as steps – to climb up beyond them. (He must, so to speak, throw away the ladder after he has climbed up it.)

He must transcend these propositions, and then he will see the world aright.

What we cannot speak about we must pass over in silence.[99]

CHAPTER 5

Active Imagination According to C.G. Jung

BY ELIE G. HUMBERT   *translated by Mrs. Julia F. Levraux and Mrs. Mireille M. Landman*

In its current form analysis takes little account of images, and when it does, it limits itself to their interpretation. It then deals with dreams and drawings, rarely daydreams. However, this approach does not fit with the experience of Jungian analysis. On the one hand the places, the people, the objects and the scenes that come to the imagination during the day deserve attention. On the other hand they are not only a source of information. They can play an irreplaceable role in dynamic analysis.

We have an example of this process in active imagination, which uses the capabilities of day-time imagination with a view to a novel relationship with the unconscious. It is the complement, and in some way the counterpart, of the interpretation of dreams.

Historical Account

Jung started to employ active imagination in response to the psychological situation in which he found himself in 1912, when he began to feel the beginning of the separation from Freud and a resulting confusion. At that time mental imagery had a name (Galton, 1883), but not yet a method. It would only be elaborated and diversified between the years 1920 to 1930. There were interesting suggestions to be found in the work of Janet and Binet but these were limited to supplying a few adjuvants to a psychiatry that was then trying new forms, 'psychological medications'.

For Jung, it was not a question of applying one method. Nothing could then replace the practice of psychoanalysis as he had experienced it in the past. It remained to allow things to develop and then confront oneself with them. It is in this way that active imagination, which today presents itself as a method, is intricately tied up with the spirit which it puts to use. It is more important to understand that than to criticize particular aspects of the practice.

These, however, only became progressively clear, as Jung became aware of what he was practising and found external points of comparison, probably in the literature which was beginning to be published on the subject at the time, by which he could define himself. The path followed by this theoretical development and its stages are quite significant. In fact, the first text of Jung's that mentions it is *The Transcendent Function* (first published in English, 1916). This study however tends to show that the axis of the development of the psyche is a two way living relationship between the conscious and the unconscious, allowing the unconscious to evolve through imagination and dreams and forming the conscious by working on the images and interpreting them. Such is the symmetrical role of the interpretation of dreams and active imagery and the perspective in which they have meaning. Concerning active imagination it is principally a question of the manner in which the images are allowed to come through and the work of the ego to put them into form and understand them. Those latter traits will subsequently vary slightly but the general aim is immediately defined.

In *The Transcendent Function* the concept used is that of 'spontaneous fantasy'. One finds it again in Jung's later works such as *Mysterium Coniunctionis*[1] but it is there distinguished from active imagination like the material of the process that works or transforms it. The difference underlines the importance of the idea of action. This appears for the first time, in 1921 in *Psychological Types* to qualify the active and passive forms of fantasy. Note that Jung still uses 'Phantasy' and not the neologism 'Imagination'. The French translator is compelled to translate Phantasy as Imagination and does not have the means to do justice to the difference between the two terms.

We can distinguish between *active* and *passive* fantasy. *Active* fantasies are the product of *intuition*, i.e. they are evoked by an *attitude* directed to the perception of unconscious contents, as a result of which the *libido* immediately invests all the elements emerging from the unconscious and, by association with parallel material, brings them into clear focus in visual form . . . It is probable that passive fantasies always have their origin in an unconscious process that is antithetical to consciousness, but invested with approximately the same amount of energy as the conscious attitude, and therefore capable of breaking through the latter's resistance. Active fantasies, on the other hand, owe their existence not so much to this unconscious process as to a conscious propensity to assimilate hints or fragments of lightly-toned unconscious complexes and, by associating them with parallel elements, to elaborate them in clearly visual form. It is not necessarily a question of a dissociated psychic state, but rather of a positive participation of consciousness.

. . . Active fantasy is one of the highest forms of psychic activity. For here the conscious and the unconscious personality of the subject flow together into a common product in which both are united.[2]

The first account of active imagination probably dates from a seminar in 1925 in Zurich, during which Jung related aspects of his experiments from 1912 to 1919. The exercise does not yet have a name, but it is sufficiently developed to be described in 1928 in *The Relations between the Ego and the Unconscious*, Part 2, Chapter 3, concerning the technique of the differentiation between the ego and the facets of the unconscious.

The actual name appears for the first time in English during the Tavistock Lectures that Jung gives in London in 1935. Then in 1936 in *The Concept of the Collective Unconscious*[3] and in *Yoga and the West*.[4] From this period it is currently used in seminars and English works: but it only takes its place in German texts from 1941, with *The Psychological Aspects of the Kore*.[5]

Description

Unlike other techniques of imagery, active imagination does not assume any pre-existing conditions: neither the position of the body, nor respiratory control or relaxation. A certain outward composure is however favourable, especially for the one who is not accustomed to it. In the same way, a superficial relaxation with respect to body weight also facilitates the initial phases. It is a question of meeting oneself where one's attention can be turned towards one's affects and phantasies, whilst the conscious mind remains what it is. The inability to produce active imagination is indicative of the state of defences. This should be analysed, however, not artificially destroyed.

For similar reasons, no theme is suggested from the start nor in the course of development of active imagination. In this sense active imagination differs from the techniques of the guided daydream as well as from meditation inspired by Mahayana Buddhism or by the Ignatian tradition. The precise starting point depends on the unconscious: A mood, an obsessive thought, the last image of a dream, an object that comes to life on its own, like a chair that seems, that night, to want to say something. The attention is thus diverted from reason and the normal activities and allows a clear field to that which seems to become animated.[6] Sometimes the image of object animates itself, sometimes there is a need to wrestle, to tear from the obscurity the phantasy or affect of which we perceive the movements and of which the defenses prevent us from capturing the image. In any case, when one wishes to throw oneself into active imagination outside of the real activity of the unconscious, one condemns oneself to meet only images that reflect in a sterile way egotism of intention.

The means of the production are many: painting, dancing, sculpting, writing dialogue or visualization.[7] The last permits most flexibility and vividness.

Up to this point the method is that of an imagination that one could call passive, or simply spontaneous, where the attention is used solely to receive. Gradually as the content of the unconscious takes form the attention changes. It focusses itself on the image that becomes an autonomous living object and no longer a component in a continuum of images. The starting image alters. Others come with the coherent intensity of actors who develop a similar scene. Will the subject remain on the outside, like the animator–spectator of a theatre of puppets? If that is the case nothing will happen. The flow of images will leave behind the effect of a diversion. On the contrary, the subject can become aware that this concerns him and enter, according to his own conscious reactions, this scene wherein different factors of his psyche[8] present and unfold themselves. Then imagination becomes active. The integration of the subject with the scene can go as far as answering by means of speech or mime to the imaginary person. This is the opposite of the dream, the tale or free association.

Whether having taken the form of a dialogue, written or spoken, of a series of paintings or visual imagery, the scene develops into a little drama. Active imagination in a story. Initially it rarely lasts longer than ten minutes. It then rapidly leads to conflict. The unconscious constellation, which provoked the active imagination, shows its opposition to the conscious order. One has the impression of arriving at a situation with no outcome. Thus a woman is given the responsibility of maintaining a sacred fire and only has at her disposal her own forest. What must she sacrifice? Her mission or her forest? After hesitating for several days she sees in a dream a little black boy. The next day she communicates with him in her imagination. He tells her: 'The man who brought the fire to earth put it into stones; where it remains forever. If you have the stones, you will always have fire.' Thus a solution is proposed. The unconscious has discovered a third option. It remains to understand what all this is about and to relate it to life.

It is, however, not sufficient that an image has appeared. Active imagination is neither a technique of emergence nor a catharsis, even if it comprises both. It is a confrontation. The practice of these exercises requires two types of treatment, the order of presentation of the form and the search for meaning. We know that Jung often insisted on the necessity to write down, each time, the protocol of what has happened. He himself took the time, even in his busy years, to depict in minute details his principal images. He then had them bound into several volumes. His commentaries on alchemy, among others, permitted the emergence of the union, the anima, the self and individuation in general, as the result of lengthy theoretical elaborations concerning that which he had initially experimented with, in active imagination. But the search for meaning does not only consist in that effort to understand. It is more a personal question: how is it possible to allow that which forms in one's imagination to inspire one's concrete existence? The risk would obviously be the action taken, the illusion of a direct transposition from the imagined to the real. One cannot however leave the phantasy world to itself. The purpose of active imagination is to help the exchange of myth and of reality, of desire and realization. It is there that one finds meaning. The figures of active imagination participate when they become regular speakers[9], over a certain period. A man, a woman or even an animal, seen in a dream, associated with in imagination, are like companions about whom it is easy to think and with whom one can enter into dialogue. It is the most intimate aspect of the development. It assists in dispelling the monopoly of the ego by founding a consciousness of many voices.

Examples

Here are the protocols of two active imaginations. The first was realized when the subject was alone, the second took place in the course of a session of analysis. Both examples are visual.

1. A female student, suffering from an acute negative maternal complex and paranoid tendencies, had rented a room from an old persecutory woman. One evening the old woman declared that henceforth she could no longer bathe in the Rhine which was flowing at the foot of the house. This had been, however, a liberty which they had both verbally agreed upon.

At that moment of imagination the young girl controlled herself and accepted the ban, but when she found herself with her books, she became the prey of long recriminations which paralysed all intellectual work. Towards the end of this wasted evening, she nevertheless managed to stop the discourse which held her emotions and to concentrate them on an image of the situation: the bank of the Rhine, the stairs she descended to go swimming, across a placard 'swimming forbidden'. Waves now hollowed out. But a critical voice murmured that all this is hardly serious, a simple representation of emotion. She did however keep her attention on the scene. The waves opened up, a gnome emerged, with frogs' legs and height of about eighty centimetres. She thought this to be a phallic production of an emotion already known to her. She did not however allow herself to be distracted by this theoretical stance and continued to imagine the scene. The gnome approached, knocked at the door. The student wondered what would happen. Should she open up? Will he blow the house up? Could he be coming to kill the old woman? In that case she could not allow him in. Finally she decided to open and to accompany the figure. The door open, the visitor asks to greet the proprietress. Again the young girl hesitated then came back to her first decision and accompanied the gnome into the 'Stube' (lounge) of the old woman. The latter invited him to sit on the couch. The gnome then started telling an erotic joke and the proprietress, laughing heartily, inviting the student to leave her alone with that so charming gentleman. This was the end of the active imagination. The student was relaxed and able to continue working.[10]

2. 'During the previous night, I slept very badly. I experienced a painful sensation in the forearms. An image recurred continually like a mirage: the white façade of a castle flanked by a tower with a pointed roof. It was perhaps the illustration of a playing card. The session of active imagination took that castle as a starting point. . .

The castle does not seem terribly ancient. It is white as if it had just been restored. The roof of the tower is equally white. One sees only a flat façade. It is the tower that is the most obvious feature. The details remain blurred, with little life. In my previous dream the card had been flat on the bed: here I try to place it vertically, but that does not work well. After a while it starts to float in the air, at an inclined angle. It floats above a thick, almost solid, dark grey-green sea; the horizon is black. The card continues to float and the sea rounds itself off into a spherical curve which becomes grooved to the right of the picture as if there was a sort of black and blurred chasm, rather disturbing. One must not fall in there. A white ghostly form seems to be walking on the sea and propels the card-castle as if it were a balloon that one throws back up each time it seems to touch the ground.

I try once again to place the castle vertically, but I do not succeed, it remains crooked. It is curious, that impression of flat façade, without thickness. There should normally be something behind it. Actually this resembles a theatre decor, a painted canvas. In fact the openings do not seem to be able to open, they are painted. The door is a kind of dark hole, indistinct and closed.

And thus I am clutching at the pointed roof of the tower which I grasp with my legs and arms as if it were a greasy pole. I say 'I', but in fact it is an adolescent dressed as in the Middle-Ages in a clinging garment and bouffant pants. One should try to see what is on the other side of that façade-decor. The tower has more body. I feel this as I am clasping it. Strange, it is gradually detaching itself from the castle. I ask myself for an instant what I could do about it, since it is only a prop. It must be possible to penetrate the façade of that castle. The tower has become a sort of ram which tries to penetrate the door with its pointed roof. The boy-me is then clutching in a horizontal position, firmly gripped. I experience a strong pain in the forearms. Disquiet. If the tower succeeds in penetrating the door, the boy will not be able to go through, he will be scraped on the way, driven back, crushed . . . There ought to be a sort of wide enough tear, allowing passage.

For a long moment the tower remains wedged, it does not progress. All of a sudden, but I do not know how, I am on the other side of the castle. It was a decor. There are a whole lot of beams and scaffoldings which are holding the decor up. They overhang a sort of enormous cliff or crevasse which seems as if cut with a knife, level with the façade. There is thus a difference in level of thirty to fifty metres. At the bottom runs a river on which I see a flat boat carrying some indistinct forms. There seem to be three persons, of which one is in red. I am spectator without being anywhere. The general colour of the back of that decor is dark, dark brown; the earth of the crevasse is dark red ochre. Curiously, the tower that succeeded in penetrating is no more a tower, but a sort of enormous penis, completely white of which the glans is particularly clear with its metal centre half open for ejaculation.

I am now squatted on the rear of the boat. This poses a problem because it is the back platform which is in the direction of the current. The barge faces the decor turn by the penis. The man in red is in front of the boat, situated at the rear, and by the manner he holds his oars he should go against the current towards the 'cliff-decor-cul-de-sac'. The remaining objects are a confused mass. In fact the barge does not move, nor do the oars, the water does not run anymore. Everything is static, immutable.

I find that absurd, illogical. That motionlessness gets on my nerves, I have had enough, I want some movement. I am now in the water and I swim with the current pulling the barge with all my strength, to make it go forward and get away from the cliff. I become exhausted pulling, but the scenery changes. The banks become flat, there is some greenery. A sort of strand runs along the river. I catch sight of my sister, standing, her feet in the water, she watches me pass. My first response is to think that she is going to offer to help me pull the barge. But I reject that idea and pass proudly in front of her pulling energetically so she does not get the impression that I am backing out.

But I have had enough of that barge! I would like to get rid of it, throw it away. As a matter of fact, there it explodes as if hit by a bomb. The debris flies through the air, I hunch my back to avoid receiving something on the head. I walk now on the bed of a large shallow river with a fast flowing current. It looks like the Tigris or the Euphrates, I do not know anymore. I am completely alone, all is deserted, in the distance are the mountains. I would like to meet someone. This solitude is extreme.

When I open my eyes, your armchair is empty. You had very softly gone to open the curtains.'

Such is the account of an imagination, half passive, half active, experienced in the course of a session by a woman under analysis. Here is the commentary she herself gives of it:

Impression that this imagination illustrates a sort of primitive sense of the primal coition when I was conceived. At the beginning, there was a sort of moonlike world without time nor space, without consistency nor colour. Everything is there, latent. Then slowly the desire of the father for the mother and the fear that the little one – me – could not pass to the other side. The idea of the necessary tear to allow the passage, is associated with the fact that at the time of my birth, my mother was torn because I was too big a baby.

Then, that barge. In reality it should go with the current but I myself and the oarsman are placed in such a way that it is rather a return backwards that seems to take place. As if I did not manage to get loose and go. Finally, I am obliged to throw myself in the water and to swim and drag the barge which is both an assurance and a dead weight, the tie to the past. For a moment, the temptation to ask for assistance from my sister who, I felt, would have given it me. But I prefer to do without and I get rid of the barge-brake by blowing it up, to find myself completely alone but walking with the current.

The unconscious content is indeed that which the commentary brings out, but locating the involvement of the ego and the nature of the image, one finds in addition, a degree of refraction according to which that unconscious content is kept at a distance as it appears. The castle is a drawing of a playing card, then a floating decor, finally a decor-façade standing on a cliff of earth. It is at first a whole, then we understand that the main building could be feminine, the tower parts itself from it, strikes the decor, and whilst the female remains façade the male becomes penis. The maternal is the passage, without an interior. One sees how the primal scene is where the subject (female) is still a young boy in the Middle Ages. The male in the form of a separated penis, is for that analysand incomparably more conscious and more humanized that the female-façade or the maternal-fake door risking forced entry.

The ego allows at first a spontaneous imagination to evolve. Then it appears and fully experiences the effort to direct itself with the current of the river. It refuses to call upon the aid of that sister who was up to now the partner of an incestuous couple, where the two sisters found the security denied to them by their parents. But the separation emerges from an all powerful motion – the blowing up of the barge – the ransom of which is the final solitude. This imaginary solitude corresponds exactly to the real solitude of which the analysand was complaining for weeks. One discovers here that all is the result of an unconscious blockage. 'If I renounce incest with my sister, I do not want to have anything to do with my past anymore.'

Characteristics

From these examples, we can determine the characteristics or distinctive traits of active imagination.

1. To give form to the affects and phantasies.

The affect which seizes an individual constitutes its vital task of the moment. One exhausts oneself allowing oneself to be rolled in the waves of mood and inner tales. In driving away the dis-ease one prepares a more serious irruption. Thinking and looking for an answer, leads the libido out of the field of emotion. It gets engulfed, for example, in representations of a better state of ourselves, which become the abstract object of desire. Psychological considerations, even the most adequate, are a trap. They feed narcissism. To deal with an emotion, one must face it, that is to say, arrest the discourse and bring the emotion to take shape. The student (Example 1) sees the situation: the stairs to her swims blocked by the placard 'forbidden'. Thus the power that possessed her becomes objective and becomes a story with which she can deal directly.

This active method is entirely different from free association. One must not let the emotion slide from image to come, for example, to the explosion of a phantasy of murder towards the mother. Jung does not try to resolve a situation by a flash-back, but by remaining in actuality, to force the unconscious to become objective in a confrontation with the conscious. The student, overcome by the murderous phantasy, would have found herself in a state of regression quite artificial and would not have had any other outlet but a rationalization of one kind or another, *viz* to identify herself with the phantasy. Here, she discovers a solution of which she had no idea: the coarse erotic joke. Instead of remaining blocked up in the only recognition of the phantasy as murder of her mother, she demystifies the super ego authority and takes a step towards the solution of her Oedipal conflict.

2. To treat the image as reality.

One often considers the work with imagination as an exercise liable to liberate some energies or as a way to obtain information. In so doing, one does not respect the image, one uses it. One brings it back to reason, which prescribes the catharsis or interprets the material. The images, in which a part of the psyche expresses itself, form however a 'just so story', animated by an original dynamism which incites us as much as an outside event. To approach this part of the psyche as it appears, allows one to relate to and engage in a story with it. To bring in an afterthought, for example: that it concerns a representation, or that the grand mythical images need to be reduced or that one risks becoming the victim of a delusion, engenders a dissociation directly related to the strength of the emotion. To guard oneself from the danger of being absorbed into the image, a danger to which we will return, one falls into the neurotic peril of denying whilst giving oneself. The motives of anal narcissism will, to manipulate the psyche and suspicion towards oneself, use psychological considerations to prevent oneself taking the image seriously.

These ulterior motives contrive to trick the course of the imagination. Example: a woman finds herself in front of the house of her birth where she suffered much. She enters and sees a sick child. Seized by a sort of rage against that house which reminds her of so many bad memories, she thinks: 'I take the child away and I set the house on fire'. Which she does. Outside, while the house burns, she considers that she cannot banish the child, that she has nowhere to leave him, and she thinks: 'Well, we start again, the house is there, it has not burned'. It is in that way that one is not serious with oneself.

To an analysand who was telling him about the following imagination: 'I am on the seashore and I see a lion approaching, but it becomes a boat', Jung answered: 'It is not true: if you are on the seashore and you see a lion approaching, you are sacred, you tremble, you ask yourself what you are going to do, and there is no question that it immediately becomes a boat'.

The image nevertheless has its measure of reality. One makes oneself neurotic playing with it, by reducing it to a fantasy or using it for preestablished ends. In the chapter 'Confrontation with the Unconscious' in *Memories, Dreams, Reflections*, Jung writes that the feeling of ethical responsibility concerning his own images has had a decisive influence on his life.

3. To commit oneself.

It is not sufficient to allow passive emergence. If the imagined situation is real, I am fully involved with it, as in a concrete situation. It is for this reason that Jung has placed in the denomination of this work the adjective 'active'.

In our first example above, the student is witness. She sees the placard, the waves . . . she hears the words of the gnome. This first form of presence supports another form: to think, hesitate, choose and assume the responsibility for the decision. The student questions granting the gnome access to the proprietress, as she would do in reality with a strange visitor. The ethical position of which the ego is the pivot is the necessary condition for a true encounter of the psychic components in question.

The subjects in whom the intellect is too important most often start by seeing themselves act or hearing themselves speak. As long as one part of the conscious remains at a distance, the active imagination is not entirely authentic.

It is to be emphasized that active imagination differs essentially from the free and easy daydream or the dialogues that unfold on the pages of an intimate diary, and that it diverges as well from the techniques that suggest the intervention of a symbol to produce a scene. It is not a question of ascent or descent, to take a magic wand or to call upon a protector. The one who engages in active imagination has no other resource than himself and what the situation offers.

4. Not to search for references.

The course of active imagination is not subject to any psychological norms. It could not be said that the student was right or wrong to allow the gnome to enter. Von Franz, who relates the case, writes that she would not have done it. That is all. Each event has its own history. We depart from all criteria that intellect tries to impose. The criterion is not a judgement of a good or better psyche, but the emotional echo of the possible decision. It is this which manifests, by a feeling of agreement or disagreement, the reaction of our psyche. Thus the student could have refused to leave the gnome with the proprietress and continue with the imagination. She did not do it, she went back to her work. It made sense for her at that moment.

Active imagination guides one to come in touch with 'the one who knows'. It is neither knowledge nor reason nor the analyst, but an original function, unique to each one, which expresses itself by some inner inclination.

Indications

Active imagination is particularly indicated in a certain number of situations that most of the time relate the conscious to the unconscious. It then accentuates some or other characteristics previously mentioned.

1. The most simple and prompt intervention depends on mental and emotional health. After a conversation, a lecture, a film on television, one feels depressed or exhilarated, preoccupied in one way or another. There has been contagion. Rather than allowing oneself to be overcome and then to unconsciously project this disturbance, it is better to evoke the agent of trouble, in imagination, and thus come to terms with it.[11] The case of the student cited above is such an example. It shows that active imagination forms a natural part of the way of life for someone who has already been through analysis. The analyst who

has to cope with communication between shadows and psychic epidemics, needs this health if he wants to avoid the unconscious reinforcement of defence mechanisms characteristic of the profession.

2. What I have just said concerns the practice of active imagination without resource to a therapist and is consequently directed to those who already have a sufficently elaborate relation with the unconscious. Such a practice is strongly discouraged for others. It might risk a psychotic breakdown or release a state of delirium without any possibility of ensuring a future grasp of reality and emotion. On the other hand, active imagination can be very useful, even in the case of a fragile ego, if it is practiced within the bounds of an analysis.[12]

Jung refers to this effectiveness at the beginning of analysis, when the unconscious of the analysand is 'overcrowded'[13]. Anamnesis remains too rational, the interpretation of dreams is too slow, the analysand must therefore be given the opportunity to paint, draw, write in order to allow the content of the unconscious, activated by the start of analysis, to take form. One would thus be working with rich material and one would keep these contents from disappearing in the sands of time. Moreover, it gives the opportunity of directly placing the analysand in touch with what is happening within him.

Certain borderline personalities have also an overcrowded unconscious. The analysis must first and foremost help them to organize their personal symbolic world, to recognize the order and meaning of the their major images. The Jungian methods are then particularly indicated. The active imagination teaches the subject the way to behave according to what, at times, was overcoming him and assists to put some order in the unconscious. It is however necessary for the analyst to feel sufficiently familiar with the imaginary world of the analysand.

3. It is rare that an analysis does not come, one day, to a point where the process seems blocked. It is a particularly important moment that cannot be treated systematically by patience alone. One would risk entering a long period in which nothing happens, until an acting out puts an end to it. Amongst the questions that the analyst must ask himself, there is the one of a change of method or, more exactly, of a change in the design of symbolization. It sometimes happens that the verbalization reaches only the intellect and that one has to defer it to take a more direct contact with the real emotion. It also happens that a conflict blocks the play of the conscious and the unconscious in such a way that neither associations, nor dreams, not interpretations will manage to open the path of a new expression. In both situations, active imagination can be useful, even necessary. Through the bias of the image experienced directly, it escapes the rationalizations and gives an

impression to the unconscious emotional flux that no longer passes through the discourse. One must be able to modify, in the course of analysis, the modalities of symbolization.

This is the case of a woman who, possessed by the animus, starts to be conscious of it. She falls on the opposite side of the possession, the feeling of non-existence, and can only find herself again in a conversation which casts off the hold of the animus. The profound request – often unconscious – is that of a land, a place, where one can exist without words, in harmony with life. An analysis, which would content itself with interpretation, could only allow the replacement of the existing dominant animus by another. On the other hand, active imagination can summon forth the land where that woman would like to find herself. It thus presents to her a sort of new mirror. In this case, the analysis risks failure by the very fact of the verbalization and active imagination offers to the conscious the means to reconstitute itself in another register.

In the second example, mentioned previously, the situation is different. The analysis was blocked by a false-mourning. The analysand was overcome by a feeling of solitude which she attributed to the unmet needs (*manques*) of her childhood. Consequently the solitude seemed a condemnation as permanent as her unmet needs were irretrievable. The analytic involvement would risk being exhausted in a vicious circle where it was said: analysis will not be able to meet my needs as the analyst cannot respond to my solitude. Active imagination brought the problem to life in another way. There is no question of unmet needs but of separation, lived out as a condition of the future. Instead of it being a yearning for an absent object, the solitude occurred in the movement of a march forward, beyond incest. The real problem becomes apparent at the primal scene. It stems from the sexual identity.

Active imagination has offered the unconscious the possibility of acting out outside the field where false problems have been created with a great deal of psychology. A certain animus had seized the conscious of this analysand and was spinning a web in which the analysis was becoming a prisoner. Despite the denouncement of the animus by dreams, it took active imagination for the analysand to be taken in by the experience of a reality in itself different from the one she wanted to see.

4. Beyond analysis, active imagination is one of the best means of keeping the relationship with the unconscious alive. It integrates with a way of life that Jung has described as individuation. In the first excerpt from *Commentary on The Secret of the Golden Flower*, Jung exposes the principle which guided him both in individuation and in active imagination.

What did these people do in order to bring about the development that set them free? As far as I could see they did nothing (*wu wei*) but let things happen. As Master Lü-tsu teaches in our text, the light circulates according to its own law if one does not give up one's ordinary occupation. The art of lettings things happen, action through non-action, letting go of oneself as taught by Meister Eckhart, became for me the key that opens the door to the way. We must be able to let things happen in the psyche. For us, this is an art of which most people know nothing. Consciousness is forever interfering, helping, correcting, and negating, never leaving the psychic processes to grow in peace. It would be simple enough, if only simplicity were not the most difficult of all things. To begin with, the task consists solely in observing objectively how a fragment of fantasy develops. Nothing could be simpler, and yet right here the difficulties begin. Apparently one has no fantasy fragments – or yes, there's one, but it is too stupid! Dozens of good reasons are brought against it. One cannot concentrate on it – it is too boring – what would come of it anyway – it is 'nothing but' this or that, and so on. The conscious mind raises innumerable objections, in fact it often seems bent on blotting out the spontaneous fantasy activity in spite of real insight and in spite of the firm determination to allow the psychic process to go forward without interference. Occasionally there is a veritable cramp of consciousness.

If one is successful in overcoming the initial difficulties, criticism is still likely to start in afterwards in the attempt to interpret the fantasy, to classify it, to aestheticize it, or to devalue it. The temptation to do this is almost irresistible. After it has been faithfully observed, free rein can be given to the impatience of the conscious mind; in fact it must be given, or obstructive resistances will develop. But each time the fantasy material is to be produced, the activity of consciousness must be switched off again.

In most cases the results of these efforts are not very encouraging at first. Usually they consist of tenuous webs of fantasy that give no clear indication of their origin or their goal. Also, the way of getting at the fantasies varies with individuals. For many people, it is easiest to write them down; others visualize them, and others again draw or paint them with or without visualization. If there is a high degree of conscious cramp, often only the hands are capable of fantasy; they model or draw figures that are sometimes quite foreign to the conscious mind.

These exercises must be continued until the cramp in the conscious mind is relaxed, in other words, until one can let things happen, which is the next goal of the exercise. In this way a new attitude is created, an attitude that accepts the irrational and the incomprehensible simply because it is happening. This attitude would be poison for a person who is already overwhelmed by the things that happen to him, but it is of the greatest value for one who selects, from among the things that happen, only those that are acceptable to his conscious judgement, and is gradually drawn out of the stream of life into a stagnant backwater.[14]

'Letting things happen' has nothing to do with passive awaiting. It is an art, an opus of which Jung read its projection in alchemy.

Take the unconscious in one of its handiest forms, say a spontaneous fantasy, a dream, an irrational mood, an affect, or something of the kind, and operate with it. Give it your special attention, concentrate on it, and observe its alterations objectively. Spare no effort to devote yourself to this task, follow the subsequent transformations of the spontaneous fantasy attentively and carefully. Above all, don't let anything from outside, that does not belong, get into it, for the fantasy-image has 'everything it needs'. In this way one is certain of not interfering by conscious caprice and of giving the unconscious a free hand. In short, the alchemical operation seems to us the equivalent of the psychological process of active imagination.[15]

This is therefore not only an exercise, it is also a process, that which continues beyond the moments where the conscious/unconscious relationship is linked by transference.

The analyst's guidance in helping him to understand the statements of his unconscious in dreams, etc. may provide the necessary insight, but when it comes to the question of real experience the analyst can no longer help him: he himself must put his hand to the work. He is then in the position of an alchemist's apprentice . . . Like him, the modern man begins with an unseemly prima materia which presents itself in unexpected form – a contemptible fantasy which, like the stone that the builders rejected, is 'flung into the street' and is so 'cheap' that people do not even look at it. He will observe it from day to day and note its alterations until his eyes are opened. . .

The light that gradually dawns on him consists in his understanding that his fantasy is a real psychic process which is happening to him personally. Although, to a certain extent, he looks on from outside, impartially, he is also an acting and suffering figure in the drama of the psyche.[16]

'Betrachten'

In comparing the texts that we have just cited, one can ask oneself if there is not a contradiction between the principle of allowing to happen and the fact of concentrating oneself on an element in order to observe the changes.

Such would be the case if letting things happen consisted of allowing the events to run their course, to passively endure the sequence of what is done and said. That is not so. It involves withholding the interventions of the conscious and to give life such attention as will break the links and give the opportunity to arrive at what is looked for elsewhere, on another scene.[17] One and the same attitude combines the availability of '*lassen*' to the power of interruption of '*geschehen*'.

This attitude isolates an image and begins to consider it. It objectifies it, takes it seriously for itself, as conjunctural or circumstantial as it may be. In so doing, it places it in a situation such

that a story comes out of it, in another way. Jung indicates the
evidence of that attitude by the verb *betrachten*, which means
'consider', but on which he gives the following commentary in one of
his seminars:

> . . . 'looking', psychologically, causes the activation of the object, as if
> something was emanating from the psychic eye to evoke or activate the
> object of the vision.
> The English verb 'to look at' does not carry that meaning, but the German
> *betrachten*, which is an equivalent, also means to make pregnant. *Trachtig*
> means 'pregnant of the young that one carries', but is only used in reference to
> animals. Thus, to look or centre the attention on one thing, *betrachten*, gives
> to the object the quality of being pregnant. And if it is, then something must
> come out of it; it is alive, it creates, it multiplies. It is the case with any image
> of fantasy. One centres on it and one discovers then that it is very difficult to
> keep it still. It moves, it changes, something joins it or it multiplies itself: one
> has filled it with a living power and it has become pregnant.[18]

Betrachten therefore means the act of considering such as objectifies
and makes pregnant all at once.

Pregnant of or with what? What is that life which animates a
fragment of imagination when one dwells on it? It seems that it
belongs to the other side of things. It is the vision that is not suitable,
the action that has no place, the pain, the desire, when they are
impossible. All that other life interferes like an opposite dynamism,
that Jung calls a *Gegenwirkung*. The word merits consideration. It
carries the strength of the object. The fragment of life considered for
itself, objectified, develops a scene the power of which assails the
subject. The image, for example, is not only a fantasmatic given, it
changes and incites the action of the subject. In the first example the
student is called upon by the gnome, to make a decision. In the second
example the barge, turned back to front, and immobile in the current
of the river, faced the analysand with the choice of interfering or not.

So the image leads the subject through the world it presents him
with, a different world. In reacting to it the subject in his turn changes,
and if he does not react to it, if he remains a spectator, he is left marked
by self-denial.

The *Gegenwirkung* is not particular to active imagination. It is one of
the modalities of the compensatory rapport between the conscious and
unconscious. One also meets it in dreams. But it does not have the
same nature and that difference explains why dreams and active
imagination do not yield the same material and cannot be interpreted
in the same manner. In fact, the *Gegenwirkung* corresponds in active
imagination to a *betrachten* which does not exist in the dream. the
position of the subject being different, the unconscious presents itself
differently.

The examination of what happens in active imagination leads to the discovery of a particular form of attention and the power of the object. Together they constitute a field where one can see clearly at what point the subject-object emerge with reference to each other. By paying attention to what happens, the conscious already takes a certain subjective position and makes its place in the unforeseen of another world whose power assails it in return and provokes it to be subjected to it.

That field is the very one of analysis. *Betrachten* defines the attention which breaks the links and, without knowing, lets things happen. *Gegenwirkung* is the action of the unconscious capable of confronting what had been happening up to then and of proposing or imposing a desire, a need, an apperception of the world, a self image, which tests the conscious, perhaps disorganizes it, and often disposes it to change. As it sets to work an interpretation capable of grasping the moment or the silent concentration on a fragment of what is happening, the analysis tends to make pregnant the point that it considers, in order to free itself and allow an 'X', which had up till this stage been unconscious, to take place.

We have analysed the relationship of 'consider/make pregnant' (*betrachten*) and of the 'contrary-dynamics' (*Gegenwirkung*) within the framework of the workings of the image. One finds it equally in an analysis which relates to the word or the behaviour.

That which concerns the termination and the consideration of the image could probably be formulated as isolation and concentration on the signifier. It is probably not the same when it concerns the development of a compensatory action. The image lends itself in a specialized way. It is a scene which resembles the world. A story can unfold from it, where the places, the things, the actors are each the significant links of multiple associations. This takes place in a period of time in which the subject involves himself. He responds to the figures that solicit him and, through that, comes into touch according to nuances of emotion and feeling, with all that converges through association in all the apparent elements of the game. The image lends itself to the ability of reorganization and the re-creation of the unconscious. In dreams and active imagination some paternal and maternal components, for example, return, evolve, resume the course of growth. The emotions of a dream and of an active imagination affect the conscious, and can set off chemical reactions. If concrete experiences provoke the organization of a complex, a lived through image has some chance of modifying that complex.

A French verb, taken in English, which translates the dynamics of the consider/make pregnant, is the verb *réaliser* (to realize), of which it is interesting to note that it is used equally to describe an intra-psychic operation as the most transitive action. The question 'do you realize what you are saying?' has two meanings: 'do you put it into practice?' and 'do you comprehend it?' The vocabulary therefore does not reduce the realization to concretization. To face what one says, imagines, feels, thinks . . . to become aware at the same time of the weight that this carries and to own it, is also a realization.

How can this verb have two significations nearly contradictory? In fact both are taken within the context of the continuity of a discourse which feeds itself. To realize breaks the links in order to objectify it, be it in an action or an attention. In both cases the objectification becomes pregnant with an opus, concrete realization or individuation.

Reflections

The exercises which aim to bring down the defences of the conscious and allow the unconscious to emerge, or even to cause the irruption, risk provoking a decompensation or even sparking off a latent psychosis. Concerning active imagination Jung knew the danger and several times warned against it[19] but at the same time he showed how the cause of the danger is the stake which gives it meaning.

Active imagination can also, on the contrary, encourage all the resistance. One regularly sees analysands for whom the evocation of anxiety in the form of a monster allows them to form an image and subsequently to ascribe to it mythological and other transformations. Jung denounces this like a puppet show in which nothing takes place[20] and insists on the importance of attention. In objectifying the movement of the images, it tends to sort out the confusion of the ego and the image, to push the ego into the backgrounds and allow it to acknowledge that the image presents something. The odds here are to 'realize'.

The ego, which has the strength to do it, has generally more distinct images, more autonomous, more surprising. On the contrary, the weaker ego has more seductive images, more trivial, more mythological and less pregnant. This mirrored relationship can become a trap, although at the same time, it is also a valuable lesson for the analyst who witnesses an active imagination during a session. He sees there, at work, the polarity of positions of the conscious and of the forms taken by the unconscious. He sees how the subject reacts to the circumstances which arise and according to which dominants he treats them. He learns, thus, to whom his interpretations are directed. In this sense, active imagination provides some light in answering the difficult question: Who is in analysis? with which type of correlation conscious/unconscious is one dealing?

In situating active imagination itself, one is struck by the way it develops most often in a state of deep relaxation and in the absence of the other. The body is able to express itself through such media as sculpture and more so dancing and mime but it (echoes) projects by synaesthetic sensations of which the most frecuently occuring form is visual. The other is equally present if the exercise takes place during analysis, but active imagination only reaches its true dimension after analysis. It then goes to the solitary limit of existence, as certain meditations did. It can be a test in itself in the proportion of the test of death.

Such conditions lead one to reflect on the exact nature of the psychic circuit which active imagination sets up. On one hand it provokes a differentiation of the ego and the representation but on the other hand is it not the conscious which permits the image to be pregnant? Is there not another side to differentiation, such that active imagination would remain to a certain extent intra-subjective, even if it reaches the objectivity of the collective unconscious?

It is significant that L.P. Clark, a Viennese psychoanalyst, tried in 1925-1926 to treat the narcissistic neuroses by means of imagination.[21] He believed that the image healed the wound related to the mother and in giving free rein to imagination one would unblock the hidden part of the relationship between the mother and the child. In fact his attempt failed and his method did not go further than passive imagination. His work had however the merit of underlining the relationship of the imaged world with the mother. That question deserves separate treatment. We want here however to point out simply what concerns the practice of active imagination.

The inspiration, the impetus, the poetry as well as the eros, is born of one participation in which one recognizes the mother, because of her regenerating capacity. The mother participation is like the door to the unconscious.

It is interesting to note that Jung proposes two models of relationship to that Mother. In the earlier writings, for example in *Symbols of Transformation*, the hero is the one who succeeds in separating himself from the Mother, by the struggle against her and the sacrifice. Towards the end of his life, especially in '*Mysterium Conjunctionis*', Jung shows, on the contrary, how the heroic task, that which passes through the trap and contradiction, is the task of incest, that is to say the return to the Mother.

One finds both these models in the practice of active imagination. For some, more introverted or closer to a pre-genital structure, it is a womb in which the subject acquires his strength and his power by challenging the unconscious powers. If he succeeds in this he will move towards the outside world with more security and a more accurate relationship. For the others, who were at the start more extroverted or simply neurotic, active imagination is, on the contrary, the exercise where they resume the ties with the Mother. We will not surprise anybody by observing that the latter are in greater need of it and can practise it with less illusion, but that the first are the ones who practise it most.

Active imagination is a method of bringing to the conscious some contents of the unconscious. It permits the use of more important material. It opens the way to the forces of compensation, and so contributes to an autoregulation of the psyche. It opens up a confrontation which can become a total internal adventure.

CHAPTER 6

From the Symbol in Psychoanalysis to the Anthropology of the Imaginary

BY LUCIE JADOT   *translated by Ann Gibson and Phillip Steinmetz*

L'imagination symbolique constitue l'activité dialectique même de l'esprit. G. Durand

This chapter[1] has a precise and limited objective, that of attempting to clarify the meaning (*signification*, to use the technical term) of the concept of 'symbol', which has been used since the beginning of the twentieth century in depth psychology and subsequently in anthropology. It will, therefore, neither concern itself with origins (noteworthy works have done so much before our contribution[2]) nor will it assume the task of presenting this concept in the field of mathematics and natural science.

The Hermeneutics

Since the second decade of the Freudian era, the problem of the symbol, specifically in its psychoanalytic signification brought about discord in the first group formed around the master of Vienna. This controversial issue affected the friendship and collaboration between Freud and Jung to the point of interrupting their association. 'I was acutely conscious then, of the loss of friendly relations with Freud, and of the lost comradeship of our work together', Jung wrote concerning the publication in 1912 of *Wandlungen und Symbole der Libido*. 'Thus this book became a landmark, set up on the spot where two ways divided'.[3]

In the preface of the fourth edition of that book (*Symbols of Transformation*), Jung explains his disagreement with the master:

I have no wish to denigrate Freud or to detract from the extraordinary merits of his investigation of the individual psyche. But the conceptual framework into which he fitted the psychic phenomenon seemed to me unendurably narrow for . . . I am thinking of the reductive causalism of his whole outlook and the almost complete disregard of the teleological directness, which is so characteristic of everything psychic.[4]

Thus, as early as 1916, Jung adopted a divergent position towards the Freudian school regarding the psychic signification of the symbol.[5] The Freudian school for its part interpreted the symbol, according to a semiotic mode, as a sign of the primitive psychosexual process. Its method is analytical and causal.

The Zürich school did recognize the scientific value of such a conception, but did and does not accept its exclusive validity. This school interprets the symbol, not only in a semiotic way in the context of historical causality, but acknowledges, moreover, its psychological signification for the present and the future. It, therefore, sees fit to add a prospective importance to the retroactive signification of the symbol. The Jungian interpretation is therefore not only analytical and causal, but also prospective and synthetic. The human psyche is characterized by 'goals' as well as 'causes'.

The Zürich school, which recognizes a teleological function to the symbol, admits that there is at present no scientific justification for such a viewpoint, since all our science is based upon causality[6]. However, says Jung, causality is only a principle, and psychology – because the life of the psyche depends equally on goals – cannot be entirely explained by causal methods.

The functional importance of the symbol is clearly illustrated in the history of civilization: for thousands of years, for example, the religious symbol has proved its efficiency in the education of humanity. When certain symbols lose their power as a consequence of analytical process and intellectual understanding, they are replaced by more adequate ones. Jung argues that the future development of humanity can only be apprehended by means of the symbol which represents something much in advance of the thought prevailing within an era, and which cannot be grasped clearly by intellectual understanding alone. The unconscious produces such symbols which are of the greatest importance to the development of personality.

Through untiring exploration of the meaning of and reflection on the function of the symbol – from myths, rituals, religions and cosmologies of primitive and modern humanity – Jung sought to understand the contemporary psyche. He was thus led to conceive of the archetype as a 'dominant structure of the psyche', unconscious, but real and universal.

Freud and the psychoanalysts had a decisive encounter with the 'disquietening strangeness', which inhabits the subject: the fantasm, the imaginary signifier of desire. Yet, is not desire at the same time (symbolic) project as well as (imaginary) regression?

This plunge into the realms of the Imaginary is taken up by the following generation in two emerging trends: the 'instaurative hermeneutics'[7] represented by G. Bachelard[8] in France and by Ernst

Cassirer[9] in Germany, and pursued specifically by Eliade, Zimmer, Corbin, Starobinski, Ricoeur and Durand;[10] and the 'reductive hermeneutics', such as the Freudian and Lacanian psychoanalytical schools, the functionalist sociologies such as that of Dumezil and the structural anthropology of Lévi-Strauss.[11]

In these two contemporary movements the attempt to achieve a structural theme of the symbol, of myth, culture and the Imaginary is notable. The *reductionist* tendency prides itself on being uniquely structural whereas the 'instaurative semantic' trend considers that the *sémantisme* as well as the structure constitutes the symbol.

Facing the 'extremism and timidity' of both forms of hermeneutics,[12] G. Durand and P. Ricoeur develop a system whereby both interwind, 'converge' and function 'coherently':

> . . . the reductive hermeneutics as well as the instaurative hermeneutics which we have examined up to now have a common flaw in restricting the explanatory field. They can only attain value when used in conjunction, psychoanalysis clarifying itself through structural sociology, and the latter referring to a philosophy of the symbol according to Cassirer, Jung and Bachelard. The corollary of dynamic pluralism and the bipolar constancy of the imaginary is, as Paul Ricoeur discovered in a decisive article,[13] the coherence of the hermeneutics.[14]

> We have established a double polarity: that of the symbol torn between the signifier and the signified, and that of symbolism as a whole: the content of symbolic imagination, the imaginary being conceived as a vast field organized by two reciprocally antagonistic forces . . . Paul Ricoeur specifies again the meaning of these two hermeneutics. Both of them being an attempt at decephering, are 'reminiscences'. But the one is archaeological, plunging in biographical, sociological and even phylogenetic past, the other is eschatological, that is to say a reminiscence, or even better, a recall to the essential order, and a ceaseless questioning of what we have named the angel.[15] The one, Freud's for example, means denunciation of the mask that images comprise . . . the other being an unveiling . . . of the essence of the spirit through the avatara of our incarnation . . . [16]

'Demystification', therefore, on the one hand: 'remythization' on the other.

Ricoeur recognizes the two hermeneutics, because any symbol is double: i.e. it organizes itself archaeologically amongst determinisms and causal links, so it is an 'effect', a symptom: but, in carrying a meaning, it is oriented towards an eschatology which is just as inalienable.[17]

However, G. Durand points out, and this is important in order to establish the anthropological meaning of the imaginary: . . . in the midst of this coherence, we would like to insist upon the fact that it is the eschatological which surpasses the archaeological. Because there are societies without scientific researchers, without psychoanalysts . . . but there are no societies without poets, without artists, without values. For man, it is always the 'dimension of appeal and hope'[18] which surpasses demystification. And hope, under the penalty of death, can never be mystification. Hope contents itself with being myth.[19]

Concluding the chapter on the levels of meaning and convergence of the hermeneutics,[20] G. Durand synthesizes the essentials of his position in relation to the imaginary and symbolism:

> From Freud to Ricoeur we have just reviewed all the directions of the hermeneutic and we have ascertained once again that the duplicity, the ambiguity of the symbol (corresponding to the duality of hermeneutics) specifies and activates even more its primary meaning of the messenger of transcendence into the world of incarnation and death. As we were writing[21] . . . symbolic imagination has a scandalous general function of ethically denying the negative.
>
> In the light of this coherent dualism that P. Ricoeur exposed in antagonistic hermeneutics (a coherent antagonism of the structure of the symbol itself being irreducible signifier, i.e. *Bild*, and meaning, i.e. *Sinn*), we could add here that symbolic imagination constitutes the very dialectic activity of the spirit, since on the level of the 'literal meaning' (*sens propre*) of the image . . . it always indicates that 'figurative meaning' (*sens figuré*) . . . the poetry of the phrase which, amidst limitation, denies the same . . . because true dialectic, as Lupasco has shown, is not a pacified synthesis, but a present tension of contradictions. And if so many symbols, so many poetical metaphors animate the spirit of man, is it not, in the final analysis because they are the 'hormones'[22] of spiritual energy?[23]

Let us do justice to Jung that he had, as early as 1916, identified the 'causal' and 'final' duplicity of the symbol, its plurality of meaning, its eschatological orientation (see above). And we do not agree with G. Durand when he estimates that Jung's interpretation of the symbol is mainly 'optimistic' and 'synthetic'.[24] For Jung clearly saw, felt and formulated the 'conflict of opposites', the 'confrontation of contraries' and the 'continuous tension' as its unavoidable result (even if he expresses that sometimes in images of completed totality, mandalas and androgynous or hierogamic symbols) as S. Lupasco, who is not guilty of submerging antagonisms in a synthesis testifies: 'The psychic is precisely the centre *par exellence* of ambivalences, tensions and contradictory tendencies as Jung so strikingly demonstrated'.[25]

Concluding this reflection on the symbolic hermeneutic we turn again to Ricoeur's words, placing himself face to face with the contradictory duality of the structural and the semantic, with the contradictory duality of archeology-eschatology. Here too he throws light upon the indissoluble reference of the symbol to a structure and a meaning:

> . . . No structural analysis, we were saying, without clear hermeneutic comprehension of the transfer of meaning (without metaphor, without

translation), without this indirect donation of meaning which establishes the semantic field, from which point structural homologies may be perceived. . . But on the other hand there is also no hermeneutic understanding without reference to an economy, an order, within which the symbolic has meaning.

Taken by themselves, symbols are threatened by their oscillation between 'stickiness' in imagination or evaporation in allegory; their richness, their exuberance, their multiplicity of meaning exposes naive symbolists to intemperance and complacency. . . What we call ambiguity (*équivocité*) regarding the exigency for univocity (*univocité*) in logical thought, results in symbols, which can only symbolize in totalities, to limit and define their signification.

Consequently, the understanding of structures is not external to an understanding which would have the task of thinking initially with symbols: today this is the necessary intermediary between symbolic naivety and hermeneutic understanding[26].

Symbolism and the Imaginary

The reader will have noticed throughout this exposé of the hermeneutics of the symbol that the symbolic imaginary of Ricoeur and Durand and the imaginary and symbolic of Lacan are not interchangeable. The following pages will try to identify the differences between the two vectors: the (semantic) hermeneutic and the structural.

For Ricoeur and Durand and definition of the symbol starts with the classical philosophical definition: 'The symbol is any concrete sign evoking, by a natural link, something which is absent or impossible to perceive.'[26] 'Symbol' refers to some concrete form, a signifier, which then awakens a sense in the symbolic imagination. But that which is thus signified is not presentable in itself[27]. G. Durand agrees with Jung's definition: A symbol is 'the best possible description or formulation of a relatively unknown fact, which is nonetheless known to exist or is postulated as existing'.[28]

G. Durand specifies:

The symbol is . . . by the very nature of the inaccessible signified, an epiphany, i.e. is the apparition, by and in the signifier, of the inexpressible. One sees . . . that which is to be the preferred domain of symbolism: the non-perceptible in all its forms: unconscious, metaphysical, supernatural and surreal.[29]

In agreement with Ricoeur, Durand argues that the signifier, the visible part of the authentic symbol, is always laden with a maximum of concreteness.[30] It is at the same time 'cosmic', 'oneiric' and 'poetic'.[31]

As for the other part of the symbol, 'this invisible and inexpressible part', it constitutes 'a very different type of logic': 'the two terms of Symbolon',[32] the signifier and the signified, are 'infinitely diverse'.[33]

This double imperative – of the signifier and the signified – is symbolic imagination specifically marks the symbolic sign and constitutes the 'flexibility'[34] of the symbol. The imperative of the signified . . . endlessly repeating the 'epiphanic' act possesses the common characteristic of redundancy. Through the ability of repetition the symbol makes up asymptotically for its fundamental inadequacy. But this repetition is not tautological: it has an always more exact tendency by means of accumulated approximations.[35]

It is possible to outline 'a summary classification of the symbolic universe':

The significant redundancy of gestures constitutes the class of ritual symbols . . . The redundancy of linguistic relationships is significant of the myth and its derivatives . . . as Lévi-Strauss has demonstrated. Finally, the painted and carved image . . . all that could be called the inconographical symbol, constitutes multiple redundancies.[36]

Corbin emphasises this 'inexhaustible epiphany': 'The symbol is never explained once and for all, but has always to be deciphered anew, just like a musical score. . .'.[37] Furthermore: 'There are variations in the symbolic intensity . . . and in the significant intensity of the system of redundancy. . . The image conveys more or less "meaning"'.[38] In brief, the symbol is 'A sign referring to an inexpressible and indivisible content or thing signified and through this, since obliged to embody concretely the totality which escapes it, by means of the keeping up of mythical, ritualistic and inconographic redundancies which send to correct and complete the inadequacy asymptotically'.[39]

We see therefore that Durand and Ricoeur, in their definitions of symbolic imagination, conjugate hermeneutic and structure, archaeology and eschatology, according to the 'method of convergence' for the one.[40] and to the 'coherence of the hermeneutics' for the other.[41]

If we now consider what there is concerning symbolic and symbolism in the Freudian and Lacanian schools we ascertain that the only dimensions of value of the symbol are archaeology and structure. It is enough to recall the criticisms formulated against Jung, specially those of Lacan.[42]

For Freud, the symbol and the symbolic are studied specifically in relation to psychoanalytic interpretation. According to Laplanche and Pontalis[43] Freudian symbolism should be understood in both a broad and in a more restricted sense:

1. Speaking broadly: a mode of indirect and figurative representation of an unconscious idea, conflict or wish. In this sense, one may in psychoanalysis hold any substitutive formation to be symbolic . . . displacement, condensation, overdetermination, figuration.[44]

In this sense, the symbol is close to the symbtom; it is 'reduced' to being the masked expression of the 'repressed' desire; in the final analysis, it will refer to the pre-history of the subject: it is archaeological.

2. In a more restricted sense: a mode of representation distinguished chiefly by the constancy of the relationship between the symbol and what it symbolizes in the unconscious. This constancy is found not only in the same individual and from one individual to the next, but also in the most varied spheres (myth, religion, folklore, language, etc.), and in the most widely separated cultures.[45]

This symbolic (*die Symbolik*) is a kind of 'basic language'[46] independent of the personal associations of the subject. In this sense, Freud's view approaches the conceptions of Durand and Jung. But it is limited, reduced to fundamental signifieds: 'Body, parents and blood relations, birth, death, nudity and above all sexuality'[47] upon which the whole Freudian theory of instincts is constructed. 'Primal fantasies'[48], these symbols often disguise the expression of a sexuality which cannot be expressed.

As we see it, the Freudian interpretation of the symbol remains hermeneutic – the semantic content being taken into consideration – viewed within a reductive and archaeological perspective. It is otherwise obvious in the work of the father of psychoanalysis that he was, by virtue of his concern with the strategies of conflicting relationships, more interested in the structure of the unconscious, then in the exploration of the symbolic semantics. If he was drawn to the symbol – and rather late, after 1914 in his written work (49) – it was a consequence of having encountered it in his exploration of the unconscious. Subsequently he was to integrate it into his general theory.

However the reductionistic tendency of the symbolic in a sexual 'schema' and the structural tendency of Freudian thought will, almost without hiatus, allow the transition of a symbolic, which still remains reductionistically hermeneutic, to the structural Lacanian '*ordre symbolique.*'

For when we admit that all signifiers finally refer to 'desire', in what way can the symbols still tell us something essential? Its forms are as innumerable as they are repetitive. The question which then arises is the articulation of desire, unspeakable signified for ever separated from the signifier which rebounds incessantly – as Rank[50] described it so masterfully – in the indefinitely renewed rebounds of compensations, symptoms, sublimations and idealisations[51] and in such an ambivalence that the game is never ending. Lacan privileged the structural to such a degree that the symbol approached the linguistic sign so closely as to almost lose all semantic relationship between signifier and signified. 'The links with what is being symbolized – the element of resemblance or isomorphism, for example – are secondary and impregnated by the Imaginary'.[52] And:

The psychoanalysable symptom, whether normal or pathological, distingushes itself from *all distrainable* form of pure expressivity, in that it is supported by a structure which is identical to the structure of language.[53]

In the *Situation de la psychanalyse* in 1956, Lacan moreover states:

Combinatory logic gives us the most radical form of this symbolic determinism. . . No prehistory allows us to obliterate the breach of this heteronomy of the symbolic. . . This exterioriety of symbolic in relation to man is the very notion of the unconscious. And Freud has constantly proved that he valued it as much as the very principle of his experience.[54]

In Lacanian symbolism it is, therefore, not only a matter of structural order, but moreover of an exogenous structural order; there it clashes with Jung's endogenous archetypal hypothesis.

For Lacan the structure of the symbol, the breach between the signifier and the signified is what is important. The significant image, the content, the semantism is secondary and, 'impregnated with the imaginary'. The symbolic order denotes the breach, the separation of desire, like the bar separating the signifier from the unspeakable signified; it is the submission to an order, to the law of separation and acknowledgement through acceptance of this order in which man is caught 'since before his birth and beyond his death' . . . 'caught like a pawn in the game of the signifier, and this even before the rules have been transmitted to him'.[55] Exogenous structure indeed! For Lacan, man is caught in the exogenous symbolicial order; for Jung, man is caught in the endogenous network of archetypal order. But in one as in the other, he has to practise an 'unglueing' of the image, a rupture in the 'coalescence of the signifier with the signified'[56] otherwise, it means the 'somewhete else', alienation, 'madness'.

According to Laplanche and Pontalis, Lacan's 'symbolic' 'covers those phenomena with which psychoanalysis deals in so far as they are structured like a language. The term also refers to the idea that the effectiveness of the cure is based on the constitutive nature of the Word (*le caractère fondateur de la parole*).'[57] They add:

Lacan's use of the notion of the Symbolic in psychoanalysis seems to us to have two aims: 1. To compare the structure of the unconscious with that of language, and to apply to the former a method which has borne fruit in its application to linguistics. 2. To show how the human subject is inserted into a pre-established order which is itself symbolic in nature, in Lévi-Strauss's sense.[58]

The Lacanian psychoanalysis therefore favours 'linguistic relations'[59] in the symbolic system.[60]

If the symbolic is for Lacan an order where the signifier Father-Phallus restores the law, cultural systems and the recognition of the Other, 'the imaginary is characterized by the prevalence of the relation to the image of the counterpart (*le semblable*).[61]

We find there all the problematics of 'specular ego' and 'narcissistic' and the 'dual relationship'[62] of which the blending relationship mother-child is the prototype. The Imaginary therefore 'implies a type of apprehension, in which factors such as resemblance and homeomorphism play a decisive role, attesting to a sort of coalescence of the signifier with the signified'.[63]

From the Imaginary to the Symbolic the deviation between the signifier and the signified stretches from the seen image to the linguistic sign:

The imaginary, coalescence of the signifier with the signified, symbolizes, in no better way, that desire is fantasized in a dual relationship, mother-uterus where the ego and the other are the same; where desire is not enunciated but is lost, submerged, embraced in the non-separate, the non-discerned, the similar.

In the linguistic sign, being the model of the symbolic order, the division between signifier and signified is impossible to resolve, as there is no internal link between them. The chain of signifiers takes meaning only through the structure of its differential oppositions.[64] Thus the definite breach of all signifiers symbolizes itself as a fundamental signified, desire.

The structure of the symbol, arising from the imaginary coalescence by means of the symbolizing breach, is a model for the structure of the unconscious. 'Structured like a language' as soon as it emerges as symbolic, it then differentiates the ego and the non-ego, it recognizes the network of order and law in which it is caught, and it knows the nostalgia of the for ever impossible desire.[55]

In the Lacanian thesis the symbol is therefore used for its structure signifier/ signified and not for its semantism or its iconography. It refers, by its very structure, to a complete symbolic system, and a whole imaginary register, that of the unconscious.

To sum up the Lacanian and Jungian theories of the symbol, we may therefore say, pushing the system's logic to its limit, that, in the symbolic, Lacanian psychoanalysis gives precedence to structure. Amongst the various symbolic systems[65] he chose the least 'iconic' – the linguistic sign – of which the lack of internal relationship between

signifier and signified[66] symbolizes the exogenous characteristic of the
order and law of cultural symbolic systems, to which language
belongs. The Lacanian symbolic order is thus devoid of symbolical
semantism because it is fundamentally structural.

On the other hand, in systematizing Jungian symbolism, the latter
appears contradictory to Lacanian symbolism. Acknowledgement of
the structure does not require it to reject the semantism of the symbol.
Mythical symbolism (linguistic or *langagier*) does not prelude
iconography. But the order and law have their fundmentally
endogenous roots in the archetypal processes. Jungian symbolism,
recognizing the archaeologic, the exogenous and the structure,
emphasises nonetheless an instaurative hermeneutic within an
eschatological meaning.

And so, the final word would be in the dialectic symbolical–
energetic because insoluble – between being and non-being: 'To be or
not to be' is not the highest drama; but in the final analysis rather, 'To
be and not to be'.[67]

Archetypal Structures, Primal Repression and the Therapeutic Relationship with Psychotics

BY GIUSEPPE MAFFEI   *translated by Anna Cortopassi*

The relationship with a psychotic is a peculiar one. At the beginning of my work, when I thought I had understood one of the possible meanings of what a psychotic patient said, or when what came forth from time to time seemed to take shape and to fit in a sort of masaic, showing the lines of a pattern, I felt relieved for a short time from the anxiety of the incomprehensible which I had felt till then. I hoped I had established a stable contact, because of the appearance of a pattern in the mosaic. The patient, unlike a neurotic, often refused to recognize himself in what we had discovered together, and I thought his difficulties were due to a wrong attitude on my part or to some emotional resistance of mind. I felty very guilty because of my failure and I did not know what to do. Even if I obtained some slight improvement in the conditions of my patients, I felt bitter and unsatisfied because there was never that therapeutic empathy so characteristic of the relationship with other patients and generally there was never a true consent concerning life. With other patients a mutual acceptance of many common structures is taken for granted and the principles of our existence and other people's are not continuously questioned. Psychic health as a goal, for instance, is hardly ever questioned in relationship with other patients, or, if it is, it is questioned at a different level. With psychotics, however, during every session, it is as if everything had to be questioned all over again. Resuming, a common dialogue is not possible: every time the patient appears to be somewhere else and not where we had left him the previous time. It is not possible to foresee where he may be found. Yet all these patients wanted to speak and to get an answer to a question I could not understand. That is why it was a difficult choice for me to go on working with these patients. Contact with the thought of Klein, Bion, Matte-Blanco, Resnik and then others allowed me to have a certain understanding of what I observed, but the decision to go on was mainly supported by a fundamental idea of Jung's. Jung's theory, in fact, always maintains that archetypal structures must be somehow activated by the relationship with others in order to develop in such a way as to allow a normal psychic condition. Psychopathologic observation, actually, allows us to notice in some situations that the process of individuation is blocked, and the archetypal structures necessary to psychic life are not activated. The fundamental characteristics of men remain as they are and do not develop in any direction. By activation of an archetypal structure I mean the coming to life of the structure itself: the existence of the soul archetype (provided that at some level we can speak of the existence of an archetype) is not possible without the relationship of men to women. Whereas in a neurotic it is a question of unblocking an already existing process imprisoned by some unconscious mechanism, in the case of a psychotic, it is often the process itself which must somehow be created and called into being. A psychotic may even give the impression that he has well understood, inside himself, the existence of a possibility of evolution, but a more careful observation will let us see how what appears in him to be a process is nothing but an imitation of what other people do or think. If a process is active at all it is active in a backward direction rather than a forward one; but one of the main characteristics of a psychotic is just that he will show, when left to himself, an absence of psychological development (and at a level of collective unconsciousness, an absence of succession in time of the representations of the archetypal structures). Perhaps there may be a parallelism with language. In order to be able to speak, it is necessary for the brain structures relative to language to be able to meet other people's speech. This is in fact the *conditio sine qua non* of the possibility of communication.

Contact with many different schools of thought, even when all of them are centred on the problem of archetypal structures, can cause a remarkable confusion and produce a series of hopeless contradictions. On the other hand, the clinical necessity of helping and understanding these patients was real and did not permit me to give up. My conclusion until now has been quite simple: it was just what I had observed, the impossibility of maintaining a contact with another person, which constitutes one of the main characteristics of the psychotic world. The patient always speaks in fact of a world different from that of the therapist.

One of these patients said one day: 'I suffer because the others are so different from me!' And starting from this sentence it is possible to find a gleam of understanding. A psychotic feels at the centre of the world in an absolute truth of his own. Isolated from affective contacts with other people, without any link, he can live with the illusion of such unity with himself that he can also represent an ideal of life for others. 'My life is really an alternative', said the same patient. Other people come to compromises, do not have a continuous coherence with their ideal ego, are continuously limited and often find they must adapt themselves. A psychotic, on the contrary, lives outside all this, and from where he lives, he watches everything happening in the world. This is why he is so sharp and sees so many things; not entering into any relationship with events, with a constituted and therefore limited self, all the events are inside him and he is inside all events. He has had to find a solution different from ours: we have built an ego, to which we have set some limits, we have limited ourselves; a psychotic has not had this possibility. When he feels bad and is anxious, we can compare his anxiety to ours, maybe to our deepest one; but we must be very careful: his crises are crises of a system different from ours. He is, from this point of view, very different from us and his anxiety comes from the impossibility of keeping the wholeness of his ideal ego. When he asks for our help, he means something different from what we understand immediately. He generally asks us to restore his own wholeness (only a part of him is aware of his illness). We understand a wholeness like ours, which is no longer a total wholeness because we have accepted castration, separation, suffering; the patient, however, means the total and ideal wholeness.

If we keep this clearly in our minds, we can avoid many misunderstandings and disappointments, but we cannot avoid a series of problems concerning our rapport with psychotics of this type. A psychotic has reached his position through a series of extremely dramatic childhood events: he has not had understanding parents, has not been able to overcome his conflicts and has had continuous disappointments. Then he has reached a shore foreign to us from which he sends us requests of help.

Now we can be more precise; with the sick part, he asks us to restore his wholeness, with the healthy part he asks us to help him leave the foreign land and come back to ours. The conflict of these two parts is very fierce and we know already which is stronger. In our work, trying to clarify his psychological situation, we side with the weaker part, with those few links our patient has established with other people. Our attempt, even if not directly addressed to the healthy part, is perceived on two sides: on the side of the restoration of omnipotence and on the side of the invitation to a relationship. As the relationship becomes deeper, it will become clearer and clearer that our help was addressed towards the healthy part. On the other hand, by showing our understanding of the problems relative to omnipotence, we implicitly provide also the sick part with an answer; and the patient's realization of this, may form a link that he may consider to be dangerous and that he may try to sabotage with a series of violent attacks.

But is it useful to undertake therapy? If we see the situation from the psychotic's point of view, is it right to work out the realization we have mentioned before and which cannot fail to create a different psychic situation, the deepest feature of which is going to be the existence of closer links than the ones previously established? In my experience with adults I have witnessed improvements in psychotics, but never have I witnessed a real overcoming of the splitting I have described. The most evident psychotic symptomatology may cease or diminish (such as delusions and hallucinations and so on), but not the split personality: I have always seen that there remains deep down an attraction for omnipotence and an intense aggressiveness against any established relationship.

I have the impression that a psychotic's injuries are too old and serious to be completely healed. What about his point of view? 'Why should I suffer so much?' a patient said to me. 'Wouldn't it be better if you left me in my delusion?'

I find it very difficult to answer this question. Actually the problem is that of working in a direction not shared by the patient. This make the situation exceptional compared to all other doctor–patient situations. The patient lives outside the social relationship, not just this particular social relationship but outside any social relationship as such. He has not developed the possibility of relating to other people. He lacks, we might say, the basic structure for relationship. At this level we find many of the modern misunderstandings between psychosis and society. I don't deny that the present social structure may favour the development of psychosis, but this is an indirect influence. In a wholly direct and primary sense a psychotic has missed those family and social relationships that make communication possible in every human society. And this is the reason why I think we can answer 'yes' to the question whether it is right to try to treat psychotics. Many things are based on the fact that we 'sane people' believe communication among men to be possible. This is our basic hypothesis. Psychotics tend to prove the opposite, but we have the duty, toward them, or rather toward their unhappiness, to propose our choice. We have chosen to associate with each other, to abandon omnipotence, we believe we are fortunate, but a psychotic may believe exactly the opposite. Through our work, we can let them perceive a possible alternative, the social one. If we avoid this task it would mean that we are somehow uncertain about our choice of living, of *ex-sistere*. To suggest implicitly, without blackmailing, an alternative difference is, in my opinion, an ethical approach to psychosis. Maybe we have not quite understood their position, as they are a continuous contradiction to our complicity, but accepting them as partners of an open dialogue at the level mentioned above, seems to be the most 'human' way that is possible today to give value to their position and to make contact with them. The deep, archetypal structures do not seem to be able to start a process of psychological development by themselves. A seed must find favourable surrounding conditions to develop into a plant. Therefore, if one is a psychotic because his experience has been marked by lack of these favourable conditions, our task is to provide him with them. It will be up to him to develop or not. A child, when left a prey to his primal fantasies, has no possibility of elaborating them; he must have, as we shall see later, a reference structure.

This type of argument does not lead necessarily to a theoretical position that sees no value in psychosis. The world of psychosis is nearer than ours to the basic libido fluxes, it is less structured than ours, and it is less tied to the 'false' structures of our social life. But when we speak to a psychotic, even starting from a theory of schizophrenia far from the traditional psychoanalytic thought (see the position of Deleuze and Guattari), we still offer our attention and we invite him to existence. And what I mean by existence, from this point of view is the activation of archetypal structures, their realization in time and space. It is this realization which leads to the formation of a structure. The Oedipal one is one of the possibilities, but the absence of any kind of structure is not consistent with psychic life.

Once we have answered positively the question whether it is right to undertake psychotherapy with psychotics, we must investigate, on the one hand, the consequences and, on the other, the ends we can aim at.

As to the first point, we can maintain that every attempt of psychotherapy brings to the constitution of bipartite structure of a psychotic a new structure which he had not known before. What we can determine with psychotherapy is, first of all, the possibility for a patient to have an image of himself and to constitute in this way a psychical structure more similar to a normal one. And what determines this process is, in my opinion, the ability of the therapist to give meaning to the feelings and emotions of his patient, which he had before only implicitly.

It is necessary to introduce first of all the idea of primal repression and in particular the definition given to this idea by De Waelhens, definition that seems to me the most useful one in facing the problem we are now discussing. I quote from a book by Rifflet-Lemaire, who refers to that author's opinion:

A. De Waelhens defines the primal repression, simultaneous with the access to language, as the act with which the subject, or more precisely what is constituting itself as 'subject', through this act avoids the immediacy of experience, providing a substitute which is not he, just as the subject is not the experience and which will constitute the real as real, the symbolic as autonomous, and the subject as subject.[1]

Now, says Rifflet-Lemaire, the primal repression is possible only if the subject places himself as something that is not the thing or the experience, just as the substitute that he gives to this experience. Consequently, such repression is possible only if the subject has a *signifiant originaire*[2] of himself that he can put as a negative of his own synaesthesia, and which will allow him to use that negation[3] inherent in primal repression. A thing is not its substitute, just as it is not the ego.

The social structure of a psychotic's psyche appears then to have as its main feature the failed constitution of primal repression. Such patients appear not to have known the possibility of distinguishing themselves from what they have lived through and this failure to distinguish themselves from themselves seems to be the cause of the serious consequences we all know.

Psychotics are continuously faced with psychic contents not repressed in a primal sense. Furthermore these unrepressed psychic contents would be excluded from consciousness through the mechanism of foreclosure* (*Verwerfung*) and could come out into reality under the various forms of hallucinations and delusions that the clinical observation of psychosis has taught us to observe. As De Waelhens[4] says, the failure of primal repression would put the psyche under the rule of foreclosure.

The problem of the constitution of primal repression is a long debated and yet unsolved problem. We can believe anyhow that such repression happens in the moment of contact between the experience and the language which provides it with meaning, only implicit before this event. Without contact with language which gives it a meaning, any experience would be destined to remain without time and dimension.

It is through the meaning implied in language that psychic life becomes history. Experience acquires meaning only if it has direction and time. Otherwise it ends in itself. It is only when I say, 'I am hungry', that I define myself as a subject who is hungry. We can formulate the same problem for archetypal structures. For a process of

---

* This term was originally used by Freud to refer to the Wolf Man's *rejection* of castration. It was Jacques Lacan though, the French structuralist-psychoanalyst who introduced it into the modern vocabulary (he rendered it into French as *forclusion* – hence its English translation) in analysing its Freudian meaning and using it to refer to a specific type of primitive negation of certain experiences or phenomena *in which they fail to become symbolized*. Unlike repression, where the negated material is symbolized and therefore becomes part of one's unconscious, the foreclosed material remains outside the unconscious (as well as, of course, the conscious part of one's psyche).

individuation to begin, it is necessary for the surroundings to recognize its necessity. Often the unconscious situation of the parents of the future psychotic prevents them from perceiving the necessity to recognize and help the process of individuation of their own child. We can certainly maintain that the process is autonomous, but autonomous does not mean that it does not depend on the activation on the part of the other. In the relationship with psychotics we have the impression that the process is blocked just because it is not activated. Sometimes the process takes place at a level that is removed from consciousness (some psychotic crises are fragments of processes that do not appear clearly) but a real development finds its source in a human relationship and the following primal repression. In order to understand this we can think of the love felt by a child for his mother, we can in fact maintain that the child's experience of love is very complex and not well defined. We can distinguish for example two aspects of this love. 'I want to join with you again, to be hugged, touched, caressed' and 'I want to come into you, to know your inside contents, to live in you'. These two aspects are confused as if they were amalgamated. The child knows them only in a chaotic mixture, they are not sorted out, but perhaps only directed by the existence of the primal fantasies. The mother instead knows diverse experiences and can answer in a partial way. She can answer 'yes' only to one of these two aspects, she can recognize, for example, in her child the need of being caressed, hugged, touched, but not his need to come inside her. The emotional, muscular, total reply can therefore make the child understand that only one aspect of experience will find an answer. The other aspect, on the contrary, will not find an answer at this moment and will constitute the 'primal repressed'. We can perceive this division also in the very use of words to signify any experience: the spoken experience never coincides perfectly with the experience that has not yet found a possibility of representation in words.

The primal repression is constituted by discrimination of a superficial level within the chaos of the primal experience, and this discrimination is determined by other people's responses. The psychotic is mainly characterized by the lack of this process. The projections he has sent out or received have been such as to prevent his recognizing himself as a subject, and he is continuously faced with unsymbolized[5] experiences of omnipotence. What determines the primal repression and so the possibility of a 'normal' psychological development lies therefore in the partial recognition of the patient's deep experiences by others. In this partial recognition an important role is played by the fantasies of the one who gives the answer, fantasies which, somehow directing his psychic life, permit contact with the child's archetypal structures, his primal fantasies.

What happens in the psychotherapy of psychotics allows us to perceive how a primal repression can be determined within the analytic relationship, and how a constitution of a bipartite structure of the psyche can be created with the presence of a nucleus of psychic experiences, signified by language. An examination of this theme will show how the constituent and fundamental side of the primal repression is represented by the acknowledgement by the psychotherapist of the meaning of mimic and verbal expression of the subject. To make my point clearer I shall give an example. It concerns a patient with progressive estrangement from reality and detachment from any emotional life experience. One day, during an analytic session, he says he feels a tiny bit crushed by strange massive forces; all the world weighs upon him and huge beams outside the door are there to crush him. On this level he is faced with a psychic content not primally repressed, therefore 'to weigh' really means that he feels the whole world weighs upon him physically together with the air around him. The word 'weigh' does not refer his mind to any other experience than the one he has expressed; his experience is actually a psychotic experience in which the weight is felt as real.

The analyst, in the light of previous experiences, understands what has been communicated by the patient and answers (evidently with the support of his own fantasies) that actually he has perception of the patient's own small weight, that it is not forbidden to have a certain weight and that moving the air around oneself or determining with one's weight changes in people near us is a possibility and not a guilt. The patient does not show logical understanding of what has been said. But at the end of session he shakes hands with the analyst for the first time after two years. Shaking hands has become for the first time a meaningful gesture. For the first time he has let his analyst feel his own weight and his own body.

What has happened? How can the effects of the analyst's intervention be understood? On the one hand with understanding, and on the other with recognition of the meaning of the word weight, the analyst in this case has performed a fundamental operation in psychic development. He has recognized the underlying meaning within one experience which had never been given meaning before. This patient had never experienced that weight might have a meaning and that it played a part in his relationship with others. Weight was perceived as a quality far from the possibility of communication with others. The analyst, with an emotional reaction, somehow had 'made psychic' what up to that moment had not had a clear psychic meaning. When we speak of archetypal structures, we do not speak of structures unconnected with the body: it is the body itself that possesses these structures, which may or may not be made psychic. The articulated expression by the analyst was only a consequence of the fact that somehow the words of the patient had awakened some of his own fantasies. The essential point lay in his emotional reaction. The first condition for the transfer of the interpretation from doctor to patient lay in the fact that the activation of his own fantasies had determined his wishing that the patient should acquire a weight for him. The analyst had stopped fearing the huge weight put on his back by such an anguishing situation as the one represented by the psychotherapy of a person who did not realize being a weight.

In my opinion it is through events of this kind that it is possible to have a primal repression: from the various meanings of weight, the analyst has in fact chosen in his communication with his patient only one or more aspects of weight. Other aspects of weight had not been supplied with a secure meaning. We may therefore be justified in thinking that part of weight connected with some drive, not understood by the analyst, tends to constitute a nucleus of primal repression. The analytic relationship has become personal: the patient finds himself in front of a subject who understands some experiences and not others.[6] If we can for a moment think of the possibility of an absolute lack in the other to recognize all meanings, I think we can well understand how for some subjects the possibility of a constitution of bipartite structure of the psyche may not arise: all the experiences are left out of the emotional communication. Any communication happens only with vain words, and therefore any 'foreclosed' representation, when it should come out, comes back to the patient from outside. In order to prove this hypothesis that the recognition of meaning allows the constitution of the primal repression, we can submit two arguments that come from ordinary observation.

1. Clinical observation demonstrates in fact that, within families of psychotics, whose psyche is characterized by total or partial lack of primal repression, communication has as its main feature very serious distortions on the level of recognition of meaning. So much has been written about this problem that it is not necessary to bring further examples. The central element missing in psychotics' families is the parents' awareness of the existence of the future patient's particular aims and wishes. The difficulty to accept the individuality and originality of a particular subject occurs often very early or even before birth; some particular situation of the parents prevents them from considering the baby's birth from the necessary emotional response.

Anamnesis and the study we can effect during a psychotherapeutic treatment of psychotics, without excluding the influence these have on their family, show clearly how the future patients have been deprived of the chance to define any vital direction with meaning for the same parents. The latter have, at once or very early, absorbed the subject exclusively in their imaginary world, though without being aware of their own intention. Some of these parents present some clearly pathological features. We can take, as an example those mothers who, even in their own life, independently from, or together with their children's experience, seem to exclude completely the 'Name-of-the-Father'.* In other words, the order of the world appears to them as thoroughly casual, dominated by rules without any deep sense. The rules exist in a certain way but might be formulated in a thousand different ways. The parents lack the awareness and the experience of a world structured according to an order in which the intention of the subject plays a fundamental, if not exclusive, role.

In this case the psychotic lives therefore in a situation foreclosing the 'Name-of-the-Father' and from this experience he draws the delusive conviction that reality should be pliable to his own imaginary level. The contact with true reality explodes the contradiction and could not help exploding it: when the pre-psychotic teenager understands that if he wants to be strong, he must really be strong and not only say so, he finds himself in front of an insuperable difficulty. The psychotic's symptomatology is often an episode reacting to this situation. When the pre-psychotic is faced with a world in which there are intentional movements incomprehensible to him and with which he should make contact with intentional movements to which he is not used, he can only react with that acute symptomatology in which we find all the tensions that up to now had been dominated by defence mechanisms exclusively alienating, such as identification with imaginary figures, disconnected from the meaning given to life by the difference of sexes and generations. Let us examine an example: if an individual is faced with a weak mother who is aware of the importance of the 'Name-of-the-Father', the father, in case the child has to be reproached, is presented as the one who justly should do so; accomplishing a function that perhaps the mother should have carried out herself. In this case a possible psychotic nucleus of the mother–child communication may be relieved by reference to the paternal order. If the mother has foreclosed the 'Name-of-the-Father', then the father will be emotionally presented as the one who acts justly, but according to a justice and order which have no authenticity and draw their strength from habit, because everybody does so. The eventual aggressiveness

---

* According to Lacan the Name-of-the-Father (*Nom-du-Père*) is the signifier of the paternal function – and, by extension, the signifier of the whole symbolic order of language (which in turn includes the broader realms of culture and civilization). Thus, foreclosure of the Name-of-the-Father (i.e. failure to enter the symbolic order) would amount to psychosis.

of the child will not be tolerable. The father will not appear to the child like a man who has found his way to face his own aggressiveness and has his own elaborated and suffered order, but rather he will appear as an identification in which signifier and signified are one thing. The reproach will refer to a 'one must' disconnected from the personal situation of the three parties and therefore remains outside a communication founding a symbolic order. This child will become convinced that in order to live one must conform to 'one must'. The impersonal 'one' may thus invade the patient's life. (Concerning this see the essay by Binswanger on mannerism.[7])

During adolescence, when the moment comes for this boy to enter the social circle, he will believe himself, for example, able to conquer a girl just because he is conforming to the rules of the world. The total conformity to the 'one' must bear its fruit. But this appears to be impossible: the world reveals to the boy a different image from the one he had expected. The girl wants a personal behaviour, it would be necessary to speak of feelings and emotions. There is no alternative. What is necessary is an experience that unfortunately the boy by now does not have. The psychotic crisis bursts out and, if we consider it in this perspective, can be interpreted as an attempt to question all over again the entire world shaped up to that moment. All the imaginary parameters explode that up to then had been used as reference points, and in their place there appear new and often terrifying psychotic contents. This is why there appear also archetypal motives, just because the attempt to repair the damages can only be radical and can bring out the deepest contents of human soul. The compensatory trend pointed out by Jung at the level of human unconsciousness seems essential if we want to understand the psychotic crisis. It is not a mere chance that it was a Jungian analyst, Perry,[8] who wrote that psychotic crises often should be interpreted as an attempt to recover. To exemplify this idea we can discuss how from this point of view we can interpret the frequent appearance at the beginning of schizophrenia of 'delusive intuitions' (the *Wahneinfall* of Schneider) and delusions of reference. In the previous world there had not been space either for intuition or for the possibility of reference. If the suggested model is valid, after the foreclosure of the 'Name-of-the-Father' all the meanings are simultaneously present and there is nothing new to discover. Everything is somehow already known and there is not therefore any joy of discovering. As that which is missing in the interpretive key can be offered only through an emotional presence, in the family communication, of the value of the differences of sexes and order of generations, there can be no search for one's place in the world: this place must be looked for only in an adjustment to superior rules over which it is not possible to have any influence. In

Demoulin's words signifier and signified mix together and the space for an objective understanding of reality is not created.[9]

When we know a pre-psychotic deeply, we can notice how thoroughly deprived he is of an interpretive key of reality; for instance if we ask him how he behaves in order to know whether a person tells him the real truth or not he will be puzzled and will offer only vague and impersonal answers. The world of a psychotic will appear, as we said above, dominated by the 'one'. The intuition has had no space for autonomous work but it has rather been coerced under the development of other functions. At the beginning of psychosis the intuition and the 'reference' take the advantage and dominate the psyche of the subject. The subject who till now had not used himself as a measure of judgement for other people's behaviour or rather had considered other people's behaviour as an unchangeable entity, suddenly upsets his own position and begins judging the outside, basing himself exclusively on the use of projective mechanisms, attaching his own projection to aspects that are present perhaps in infinitesimal way in the people surrounding him. By now nobody can understand: how is it possible for a son or a brother to have become so strange and incomprehensible? And really that brother or that son has become very strange, but especially in relation to his past in which he had been completely far from his unconscious contents. The crisis accompanies the emergence of these, for which, however, because of the previous history, there can be brought into play only the mechanism of foreclosure and thus, through alienation and dangerousness, the road to hospitalization and psychiatry. If psychiatry accepts the formulation of the problem the family has given, that is if psychiatry itself considers the situation incomprehensible, it will be difficult for the man who has now become a patient to be able to make sense of what is happening. Many exclusion mechanisms will be set to work and he will slide down the slope of a deeper and deeper regression. If on the contrary psychiatry does not accept the role the family imposes on it, it will be able to side with the patient and try to stop this terrible descent. It is well known, for example, how the motherly attitude of a nurse can arrest or temporarily relieve a psychotic situation.

After clarifying by these specific examples what we described in theory, and before concluding this first point, it is necessary to go back to a problem already touched upon, but needing further consideration. I refer to the fact that in the families of psychotics, within an interpersonal communication which seems to us deeply distorted, not all children become psychotics. Many questions arise therefore: what is the psychic trouble affecting the parents? When in the family history was such a situation created, that made a child's psychosis inevitable? We cannot give a full answer to these questions as yet. Waiting to understand these problems better, we can only assemble some facts. As for the psychic disturbance presented by the parents, this reveals, in a number of cases, a successful and total conformity to a set of completely impersonal rules of behaviour. We can often observe a mother so well identified with her motherly function that she behaves in compliance with certain rules in an apparently perfect way. Responsibility, sacrifice, devotion to the other are present, but they are addressed to an *abstract* one, not to a *concrete* one; they are human qualities that somehow have become cold and impersonal. These mothers seems to have never known an affective life and real suffering derived from deep experience. But when did they slip so far from any possibility of real and affective communication? It is with regard to this that anamnesis sometimes permits the observation of a particular meaning taken into the mother's life with the birth of that son who later will become a psychotic. This observation allows us also to have a glimpse of the answer to the other questions that are formulated above.

A child's birth always has a very deep importance in the parent's unconscious and all the infantile themes are awakened by the presence of this new human being who is particularly puzzling because, on one side he has many needs, and on the other he is so pliable and helpless as to provide opportunity of receiving all possible projections. Besides, any physical problems in the mother acquire through pregnancy and delivery an importance that may not have been noticed until then. Previous psychic conflicts may be mobilized relative to pain, to death, to the deepest and most complex themes which may formerly have been far from consciousness. Before such problems the hope may have arisen not to have any need of the integrated functions of the Ego and the secondary process in respect of the newborn child. One may say, 'Let us hope my son will grow well and will not give me any worries'. But this sentence often means: 'Let us hope he will not need my intervention'. In this case the son finds he is living in a world where there is for him only a deprivation of the gift of the meaning and therefore of the possibility of entering the symbolic order. Other children however may not produce the same kind of reaction and so may have a different place in the personal history of their parents.

Finally we could argue that the parents of psychotics may be subjects who, if they have had access to the symbolic order, have had access to it only with a certain fragility and inconsistency. As a result there may still exist the possibility of regression to the imaginary level, which the birth of a child may precipitate, causing a series of reactions through which the son may find himself living in a world devoid of any meaning for him. For the psychotic child the possibility of the development of a bi-polar structure of the psyche has not been created. Consequently it becomes necessary to employ that particular psychic mechanism of foreclosure, substantially the refusal of something which for the psychotic has remained outside any possible psychic representation. When the refusal is at the level of 'It is not true that', the object of negation is somehow representable to the subject himself; when the refusal takes place, as in foreclosure, the subject is being deprived of the possibility of perceiving the existence of the 'Name-of-the-Father'. This is why the psychotic finds it so difficult to relate to another person. Any relationship with the other implies the acceptance of a sense of relationship, but this implies in turn (as we have seen) the prior existence of a bipartite structure of the psyche, which the psychotic does not in fact know. From this situation arises the circumstance that the psychotic cannot understand how a smile can refer to a series of contrasting emotions, because smiling equals laughing and he knows only his own subjective laughter, i.e. laughing at the 'strange' efforts that other people make, to do things whose meaning he has never understood.

What meaning can there be in the useless attempt to live one's own life if one starts from the conviction of the illusoriness of the foundation of mutual exchanges? His experience of laughing is only his own and he finds it intact (i.e. not 'shared') in other people's smiles: the smiles of others are therefore always seen to mock an incompleteness or difficulty of his.

This is precisely why psychotics are so sensitive to any form of message sent to them: in fact, without a symbolic order, the distinction between a part and the whole has no meaning and consequently every part is representative of the whole and *vice versa*. If a fellow patient asks a psychotic to give *him* a cigarette, this request becomes immediately (or rather it is at the same moment of being made) a request to give away something that belongs to him, a thing of his own, himself. For a subject who is not psychotic the request of a cigarette refers to a series of precise meanings. It is taken for granted, for example, that what is requested is something completely separate from the subject who has been asked for it, also that the absolute goodness of the subject is not required, that he knows that the request does not deeply concern the person who makes it and so on. A psychotic subject lacks completely this series of references even at that level. What the companion wants is not clear to him, whether he wants a cigarette or love, because according to the laws that rule the psychotic's world there is no clear distinction between giving a part of oneself or all of oneself. I think that an understanding and affectionate attitude towards a psychotic may give very interesting results for precisely this reason; any openness or benevolence is for him total openness and benevolence.

The psychotic can trust the other totally if the other is benevolent, because he will believe him to be totally and really and truly benevolent (while the other will understand that the benevolence is not total but partial and also conditional).

2. That the gift of meaning creates the possibility of the development of this bi-polar structure of the psyche is proved furthermore, in my opinion, by two clinical facts quite often observed and which point to the same conclusion. The first is that the experience of some psychotics in young people's protest movements has produced in them an opening to the symbolic order. Finding themselves confronted by basic themes such as those proposed by the protest, the attempt to find answers without starting from already fixed codes has constituted for many psychotics such an important experience that, owing to their active participation in the attempt to create new symbols, some have been able to perceive the possibility of the existence of a separate symbolic order. The questioning of every problem, never taking anything for certain or granted, has limited the imaginary dimension and widened and opened the symbolic one, in terms of concrete experiences. The same observation holds true also for participation in the experiences of therapeutic communities. The analysis of a psychotic who had lived for a long time in a therapeutic community, from which he had nevertheless ultimately been dismissed because he was considered dangerous, permits the observation of some interesting later effects of the experience itself. Its greatest usefulness appears to have been in the fact that this patient, after terrible personal experiences, found himself suddenly in a place where he could look for a personal contact beyond his psychosis.

This situation was completely new to him. The experience became a positive nucleus of the utmost importance for the rest of his life. These observations also seem to provide a basis for a theory with a psychoanalytic and objective underpinning of a new psychiatry, which will reject the role to which society wants to confine it and will take upon itself the task of recognizing the meaning of life of individuals who have always been denied such recognition. In this context the proposals of Tosquelles and of the *Revue de Psychothérapie Institutionnelle* seem to be of the utmost importance.

The other clinical fact, just as easily observed, is demonstrated by the remarkable influence that very simple words can have on the psyche of the psychotic, when these words are supported by a positive affect and so imply the recognition of separate meaning. Generally during a dialogue, the psychotic manages to get involved in a series of problems and statements on an imaginary level, and it is difficult to bring him to an independent symbolic dimension.

In order to establish human contact a qualitative change is required and this may be represented by statements proving that the psychotic's words have been listened to and have also acquired a personal meaning for the listener. These statements, pointing to a personal interest, when such really exists, may determine the passage from the level of abstract speech to that of concrete speech, so permitting a less unpleasant subjective experience.

I maintain that the arguments presented here clearly enough indicate the *recognition of meaning* as the event capable of determining that primal repression (the activation of archetypes) that alone can subsequently permit the existence of that secondary repression, the constitution of a personal unconsciousness and the access to normality and to neurosis.

Our work, if successful, will thus take the psychotic towards a psychic structure different from the one he has known before. He will be recognized in his individuality and this fact will lead him to approach a sort of complicity with us. In taking care of him, a therapist tells him implicitly: 'You are important to me', and the psychotic has never heard such an acknowledgement of his individuality. It is necessary, in fact, to pay great attention to the meaning of 'you' and 'me'. This you and me must be in fact completely individual: the mother generally had never been clear in her unconsciousness that the 'you' she was speaking to was one of the various 'yous' she came into contact with ('You son are important for me') and the 'me' she was referring to was a 'me' that had a precise relationship with other 'yous' ('You, son, are important for me, mother'). If the sentence had been formulated in this way the son would have found himself in a clear and defined historical dimension. Every situation would have become defined and the son could have taken his own place. Feelings of omnipotence both at the level of you ('You, son, come, you omnipotent, to restore the order broken by the castration I suffered') and at the level of me ('You, son, come to rest on my omnipotence totally intact from yielding to your father') have instead drawn the future psychotic first into the universe of symbiosis and then into the tragedy of psychosis. The therapist proposes a possibility of contact, against the background of the 'Other' (Lacan) and so highly individualized. This contact can establish relations which are completely new for the patient. Under these conditions the psychotic sometimes seems to be willing to know us and to let us know him.

CHAPTER 8

Tentative Views on Dream Therapy by Xhosa Diviners

BY M. VERA BÜHRMANN

Introduction

This is a report on field work that was undertaken to assess the therapeutic techniques of Xhosa diviners. The Xhosa-speaking people inhabit an area along the south-eastern coast of South Africa, and this article deals with their attitude to, and use of, dreams. An effort is made to see it in an historical framework and to discuss its relevance to present-day practices and research work.

In view of the cultural differences between most research workers and their clients it was regarded as important to use an approach that would decrease this as much as possible. It could be described as a phenomenological approach. The attitude of the research worker had to be as free as possible of preconceived theories and prejudices. This attitude of participant observer then permits the material to speak for itself, meaning becomes apparent, and the material, which at first may appear chaotic or senseless, orders itself into meaningful constructs for the Western-trained professional.

Eight days were spent with the diviner, Mr T., his diviner wife, their novices and some of their patients. They were observed in a variety of situations. They performed ceremonies as a group and Mr T. functioned as a group and family therapist, unravelling conflicts, discontents and tensions within the family and clan. It was also possible to gain some insight into his way of dealing with individual patients.

I should like to focus on my impressions of, and ideas about, their use of dreams. This aspect was chosen for a variety of reasons, but primarily on account of his emphatic statement, 'If they don't dream I can't work with them'. This central place of unconscious material in therapy indicated some similarity in his, and my, techniques – it served to open doors and build bridges of communication between us. He aids dreaming by prescribing 'medicine', which he prepares from the roots, stem and bark of plants. The head, face and upper parts of the body must be washed with it and it must also be imbibed. Those patients who seek his help but in his opinion require 'medicine' he sends to herbalists; those who are 'mad' he sends to the European doctor. 'White doctor' is a confusing term because he as a diviner is also regarded as a 'white doctor', which I interpreted as an 'enlightened doctor', i.e. in touch with the ancestors of the river who are white.

Dreams were also chosen because one was struck by the natural and automatic value attached to them, in marked contrast to the Western attitude. Dreams are regarded as communications from the ancestors which can be understood and interpreted by the diviner. The authenticity and the meaning is never questioned, and the injunctions must be obeyed. The effects of ignoring these messages would result in the displeasure and even anger of the ancestors who could then cause misfortune, illness and even madness.

I was fortune enough to get a good history and dream series from one of Mr T.'s patients who spoke English well and who was eager to discuss her illness and treatment.

History (condensed).

The patient, S.-A., was twenty-two years of age, married for five years but still childless. Born at Keiskamahoek – a rural area – she attended a nearby high school up to Standard VIII.

Her father was a carpenter, but drank heavily and they were often short of money. Her mother left him when S.-A. was eight months old and she was reared by her paternal grandmother who lived with them. In 1969 S.-A. left home to work in Cape Town. Early in 1970 she met a man, they got married and in May 1970 she stopped working. After some months she became 'ill', and on visiting a European doctor her husband told him that 'he wanted a child'. On a subsequent visit to a witch-doctor in Cape Town her husband said, 'She's lazy, does funny things, refuses me – I think she has other men'. This witch-doctor and another one said she had the 'black people's sickness'. A male relative deputising for her father performed a healing ceremony called *isiko* with temporary improvement of her mental state, but still no pregnancy resulted.

In December 1970 her husband took her to his people at Keiskamahoek and left her at the home of his grandfather. At this stage of the interview she started reporting dreams and these are given verbatim.

1971

A1. 'While sleeping I saw a gang of people who wanted to take me to the forest. I asked; "What do you want with me?" They said: "We want you to be our fool and play with you." I said: "Go away. I don't like you." I was scared and poured urine all round the house.'

A2. She said to me: 'Really a vision. Next day at 8.30 a.m. I saw three dwarfs at the half-door looking at me. I was very frightened.' ('Half-door' was her word for stable door and they sat on the lower half.)

A3. 'Sleeping, I saw a yellow snake – I shouted, afraid and my heart went like this (palpitations). I told my dreams to a witch-doctor and he gave me medicine to pour round the house.'

A4. 'The other day while sleeping I saw my father's grandfather, dead long ago, who told me to make Xhosa beer for the family.' She added: 'I wrote a letter to my family and told him, but he said, "Nothing like that for you, my child." ' (In other words, there was a conflict between the living father and the voice of the ancestor in the dream.)

1972

A5. 'My father's grandfather in a dream said father had to make *itambo esiko* (neck rope: the correct term is *isiko lentambo* – it is a healing ceremony).'

'My father refused and I became very ill. I was always sleeping, didn't work, couldn't eat, was taken to Dr. M. who found nothing wrong but sent me to Cape Town.' There she was examined and treated and had 'an operation', presumably a curettage. She was now living again with her husband at Langa, i.e. Cape Town, but got worse, 'very weak, couldn't even pick up a spoon, only took milk, very weak and thin – head got foolish.'

Her husband then took her to Mr T. who referred her to his wife for the *uvumisa* (a divinatory or diagnostic session). She said: 'I'm very ill, my heart is running wrongly, afraid to stay alone, don't want any person to be angry with me – Xhosa sickness. My mind not all right, takes me a long time to think, do funny things which my husband doesn't like. Do not want him to touch me, or sleep with him. I cried a lot for nothing. Mr T. said you can't have a child unless I go to the river for *masiga*.' (Here she is using a word for a healing ceremony.) She continued: 'Mr T. gave me and my husband medicine for three weeks'. (In order to promote conception.) Her husband then returned to Cape Town after an initial four weeks, while she stayed behind and started treatment with Mr T. in January 1975.

1975

Treatment (as described by the patient): 'Medicine to drink and medicine to wash to keep dirty things away from me so that I can be pure.'

She had to tell him her dreams every day. She related the following dreams:

B1. 'Being near the river washing clothes, took white towel washing in the water – soap was taken by the water. Woman person told me not to wash in the water but outside.'

B2. 'At my home. Father's brother in grass house with father's family – drinking Xhosa beer.'

B3. 'At Mr T.'s home all doing the *inhlombe*' (a diviner's public function, with singing and dancing). 'There came Bushmen doing their dance, with their skin clothing. Other Bushman said: "My child, you must sing this song, *Vumani, batshayi bomhlahlo*" (a special diviner's song to hasten the coming of the spirit from whom he gets the information he is seeking). 'When it is black and darkness in the house I started to sing in the dream and woke up singing with the others in our beat.'

B4. 'There came a voice from Mr T.'s house saying I must go to my father for the beads, i.e. head beads. I started to go. On reaching the house, home, I see father's grandmother, who's dead. She said to my father he must do everything for me, this sickness does not belong to me only, it's for the whole family.'

'I started to wake up and told Mr T., and he said: "Go home and remind your father about those things."' She said to me: 'I went home.'

Three days later: 'My father agreed and said I must go (on a certain date) with witch-doctors to welcome me for the sickness to *umlambo*'. (A special river ceremony to introduce the patient trainee to the ancestors who live in the river. Their acceptance of the potential trainee is an essential preliminary.) A few days after the final consent by her father she had the following dream:

B5. 'I'm making food for Mr T. After eating, his stomach is so full and I ask him what is wrong, and he said he had pain. He asked me to work with Mrs T. and his two brothers and to bring medicine from the veldt. I found the plant with the yellow flower.

'I woke up and told it.' (Some dreams need to be told immediately.)

S.-A. had been helpful and pleasant during the week of our fairly close contact with her, but after this dream her mental and physical well-being was striking – she radiated health. She participated fully in the ceremonies, dancing and singing during the whole period, and attended to our needs in a quiet efficient way. Her attitude towards Mr T. was that of a daughter who had to serve him in many little ways. She was clearly devoted to him and expressed her heartfelt gratitude to him for her restored health and called him 'my father'.

Discussion

DREAM AND SLEEP THERAPY IN ANCIENT CIVILIZATIONS:
A COMPARISON AND CLASSIFICATION

The use of dreams to heal a large variety of illnesses was practised in all the countries of the Ancient World, i.e. the Middle East, Greece, Egypt, and by the Aryans of Ancient India. I have drawn much of the material on ancient healing practices from Meier[1] and Jayne.[2] At Epidauros in Greece the healing cult of Aesculapius lasted for 800 years, from 600 BC until about 200 AD. Modern doctors still have a link with it – the universal snake symbol. There and at other centres the temple disciplines of purification, temple-sleep and hypnotic rest states were used, apparently arousing bodily and psychic processes which in turn furthered healing.

The belief was universally held that illness was caused by a supernatural being such as a god and that the cure was effected by communication with this being and getting to know his will. This communication occurred through dreams which had to be explained, 'made clear', by the priest or healer.

To the patients the dreams were vital experiences and there are many records of a single healing dream. The most famous example of the effect of a dream as far as medicine is concerned is that of Galen, the father of modern medicine. He became a healer as the result of a dream his father had in which Aesculapius cured him (Galen) of a fatal illness. He used dreams for diagnostic purposes and Aesculapius also advised him in dreams about therapy and even about operations.

Illness, as coming from a god, was treated with reverence and had dignity and dreams as communications from the god had extraordinary power and numinosity.

Patients came to the healing centres, sacred places or temples because of illnesses, physical or mental, or troubled minds, or were sent by dreams. They were dealt with in a variety of ways. Sometimes they stayed only for a few days, spent one night in the sanctuary and left cured after a single healing dream. Some stayed for several months, i.e. until they were considered 'ready' for the 'healing dream or dreams'.

They had to undergo a ritual bath to free the mind of the contamination of the body and thus release it for uninhibited dream experiences and this, in turn, resulted in the 'healing dream' and at times in a conviction of having been re-born. A special section of the sanctuary was set aside for this purpose and sleeping draughts were often given. The dreams were then interpreted by the priests of Aesculapius under his direction and inspiration.

Music, singing, dancing and acting were used as aids to healing, and presumably to induce a receptive attitude and mood. Plato wrote about 'rhythm and harmony descending to the depth of the soul, which it grips powerfully' (*Republic III*, 401D).

Dream Therapy as used by Xhosa Diviners

There are many similarities between these ancient practices and the present-day methods of the 'Xhosa diviner' ('witch-doctor').

The atmosphere at certain times and during ceremonies was charged with meaning and had a numinous quality that could not be ignored. Everything in their world had meaning and they lived in an undivided world in close contact with each other and with their ancestors. The meaningfulness did not consist of rational, intellectual 'scientific' concepts but something whole, embracing a totality of being.

Marie-Louise von Franz, in commenting on fairy tales, writes about the hidden meaning which is difficult for modern thinking to perceive but 'a meaning that might be intuitively seen and effortlessly expressed by a primitive medicine man still living in the field of such ideas but of which we today have little inkling'.[3]

Leopold Senghor writes 'classical Europe presents us with a civilization of discussive reason; classical Africa with a civilization of intuitive reason'.[4]

As during ancient times, the Xhosa patients come on account of physical illness, or troubled minds, because of misfortune, or because their dreams send them. These dreams are regarded as communications from the ancestors, and to ignore these would lead to serious illness or to catastrophes of some kind, not only for the individual but for his family or clan.

Patients come to the diviner from far and wide and stay at his homestead or adjoining ones. Every effort is made to integrate them in the day-to-day activities and chores – 'everyone must work'. The diviner becomes and is called 'our father'. Dreams must be told to him daily and he deals with these appropriately. If a dream is too complex or confused 'one keeps it to oneself knowing it will come back'. A dream must be related immediately 'otherwise it disappears like a whiff of air'. Dreams are taken seriously and once the message has been made clear, must be acted on to prevent more serious illness. This is clearly portrayed in the history of S.-A. whose father repeatedly refused to co-operate, and her condition got worse.

It is not clear whether all dreams are dealt with by talking, or also by singing and dancing to the beat of a drum, thus invoking the help of the ancestors. More research on this point is required.

Other similarities to ancient healing practices are the use of medicine to induce sleep and the process of purification. Like the ritual bath which had to free the mind of the contamination of the body, S.-A. had to drink medicine and wash her body with it to keep dirty things away '. . . so that I can be pure'.

Without the aid of Mr T., the diviner, this orderly growth and development could not have occurred. Through his attitude, respect and understanding of psychic processes the autonomous functioning of the archetypes of the collective unconscious would have been interfered with. He functioned as a midwife and permitted the normal delivery of a healthy, happy and potentially whole personality. By these means he proved himself to be truly a psychic healer in the very best tradition.

In what follows I should like to keep as close as possible to Mr T.'s mode of expression and ideas about the use of dreams in general, and also his comments on this particular series of dreams.

Dream Therapy as used by Mr T.

For the understanding and use of dreams the body must be 'fresh', i.e. 'alive', 'exhilarated'. Dancing, singing and medicine can be used to make the body 'fresh'.

The medicine which is used is *bulaw*. The crushed stem, bark and root is whipped into a froth. With it the body is washed and, at times, it is drunk to the extent that it induces vomiting. This makes the body 'fresh' and dreams, *amathonga*, which are dreams about 'good' things and which come from the ancestors, are induced. With *bulaw* the dreams become clear and are remembered. If dreams are not remembered or remain unclear *bulaw* must be used again as indicated by the diviner. He himself takes this when necessary, i.e. when he needs it for his own dreaming or to help him 'to see the dreams of patients better'.

Dancing and singing, which always go together, help with dreams in the same way as *bulaw*. It helps the diviner to see clearly if things are 'good' or 'bad'. The dancing and singing for this work is always special and there must be clapping of the hands from the audience in tune with a particular stamping rhythm. The songs and dancing wake up the *umbelini*. *Umbelini* is like *umoya*, wind, spirit. 'You'll never be a person without *umbelini* – nothing lives without *umbelini*.' The songs and dancing 'wake up' the *umbelini*, which is often at first felt in the lower half of the body and then the body feels 'heavy'. Mr T. continued:

> You can never be a diviner if the *umbelini* remains in the lower part. It must come up and go to the head, but it must come up in the 'right' way to enable you to say the right things. If it goes up the wrong way you become mad. The

umbelini must not be above you. The girl in the hut is getting worse because the *umbelini* is getting above her – on top of her. *Umbelini* when caused by the ancestors does not make one violent or mad – it makes one just right, like me. If people come for *vumisa* my *umbelini* wakes up and I'm able to say what I want to say! *Umbelini* can also be caused by 'dirty things' and then it is bad.

Everything which is being done is to make the 'blood fresh'. When the songs and dancing are 'weak' my blood will not be fresh – I shall not feel well and not feel fresh.

Dreams are of two kinds and usually only the diviner can know the difference:

1. *Uguphupa* can be bad dreams, they need not come from the ancestors but from people. 'Bad' dreams can be following by 'good' ones which then remove the 'bad' ones. Bad dreams can come from the ancestors when they are dissatisfied but they can also come when the 'blood is bad'. 'When I have a "bad dream" I urinate in my hands, take it in my mouth and spit it outside to chase them, the bad spirits, away.'

2. *Amathonga* are dreams about 'good' things and come from the ancestors. 'These are the ones which we interpret by dancing and singing. We want them to be clarified, the blood to flow nicely and the sweat to pour, therefore hard stamping with the feet is necessary.'

Some dreams are private and to be shared only with the diviner for interpretation. As Mr T. said:

If we share a room they can wake me up and tell me immediately or just wake me and tell me that they have dreamt. If we sleep in different homes, they wait for me to wake up and find an opportunity to talk to me alone. Others should not hear. They can then say they had dreamt the same and thus exploit my power.

If dreams are being interpreted with singing and dancing the diviner will stop it if it becomes clear that it is a 'bad dream', or 'there are things in this house', or 'when it is a dream which should not be treated publicly'. At a subsequent interview, however, this statement was to some extent contradicted. Many points about dreams require further research and clarificiation.

The Pre-Treatment Dreams Considered Further

GENERAL COMMENTS AND COMPARATIVE INTERPRETATION

In a recent publication Rossi explores the creative problem-solving processes, and growth-promoting functions of dreams.[5] This is also a basic thesis of analytic psychology, and the use of dreams as a therapeutic tool is regarded as indispensable for the understanding of the unconscious. In this series the gradual integration of unconscious material and the autonomous functioning of the archetypes can be seen.

From the first dream in 1971, in which the dreamer felt threatened and scared, to the final dream in June 1975, where she became a 'healer' and found the yellow flower, there is a logical sequence and evolution with a resolution of her psychic problem and an implied solution to the problems of her life.

It is also important to note the difference in quality between the earlier dreams and the later ones. The earlier ones, especially the first three, are frightening to the extent that measures were taken to protect her against the visits from evil spirits by the pouring of urine and, later, 'medicine' from a 'witch-doctor', round the house. The later dreams, especially the 1975 dreams, are positive and helpful.

In *Two essays on analytical psychology*, Jung makes it very clear that the attitude to the ego towards dreams and the unconscious generally determines the content of the latter as it presents itself in dreams. The more rejecting and non-accepting the ego attitude the more aggressive, hostile and incompatible the objective psyche becomes. With a change in the ego attitude communication and reconciliation can occur.[6] It seems as though this was an important factor in the dream series of this patient.

A brief discussion follows of the most salient points in each of the dreams reported above as seen through Western eyes. (Author's interpretation.) The patient's dreams were discussed with Mr T. (her native therapist) and his responses, twelve months later, are added here more or less verbatim.

A1. The gang of people coming from the forest, ancestors from the forest, represent archetypal images of her unconscious masculine side. Jung claims that the animus in woman usually consists of multiple figures. In his case it is contaminated by the shadow. The forest is an image presenting the collective unconscious. They invite her to play, i.e. to intercourse, to be made into a 'fool' as if to indicate how foolish her attitude is and also to demonstrate the power of the unconscious. She chased them away expressing her dislike, refusing to have intercourse with them. The dream also emphasises her real sexual attitude to her husband.

These attitudes of the patient resulted in fear and anxiety and she resorted to magic to erect a barrier between the ego and the unconscious areas of her psyche by pouring urine round the hut.

Mr T.'s comment: 'There was a dirty spirit. The spirit can be removed by herbs. Sometimes there are ancestors and bad spirits in the forests' (a reference to the fact that they came from the forest which is a place where ancestors normally reside).

A2. This was really a vision. The unconscious now expresses itself in even more direct imagery. The animus which is still contaminated by the shadow, again appears as a multiple figure. The figure three can have many other meanings, e.g. it can indicate her undeveloped functions which together with her superior function, can form a totality or quaternity, i.e. a symbol of wholeness. Three being an uneven number is generally accepted as masculine as opposed to even numbers which are feminine. It is significant that she was failing in her feminine functions. In her amplification of the dream she said they were sitting on the lower half of a stable door, again indicating the split in her psyche.

The problem is getting more clearly defined as one of a lack of wholeness, of unconscious shadow and animus contents clamouring for integration. It also emphasises her unrelatedness to her husband and her sexual attitude.

Mr T.'s comment: 'Those three who looked like dwarfs are her ancestors, trying to bring her closer to them so as to lead a better life.'

A3. The snake is a very pregnant symbol and occurs everywhere. In its instinctual manifestations it has negative unreliable aspects but even these may be a prelude to change. It is very frequently met as a symbol of healing, regeneration and transformation. In Kundalini Yoga the serpent is a symbol of renewal of the personality.[7] The medical profession still uses the healing serpent of Aesculapius on its badge. Among the Ophites the snake was the symbol of Christ. In the mysteries of Sabazius, 'a golden snake was let down into bosom of the initiated and taken away from the lower parts'.[7]

It is also a universal sexual symbol. This patient was obsessed with her sexual and biological problems. This is clear from her history and also from her reaction to her dream symbols up to this stage. There are, however, indications in this dream that a healing and transforming process was possible. The golden colour is significant. Gold and yellow indicate treasure in terms of renewal as the light of the new day. It seems to foreshadow the emergence of the yellow flower in the final dream.

She still reacts, however, to the snake symbol in a negative way with much fear and anxiety. She is not yet ready to integrate and relate positively to the powerful archetypes of the collective unconscious.

Mr T.'s comment: 'What she called palpitations is really *umbelini*. Seeing such a snake should cause fear because it does not belong to her.'

Author: 'Has the yellow colour any meaning?'

Mr T.: 'Yellow snakes can be made by herbs – bad ('dirty') herbs.

I never use these herbs. Good and bad herbs cannot be mixed. I can't cure people if I also use bad herbs.'

A4., A5. These are more personal dreams and have direct bearing on Xhosa culture and belief systems. In these the paternal grandfather, as an ancestor, first gives her a message for her father and in the second instructs him directly. These dreams refer to Xhosa customs and rituals which pertain to psychic healing and to initiation as a novice, and which must be obeyed. In terms of analytical psychology these are demands for the recognition of repressed and denied psychic contents and, as Jung says, if this is not acceded to, it leads to serious mental symptoms and illness.[6] The Xhosa hold similar views and the patient, in fact, developed a serious and classical depressive illness, which led to her being taken to Mr T.

A4. Mr T.'s comment: 'Very simple! I never tasted beer, but in a dream my mother, long dead, told me to make beer. When I asked why she said, "For your father and I will come". I made it and bought a special calabash to have it ready. Beer calls the ancestors. That is the message of the dream.'

A5. Mr T.'s comment: 'The father's grandfather was serious and said she was not malingering. She cannot make the sacrifice herself. It must be under the father's auspices, but she herself may contribute. In the previous dream the father's answer was wrong.'

Isiko lentambo – a healing ceremony – indicates that she should become a diviner. It is the first ceremony in the treatment and training (treatment and training run concurrently in certain diagnostic categories).

The Treatment Dreams Considered Further

AUTHOR'S INTERPRETATIONS AND COMMENTS BY THE DIVINER

B1. This dream deals with therapy and the ambivalent aspects of the unconscious. The water and river present unconscious libido and in this case also cleansing or purifying. By washing in the stream the soap is carried away in the same way as the ego can be overcome by the dynamic power of the unconscious. The white towel is the special headgear of diviners (they may also wear yellow). The 'female person', therefore, warns her to keep a safe distance to avoid being carried away or submerged by the forces of the unconscious.

Mr T.'s comment: 'This again told her that the river ceremony must be performed. The soap is calling her.' (Soap is the only article which patients must bring to the diviner's home when they commence treatment.) 'Washing inside the river is disrespectful. She was giving the "river people" (i.e. the ancestors who live under water) dirty water and one of her own people – an ancestor – corrected her.'

Author: 'Respect?'

Mr T.: 'If she can't respect the "river people" how can she respect me and those she lives with? The soap was taken by the ancestors for what she was doing to them.'

B2. 'At my home' signifies a step towards finding herself – her ego was rescued from submergence. 'My home' could also indicate the emergence of the self. The significance of the 'grass house' will be discussed later.

She is with her paternal family – united and participating in something the ancestors demanded. The Xhosa society is patrilineal and the paternal ancestors are the decisive ones.

Mr T.'s comment: 'A good dream – meaning "togetherness".'

B3. At the house of the diviner, healer and her spiritual father, i.e. in a safe and protected environment, she can face the demanding task of integrating her shadow side. The Bushmen are the traditional enemies of the Xhosa. Here they appear in their primitive clothing, dancing their special dance. Dancing has considerable archetypal significance. It is in the service of the god, it generates power, is the ritual of fertilization and effects reconciliation. In the shadow side of the psyche, here represented by the primitive Bushmen, most valuable aspects of the personality are often buried. This dream confirms it. She is addressed as 'my child', and she is given a special song and wakes up singing. The 'skin clothing' could also refer to the skirt made of animal skins which the diviner is presented with at the end of his training to signify his qualified state.

Mr T.'s comment: 'The arrival of the Bushmen at this ceremony means that one day she'll make the *inhlombe* at her own home in her own skins. Bushmen live in the forest and they have come to fetch her to the woods. Ancestors can take people to the forest or to the river.'

Author: 'The song?'

Mr T.: 'This is a song the Bushmen like to sing – it leads people on the diviner's path. *Vumani* means "to sing". There are diviners who tell everything and those that tell just a little bit. That is what *umhlahlo* points to.'

B4. Being sent for the head beads is an important step in personality development and mental health. Head beads are used in the river ceremony which is the first ceremony to be performed when a person has been accepted by his relatives as a potential novice, but he must still be introduced by his river ancestors for their acceptance or rejection.

The paternal grandmother now addresses the father. She is the symbol of the Great Mother, who has wisdom and power and must be obeyed. Her remark that, 'it is for the whole family', will be generally accepted by modern family therapists and analytical psychologists. The father agreed and the final dream sets the seal on the process.

Mr T.'s comment: 'The father's grandmother can appear in dreams. It is customary for the men to go first and the women to follow and thus close the family.'

B5. The discomfort and distention of her therapist, as a result of her food, could be that she had an inflated and idealized image of him and this had to be corrected by his pain, i.e. illness and disintegration. He was no longer superhuman, but had become vulnerable; he had become the 'wounded healer'. She, on the other hand, is shown the way to become a healer and his equal and their roles are reversed.

Perhaps she was also over-zealous and one-sided. The instruction she received is to the effect that she must work and realize her other functions so as to become whole. She must work with Mrs T. and Mr T.'s two brothers, thus forming a group of two females and two males, the number four which is a quantity, and also a union of the opposites. In this state of psychic wholeness she finds the plant with the yellow flower which is the symbol of self-realization.[8]

Mr T.'s comment: 'I had pain in the stomach and S.-A. was telling me to look for medicine to cure myself. The ancestors worked through her. All along I trust my wife more than my brothers, who are also *amagqira* (the Xhosa word for "witch-doctors") but not qualified so I always send her along.'

Author: 'Yellow flowers?'

Mr T.: 'Has no meaning.'

Author: 'S.-A.'s food making you ill?'

Mr T.: 'Something is wrong or it has no meaning. Even if I tell her she is really telling me. This dream could be good or bad.'

The next day he enlarged as follows: 'She was shown what she had done. It came to her that she had given me the food that made me ill. The ancestors then showed her what medicine to give. Bad dream in that I was given something bad while asleep. Good in that she got the medicine to give me.'

This discussion took place twelve months after the dreams were told to me. This is important because on previous occasions when his own and other people's dreams were discussed immediately, I noted that more relevant and wider associations were obtained.

Comparative Dream Elucidations

My analysis of the dream series was arrived at completely independently of any discussion with Mr T. It seems to me, however, as though there are no essential contradictions in spite of the different modes of expression, except for the final dream.

His approach and opinions are coloured by some rigidity of cultural rituals and beliefs, but I know from experience over the years that he goes by an immediacy of experience in response to dreams or other psychic materials at the time it is presented to him by the patient. His *umbelini* tells him at the time what the meaning is, what the ancestors want, and what he must say. To deal with dreams in the 'cold' is therefore not a true reflection of his views or responses.

His attitude to dreams, dream content and the dreamer is one of respect and to them the term 'respect' has deep meaning. It can perhaps be described as 'reverence', 'respectful awe' and an 'attitude of non-violation'. This attitude is shared by the community as a whole if they are still culturally linked and still have roots in tradition. This attitude seems to me to be decisive in the development of the dream series and the recovery of the patient.

The dreams fall into two distinct categories.

The first five dreams that she related occurred during 1971 and 1972. During this time she was seen by Western-trained doctors and at least three 'witch-doctors' who practise in urban areas with no improvement. In fact after the fifth dream she became very ill. It seems that no one was able to deal with her conflicts, and with the demands of unconscious psychic material for a hearing.

It is both revealing and moving to observe how her unconscious, through dreams, indicated the problem and also the path towards healing, how it invoked the help of the ancestors and how it persisted in spite of the non-co-operaton and even obstruction of the external world, e.g. her father's response, 'nothing like that for you, my child'.

The first dream series therefore ends with frustration, despair and a serious depressive illness.

The second group of five dreams are very different. She is now in treatment with the T.'s at their homestead in a traditional rural setting. From the first dream where she encounters the unconscious (river and river people) albeit still not in the correct way, there is progress and development with termination in self-realization – the finding of the yellow flower. This period lasted six and a half months and from my observation over the two years the treatment can be intense.

Author's Evaluation of the Comparative Interpretations

A1. Mr T. succinctly described the very essence of the collective unconscious, the forest, where there can be good and bad spirits. A cure for the 'dirty spirit' can be achieved by the use of herbs – a remedy from nature. The positive stance of the healer is present.

My interpretation concerns itself with the separation of the collective unconscious into archetypes, naming them the animus and shadow and indicating her inability to relate to them, thus seeing the problem and the way towards healing the split. Mine is more discriminating and analytic, his more synthetic.

A2. Mr T. sees the dwarfs as ancestors trying to overcome the separation or healing of the split, i.e. integration. I interpret it as a more direct confrontation with the collective unconscious, an indication of the presence of unintegrated and inferior aspects and an effort at establishing integration or wholeness.

A3. Mr T. agrees that she should be frightened by seeing such a snake 'because it does not belong to her'! His answers to my questions have bearing on 'bad' and 'dirty medicines' and 'herbs' that are used in witchcraft, of which he and his group have a real horror, and from which they dissociate themselves completely. This aspect, however, cannot be discussed here.

My interpretation deals very briefly with some of the aspects of the snake symbol indicating its extremely wide and deep significance. It is one of the most universal and numinous symbols of the collective unconscious which can be really frightening and truly does not 'belong' to us. I also see its positive aspects and that it could foreshadow the yellow flower. I think Mr T.'s inability to see this is caused by a culturally shared anxiety about witchcraft.

A4. Mr T. says 'beer calls the ancestors'.

A5. The ancestors correct and direct the living about the way in which they should behave and that they should obey. My comments are essentially similar, using the terminology of analytical psychology.

I have called the second series the treatment dreams.

B1. Mr T. sees this as emphasising the fact that the 'river ceremony' must be performed. She and her people have accepted her illness as coming from the ancestors and that she needs treatment and training but she must still get the acceptance and approval of the ancestors who live under the water. The emphasis on respect is germane because the forces of the collective unconscious must be approached with respect and caution. The soap calling her seems to refer to her personal and ego involvement. A female ancestor corrects her and acts as her guide and mentor.

In my interpretation the aspect of respect was under-stressed even though I stressed the dangers of coming too close to the dynamic powers of the unconscious. For the rest there is no essential difference in our understanding of this dream.

B2. Mr T. sees 'togetherness'; so do I, but at various levels. She is united with her paternal ancestors, i.e. contents in her personal and collective unconscious. I also see the emergence of the self, especially on account of the 'grass house'. The Xhosa people do not live in 'grass houses'. The 'grass house' is vital and specially constructed for the passing–out or graduation of the trainee diviner as described in another article. It represents his uniqueness, separation, strength, independence and self-reliance. This is an example of the cultural collective area of human activities and thinking as mentioned by Plaut.[9]

B3. Mr T. sees the arrival of the Bushmen – The opinion has been expressed that all good Xhosa diviners have Bushman blood: the Bushman, although their traditional enemy, carries a mystical aura – as an indication that she will one day be a diviner in her own right and at her own home. She is being led on the 'diviner's path', i.e. the path of knowledge and enlightenment and is given her diviner's song.

I saw this dream as an integration of the shadow without which no one is whole and healthy and cannot be a therapist or diviner. My comments using different language express the same idea, i.e progress towards wholeness.

B4. Mr T. comments on the presence of the female ancestor to 'close the family'. To me he seems to refer to the acceptance of the female principle to effect completeness. This is especially significant as female members of a clan rarely figure as ancestors unless she was of special significance or had outstanding gifts.

His ignoring of her being sent for the white head beads is natural because to him it is self–evident. It is another instance of the cultural collective area of functioning. I enlarged on the importance of the white head beads because of their symbolic meaning. The paternal grandmother I saw as a symbol of the Great Mother because of her authority and wisdom. I think there is room for both Mr T.'s and my interpretation or my interpretation of what Mr T. said.

B5. This dream is interesting because it shows up considerable differences in understanding and interpretation between Mr T. and myself. (This article is not the place to go into detail because it would lead to discussion of cultural beliefs, attitudes, practices and general psychopathology.) It is, however, interesting that it was the only topic or dream that he wanted to comment on the next day, saying, 'talking to you makes me think, and see things deeper'.

The aspects on which we agreed were the activity and help of the ancestors, and that they led her to the correct medicine.

Her inner development towards wholeness and self-realization was overlooked by him and instead there was a paranoid flavour.

From my research in general and this case in particular a considerable amount of evidence has been collected to indicate that some Xhosa diviners use the dreams of their patients to further therapy. Their methods appear on the whole to be intuitive and experiential and the rational functions, especially thinking, seem to play a relatively unimportant role. Thinking is, however, not denigrated by them as one of them has repeatedly said that our discussions are of help to him because they make him 'think and see deeper'.

Summary

I have described how a dream series had been viewed from two culturally widely different backgrounds, and it is hoped that the effort towards comparative analysis has shown basic similarities between the concepts of a Xhosa diviner and the analytical psychologist. The therapeutic techniques, however, are very different, and much research is still required in this area. The diviners work on a less verbal level than we do, a level I should like to call psycho-physiological.

CHAPTER 9

The Health Care of an *Igqira* (Indigenous Healer)

BY M. VERA BÜHRMANN

Introduction

For a considerable number of years I have been researching the healing procedures used by the healers of the Xhosa people who inhabit the rural areas of the Transkei and Ciskei, areas situated on the northeastern coast of South Africa. The Xhosa form part of the bigger Nguni group including the Zulu and Swazi[1].

The research method used was that of a participant observer. This experiential attitude was the most fruitful because much of what goes on at the rituals and ceremonies is of a non-verbal nature. The attitude is very similar to that of the therapist during play therapy with young children. Discussions with those closely involved in a particular ceremony had great value but much of the symbolic meaning which I attach to the material is derived from the theory and practice of analytical psychology and related fields.

Many terms have been used to designate these healers, such as 'witch-doctors', 'diviners', 'medicine-men'. These terms are all unsatisfactory in one way or another because they describe only one aspect of the total function of indigenous healers or because they have negative overtones. The Xhosa word *igqira* (plural *amagqira*), meaning healer, will be used in this paper. The disadvantage of the word is that it is Xhosa only and not known to some other Black people in South Africa. The Xhosa are however my special field of study and therefore the term seems appropriate. They have a variety of healers but my special concern is with those whose methods are comparable to the methods of analysts and psychotherapists.[2] They undergo a prolonged period of treatment and training and primarily use psychotherapeutic techniques in their practices. They use herbal remedies only sparingly. Their techniques consist of dream therapy including interpretation,[3,4] rituals, sacrifices, healing dances called *intlombe* and milieu therapy. These methods are not used only to treat the sick and troubled in their care but also to attend to their own health and to keep their powers on a high level of efficiency. Material from the life of a qualified *igqira* will be used in this paper to illustrate the latter aspects.

To appreciate their views on health and ill-health and hence the rationale of their treatment it is necessary to have some knowledge of this people's cosmology. They do not separate health and ill-health into mental and physical aspects as is customary in the West. They say 'when I am ill the whole of me is ill'. Their world view expresses the same wholeness and unity expecially in terms of their relationship with their ancestors. In anthropology the term 'shades' is commonly used. For many reasons the term 'living dead' is more descriptive, but for psychological reasons the term 'ancestor' is preferable because it indicates the all-important aspect of relatedness and the familial nature of these 'beings' who are deceased kinsmen and not strangers.

The ancestors share in these tribespeople's daily living in a way which is difficult for the rational-minded Westerner to understand. The existence, presence and influence of the ancestors are never doubted and life without them is unthinkable. On the whole the ancestors are friendly protectors, guides and mentors, but their displeasure can be aroused and then they can withdraw their protection and even cause ill-health, unhappiness and misfortune for a particular individual, his family or even his clan. The worst effect of the withdrawal of the ancestors' protection is, however, that their living kin are then exposed to the evil effects of witchcraft.

For health, success and good fortune constant communication between the living and the ancestors is highly desirable. The ancestors communicate with the living in a variety of ways, mostly through dreams, synchronistic events, the behaviour of wild and domestic animals, omens, events in nature such as lightning, and also through illness and misfortune. The living in turn communicate with their ancestors through their rituals and ceremonies. In these they may ask for forgiveness, give praise and thanks or ask for guidance about managing their lives. They may also ask how to correct things that have gone wrong in the life of the individual or of the whole family. When they have obscure dreams they ask for clarification. They want answers to two main questions: '*how* did these events come about, and *why* did it happen to me and not to others?' In some cases they also ask *who* is responsible.

Ancestors are omnipresent but there are certain areas which they like particularly and where they congregate. As they have retained many of their human qualities they exhibit preferences depending on the circumstances of a situation. Apart from the kinship ancestors discussed above there are others. These are the 'River People' and the 'Forest Ancestors' who are more collective and universal and have a numinous quality about them which is absent from what can be called the kinship and domestic ancestors. Their particular functions as archetypes representing the collective unconscious cannot be enlarged on here. The kinship ancestors have favourite areas around the homestead, and a special place in the main hut of the homestead complex. Another constant area where they reside is in the cattle pen opposite the gate. In the body, even though they move around, they favour certain areas, for example the gallbladder, head, back, shoulder blades and organs of procreation. These ideas apply to both the animal and human body. A woman said: 'They are in me – I feel them. They are happy with me. I think of them always. They know I am thinking of them.'[5]

The ancestors have retained some of their human attributes and can for example experience hunger and thirst, or feel cold and neglected. They can make their wishes and feelings known, sometimes clearly, often obscurely, through dreams, visions and, as described, in the body. The expert knowledge of an *igqira* is often required to clarify these phenomena. It seems that a symbiotic relationship exists between the ancestors and the living, one of mutual interdependence with each having a well-defined function and each meeting the needs of the other.

The *igqira* is the main mediator between the living and the ancestors. He has acquired this function because he 'was called by the ancestors to become their servant'. The process starts with an illness called *thwasa* which may manifest in various ways. It may be experienced for example as discomfort of the body, or as a state of confusion and isolation, but it is always associated with frequent and vivid dreams. At the onset of *thwasa* persons often behave strangely, disappearing from home and wandering in the veldt or forest. It has been reported that they 'visit the people who live under the water' – the River Ancestors. This condition, behaviour and experience can appear so bizarre to the Western psychiatrist that a diagnosis of psychotic illness if often made.

When a person in the family behaves in this strange way he or she is taken to an *igqira* by relatives or close friends to find out what ails him or her. If the findings indicate that the person is suffering from *thwasa*, i.e. that the ancestors are calling him, it is suggested that he should undergo the necessary treatment which also often includes training to become an *igqira*. The choice to come for treatment is left to the individual and his family. If a decision is delayed he usually becomes worse and if the call is ignored it can lead to serious illness and even insanity. If treatment is chosen, the individual may go to any *igqira*, not necessarily to the one who made the diagnosis. Amongst the Xhosa there seems to be little difference between the sexes in the incidence of *thwasa* and of those who eventually themselves qualify as *amagqira*.

The treatment and the training in particular, is long, rigorous and expensive and only a small percentage eventually emerge as fully qualified *amagqira*. The practice is also demanding for a variety of reasons – two of the less obvious may be mentioned.

Firstly, much of the work consists of divining, i.e. *vumisa* (diagnostic sessions). These consist of sessions at which they must determine the nature and the cause of the illness, misfortunes and troubles of those consulting them, as well as steps necessary to resolve the problems. To do this they have to establish contact with the ancestors who are regarded as wise and even omniscient and consult with them. He, the *igqira*, must then communicate the wishes and advice of the ancestors to the troubled ones and give guidance about practical details. This is the *igqira*'s mediating function and it can lead to further actions in which they may be involved, e.g. performance of sacrifices or attending a herbalist. It has often been observed that at the end of such a session the *igqira* can look tired and strained. They admit it is 'hard work' and even experienced *amagqira* can fail to clarify matters to the satisfaction of their clients. As the bulk of their work consists of private *vumisa* sessions the strain is due to their intense concentration and involvement with the clients and their problems. The exhaustion is mental and emotional and appears to be similar to that experienced by a psychiatrist after a difficult dynamic diagnostic session.

The second reason why the work is taxing and why many 'called ones' are reluctant to obey is because it is associated with specific dangers. This danger is in the so-called '*fukamisa*' (brooding) of the ancestors. *Fukamisa* means to hatch and to generate, and the person over whom the ancestors brood becomes 'something else'. This process has positive and negative effects. Berglund[6] writes: 'Without this constant brooding of the shades (ancestors) the diviner is not able to divine satisfactorily. But necessary as the brooding is, it is also dangerous and to be handled with care.' Excessive brooding of the ancestors is much feared as it can lead to madness. It seems that *amagqira* take medicines to 'make them strong' so as 'to be able to take it'. Brooding can be equated with introversion and extreme pre-occupation with unconscious images.

The aim of this paper is to illustrate what can happen to an individual (a woman) who had been called by the ancestors to serve them, who responded to the call, had her training and qualified, but subsequently failed to use it as she should have. By practising as an *igqira* in a half-hearted way she by implication did not accept the responsibility of her call and did not serve them. The ceremony which will be described indicates how this shortcoming was rectified in this particular instance. Certain similarities and differences with concepts and practices of analytical psychology will also be explored and discussed. The influence of dreams in the life of this female *igqira* will be traced and parts of a ceremony will be used as illustrative material. The part of the ceremony which will be focussed upon is the *intlombe* which I call the 'healing dance' and which is accompanied by singing, clapping of hands and drumming, the whole forming a mandala in action.[7]

The material is presented in the first instance in a descriptive way because much of what transpires at any healing procedure is non-verbal, while the researcher is a participant and involved observer.

Case Material

M.G., a forty-six year old widow with four children, had qualified as an *igqira* about ten years previously. She was running a store and practising as a healer during her 'spare time'. She belongs to the Majola family whose 'clan animal' is a snake.

I attended an *intlombe* at her home without any idea of what it was about. I was introduced to an obese, sad-looking woman who immediately apologised because she could not offer the attending *amagqira* and visitors the customary drink, i.e. neat brandy, because she was 'too busy at the store' and did not have time to make the necessary purchases. The absence of brandy was a serious matter because the offering of alcohol is for the ancestors also – they are major participants. Previously, i.e. a few decades ago, the offering was home-brewed beer. It is said: 'Beer calls the ancestors.'

At the usual introductory phase of the *intlombe* M.G. very briefly gave the reasons for the ceremony: it was a long time since she last danced or arranged an *intlombe* – about two years back, and that was why she was ill so often. She was told in a dream to go and rub her face with a special clay. She was surprised at this instruction because ordinarily it is only for the use of expectant mothers. After this dream she knew she had to do an *intlombe* and a sacrifice.

She now stopped speaking but continued to dance with the other trained and semi-trained participants. Dancing and singing of significant songs always precede the *vumisa* which is part of this particular type of *intlombe*. The dancing and singing is necessary to create atmosphere, tension and concentration. It is a kind of *rites d'entrée* – a canalisation of libido into the activity to be undertaken.[8]

At first M.G. danced in a lethargic disinterested manner. This languidness gradually changed, she became more involved, she moved her body with increasing vigour and the rhythmic stamping of the ground with her bare feet became hard and intentional. Her facial expression changed from a rather dull expressionless mask to one showing increasing animation and emotion. Later she was moved to tears and in the end she looked clearly relieved and bore what could be described as an expression of joyful resignation.

Some of the significant songs will be mentioned and briefly discussed later: 'It is calling, the crab is calling'; 'I have been called, I have been called, I have been called by the crab'; 'It makes beer, the crab makes beer'; 'I dream badly, I dream of drunkards'.

Each song is always repeated many times and is often interrupted by verbal comments from the dancers. The request for the songs comes from the dancing group.

After some time and when the dancing and singing had become animated the officiating *igqira* said: 'Please repeat the songs. It looks as if it is going to be alright. I am not going to say anything now. Freshen up these *amagqira* so that they should look at what is wrong.'

A senior female *igqira* in the dancing group now took over the proceedings for a while and asked amongst others for the following songs: 'Let darkness depart and light appear'; 'I thank this lovely sickness that I have'; 'I bow to the Majola ancestors'; 'I hope I will be well in this house and this fever perhaps will end'.

The officiating *igqira* then started to *vumisa*. The gist of it was 'that you, Radebe [M.G.'s clan name], are an *igqira* but you have stopped taking your family stick' (stopped working as an *igqira*). 'You also have a habit of not telling people when you are worried' (i.e. not telling the ancestors). 'It is seen that there is a woman here who is an invalid, that is why we [the ancestors] are here. You are now correct in saying "I am sorry" here at your home.' (I have inserted the word and concept ancestor because I know from observations that the one who does the *vumisa* becomes identified with the ancestors and functions as their mouthpiece, talking in the first person.)

M.G. then spoke, agreeing with the *vumisa*, and continued: 'Here at home we ask for forgiveness from the Majola animal which was injured. I ask for mercy because this thing has made a disturbance inside my blood. My blood is not running well and the cause must be uncovered. I bless the Majola animal [snake] which appears whether one is in hospital or in jail. I ask it to let my work prosper.' It appeared that since starting to contemplate and prepare for this ceremony her deceased father had frequently been visiting her home. She gave thanks and asked that he should always look after her. She asked for forgiveness from the people of the Radebe clan. 'Even though I am alone here now [i.e. without a husband] I am not afraid of Majola, Mntakwende, Radebe and Ngqosini.' (These last are ancestral clan names.)

Her older brother now interjected and urged her to leave the pills of the white man: 'They won't cure you – we have been asking you for a long time to do the proper thing.'

She finished by telling the ancestors that she 'bows to them' and wishes that they will look after her. 'You were going to give up where I was concerned. It was said to me "this is the third time that we have been telling you to leave the European pills alone – you are supposed to be treated the Xhosa way". I replied "that I will not refuse that now. I do not know if you will be able to bear this, but in my dream I was told to wear a white blanket, called a mantle, that will cover me from head to foot. Even there I am not refusing".'

This speech terminated the indoors part of the proceedings. Accompanied by singing and clapping and with dancing steps all the participants now left for the cattle pen for the sacrifice of a white goat which was the next stage of the ceremony.

At a discussion subsequent to the ceremony more facts were obtained from a visibly moved M.G. She was very different from the dull depressed-looking woman whom I had met on arrival.

She lost her husband about five years previously. She had been in poor health for several years, especially with asthma and headaches and had been treated by European doctors with little lasting effects. The business had been claiming most of her time and energy and even though she is a qualified *igqira* she had not been very active as such.

On a later visit of mine when she was already working as an *igqira* and beginning to feel better, M.G. spoke more freely and gave more details. The family and personal history have direct bearing on the development of events and the situation which resulted in the *intlombe*. I therefore report this below as background material, which I will not, however, analyse.

Her paternal grandfather was an *igqira*. 'He stayed under the river with the "River People" for several days and came out as an *igqira*.' One of her brothers is also an *igqira* who practises from the paternal home some distance away.

Already from the time that she was a small child her parents noticed that she was different from the other children – there were signs that she had special gifts. At the age of seventeen she 'became ill'. She wanted to stay in bed, she suffered from severe *umbelini* (anxiety, inner turmoil) and was afraid of everything 'even my people at home'. Her sleep was disturbed by strange dreams and on being taken to an *igqira* he said she had the 'white illness' i.e. *thwasa*.

One of the dreams she had at the time was as follows. 'The animals of the forest came to me strangely, but I knew them also. But my dreams showed me that I am an *igqira yemlambo* [of the river] as my grandfather was.'

She did not go for the customary treatment, however, and her dreams continued, mostly about the river. 'You're told in dreams that you are a river doctor. Dreams are many and come in succession. You bring them together to get their meaning.'

At the age of about thirty (1960–1961) she had the following dream. 'I was in the river with a piece of plank playing with the water. I played a long time. There came an old grandfather who stayed near me and he asked "What are you doing?" and I said "I am playing". He stayed and I played my games. There came another old man exactly like the first one. I knew the second one but I did not know the first one. The second one asked the first one "Why are you staying here watching this child at her play?" and he answered "I am watching her and I have come to tell her that she is a river doctor." '

It became increasingly clear to her that she was being called but it was difficult to go. For a married woman with children the commitments of the training program are particularly burdensome. She delayed going for treatment and training until 1964. 'At that time I had visions in my sleep. For example that I was standing in the river and seeing someone coming out of the river saying what he wishes and asking me for *utywala* [Bantu beer]. Dreams are the guidance of our illness. During treatment you tell them to your *igqira*. But now that I am not under him any more I have ways of dealing with them myself.'

She completed her training in 1968. From her training *igqira* I received the information that she was a good pupil and is a gifted healer. He was sorry that she was not more active as an *igqira*.

Some while later, when conducting a river ceremony for a patient she encountered a real snake (snakes are common in that area), but because it was the ancestor snake of the Amajola family it did not harm her. She later found the snake at her home and bid it welcome, knowing it would not harm any visitors. But the children unfortunately knew nothing about its significance and killed it. M.G. was very upset and knew that a ceremony had to be performed as soon as possible 'otherwise one could become ill and even die'. She delayed executing this. She often saw the snake in her dreams, however. Her health deteriorated. A subsequent dream made it clear that she had to act without further delay. 'In the dream I was told to smear my face with *ingxwala* [the name of a particular clay]. I was even told where to find it'. She was surprised because this clay is normally only used on the faces of pregnant woman. She however went, following the path indicated in the dream and found the clay. She then fully understood the meaning of the dream, hence her sacrifice this day.

She was visited by me eighteen months later. She looked happier and more animated and said it was since she had carried out the ceremony. A relative was now running the store and she was very busy as an *igqira*. 'Now since I am well I can experience pleasure, previously I could not.'

Discussion

When first seen M.G. presented a picture of clinical depression in Western terms. There were several significant factors.

The death of her husband cannot be ignored but was not explored. It was however briefly referred to in the *intlombe*: 'Even though I am alone here now, I am not afraid of . . . . . ' (clan names). His death probably contributed to her involvement in the store and also to her depressed state. It certainly caused loneliness and feelings of fear.

In terms of Xhosa cosmology there are other important factors. Her associates had for a long time been telling her that she was ill because she rarely attended *intlombes*, i.e. those conducted by other *amagqira* in the vicinity. This is customary and a necessary practice for an *igqira*.

There was another important factor. M.G.'s family history as well as her personal history, taken together with the early dreams which she reported indicated clearly that she was destined to be a healer and to serve the ancestors. This she did not do. She ran a business instead which left her little time for her real, psychologically determined work.

From the *vumisa* it appeared that a pivotal factor was that she had to a large extent stopped practising as an *igqira*: 'You had stopped taking your family stick'. She was therefore unfaithful to her calling and disobedient to her ancestors. Although called and trained she was not serving them. This applied both to her inner relationship with them and also as mediator between them and the ill in the community. She had also disappointed and offended her ancestors in yet another sphere. She failed to educate her children in their customs and beliefs to the extent that they did not know that the snake was an ancestor animal of the Amajola. This seems like gross neglect of children and ancestors and her inner turmoil is therefore understandable.

The above account confirms Jung's concept concerning unused gifts and undeveloped potential. Such neglect usually leads to a neurotic illness or psychological problems which force the individual to take stock of himself. The illness then is an effort to restore the psychic balance. It is significant that her involvement with her business was such that she failed to attend to very important details required for the ceremony. From the perspective of Xhosa cosmology, she did not bid the ancestors welcome to her home to participate in the very important work on hand. One can say in the word of the song that 'the crab did not brew beer at the river' to call the ancestors.

According to her history she started developing psychosomatic illnesses especially asthma and became obese a few years ago. She went to Western doctors who could only give her symptomatic treatment with ever-decreasing effectiveness.

Clear evidence of ancestor involvement was given to M.G. by the appearance of the snake while she was conducting a river ceremony for a patient. This snake has special significance for her clan and she bade it welcome to her home. Psychologically the snake appearing in her dreams can be seen as an image of the collective unconscious in its compensatory function. By her bidding it welcome to her home, i.e. taking it into her home where she knew it would harm nobody she indicated her psychological readiness to relate to and even integrate up to now neglected aspects of her psychic apparatus. This snake symbol in its healing and rebirth function is the forerunner of the subsequent dream where she was in fact told in no uncertain terms that the psychic situation was 'pregnant'. Having to apply the clay to her face, indicating her pregnant state, meant that there were unconscious psychic elements in her which were ready to emerge into consciousness.

The killing of the snake was a major offence and she knew she ought to deal with it immediately but she delayed, ostensibly because she was too busy with external materialistic affairs. Such an offence in their cosmology calls forth the wrath of the ancestors and she knew it, so one must look for more deep-seated reasons for her inaction. In spite of being greatly perturbed and knowing that a ceremony to communicate with the ancestors was required, otherwise 'one could become ill and even die', she did nothing. She ignored the situation and the obligation in the face of general beliefs and betrayed her knowledge and function 'as a servant of the ancestors'. This reluctance indicates the general opposition to change which is so typical of the human psyche. It was as though she tried to get rid of the troublesome prompting by the ancestors – the dynamic unconscious as I see it – by well-known defence mechanisms, most probably denial and repression. This denial or resistance to the prompting from the unconscious can also be viewed as an insult to the ancestors. Counter-responses were evoked from the unconscious. She often saw the snake in her dreams and her health deteriorated. A dream then followed in which the unconscious expressed itself in unequivocal terms. In this dream she was not only told what to do but the path to follow was also indicated. She was left no choice.

The indication of the path is a common theme in the writing of analytical psychologists. Meier[9] writes about the indication of the path to the healing fountain-head and the aetiological connection between the snake and the place of healing. Von Franz[10] cites numerous examples of animals indicating the way and leading the hero on the path to integration and wholeness. In Jung's[11] work, Mercurius, in some of his protean manifestations acting as psychopomp, indicates the way and acts as a uniting symbol.

Being told in an *ithongo* (a special kind of dream which always comes from the ancestors) what to do and being shown the path is therefore seen as the mediating function of the psyche, mediating, that is, between the conscious and unconscious, the ego and non-ego.

In the Xhosa culture this mediation or communication is achieved by a variety of rituals and ceremonies in which the *igqira* plays a major role. Through ritual and sacrifice by the living, varying with the particular circumstances, communication and communion with the ancestors are established. I see such communication as a healing of the breach between the ego and the unconscious, especially the collective unconscious. This psychic integration seems to have started in M.G.'s case from the time she contemplated this ceremony. Since then her deceased 'father started visiting my home'. The snake had been transformed into the ancestor father, who in this instance was the carrier of positive and spiritual aspects of the animus. The accusation of the ancestors 'you have stopped carrying your family stick' is beautifully descriptive and is the essence of her problem. The 'family stick' is symbolic of her masculine or *logos* function which has to clarify and bring unconscious factors into consciousness – i.e. her divining function. *Amagqira* have, and at times carry, a variety of sticks to indicate their qualified state.

The sacrifice of the goals of the ego and submission to the greater wisdom and guidance of the unconscious is well expressed by M.G.'s final communication to the ancestors. She undertakes to bow to the ancestors and she asks their pardon and their help. She also confesses to her obstinacy and that they could well have despaired of guiding her. 'This is the third time' that they had to point out her erroneous ways and tried to get her to accept them as the true healers.

The instruction to wear and cover herself 'from head to foot' in a white blanket refers to an aspect of the final initiation and passing out or qualifying ceremony of an *igqira*. Having successfully completed his training as an *igqira* he then becomes a 'white doctor' and 'a servant of the ancestors who live under the water', who are reputed to be white. The initiant not only becomes their servant but becomes identified with them. This process is symbolized by being cloaked with a white blanket at a particular moment during the initiation ceremony. M.G. must now wrap a white blanket round herself on their instruction. They are therefore demanding a second graduation and re-affirmation of her dedication. In terms of Western practices it can be seen as doctors repeating the Hippocratic oath. She says 'even there I am not refusing', i.e. I am accepting my calling and will resume my work as a healer in the dedicated way demanded by you, my ancestors.

This she apparently did with the beneficial results as observed during a subsequent visit.

M. Vera Bührmann   163

The songs which were selected for comment deal in the first instance with the crab, which is an all-important and significant symbol in their cosmology. The crab is: 'The keeper of the river'; 'The crab brews beer by the river'; 'Beer calls the ancestors'; 'Most of us get sick by the river'; 'Healing is also by the river'.

In view of M.G.'s dreams during her youth and as an adult, about the river, water and people associated with the river the songs about the crab are also to the point: 'It is calling, the crab is calling'; 'I have been called, I have been called by the crab'. River ceremonies are common for a variety of illnesses, accidents and misfortunes. The river also figures largely in the training to become an *igqira*.

'Dreaming about drunkards' can be seen in terms of reality, as it is fairly common in the community and the source of considerable trouble. But in terms of the crab it seems to refer to the 'divine intoxication', the holy drunkenness of inspiration, and the mead of immortality.[12]

The song praying for darkness to depart and for light to appear is a constant one at their ceremonies. It is aimed at invoking the aid of the ancestors, asking them to clarify problems and to throw light on what is obscure and unknown and therefore anxiety-provoking to the participants. This is also a frequent 'prayer' of both Western patients and psychotherapists. We are frequently in the dark about what is going on in the therapeutic situation when dream messages are obscure and therapy at a standstill. We often feel as though we are in a thick fog and any glimmering of light is welcomed. This is especially so when the patient is in a depressive phase, as in the 'night sea journey'.[13]

In the second series of songs the illness is seen as positive, with an acceptance of the superior wisdom of the supra-personal. It implies that the illness holds the promise of a change of something emergent as a new birth: 'I thank this lovely illness that I have'; 'I hope I will be well in this house'; 'I bow to the Majola ancestors'. This seems like profound wisdom and submission to superior forces. Not my will but thine be done!

Conclusion

I have attempted to describe what happened, what was said and done in M.G.'s case, and to draw some analogies with the thinking in analytical psychology. In Western analytic treatment the above material would probably have emerged over a number of sessions. Here it was dealt with during a few hours partly on account of the constellation of archetypal material which by-passed ego defenses.

Pfister[14] who analysed the methods of Shamans concluded that the unconscious of the medicine man speaks directly to the unconscious of his patients and thus circumvents consciousness and its defence mechanisms.

To a large extent the Xhosa people still have a mythology by which they live and which directs their lives. The 'River People' and the idea of being wrapped in a white blanket as an indication of identity with them has not been stripped of its mythological meaning. The officiating *igqira* incarnates the ancestors or living dead and addresses himself to the *whole* of the other not just to his or her ego. Western man usually grasps these events with his ego and intellect, is not deeply stirred, and they are not deeply meaningful to him.

Other symbols and symbolic acts in the reported ceremony carry a meaningfulness and a numinosity which the Xhosa cannot ignore. The crab is the keeper of the river, i.e. he is the guardian of the unconscious where the treasure of the healing potential is found. Western man usually only experiences the power of these symbols in dreams with archetypal content, they experience it in daily living.

The *intlombe* or healing dance as described elsewhere[7] is composed of many archetypal opposites. This can be seen in its structure and also in the behaviour and apparel of the participants. One of the functions of the *intlombe* is to bring these opposites together and thus further wholeness and health. In the case of M.G. her ego was confronted by archetypal images, and because of her eventual positive attitude towards the latter the breach between these two opposites could be healed.

What I have not so far mentioned is the quality of the atmosphere because I find this difficult to put into words – words tend to destroy. I, as a participant observer, was drawn into an atmosphere of numinosity which had the magical effect of transporting me to non-verbal levels of human experience. These experiences are not unknown in Western psychotherapy – they occur when archetypal layers of the psyche are constellated as during emotionally highly charged moments. In my opinion those are the uniting and healing moments.[15]

CHAPTER 10

On the Relation of the Doctrines of Yoga to Jung's Psychology

BY PHILLIP A. FABER AND GRAHAM S. SAAYMAN[1]

Introduction

An examination of Jung's psychology in relation to Eastern philosophical systems and religious doctrines is of interest for a number of reasons. Firstly, Jung formulated his concepts in general ignorance of those of the East and a comparison of his psychology with Eastern systems may therefore provide an objective, external reference point from which his work may be evaluated. Secondly, Jung later examined several Eastern texts and commented on Eastern meditational practices from the perspective of analytical psychology.[2-6] Thirdly, Jung stated that there were intrinsic similarities between the theory and practice of analytical psychology and Eastern systems: ' . . . I had been unconsciously led along that secret way which has been the preoccupation of the best minds of the East for centuries'.[5]

Nevertheless, despite the increasing interest of contemporary Western psychology in the theory and practice of meditation, comparatively little has been written from within the framework of analytical psychology, subsequent to Jung's own commentaries, on Eastern conceptions concerning the nature of the psyche. It is the purpose of this paper to make explicit some points of comparison between Jung's psychology and the doctrine of Yoga. The classic tradition of Eastern thought is said to have had its origins in India.[7] Out of the philosophies of Brahmanism, Jainism, Sankya and Yoga developed Buddhism, which carried the fundamental tenets of Indian thought to the rest of Asia. Perhaps the most systematized statement of Indian philosophical and religious thought is to be found in the classic 'Yoga Sutras' as expounded by Patanjali[8].

Accordingly, the discussion to follow will take the form of a comparison of relevant formulations in Patanjali's Sutras and Jung's psychology.

The Concept of Psychic Reality

Jung emphasised the considerable difficulties encountered by a Westerner in attempting to integrate the ideas developed in Eastern cultures over thousands of years. The historical split in Western thought between science, on the one hand, and philosophy and religion on the other, has almost inevitably led to the dismissal of the Eastern standpoint as mystical and metaphysical speculation, not deserving of serious scientific comment.[3] Jung maintained that analytical psychology is an empirical science, because it deals with the phenomenological *reality* of intrapsychic processes. Thus, in coping with the problem of Eastern metaphysics, Jung adopted an approach compatible with his own psychology: 'Metaphysical assertions are *statements of the psyche*, and are therefore psychological'.[2] Jung also replies as follows to the assertion that metaphysical systems, and the psychological experiences from which they are largely derived, are not susceptible to objective, empirical assessment.

. . . Restriction to *material* reality carves an exceedingly large chunk out of reality as a whole, but it nevertheless remains a fragment only, and all around it is a dark penumbra which one would have to call unreal or surreal. This narrow perspective is alien to the Eastern view of the world, which therefore has no need of any philosophical conception of super-reality. Our arbitrarily delimited reality is continually menaced by the 'supersensual', the 'supernatural', the 'superhuman', and a whole lot more besides. Eastern reality includes all this as a matter of course. For us the zone of disturbance already begins with the concept of the 'psychic'. In our reality the psychic cannot be anything except an effect at third hand, produced originally by physical causes; a 'secretion of the brain', or something equally savoury . . . Far too little in theory, and almost never in practice, do we remember that consciousness has no direct relation to any material objects. We perceive nothing but images, transmitted to us indirectly by a complicated nervous apparatus . . . The consequence of this is, that what appears to us as immediate reality consists of carefully processed images, and that, furthermore, we live immediately only in a world of images . . . Far, therefore, from being a material world, this is a psychic world, which allows us to make only indirect and hypothetical inferences about the real nature of matter. The psychic alone has immediate reality, and this includes all forms of the psychic, even 'unreal' ideas and thoughts which refer to nothing 'external'. We may call them 'imagination' or 'delusion', but that does not detract in any way from their effectiveness . . . From this we can judge the magnitude of the error which our Western consciousness commits when it allows the psyche only a reality derived from physical causes. The East is wiser, for it finds the essence of all things grounded in the psyche. Between the unknown essences of spirit and matter stands the reality of the psyche – psychic reality, the only reality we can experience immediately.[9]

Thus, in Jung's view, intrapsychic phenomena are amenable to empirical, psychological analysis. Eastern systems are also susceptible to psychological examination from a phenomenological perspective. It is therefore possible that Western conceptualizations of intrapsychic phenomena might benefit from the translation of Eastern formulations into a frame of reference compatible with depth psychology.

The Ego and the Concept of Consciousness

Jung used the term 'psyche' to designate the totality of all psychological phenomena, including both conscious and unconscious processes.[10] He stated further: '. . . the psyche consists essentially of images. It is a series of images in the truest sense, not an accidental juxtaposition or sequence, but a structure that is throughout full of meaning and purpose; it is a 'picturing' of vital activities.'[11]

Jung held that psychic images reflect processes in the brain and are reproducible in '. . . an almost infinite series'. Although he wrote, 'the nature of consciousness is a riddle whose solution I do not know', he maintained that the series of images has '. . . the quality of consciousness'. Observation indicates that we are only aware of a small part of this totality, and that awareness is variable, undergoing continual modification as attention shifts. If we are only aware of the psychic images of 'internal' and 'external' processes and objects, then that of which we are aware at any given moment in time constitutes the field of consciousness. Whereas consciousness can potentially encompass the totality of the psyche, in practice it moves within a very circumscribed area or field, *due to its association with the ego*. This point is of central importance and will be elaborated further in Patanjali's treatment of the ego-sense.

Jung's definitions of consciousness and of the ego are to a large extent interdependent. He defines consciousness as '. . . the function of activity which maintains the relation of psychic contents with the ego'.[10] Elsewhere, he compares consciousness '. . . to the beam of a searchlight. Only those objects upon which the cone of light falls enter the field of perception.'[11]

In defining the ego, Jung writes, 'there can be no consciousness when there is no one to say "I am conscious" '.[12] Knowledge of phenomena depends, therefore, upon a relation of identity with a *subject*, the ego, which is in turn defined as '. . . a complex of representations which constitutes the centre of my field of consciousness and appears to possess a very high degree of continuity and identity'. He comments further: 'The ego is the subject of consciousness. All our experience of the outer and inner world must pass through the ego in order to be perceived'.[10]

It follows therefore that the ego is not synonymous with consciousness in Jung's system, although it determines the quality and orientation of consciousness to a major degree. Indeed, it has the properties of a 'filtering mechanism' which may exclude from awareness a wide variety of stimuli, images, thoughts and other potential contents of consciousness. In addition to the clinical evidence derived from depth psychology, this contention is supported by a considerable body of evidence derived from modern experimental psychology (see for example Ornstein, 1972[13]). Accordingly, '. . . relations to the ego, in so far as they are not sensed as such by the ego, are unconscious'.[10] The unconscious is defined simply as '. . . the totality of all psychic phenomena that lack the quality of consciousness'.[10]

We now turn to a consideration of Eastern formulations of the nature of consciousness and the role of the ego. As indicated above, Western thought rests upon the assumption of the reality of matter as opposed to the reality of the psyche, which is seen as a derivative of material processes. In marked contrast, Eastern thought commences with the opposite assumption and locates reality in the fact of consciousness itself. Physical processes are thus seen to be a derivative of consciousness. Between these two polarities, Jung interposes the concept of psychic reality.

In his Yoga Sutras, Patanjali postulates an underlying and interpenetrating unity of all phenomena. This primary quality of unity is held to be absolute, is said to be indefinable and inexpressible conceptually, and corresponds to *Brahman* of the Upanishads and Vedanta. The individual human organism can, however, come to experience itself as this unity in terms of the Self, which is designated by the terms *Ātmān* or *Purusha*. From a psychological perspective, the Self is said to be experienceable as 'pure consciousness', or as 'consciousness absolutely unqualified'.[7] The Self as pure consciousness is 'that' which remains after all attributes or phenomenal characteristics ascribed to it have been removed. The forms and patterns of the phenomenal world (*praktri*), that is, those factors which give reality the quality of multiplicity and separateness, are therefore held to be illusory (*Māyā*) from the perspective of pure consciousness. It follows therefore that 'reality' is synonomous with the Self as pure consciousness; ignorance of the nature of reality is ascribed to the mistaken identification of consciousness with the 'mind' (*citta*), defined as the 'universal medium through which consciousnss functions on all planes of the manifested universe'.[14] The mind is conceptualized as the product of the interaction between consciousness and matter, and is thus the focal point, as it were, where change occurs. When identified with the mind, consciousness is therefore experienced as being subject to its vicissitudes or modifications (*vrtti*), which are held to be ultimately painful (*kleśa*) as compared to apprehension of reality as pure consciousness. The overall aim of Yoga practice is therefore to free consciousness from the action of the mind.

Patanjali conceptualizes the mind as being 'inert', in the sense that it is not inherently intelligent and conscious. Like the physiological sense organs, it is thought to function only as the medium by means of which phenomena are apprehended. Moreover, the mind comprises three fundamental systems, *manas, buddhi,* and *ahamkar.* The last named denotes the ego sense which, so to speak, claims ownership of all phenomenal experiences arising out of the interaction of mind and matter and thus results in a sense of individual conscious identity. *The ego sense does not constitute the real identity, since it is by definition a mental system.* In this regard, Zimmer writes: 'The seeming consciousness of phenomenal beings can be described, approximately, as a reflection, or specification of the pure and primary consciousness of Brahman.'[7] A major objective of Yoga practice is therefore to modify the ego sense with a resulting cessation of the attachment of consciousness to the mental modifications, which in turn leads to the elimination of suffering.

In Jung's psychology, the function of consciousness is theoretically capable of so developing as to completely approximate the psyche, that is, individual consciousness may so develop or expand as to encompass all possible psychic images (e.g. Jung 1951[15]). While Jung views consciousness as developing phylogenetically and ontogenetically out of the unconscious, Patanjali, on the other hand, asserts that *consciousness is pre-existent*, immutable, unchanging and underlies all phenomenal appearances. Thus, for Patanjali, it is not so much a question of the development of consciousness, but rather of a progressive dissolution or elimination of phenomenal appearances, so that the pre-existent, underlying nature of pure consciousness is revealed. For Jung, *the unconscious is pre-existent*, which in turn implies the potentiality for an increase in or expansion of consciousness, achieved through a progressive increase in awareness of previously unconscious contents. However, these differences, perhaps ascribable to Jung's Western extraverted bias on the one hand and the typically introverted attitude of Yoga on the other, are only apparent, since both systems recognise that *empirically*, the expansion or unveiling of consciousness is hampered by its association with a mental ego-complex or ego-sense. As will become apparent in the later discussion of their practical application, both systems seek to modify the ego-consciousness relationship in order to stimulate or facilitate a higher level of personality functioning in the direction of increased mental health or 'self-realization'. Moreover, both systems are similar *in practice* in that they both require the elimination of unconscious factors which bias and distort our perception of 'reality'. In Jungian terms, this is achieved by the progressive withdrawal of the projections of unconscious contents which may, in particular, adversely affect interpersonal relations. In Yogic terms, an increase in awareness, alertness or vigilance accompanies Yogic practices and results in the progressive dissolution of superficial phenomenal appearances described as 'ignorance' (*Māyā*).

Jung's Concept of the Unconscious: Instinct and Archetype

Jung's model of the psyche postulates a personal and an impersonal or collective system of the unconscious. The personal system comprises '. . . forgotten, repressed, subliminally perceived, thought and felt matter of every kind'.[10] The repressed material aggregates to form complexes or 'feeling toned ideas'.[16] The adjective 'personal' is used to describe this system of the unconscious precisely because its contents are of ontogenetic origin; they were either once conscious or else have the capacity of achieving consciousness, and are closely co-ordinated with the needs of the ego.

The collective system, on the other hand, is defined as '. . . a part of the psyche which can be negatively distinguished from the personal unconscious by the fact that it does not owe its existence to personal experience, and consequently is not a personal acquisition'.[17]

Jung characterized it as a 'phylogenetic substratum',[12] structured according to patterns of life and behaviour selected during the process of evolution. He thus ascribed a pivotal role to the evolutionary process as a factor influencing human behaviour and his theory thus contains a biological thrust. It implies that there is an inherent and therefore universal (collective) predisposition or preprogrammed blueprint for all human beings to respond similarly in the primal situations of life (birth, death, love, parenthood and so on) experienced during the developmental passage from birth to death. The collective unconscious thus contains, in potentia, all of the 'instincts', as well as their associated archetypal images, and this implies a series of critical transitions, as developmental nodal points are negotiated during the maturation process of a human life: '. . . (man) has in him these *a priori* instinct-types which provide the occasion and the pattern for his activities, in so far as he functions instinctively. As a biological being he has no choice but to act in a specifically human way and fulfil his pattern of behaviour.'[18]

The second, related component comprising the collective unconsciousness, the associated archetypal image, guides the instinct, providing it with both its meaning and its direction. The archetypal images shape the development of human life and are particularly prominent at critical points of transition, for example at adolescence, middle age, preparation for death: 'Archetypes are typical modes of apprehension, and wherever we meet with uniform and regularly occurring modes of apprehension we are dealing with an archetype, no matter whether its mythological character is recognised or not.'[19] Archetypes are further defined as '. . . factors which arrange the psychic elements into certain images, characterized as archetypal, but in such a way that they can only be recognised from the effects which they produce'.[20] Moreover, archetypes are '. . . the necessary a-priori determinants of all psychic processes . . . just as his instincts compel man to a specifically human mode of existence, so the archetypes force his ways of perception and apprehension into specifically human patterns'.[19]

Jung's investigation of archetypal images ranged from his studies of ancient myths, modern fairy tales, the religions of East and West, to his studies of medieval alchemy, the dreams and visions of normal individuals, the hallucinations of the insane and his own experimental research.

In summary, 'instincts' can be conceptualized as dynamic, biological predispositions, actualized in behaviour. The archetypal image is psychic in manifestation and corresponds to the psychic 'portrayal' or 'picturing' of the critical phases in the development of instinctual processes: 'The primordial image might suitably be described as the *instinct's perception of itself*, or as the self-portrait of the instinct . . . '[19]

Jung was later to develop these earlier formulations and, from 1946 onwards, extracted two separate propositions from the above definitions: on the one hand, there is the concept of a 'factor' termed the archetype *per se*, conceptualized as an a priori conditioning factor, and, on the other hand, the concept of the psychic representation or content of that factor, the archetypal image. He therefore conceived of the archetypes as being in a pre-existent state of potentiality which occurs prior to the differentiation of any psychic or physical manifestation as archetypal motif or behaviour pattern. He used the term 'psychoid' which means 'psyche-like' or 'quasi–psychic' to denote this condition of the undifferentiated potentiality of the archetype *per se*. This psychoid state is described as 'transcendent' due to the fact that '. . . the real nature of the archetype "as such" is not capable of being made conscious'.[18] Elsewhere he writes: 'The collective unconscious represents a psyche that cannot be directly perceived or represented, in contrast to the perceptible psychic phenomena, and on account of its irrepresentable nature I have called it psychoid.'[18] The psychoid archetype, as a structuring principle, is compared to the

. . . axial system of a crystal, which, as it were, preforms the crystalline structure in the mother liquid, although it has no material existence of its own. This first appears according to the specific way in which the ions and molecules aggregate. The archetype in itself is empty and purely formal . . . it is nothing but a possibility of representation which is given a-priori.[17]

Jung further hinted that this irrepresentable and unknowable psychoid condition is '. . . an altogether different form of being' and commented '. . . for lack of empirical data I have no knowledge of such forms of being, which are commonly called spiritual'.

The Concept of the Subconscious in Yoga: Vāsanā *and* Samskāra

The doctrines of Yoga allocate a central position to what is termed the 'subconscious'. Eliade[8] conceptualizes this 'psychomental system' as comprising subliminal latencies termed '*vāsanās*'. It is contended that an immense reservoir of these latencies exist in the subconscious in a potential condition. The origin of the latencies is ascribed to memory, which is conceptualized as being both personal and impersonal. The impersonal system arises as the result of cultural transmission (language, mores, civilization) from generation to generation. Direct transmission may also occur through the agency of what is termed 'karmic transmigration'. In the latter case, the *vāsanās* which have been actualized in previous existences are said to form subtle mental residues '. . . of all the perceptions, acts, desires and movements of will of the past, all the propensities and trends, the heritage of habits and inclination, and the peculiar readiness to react this way or that, or not to react at all'.[7] Personal memory arises from the stored experiences of one lifetime, which is patterned by the *vāsanās* after the experiences of previous lifetimes. The subconscious is conceptualized as being a dynamic system, in which there is a continual process of actualization of a state of potentiality, this continual circuit, as it were, giving rise to the dynamism of mental life. The basis of all human behaviour is therefore ascribed to the action of the subconscious which predisposes the individual towards specific modes of perception and behaviour. These modes perpetuate themselves in an endless cycle of action and reaction.

A considerable part of human experience is owing to this racial and intellectual heritage, to these forms of action and thought which are created by the play of the *vāsanās*. These subconscious forces determine the lives of the majorty of men. It is only through Yoga that they can be known, controlled, "burned".[8]

Furthermore:

> . . . the *vāsanās* constitute an immense obstacle – for they are in the highest degree elusive and difficult to master. By the very fact that their mode of being is that of potentiality, their own dynamism forces the *vāsanās* to manifest, to actualize themselves under the form of acts of consciousness.[8]

The continual actualization of the latencies is conceptualized as resulting in the formation of psychic impressions, termed *samskāras*[7], which accumulate in the subconscious. These impressions, once formed, continually influence the pattern of actualization of the latencies, and are in turn elaborated or built up, as it were, by the ongoing actualization process. Thus, the *samskāras* may be conceptualized as *personal* predispositions, unique to the individual, which nevertheless derive from the dynamism of the *vāsanās*, which are *impersonal, collective* tendencies, inherent in the structure of the human organism. At this point, the marked correspondences between Jungian theory and the doctrine of Yoga become apparent.

By first disciplining, and later 'destroying' the *vāsanās*, mental activity is stilled to the point where the mind can become a purified and perfect reflecting medium for consciousness, thereby enabling experience of the true nature of the individual as the Self. It thus follows from the above discussion that the overall aim of Yoga practice is to inhibit the actualization of the subconscious, hence Patanjali's definition of Yoga as 'the inhibition of the modifications of the mind',[14] or the 'suppression of states of consciousness'.[8]

The Yogic Path to Self-Realisation: The Role of Meditation

Patanjali recognizes four states of consciousness, namely waking consciousness, the dream state, dreamless sleep and transcendental or pure consciousness, which is conceptualized as a synthesis of the preceding three, and corresponds to *samādhi*. The procedure for achieving experience of the Self is classified in an eightfold system, the 'eight limbs' of Yoga. The first two limbs, *Yama* and *Niyama* are designed to provide an adequate moral foundation for more advanced practice. The term 'morality' is used in the sense of eliminating those mental disturbances caused by uncontrolled emotions and desires, notably sexuality and aggression, hence the practice of sexual continence (*brahmacarya*) and non-violence (*ahimsā*). The next three steps of Yoga, designated *āsanas, prānāyāma* and *pratyāhāra*, are designed to reduce proprioceptive input, to reduce breathing rate to approximate that of sleep, and to reduce sensory stimulation of the brain respectively, whilst nevertheless maintaining a state of alert awareness. The Yogi is thus able to enter the sleep states without relinquishing the continuity of consciousness[8] and is then in a position to work with the 'purely mental'[14] memories of past experiences and images connected with the future which become more visible, as it were, given the inhibition of distracting phenomenal stimuli achieved during practice of the preceding steps. The sixth limb, *dhāranā*, or concentration, constitutes the '. . . confining of the mind within a limited mental area'.[14] An object (or image) of concentration is selected, and the mind is limited in its movement to the aspects or attributes of that object. The concentration object is generally selected with a view to its powerful, symbolically unitive associations, hence the use of, for examply, the mandala. When unbroken attention to the subject can be maintained, the seventh limb, *dhyāna* or contemplation ('one-pointedness'), is attained. The mind comes to know the object much more intimately than is possible by means of the ordinary attentional cognitive processes characteristic of waking, everyday consciousness. The goal then becomes experience of the underlying reality of the object, namely the Self. That which prevents the complete fusion or 'Yoga' of subject and object is the very subjectivity of the mind, characterized as the 'residual consciousness of its own role or action in the process of *dhyāna*'.[14] With the elimination of this residue, the only object which can fill the mind is the object of meditation itself. When this occurs, the perceiver, the object of perception and the perception process itself become fused in one transcendent state of consciousness, termed *samādhi*, the eighth and final limb of Patanjali's system.

Patanjali distinguishes several conditions of *samādhi*, the technicalities of which need not detain us here. Relevant for our purposes is the ongoing process of contemplation which results in the ultimate experience of pure consciousness. *Samādhi* is defined as a '. . . process of diving into the deeper layers of one's consciousness, which functions through different grades of the mind'.[14] The mind, now in a state of union with the object of contemplation, is perceived as consisting of several levels, which correspond to the levels of the object. Thus:

. . . each successive stage of *samādhi* reveals to our consciousness a different and deeper layer of the reality of the object, and by continuing the process of *samyama* through the successive stages, we ultimately arrive at the innermost reality of the object . . . *samyama* is really a means of passing from the outer expression to the reality within whatever may be the nature of the relationship between the outer expression and the inner reality. Since the reality underlying all objects is contained in the Divine Mind (Brahman), and the object of *Samyama* in *samādhi* is to know this reality, it follows that what the yogi does in *samyama* is to sink into his own consciousness until he reaches the level of Divine Mind in which the reality of the object is to be found. The seed (object) on which *samyama* is performed merely determines the line along which consciousness has to sink.[14]

This process is rendered more comprehensible when the nature of the objects or 'seeds' is examined more closely. Every phenomenon is said to have two basic forms, an outward form from which we are familiar, and an inner form termed an *archetype*, of which we are unaware in normal waking consciousness.[14] The archetype is conceptualized as a corresponding reality at the level of 'Divine Mind'. At this extremely 'subtle' (Taimni's word) level of archetypal form, the yogi is but a step away, so to speak, from the final goal, that of formless, pure consciousness. It is the perception of the archetypal properties of the object that fill consciousness, and with the successful practice of *samyama* on these properties, the final level of form is transcended, and pure formless consciousness is experienced. 'The light which was up to this stage illuminating other objects now illuminates itself, for it has withdrawn beyond the realm of these objects. The seer is now established in his own Self'.[14]

The Process of Individuation: The Role of Active Imagination

Jacobi[21] has stated that in its practical application, Jung's psychology constitutes a 'way of healing and a way of salvation'. In this sense then, it constitutes the psychological concomitant of a religious system. The psychological parallelism with religion is apparent in Jung's definition of the central concept of individuation, which, he states: '. . . means becoming an "individual", and insofar as individuality embraces our innermost, last and incomparable uniqueness, it also implies becoming one's own self. We could, therefore translate individuation as "coming to selfhood" or "self realization".'[22]

Two aspects of the concept of individuation can be distinguished. On the one hand, it denotes the ongoing self-regulatory activity of the psyche, which exhibits a prospective or purposive tendency when viewed over the development of a human life. This tendency is empirically observable in dreams.

. . . our dream life creates a meandering pattern in which individual strands or tendencies become visible, then vanish, then return again. If one watches this meandering design over a long period of time, one can observe a sort of hidden regulating or direct tendency at work, creating a slow, imperceptible process of psychic growth – the process of individuation.[23]

On the other hand, the concept is used in a narrower sense to denote a specific means of personality development, which takes the form of 'a maturation process . . . induced by an analysis of the unconscious'.[24] Individuation in the narrower sense consists essentially of the reconciliation of the conscious and unconscious systems of the psyche by means of the transcendent function.

Essentially, this consists of a dialectical process, a 'dialogue' between conscious, cognitive aspects of the personality and unconscious, emotionally toned components: the autonomous, archetypal complexes. Jung's method of *active imagination* plays an important role in this process. The method, characterised as a form of 'visionary meditation',[25] attempts to make conscious the spontaneous, unconscious natural process of psychic growth, and thereby to stimulate or accelerate it.[26] Technically, this entails a form of concentration upon spontaneously arising images following the induction of a reduced intensity of consciousness:

Active imagination is a method of introspection, for observing the stream of interior images. One concentrates one's attention on some impressive but unintelligible dream image, or on a spontaneous visual impression, and observes the changes taking place in it. Meanwhile, of course, all criticism must be suspended, and the happenings observed and noted with complete objectivity.[27]

The patient is trained to suspend the directive, outward orientation of consciousness. A 'deliberate weakening of consciousness'[27] or 'abaissement du niveau mental' is thus brought about, with the result that unconscious material floods the field of consciousness, taking the form of 'a long and often very dramatic series of fantasies'. Jung comments further: '. . . these images differ from dreams only by reason of their better form, which comes from the fact that the contents are perceived not by a dreaming, but by a waking consciousness'. The pivotal role played by the analysis of dreams and the use of active imagination in Jungian analysis becomes clear when it is considered that it is the Self which generates the phenomena experienced in these states of consciousness:

The organizing center from which the regulatory effect stems seems to be a sort of 'nuclear atom' in our psychic system. One could call it the inventor, organizer, and source of dream images. Jung called this center the 'Self' and described it as the totality of the whole psyche, in order to distinguish it from the 'ego', which constitutes only a small part of the total psyche.[23]

The concept of the Self can be more readily grasped when it is considered that in Jung's view, consciousness arises out of the unconscious. He writes:

Consciousness is always only a temporary state based upon an optimal physiological performance, and is therefore regularly interrupted by phases of unconsciousness . . . from this arises the important conclusion that the real and authentic psyche is the unconscious, whereas the ego consciousness can be regarded only as a temporary epiphenomenon.[28]

Consciousness can therefore be regarded as the manifestation of certain unknown tendencies and potentialities of the psychoid substratum of the psyche. The unconscious is '. . . the ever present mother of consciousness'[29] precisely because in historical terms the unconscious is immeasurably older than consciousness. The ego, being the centre of consciousness, is likewise a recent phenomenon. Jung writes: 'We cannot overlook the fact that, just as consciousness arises from the unconscious, the ego-centre too crystallizes out of a dark depth in which it was somehow contained in potentia.'[12] The ego is therefore a prefiguration, as it were, of a more all embracing potential identity which lies dormant, but whose synthesis is the goal of individuaton. Thus

. . . unconscious processes stand in a compensatory relation to the conscious mind. I expressly use the word 'compensatory' and not contrary, because conscious and unconscious are not necessarily in opposition to one another, but complement one another to form a totality, the Self . . . the Self is a quantity that is superordinate to the conscious ego. It embraces not only the conscious but also the unconscious psyche, and is therefore a personality which so to speak we also are.[22]

Our earlier discussion concerning the nature of the unconscious revealed this to be a matrix of structuring principles which exist in a potential, psychoid condition until elicited or activited by the experiences undergone by consciousness. These experiences are themselves patterned in accordance with the psychoid, unconscious archetypal potentiality. The nucleus of all psychoid potentialities is the Self, the superordinate nodal point or centre from which all other archetypal principles emanate. Thus, the experience, confrontation and integration of phenomenological material derived from both dream and meditative states provide access to the Self, which unfolds and manifests during the dialectical process described above.

Jung observed a characteristic, developmental progression as individuation proceeds: in the early stages, the imagery reflects emotionally toned, repressed material, often personified in archetypal images portraying the Shadow, or the dark, unacceptable aspects of the personality. As the process proceeds, however, the formal, impersonal, underlying structuring principles begin to become apparent:

The spontaneous fantasy products . . . become more profound and concentrate themselves gradually around abstract structures which apparently represent 'principles', true Gnostic *archai*. When the fantasies are chiefly expressed in thoughts, the results are intuitive formulations of dimly felt laws or principles, which at first tend to be dramatised or personified . . . If the fantasies are expressed in drawings, symbols appear which are chiefly of the so-called mandala type.[5]

Thus, the procedures of analytical psychology appear to achieve results similar to those of yogic practice, at the phenomenological level at least. In both cases, the initial psychic flux is stilled, thus allowing the more subtle, underlying unitive and generative principles to be apprehended by and integrated into consciousness. As noted above, Jung observed that mandalas (symbols of centrality portraying the intrinsic structure of the Self) may be spontaneously produced by individuals ignorant of their significance in Eastern doctrine, after a great deal of dramatic, personal imagery has been worked through. It would appear, then, that at an advanced stage of analysis, active imagination becomes *naturally and spontaneously* focussed upon symbols of the Self, an outcome prescribed *at the outset* by the 'mind-emptying' yogic meditation techniques. Thus in the latter case, an attempt is made to 'inhibit the modifications of the mind' or to still the psychic flux *by an act of will*.

Conclusions

In its *practical application*, Yoga is a highly evolved and systematized method of self-realization; it was conceptualized by Jung as a type of religious initiation ceremony, of which active imagination is the 'natural analogue'.[2] The initiation ceremonies '. . . do however differ in principle from the natural process in that they forestall the natural course of development, and substitute for the spontaneous production of symbols a deliberately selected set of symbols prescribed by tradition'. Jung accordingly conceived of Yoga as a form of 'technical transformation of the personality'.[30] Jung's position is supported by the fact that in the *dhāranā* phase of the eight limbs, a concentration object is deliberately selected, contemplation of which is said to inhibit spontaneous mental activity. In spite of this fundamental difference, however, Jung recognized the final aim of Yoga (and other Eastern methods) as being identical to that of individuation by means of active imagination, namely the synthesis or realization of the Self. Jung in fact conceived of the Self as being 'a figure comparable to *Purusha, Ātman* and the Mystic Buddha',[30] but nevertheless emphasized that the methods which have been developed to approach this final goal must of necessity differ in Western and Eastern cultures, since the given psychic conditions are different at the outset. Thus, in Jung's view, the method of active imagination is especially applicable in cases where there is a marked dissociation between consciousness and the unconscious, since the method consists essentially of bringing consciousness into contact with its archetypal, collective basis. This dissociation is particularly pronounced in Western culture,[31] and is ascribed to the ontogenetic emphasis upon the rational, logical and directed form of consciousness which is so highly valued and cultivated in the West.

In Jung's view, 'Yoga technique applies itself exclusively to the conscious mind and will'.[3] This process constitutes the exact reverse of the method of active imagination. From the perspective of Jung's psychology, the eight limbs of Yoga appear to be a highly developed system of techniques for strengthening consciousness, whereas during active imagination a deliberate weakening of the critical, rational functions of consciousness is induced. Jung felt that the application of Yogic techniques to the Western psyche is unwise. He writes:

I do not apply Yoga methods in principle, because in the West nothing ought to be forced upon the unconscious. Usually consciousness is characterized by an intensity and narrowness that have a cramping effect, and this ought not to be emphasized still further. On the contrary, everything must be done to help the unconscious reach the conscious mind, and to free it from its rigidity.[3]

Both systems are, however, in agreement that the unconscious or subconscious area of man's psychic constitution must be overcome or depotentiated in order for individuation or self-realization to proceed. Jung's solution is to 'deflate' the unconscious by facilitating or accelerating the natural rate of actualization of the unconscious factors in consciousness by means of the method of active imagination. Eastern Yoga, applying itself to a consciousness already overburdened by the action of the subconscious, attempts to suppress and ultimately 'destroy' the action of this mental system by controlling or inhibiting the actualization process through direct experiences of the archetypal basis and latent conditions which generate it. Access to the generative source must, as has already been suggested, entail experience of the realms of personal and impersonal memory; if these concepts can be viewed as metaphysical parallels to Jung's concepts of a personal and an impersonal or collective unconscious, then the concurrence of the two systems on the structural continuity or opposition between personal and impersonal factors in the psyche is paralleled by their postulation of a progression of experience from personal psychic material to impersonal (archetypal) material during the process of individuation or self-realization.

Both systems lay claim to an empirical, scientific methodology in that they both rest upon an experiential basis. In their practical application this experiential component is, at least partially, derived from the induction of a meditative state. Further parallels become apparent at this point. As we have mentioned above, the practitioner of Yoga attempts to enter the sleep states without relinquishing the continuity principles underlying mental phenomena. Jung noted the correspondence between the initiation of active imagination and the hypnagogic state characteristic of sleep onset, and held the view that the images experienced by a waking consciousness emerged in a more creative form than in the nocturnal dream state, thereby providing more advantageous conditions for the integration of unconscious material into consciousness.[26] Thus it would appear that both systems recognize the maintenance of a lucid state of consciousness as the crucial factor in their respective meditational techniques. Moreover, as noted, the mere act of meditation does not necessarily imply access to or integration of material from the collective unconscious. The key word is *integration* and this requires a moral and ethical response to the insights or 'hints' received during meditation. Indeed, this is precisely why Jung called his method *'active'* imagination, since it requires active participation not only during the events witnessed during the process itself, but also during the subsequent business of everyday living. He refers to a resultant *change in attitude* to life's problems as a consequence of 'Self-Realization', and in so doing, adopts a psychological perspective which is firmly rooted in the earth of everyday reality as opposed to the 'ineffable', 'transcendent' and 'mystical' flavour which is often associated with this term. For example, Jung writes:

This 'outgrowing', as I formerly called it on further experience was seen to consist in a new level of consciousness. Some higher or wider interest arose on the person's horizon, and through this widening of his view the insoluble problem lost its urgency. It was not solved logically in its own terms, but faded out when confronted with a new and stronger life-tendency. It was not repressed and made unconscious, but merely appeared in a different light, and so did indeed become different. What, on a lower level, had led to the wildest conflicts and to panicky outbursts of emotion, viewed from the higher level of the personality, now seemed like a storm in the valley seen from a high mountain-top. This does not mean that the thunderstorm is robbed of its reality, but instead of being in it, one is now above it. However, since we are both valley and mountain with respect to the psyche, it might seem a vain illusion to feel oneself beyond what is human. One certainly does feel the effect and is shaken and tormented by it, yet at the same time one is aware of a higher consciousness, which prevents one from becoming identical with the affect, a consciousness which takes the affect objectively, and can say, 'I know that I suffer'.[5]

From *a theoretical perspective* both systems would appear to adopt the general position that a *potential* factor actualizes itself in and through the psyche, determining patterns of perception, ideation and behaviour. In Jung's theory, the instincts and their corresponding archetypal images comprise the collective unconscious, whereas in Yogic doctrines, the subconscious is viewed as a dynamic 'bio-mental circuit' comprised of latent, inborn predispositions or *vāsanās* which seek actualization and expression in behaviour.

Second, the potential psychic aspect of Jung's psychoid archetype might be viewed as analogous to the 'inner form' or structuring principles of outwardly experienced phenomenal forms, or 'archetypes' of Yogic doctrine, which are said to become perceptible during certain states of consciousness, achieved as the result of advanced practice of Yogic technique. The archetype, then, as conceptualized in Yogic doctrine, appears to be very similar to the Platonic concept of the pure and immutable Idea which is transcendent, existing prior to all experience. However, this statement must be qualified by the consideration that, in Jungian theory at least, the evolutionary process of Darwinian selection is introduced as a factor in the development of man's consciousness and the archetype is thus *not* necessarily immutable, but is subject to historical modification.

Third, aspects of Jung's concept of the 'complex' and the Yogic *samskāra* would appear to be more or less equivalent, in that they imply accumulated energic psychic structures mediating personally acquired habits and predispositions, which nevertheless derive from the fundamental and impersonal systems of the collective unconscious or subconscious respectively. Thus, in Yogic doctrine, there appear to be equivalents of Jung's demarcation of the psyche into personal and impersonal or collective systems. We note, however, Jung's more than once expressed caution against drawing too close a parallel between his ideas and those of the East.[6]

The above reasoning is nevertheless corroborated by several additional considerations. In the first instance, both Jung and Patanjali conceive of some form of continuity or opposition between personal and impersonal factors constituting the psyche. Progressive experience in Yoga implies an ongoing penetration of impersonal, universalized factors. Jung, likewise, emphasizes the necessity of experience of the impersonal substratum of the psyche in order for self-knowledge to accrue. In practice, this takes the form, in Jung's model, of a preliminary integration of the contents of the personal unconscious into consciousness, with the concomitant dissolution of the complexes. This opens the way, so to speak, for experience of the archetypal levels of the psyche. Yoga, similarly, conceives of the neutralization of the *samskāras*, which are by definition personal in nature, as being an essential prerequisite for experience of the Self. The two systems thus appear to exhibit a common conceptual progression from personal *samskāras*/complexes to impersonal *vāsanās*/archetypal structuring elements.

The foregoing arguments are supported by Kirsch's assertions regarding the Dharma-kaya or Self of Tibetan Buddhism. He writes:

The collective unconscious is the matrix of everything. It is the womb of everything, even of the Dharma-kaya. It is the Dharma-kaya itself.[32]

CHAPTER 11

Jung as Philosopher and Theologian

BY MORTON T. KELSEY

The contribution of C.G. Jung to medicine and psychology, to anthropology, as well as to man's present ability to understand himself in depth, is well known. Concepts of his are part of the very vocabulary now used to describe man's functioning. There is a growing appreciation of his importance psychologically that cuts across academic lines. Yet few people recognize that in still another area Jung made a contribution which may prove equally significant as the twentieth century draws to a close. Jung's thought in the fields of philosophy and theology may well provide these two disciplines with a way out of the sterile desert in which they have been stranded for more than two centuries. [1]

Philosophy and theology are closely linked, despite the thinking of some theologians who keep looking through the wrong end of the binoculars. When philosophy provides man with some base for a viable relationship with transpersonal meaning (or the 'divine'), then the task of theology is within the realm of possibility. It then has the plausible task of exploring and elaborating man's relation with that meaning. When philosophy provides no such base, theology may whistle in the dark or concoct all sorts of intellectual ideas about meaning, but practically no one is taken in. Jung has offered such a base, and also a method for exploration.

Just how unique is Jung's contribution in this area? To see this aspect in relief, let us review the main developments of modern philosophy, presumptuous as this seems, in a few sentences. Starting with the skeptical certainty of Descartes, backed up by the Enlightenment, practical philosophers gradually came to have great confidence in man's reason and his knowledge of the world around him. By the nineteenth century this point of view had solidified into dogma, a dogma that the material alone was real and that it developed through rational and mechanical laws which would eventually be understood *in toto*. Man himself was a prisoner in this closed and unalterable system, since his psyche was merely an epiphenomenal by-product, 'nothing but' the result of this material process.

Since then most philosophy has been an attempt to support or attack this dogma. Popular thinkers from Comte to Mach and Skinner developed the implications of this point of view. Hegel, on the other hand, tried to support the autonomy of 'mind' and 'idea' by viewing the entire experienced world as a manifestation of mind. But with no place for the individual, Hegel's 'ideal' system left man as much the prisoner of an unvarying order as he had been in the materialistic system.

Kierkegaard and the existentialists who followed him reacted violently. Realizing that man's unique individuality was lost in Hegel's magnificent dialectic, they turned attention to the individual, but without questioning the idea that man was caught in a closed, physical system. Since they saw no way for extraneous meaning to break through, all they could offer was a blind jump of faith in the tension of dread and anxiety. In phenomenology the lead of Hegel was picked up again by Edmund Husserl in the effort to base a whole philosophy on the logical presuppositions of man's conscious intentional act. Husserl saw no way by which man could reach *meaning* except through intellectual analysis.

Meanwhile philosophers in Britain took a different tack. Building on the genius of Wittgenstein, Russell, and Whitehead, they developed a school of empiricism in which logic was seen as tautological; it could bring no new knowledge. Rather they saw all knowledge as derived from empirical observations. Since one never knows with logical certainty what new experience will bring, all knowledge is then only probable and hypothetical. They did not deny that men might have other levels of experience than sense experience. But by pushing aside any other possibilities, they wrote off moral theory, metaphysics and theology with a stroke of the pen.[2]

All of these major schools of philosophy deny that man has any significant immediate relationship with a meaningful reality that transcends this rational space-time world. Therefore, theology is hard put and the intelligent modern man looks in vain to find any substantial meaning for his life. It is at this point that Jung enters the picture.

Jung did not become interested in philosophical questions out of theoretical curiosity, but for a very practical reason. Intelligent men came to him who were sick for no apparent reason, and yet were unable to reason themselves out of the sickness. They were suffering from psychological distress, and also a host of physical symptoms which resulted at least in part from this distress. Jung discovered that mere loss of meaning could result in exactly this kind of sickness. Being a committed physician, he set about to heal this neurotic illness by finding some meaning that could fill the gap which the absence of traditional religion left in these lives.

In this task Jung was singularly successful. He was particularly well qualified for it; he had been trained in the most rigorous scientific method, he had a competence in historical philosophy shared by few psychologists and scientists, and he had a wealth of empirical data about man and meaning. He also enjoyed the practical undertaking, and in it he laid the foundations for a new philosophical and theological understanding. At the same time he was participating in the growth of a new attitude within the scientific community itself.

Early in the twentieth century awareness was growing that the outlook of nineteenth century rational materialism was too narrow to take in the data becoming known about our world. Through the work of Becquerel and the Curies, of Planck, Heisenberg and others, the substantial atom exploded into an increasing number of particles which could not be understood on the basis of Newtonian mechanics. Einstein, in one of the greatest intuitions of this age, came to the conclusion that space might not be Euclidian in nature, and his studies of the speed of light brought a new concept of time. Man's whole conception of time and matter and scientific truth were going through a traumatic change. The scientific method had not produced final and certain truths after all, but hypotheses which could be overturned by new research and replaced with new understanding. Scientific 'laws' could no longer be seen as ultimate truths. They were like maps, increasingly accurate, but still only maps of a territory that could never be fully known.

In *biology* and *paleontology* it was found that the idea of survival of the fittest does not always fit the facts, and that the relation between genetic factors and what Darwin observed appears to be directed in too complex a way to express without some idea of purpose. Thus, through thinking about evolution, the idea of teleology was reintroduced into the study of man. Pierre Teilhard de Chardin has drawn this point of view with brilliance and clarity in his many books.

From a medical standpoint it has become increasingly clear that man can no longer be treated as a passive assortment of physical parts, operating in a purely material environment. His hopes and fears, even hopes and fears about transcendental things, can well alter the whole course of an illness, a thesis supported by Dr. Flanders Dunbar in her scholarly study, *Emotions and Bodily Changes*, and by Dr. Jerome Frank in his equally well documented *Persuasion and Healing*.

This thinking has not taken hold generally, however. It has begun to make a deep impression on the philosophy of science, but the idea that these new conceptions may have a relation to man's own life, and his finding meaning in this universe, has not occurred to other philosophers. Jung stands quite alone in his effort to demonstrate that man's experiences actually do bridge this gap.

Jung and Modern Thought

One great contribution of analytical psychology to modern thought is that it finds a direct, inner verification of the findings of the other natural sciences. Jung has described from direct encounter the processes which Teilhard de Chardin and others described from the outside. Building quite consciously on the work of Janet, Charcot and Freud, Jung began to record the contents of an unconscious stratum of personality which was disclosed through neurotic disturbances, human error, intuitions, and most significantly, through the dream. He carefully sketched out an empirical framework in which man's purely psychic, unconscious experiences were given the same value as experiences of the physical world.

A second contribution of Jung was his realization that theories of the unconscious were as difficult to accept from a nineteenth century world view, as difficult to understand, as theories of quantum mechanics. In fact Jung often drew attention to the analogy between quantum mechanics and depth psychology. He realized that in taking the unconscious seriously as an operative part of man's personality, he was breaking with both Western philosophy and the popular psychological tradition of Wundt, in which the psychic was viewed only from the standpoint of consciousness. He was prepared to support his position. While he did not write a great deal about his methodology and philosophical presuppositions, he was well aware of them and they were clearly formulated. In various places in his writings he spoke of the relation of historical and current philosophy to his approach. His findings were presented within a careful and critical philosophical framework, which is seldom found among empirical scientists today. In addition he had the knowledge and the interest to do an adequate job.

To begin with, Jung quite frankly accepted a philosophical realism, the organic realism of modern science with its empirical emphasis. He anticipated the work of Wittgenstein, Ayer, Carnap, and Popper, who have come to understand that man's reason can bring him no new knowledge, but only possibilities which must be verified in experience.

But Jung did not limit his empiricism to sense experience alone – to that which can be objectively verified in a physical sense. In studying personal encounters with the autonomous unconscious, he applied basically the same test as the physical sciences: How does it work? What is the result of the individual? Does it recur? Father Hostie has described this empiricism at some length in *Religion and the Psychology of Jung*, defining Jung's method as 'non-experimental empiricism.'[3] Jung was fond of remarking that in scientific experiments the scientist asks the question, while in clinical practice the patient and nature ask it, and that it is not hard to see which asks the more difficult questions. Scientific experiment gives careful defined data about a small area of matter. Jung's method gives less defined data about the nature of man himself, data which man needs for survival.

Jung also accepted, quite consciously, Kant's basic idea that man has contact with two kinds of phenomenal experience, one related to the objective, external world, the other to the subjective or psychic world. To Kant, however, the subjective was exhausted by consciousness, while Jung dealt with the phenomena of an expanded subjective world which included unconscious contents and processes. And this large component – perhaps the major component – was made up of contents that were not always as personally subjective as they might appear. They were experienced subjectively – as, after all, our experiences of the physical world are also given – but they often seemed to come into the psyche from outside itself.

Thus Jung maintained that man has contact with an objectively real physical world, which of necessity is experienced subjectively; and an equally real world of autonomous psychic contents which are experienced directly, inwardly, subjectively. Both these experiences give only phenomenal knowledge. Neither kind gives final, apodictic knowledge of the 'thing-in-itself' but only what can become known through its reaction with the subject. But this phenomenal knowledge can be made more certain as more attention is directed to the phenomena themselves. Either the physical object, or the psychic contents which Jung described, can become known through experience. What Jung wrote to me in 1958 summarizes his understanding as well as any of his writings; in this letter he said:

The real nature of the objects of human experience is still shrouded in darkness. The scientists cannot concede a higher intelligence to Theology than to any other branch of human cognition. We know as little of a Supreme Being as of Matter. But there is as little doubt of the existence of a Supreme Being as of Matter. The world beyond is a reality, an experiential fact. We only don't understand it.

The failure of most people to realize that he was talking about the experience of contents that influence the psyche, not merely subjective ideas, exasperated Jung. When I was visiting him, a proof copy of a book titled *Jung and St. Paul* lay on his coffee table, and I asked him what he thought of it. His only reply was that the author had failed to grasp this most elementary point. As a practical matter it is impossible to understand Jung merely by reading him, but only by dealing directly with the realities of which he has written.

In fact, one of Jung's important statements was that 'natural science is not a science of words and ideas, but of facts'.[4]Let us look for a moment at how the physical scientist handles these facts. He does not question that they are only empirical observations, the experiences someone has had with matter. He asked what they mean, and then by induction or analogy, or often intuitive insight, he makes an educated guess – a hypothesis which he proceeds to test. In this way he reaches a theory which takes all the facts into relationship. Each new experience that does not fit requires an expanded or often an entirely new theory. One inconsistent fact, small enough to be overlooked by most observers, may even require a whole new world view. It is at this point that logical thought is most needed. The possibilities that have been developed through logic, pure mathematics, or imagination can fill the gap, and even new systems of such thought may be required.

Changes in hypothetical construction are probably easiest to see by looking at a nutshell outline of our growing understanding of matter. From experiences of distinct atomic properties came the idea of hard little balls of matter. Next by various stages, including the observations of Copernicus and Kepler, these were seen to be working in the macrocosm according to the genius of Newtonian mechanics. Then came the developments we have spoken of, which began in 1896, when Becquerel was looking for light-induced radiation and instead found his sealed photographic plates mysteriously exposed by a substance that had not even seen the light. This was followed by the experiments of the Curies, Rutherford, and others, and the work of Planck, Einstein, Bohr, Meitner, Fermi . . . and the blast; and it was brought home to most people that matter does not always conform to the laws of mechanics.

Jung, who began his work a few years later, came upon his evidence almost as unexpectedly as Becquerel. He listened to the people who came to him for healing, and found that unconscious contents were pushing towards the threshold of consciousness. Many of these people were practical scientists who had neglected the whole area of feeling and unconscious experience. As they encountered these unconscious contents and dealt with them consciously, they not only found healing, but their experiences often involved strange elements of mythology and extra-sensory perception. In many instances it was through an experience of this nature that a patient began to find meaning and new energy. Thus Jung was led to make careful studies of mythology and dream symbols, synchronicity, and other such experiences.

This new and detailed knowledge of the unconscious – coming from the most complex pieces of matter, human beings – showed that a new hypothesis was needed to understand both consciousness and the unconscious, and their relation to the material world. The older theories were no longer adequate, and Jung suggested a new hypothesis which stepped beyond the deterministic naturalism of the nineteenth century, and therefore was loaded. The implications of his theory were both philosophical and theological.

Jung's direction had the support of a strong pragmatic bent in his thinking. He believed that electing a course of action that results in permanent healing, in human wholeness, comes closest to living with reality as it is. Jung was much influenced by James' pragmatism; he knew James' writings well and often quoted him. In pragmatism there is a further hypothesis, which Jung accepted, that life is more than just a chance and meaningless epiphenomenon. If there is ultimate meaning in the universe, and if man's life expresses a high level or stage of that meaning, then what furthers and develops human life is likely to correspond to the meaning of the universe. Living life as fully and completely as possible is then likely to express something true about the world in which we live. Jung offered the theory that nature is meaningful in itself, and then adduced volumes of evidence from man's inner life to corroborate this thesis.

His approach was also reinforced by experiences of unconscious contents rather than merely primitive and atavistic elements. The unconscious offers understandings which can be superior to consciousness, although they are usually expressed in images rather than abstract concepts. In the introduction to *Symbols of Transformation*, Jung carefully differentiated the two kinds of thinking of which man is capable – the directed, conceptual thinking characteristic of most logic, scientific demonstrations, mathematics and philosophy, and the intuitive, symbolic 'thinking' that comes from the unconscious.[5] It is by this thinking in images that man conveys his deepest meanings, particularly his emotional meaning. Art, drama, liturgy, folktales, mythology, all use archetypal images, and each night the dream also presents its meaning in symbols and pictures. Most of us, however, have lost touch with the capacity to think symbolically and so we fail to understand either man's myth or his dreams.

Mapping a New Understanding

If Jung's evidence from the unconscious is taken seriously, then man clearly has need for a new understanding of the total world of experience and of his place within that world. The hypothesis that Jung offers is very different from the materialistic rationalism which has swept the house bare for most of us. Instead, it finds man faced with an *experiential* dualism. From this point of view, man is not only confronted with the objective reality of a physical world, but he is also given experience which relates to the objective, autonomous reality of a psychic world, and man himself is a bridge between these two worlds of experience. He also finds a non-conscious organizing function at work within the unconscious, in addition to rational consciousness.

Through these unconscious contents and meanings, Jung found, man is presented with a vast psychic world, as objectively real, as meaningful and experienceable as the material and physical world, and not reducible to the physical. In this view he came very close to Plato's understanding of 'the ideas' – which Jung saw not as eternal concepts, however, but rather as the philosophical version of his 'psychically concrete' archetypes.[6] He further agreed in principle with Plato that man does not come to know and experience the realm of 'the ideas' through the exercise of reason, but only through irrational means like those Plato described as prophecy, dreams and healing, art, and love. Indeed in 'Psychology of the Transference'[7] and in certain pages of *Memories, Dreams, Reflections* Jung expressed his appreciation of the cognitive value of love in a way very similar to Plato.[8]

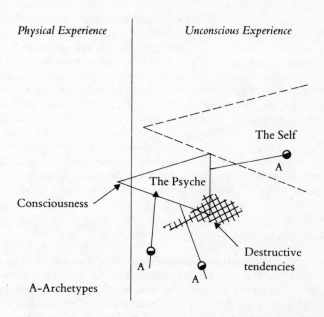

This point of view can be shown in the above schema. The two realms diagrammed both present man with valid *phenomenal*

experience. Either one can be understood better and better as one opens himself to more and more significant experiences, and then lets his rational and analytical capacities play upon them. Both are worlds of great complexity. Man's psyche itself is based in the unconscious realm. 'The Self' (dotted lines, open-ended) represents those creative and suprapersonal contents which are so meaningful for human development. The destructive tendencies (shaded) are those described, for instance, in Jung's account of his encounter with the unconscious in *Memories, Dreams, Reflections*.[9] A few of the possible archetypes are shown, presenting both creative and destructive aspects. All of these realities impinge upon the psyche, with consciousness usually directed towards the outer physical world.

Such a diagram obviously has as many faults as a word-picture of a theory. It is over-simplified and maps the territory about as an oil engineer's map of Colorado shows what the Rocky Mountains are like. But it does try to represent the most developed points of Jung's philosophical thinking in a form that shows where to look for significant data. With some supplemental designations, it also suggests quite clearly the implications of Jung's thinking for philosophy and theology.

If Jung has mapped the territory correctly, then man is indeed in touch with complex realities which he cannot handle physically, which can only be known as men have the courage to encounter this other realm and try to understand and be understood by it. In fact, Jung's thinking can provide a philosophical base for a modern, experiental theology just as Plato's world view provided such a framework for the church fathers to express their Christian experiences. This Platonic base lasted for the first twelve centuries in the West and is still the basis of Eastern Orthodox thinking.

Religious people in all ages and among all peoples have spoken of a 'spiritual world' apart from the physical world. As one of the greatest modern physicists, Werner Heisenberg, has reminded us, words like these which come from the natural language express a more direct connection with reality than even the most precise abstractions of science.[10] Since Jung's evidence also shows that there is such a realm in which men have come into contact with a meaning superior to human consciousness, it appears that the idea of God is not metaphysical speculation, but rather the name which religious people have applied to their experience of such a reality. From Jung's world view the religious undertaking and the religious object are not only potentially meaningful, but necessary if man is to survive. Jung has laid the foundation and empirical theologians can build upon that base.

Two of Jung's own statements, late in his work, clearly point out what we have sketched. In the first he wrote:

I have, therefore, even hazarded the postulate that. the phenomenon of archetypal configurations – which are psychic events *par excellence* – may be founded upon a *psychoid* base, that is, upon an only partially psychic and possibly altogether different form of being. For lack of empirical data I have neither knowledge nor understanding of such forms of being, which are commonly called spiritual. From the point of view of science, it is immaterial what I may *believe* on that score, and I must accept my ignorance . . . Nevertheless, we have good reason to suppose that behind this veil there exists the uncomprehended absolute object which affects and influences us – and to suppose it even, or particularly, in the case of psychic phenomena about which no verifiable statements can be made.[11]

The second remark, made by Jung in his British Broadcasting Corporation interview, is also too well known to be repeated, but it crystallizes all the other ways he tried to put this over: 'Suddenly I understood that God was, for me at least, one of the most certain and immediate experiences . . . I do not believe; I know. I *know*.' Philosophically Jung presents a consistent pragmatic realism within a phenomenological base which can deal with religious experience.

Jung also suggested that empirical theologians take the problem of evil more seriously. His experience made him balk at the Aristotelian position that evil is only the absence or deprivation of good, the *privatio boni* – with good naturally belonging to man – and so he had to meet this problem directly. He dealt with it as creatively as any one in our time, and set the stage for further theological encounter.

He would have agreed with the author of Ephesians: 'For our fight is not against human foes, but . . . against the superhuman forces of evil in the heavens.'[12] Man has to wrestle with darkness to find out its nature, and then either integrate or reject it. Jung believed that the doctrine of the *privatio boni*, first laid down for the church by Augustine and later developed by Aquinas, crippled man in this struggle. It deceived man about the seriousness of his struggle. 'The growing awareness of the inferior part of the personality,' Jung wrote, 'should not be twisted into an intellectual activity, for it has far more the meaning of a suffering and a passion that implicate the whole man.'[13] Dealing with unconscious contents or with God can be a painful process, a *via crucis*, which most men will avoid at any cost. This emphasis on creative suffering has much in common with the teaching of Jesus of Nazareth.

There is another very important element, if anything the crucial element. This process of dealing with the unconscious, or the spiritual world, is not a process characterized by detachment and lack of personal involvement. One does not get far by detached objectivity. Nor does one need worry about God's being reduced in stature by familiarity. Furthermore, this encounter is seldom possible outside of a deep concern for another person involved in the same encounter.

In one of the concluding paragraphs of his autobiography, Jung all but stated that only as one gives in to love can he know the way of wholeness, and thus the reality of the Self, or of God. Love for Jung was as much the powerful, revealing daemon as it was for Plato. For most people the process of coming to creative relationship with the unconscious involves the whole person in contact with another human being. The process of integration requires and results in deepened human relationships. John put it well in his first letter in the New Testament when he said that no man could love God who did not love his brother. Allowing one's self to have this kind of relationship is a costing experience. Often, if one is capable of it, he will find himself deluged, because men hunger so for this kind of reality. He will also find more material for theological examination than he can integrate and develop in less than a lifetime. The time is ripe for philosophers and theologians to take up the task which Jung has made possible and shown is necessary for modern man.

CHAPTER 12

Jung and Religion:
A Theological Assessment

BY JOHN W. DE GRUCHY

James Heisig commences his bibliographical essay 'Jung and Theology' with the comment: 'It would, I think, be fair to characterize the present state of scholarly relations between Jungian psychology and theology as chaotic.'[1] Heisig amply demonstrates his opinion, and his essay also serves as a comprehensive introduction to the literature up to 1973. Moreover, he confirms the general impression one has that after an initial period of considerable antipathy, the thought of Carl Jung has gained the positive attention and interest of a growing number of Christian theologians, historians of religion, and pastoral psychologists. Since 1973 this trend has continued, and it is now not uncommon to find ample reference to Jungian ideas in contemporary textbooks on Christian theology and psychology.[2-4] References naturally abound in the literature of the more esoteric religious traditions, or on subjects such as mysticism.

At the same time there remains an ambivalence to Jung's understanding of religion even amongst those who respond most favourably to his ideas. Theologians remain cautious. This wariness derives largely from Jung's highly original interpretation of religion in general and Christianity in particular. An interpretation which is based not only on the great religious traditions of the East and West, but also on his own investigations into such subjects as alchemy and his study of the dreams of his patients as well as his own. It is not just that Jung attacks the sterility of much that passes for Christian orthodoxy, or that he expresses dissatisfaction with some traditional dogmas such as the Trinity, but that he appears to accept a vast array of seemingly disparate religious ideas without too much critical discernment. His handling of biblical texts, for example, would make most, if not all exegetes' hair stand on end, a not inappropriate metaphor for what he writes in his *Answer to Job*, where he also openly acknowledges his approach:

I shall not give a cool and carefully considered exegesis that tries to be fair to every detail, but a purely subjective reaction. In this way I hope to act as a voice for many who feel the same as I do, and to give expression to the shattering emotion which the unvarnished spectacle of divine savagery and ruthlessness produces in us.[5]

In fairness to Jung it must be recognised at the outset that he did not claim to be either a theologian or a metaphysician, nor, as we have seen did he suggest that he was approaching religious traditions according to the accepted canons of scientific theological enquiry. Jung was a therapist. His concern was the cure of souls not the satisfaction of eminent divines. This does not mean that Jung regarded his work as unscientific. His attack on the rationalism of much Christianity did not mean that he rejected reason as a tool of paramount importance in his investigations. On the contrary, in *The Secret of the Golden Flower* he explicitly acknowledges that 'science is the tool of the Western mind, and with it one can open more doors than with bare hands . . . it obscures our insight only when it claims that the understanding it conveys is the only kind there is.'[6] Jung certainly felt an affinity with the intuitive approach to knowledge characteristic of the East and the mystic, but he also regarded it as a mistake when Western man 'turns his back on science and, carried away by Eastern occultism' becomes a 'pitiable imitator'. Theosophy, he wrote, 'is our best example of this'.

Whether or not Jung finally satisfies the Christian theologian, there can be little doubt that he does disturb and challenge the complacent interpreter of the tradition. What the theologian has to avoid is missing Jung's point because of the way in which Jung expresses himself. In one sense the theologian and the psychologist are playing different language games, just as they are approaching reality from different perspectives. Because the same word does not necessarily mean the same thing to both parties, they can easily misunderstand each other. At the very least, the theologian must try to penetrate beneath Jung's expressions to see what he is in fact getting at. Only then can he discover insights that may be of theological significance, and only then may he express his critical reservations. In this short essay I will outline what I regard as of the essence of Jung's understanding of religion, and then offer a brief theological critique of the major issues that have been raised by theologians in responding to his thought. In doing so, it will become evident that I am a critical admirer of Jung's remarkable contribution to the psychology of religion, and to religious thought as a whole, but remain a theologian committed to the mainstream of the Christian tradition.

1. Jung and Religion

While still at school, and shortly after his confirmation in the Swiss Reformed Church of which his father was a pastor, Jung experienced a great emptiness in his life. 'For God's sake I now found myself cut off from the Church and from my father's and everybody else's faith. Insofar as they all represented the Christian religion, I was an outsider. This knowledge filled me with a sadness which was to overshadow all the years until the time I entered the University.'[7] It will be recalled that the reason for this sadness was that the young Jung found a vast gulf between the somewhat sterile teaching of the catechism, and his 'secret', or, what he later referred to as an experience of the 'numinosum'. For Jung, the dogmas of conventional Protestantism as they had been explained to him were empty of that very *mysterium* which he regarded as the *sine qua non* of religion. Many years afterwards, after he had modified his views on both Christianity and dogma, Jung defined religion as that which 'designates the attitude peculiar to a consciousness which has been altered by the experience of the numinosum'.[5] Moreover, by then he had broken with Sigmund Freud and concluded that just as this experience of the 'numinous' was of the essence of religion, so religion itself is of the essence of life. Man cannot live without gods – or demons!

Jung's early disenchantment with Protestantism as he had then experienced it, and his later affirmation of 'a *positive* Christianity, which is as much Catholic as it is Protestant',[8] indicate that he did not regard all religion as good and helpful. In rejecting Freud's wholly negative attitude towards religion, Jung was not suggesting that all forms of religion are unharmful. On the contrary, Jung makes the clear distinction between true religion in and through which the 'numinous' is experienced, and degenerate religion 'corrupted by worldliness and mob instincts'.[5]

'Worldly religion' is religion which has lost touch with the living mystery at the heart of all reality, and, 'it is readily understandable,' says Jung, 'that such a religion is incapable of giving help or having any other moral effect'. Indeed, the tragedy of 'worldly religion' goes far beyond its failure to help the individual discover meaning and healing, it affects society at large. It produces a cultural and spiritual malaise, a vacuum, in which ersatz religion with its mob instincts flourishes.

By the end of the nineteenth century much Protestant religion in Europe had succumbed to rationalism, moralism or pseudo-pietism. For Karl Barth, Jung's great theological contemporary and fellow-countryman, Protestantism had lost its sense of the divine mystery, the 'wholly other', or what Rudolf Otto called the 'mysterium tremendum'.[9,10] It was impotent to deal with the crisis that shattered European Christendom in 1914–18. Human optimism and confidence in man's inherent rationality and goodness had replaced a sense of awe and humility before the divine reality. It was precisely this that Jung had encountered earlier on in his own personal experience. And the emptiness of the religion he was taught in his confirmation class not only affected sensitive people such as he, it affected the whole life of society. Writing in 1937 while Nazi tyranny was driving Europe once again to the brink of war, Jung declared:

> The catastrophe of the first World War and the extraordinary manifestations of profound spiritual malaise that came afterwards were needed to arouse a doubt as to whether all was well with the white man's mind. Before the war broke out in 1914 we were all quite certain that the world could be righted by rational means. Now we behold the amazing spectacle of states taking over the age-old totalitarian claims of theocracy, which are inevitably accompanied by suppression of free opinion . . . It is not very difficult to see that the powers of the underworld – not to say of hell – which in former times were more or less successfully chained up in a gigantic spiritual edifice where they could be of some use, are now creating, or trying to create, a State slavery, and a State prison devoid of any mental or spiritual charm.[5]

These words have not lost any of their significance for us in our time. And it is important to bear this in mind in evaluating Jung's contribution to religious thought. His contribution is by no means confined to the area of individual therapy. On the contrary, his profound insight into what he described as the 'collective unconscious' of the human race, has enabled us to understand better the impersonal forces, the demons, which lurk deep in man's unconscious erupting again and again in irrational deeds done en masse. It was religion, false religion, that crucified Jesus, burnt witches, and created Auschwitz. So Jung gives us some important clues for understanding why apparently good religious people can, and do, perpetrate ghastly crimes against their fellows. There are 'beasts or demons that lie dormant in every person until he is part of a mob'. At this point, we are not very far from what St Paul labelled 'the principalities and powers of this passing age', those sinister, irrational forces in the human underworld which attack and undermine even the structures created for human good in the world (see Caird[11]).

According to Jung, the problem with Christianity in the West, since the demise of the 'gigantic spiritual edifice' the Middle Ages, is that the experience of the god-image in Christ has remained superficial:

> Christian civilization has proved hollow to a terrifying degree: it is all veneer, but the inner man has remained untouched and therefore unchanged . . . Inside reign the archaic gods, supreme as of old . . . Too few people have experienced the divine image as the innermost possession of their own souls. Christ only meets them from without, never from within the soul; that is why dark paganism still reigns there, a paganism which, now in a form so blatant that it can no longer be denied and now in all too threadbare disguise, is swamping the world of so-called Christian culture.[12]

In other words, the cultural crisis in the West as Jung saw it, is a religious crisis. Genuine religion and religious experience has largely departed, with the result that false religion flourishes. His solution, whether for the individual person or society at large, was a rediscovery of the integrating power of true religion, a fresh experience of the 'numinous'. 'Freud', wrote Jung, 'has unfortunately overlooked the fact that man has never been able singlehanded to hold his own against the powers of darkness – that is, of the unconscious. Man has always stood in need of spiritual help which each individual's own religion held out to him.'[13] Or, as he wrote in his *Answer to Job*:

Everything now depends on man: immense power of destruction is given into his hand, and the question is whether he can resist the will to use it, and can temper his will in the spirit of love and wisdom. *He will hardly be capable of doing so on his own unaided resources.* He needs the help of an 'advocate' in heaven, that is, of the child who was caught up to God and who brings the 'healing' and making whole of the hitherto fragmentary man.[5]

Having reflected on the cultural dimension of religion let us shift our focus to the personal. In doing so, however, we must not lose sight of the fact that for Jung the personal and the social belong together. The religious crisis in Western culture is integrally related to the spiritual crisis of the individual Westerner, who, according to Jung, has been left without help by the Church. This was Jung's own experience. And as he sought to heal his patients he became aware 'that every one of them fell ill because he had lost that which the living religions of every age have given their followers, and none of them has been really healed who did not regain his religious outlook'.[13] Which point brings us to the role of religion in the process of individuation.

The process of individuation, or Self-realization, is the process by which healing takes place through the re-integration of the person around a new centre, the Self. A crucial part of this process is the recognition of the dark side of our personality, our shadow, our own netherworld, not as something to be shunned, but as something full of potential which needs to be reconciled with the rest of the psyche in order for it to become creative and not remain destructive. Jolande Jacobi expressed this well in *The Way of Individuation*:

Man must become relentlessly aware of the potentiality for good and evil within him, taking care not to think that the one is real and the other illusory. Both are true as possibilities in him. He cannot completely escape from either if, as he should from the outset, he lives his life without self-deception.[14]

And again, this time from her book *The Psychology of C.G. Jung*,

Only as we learn to distinguish ourselves from our shadow by recognising its reality as part of our nature, and only if we keep this insight persistently in mind, can our confrontation with the other pairs of the psychic opposites be successful. For this is the beginning of the objective attitude toward our own personality without which no progress can be made along the path of wholeness.[15]

It is at this point that we begin to see the crucial role which religion places in making people whole.

In his researches into the symbols and images which his patients revealed in their dreams, fantasies and so forth, Jung continually came up against what he called 'reconciling symbols'. That is, symbols which point to the wholeness of the personality. There is, he maintained, a movement within each of us toward completion and perfection (*telos*), and it is this *telos* or goal that is represented by the Self. Thus, Self-realization is not ego–fulfilment, but the creation of a new personality through the discovery of a new centre, the Self, in and through which both the conscious and the unconscious as well as the opposing elements and forces in the personality are reconciled in a new creative synthesis. Religion enables us to give expression to the archetypes of the unconscious, both personal and collective, and thereby provides the resources by which we can know ourselves and especially the hidden conflicts within us. But it does more, it provides the reconciling symbols, the symbols of the Self.

The more Jung studied the material that emerged in the dreams of his patients, the more he became aware of the correspondence between their images and the symbols of the great religious traditions, and the more he studied the latter the more convinced he became of the correlation. This was, perhaps, his greatest contribution to religious knowledge. To quote R.C. Zaehner:

Jung. . .has illumined so much that was dark before that we would do well to reconsider some of his leading ideas as seen against the background of Christian and other theologies. According to him the God–archetype dwells deep down in the unconscious, and is liable to come to the surface in various symbolic forms. Now, this is precisely what all higher religions, in so far as they are theistic, also assert.[16]

Although Jung had his roots in Western Christianity and rational enquiry, he was profoundly influenced by Eastern religious thought and mysticism. For example, his idea of the Self as not only the centre of the personality but also its circumference, is similar to the Upanishadic teaching on the unity between Brahman and Atman. And the Mandala, which is so central to Eastern religion, is, for Jung, the symbol that most clearly reveals man's search for wholeness. It is not just a focus for contemplation, it is the ultimate expression of the Self.[7] Related to the Mandala is the symbol of quarternity. Jung maintains that this is an improvement on the symbol of the Trinity because it includes evil as part of ultimate reality. Without this, goodness could not have any substance.[5] This is very close to certain Eastern interpretations of God. In Hinduism, for example, the dark forces, what are regarded as evil and symbolized by the Devil in Christianity, are included in the 'Godhead' rather than being rejected as outcasts or as the absence of the good (*privatio boni*). Understandably, then, Jung's religious insights have often been regarded as much more akin to the East than the West, and more illuminating for Oriental religion than the Judaeo-Christian tradition.

Yet this is not the total picture, for whereas the Buddha is the symbol of the Self in the East, Christ fulfills the same role in the West. Traditionally, until the rise of secularization, Christ was at the centre of the Western Mandala, as seen, for example in the great rose-windows in European cathedrals. 'He', wrote Jung, 'is our culture hero, who, regardless of his historical existence, embodies the myth of the Primordial Man, the mystic Adam.'[17] Jung clearly attaches little importance to the historical Jesus compared with the significance he places on the living and immediate presence of the Christ archetype in the unconscious experience of the West. It is the mythical Christ who is the perfect man (*teliosios anthropos*), he is that to which the ego strives in searching for healing. So Jung refers to the words of St Paul: 'I live, yet not I, but Christ lives in me' as an expression of the journey to Self-realization. But whether the symbol for the Self is Christ, Buddha or Brahman, apparently does not matter. What is crucial is that man should experience this god-image in himself: 'and feel its correspondence with the forms that his religion gives to it. If this does not happen there is a split in his nature; he may be outwardly civilized, but inwardly he is a barbarian ruled by an archaic god.' (Fordham[18]; and see also Jung[7]).

2. Theological Assessment

Heisig's summary of H.M.M. Fortmann's study[19] on religion in Marx, Freud and Jung provides us with an appropriate point of departure. Fortmann, Heisig writes, 'considers Jung to have given us the best psychology of religion to date: full of brilliant questions and untenable answers!'[1] So let us consider some of the questions which Jung's treatment of religion causes theology to consider afresh and see if his answers are untenable from a Judaeo-Christian perspective.

Jung's sincerity with regard to the importance and role of religion cannot be questioned, and we are indebted to him for reminding us of the integral relationship between religion and the mental health of both individuals and society. Further, we would not dare to doubt the reality for him of his own religious experience, his claim to *know* God, and his assertion that he has nowhere denied God (see White[8]). And certainly, his research has made a significant and distinctive contribution to the study of religion, and thereby to theological reflection. Nevertheless his contribution to Christian theology is ambivalent because in spite of his positive attitude towards religion, and in spite of his pleas to the contrary, taken without critical reservation his views undermine the foundations of the Judaeo-Christian tradition. Of course, some may well respond by saying, if that is so, let it be so! We just do not think, however, that the foundations can be so easily shattered.

One of the more helpful recent attempts to relate theology and phenomenology in a way which also embodies some of Jung's key insights, is Jennings' *Introduction to Theology: An Invitation to Reflection upon the Christian Mythos*.[2] Jennings maintains that 'the practical and irreplaceable function of the image or symbol is that it provides the only access to reality'. He further maintains, along with Jung, that symbols can become destructive, they can be 'imposed by the rulers who now manipulate these images to their own ends or as imposed by the dead hand of the past whose cadaverous representatives exercise authority amidst the order of sanctity and decay'. Jennings is not saying anything new, but we quote him as an illustration of the fact that Jung has been largely responsible for helping us to see the importance and power of symbols and myths, not just as something of significance for primitive man (see Frankfort[20]), but as much if not more significant for modern man. Jung has dramatically reminded us that man cannot live and find meaning without myths. And this is so important, that if man does not have proper access to the great religious myths then he will create his own, and will invariably let loose a myriad of demons in the process.

Many Christians react negatively to the word 'myth' because of its popular misuse, and, unfortunately the way in which Jung separates the Jesus of history from the Christ-symbol, or vice-versa, is open to serious question. Indeed, Jung seems to be oblivious of the fact that for most of the nineteenth century theologians wrestled with this issue, and that the only meaningful resolution to the problem which makes sense of the data is to assert that the 'Christ of faith is the Jesus of history' (see, for example, Neill[21]). Jung is, or so it would appear, notoriously cavalier in his treatment of history, and this is particularly so in his handling of the historical foundations of Christian faith. The Christ-symbol is reduced to an unbiblical gnostic myth the moment it is separated from Jesus the Jew of Nazareth and his proclamation of the Kingdom of God, and is no longer recognizably Christian.

Having lodged our protest, however, we can still respond positively to Jung's insistence on the importance of myth, for genuine myth can arise out of historical event and experience. Thus, as Mircea Eliade, one of the great contemporary historians of religion reminds us, Jesus Christ is no mythical person but the fact that the Christian participates in his death and resurrection *now* is essentially and correctly 'mythical behaviour'.[22] To a highly dangerous degree modern man has lost his anchorage because a psuedo-rationalism has severed the connection between him and those myths and symbols that give meaning to life. We are indebted to Jung for helping to awaken us to this danger of secularization and the personal and social havoc it has caused. At the same time, the Christian theologian insists that the 'truth claims' of mythology must stand the test of historical and rational enquiry else, like those of Nazism, they can and often do become demonic. The task of the theologian is not to reject myth as such but to subject all myths to critical reflection.

The Christian theologian must readily concede that Jung has made an important contribution to our struggling with the problem of evil. For the classical Augustinian tradition, which lies behind both Catholic and Protestant orthodoxy, evil is the absence of the good, i.e. *privatio boni*. However, as John Hick has shown, this solution to the problem has serious deficiencies,[23,24] and Jung has helped us to re-examine the possibility that evil is not merely the absence of good but the dynamic presence of a power that must be taken more seriously than has been our custom since the Enlightenment. However, and unfortunately from a Judaeo-Christian perspective, Jung goes much further and develops a dualistic understanding of God in which both good and evil co-exist. Here he is a latter day Manichaean, or a Hindu, but certainly not a Christian. God, for Jung, is no longer wholly good, he includes Satan or Shakti within himself.[8] Having posited this for God, Jung then proceeds to do the same for man. Zaehner sums up:

The 'dark, feminine', instinctive side of human nature is what we have inherited from the animals; it is neither good nor evil, but has, as Jung has demonstrated, great potentialities for both. That it must be integrated into the total psyche, few will deny; but to equate it with moral evil or the Devil, and then to assert that evil as such has to be integrated into the whole psyche, shows a certain confusion of thought.[16]

Nevertheless, Jung has rightly reminded us that the material, instinctive, non-rational and intuitive sides of our nature, must be given their proper place if the psyche is to be integrated.

Jung's empirical investigations have not only show that religion is man's most important instinct, but they have also gone further and suggested a basic correspondence between the symbols of Christianity and the needs of the unconscious. In other words, Jung is saying that what Western man deeply needs, Christianity profoundly supplies. In these days of rampant religious pluralism in the West, and also the East, one may wonder, of course, why some Westerners are attracted to Buddha as the symbol of the Self, and why some Easterners to Christ.

In speaking about Christ as the symbol of the Self, and in his use of the phrase *imago dei*, Jung has been criticized for equating the psychic totality, Self, with a purely immanent God. Jung rejects this criticism by saying that the Self can never take the place of God, although it may be a receptacle for divine grace. The Self represents a purely human wholeness. What Jung is talking about is the *image* of God in man. He writes:

It is impossible for *psychology* to establish the difference between the image of God (or the Self) and God himself (i.e. in reality, not merely conceptually). For even the concept of the Self indicates something transcendental; and empirical science is incapable of making positive statements about it. So great is the 'numinousnes' in our experience of the Self, that it is only too easy to experience the manifestation of the Self as a manifestation of God. It is not possible to distinguish between Symbols of God and symbols of the Self, i.e. it is not possible to *observe* the distinction empirically.

He added characteristically, 'I cannot help this being so; I mean that the manifestation of the Self should have this God-like character. I did not make it so' (see also White[8]). As long as Christians do not misuse this insight through questionable apologetics (e.g. that there is some kind of 'God-gap' in everyman), or begin to think in terms of the divinization of man as the way of redemption, it is a suggestive and helpful one. In this connection, it should be noted that while for Jung the symbols and dogmas of Christianity seem to originate from the deep unconscious needs of the human psyche, for the Christian theologian they arise on the level of consciousness, that is through man's response to revelation within historical contexts. For the Christian this gives them their validity, a validity which is then tested by experience. However, the fact that Jung as a psychologist should approach the subject from a different starting-point does not mean that there is no connection between the two approaches, even though there is a difference of description, emphasis, and basis for what is said.

Another problem which the theologian has in responding to Jung's understanding of religion arises from the huge amount of empirical material which he has unearthed, data which is not only unique but almost too enormous to evaluate. He has made what Antonio Moreno calls 'a priceless contribution to the phenomenology of religion'.[25] The problem is not the amount of data, however, it is the manner in which Jung uses this material. Again and again he appears to be indiscriminate in the choice of his sources which he uses to substantiate his ideas – alchemy, gnosticism and tantrism, to mention but a few of the most important. Furthermore, he tends to use his sources eclectically and uncritically in order to serve his own hypotheses. This does not necessarily mean that his insights are invalid, but that the theologian has his time cut out trying to sift the wheat from the chaff. For example, to quote Zaehner, 'even if we are prepared to admit the truth of Jung's explanation of the *Hieros Gamos* in pagan religions, alchemy and tantrism, it is doubtful whether there is any validity in his transference of this myth to the mythical nuptials of the Christian soul with Christ', as we find in the great Christian mystics. [16]

It would have been much easier to approach Jung simply from the perspective of religion in general, or perhaps from the perspective of Eastern religious experience or mysticism. But we have chosen to speak out of the circle of Christian commitment while being open to the insights and truths of other traditions. Perhaps the major difficulty that a Christian theologian has with Jung is that, in spite of his disclaimer to the contrary, he does move beyond empirical investigation, where he is an authority in his own right, to theological speculation, where he claims no special training or skill. But we are glad that he did so, because his intuitive awareness has been of immense value in providing insight not only for the poet and writer, but also the theologian. Thus, we affirm as strongly as possible what he wrote in *Modern Man in Search of a Soul*, and what he reiterated at the end of that memorable TV interview with John Freeman, that man cannot live without meaning, and agree with him that much contemporary as well as traditional religion and philosophy is impotent in providing such meaning for modern man. Jung's great contribution from our perspective is therefore the challenge which he has presented and the insights he has offered to theology in the interests of the re-birth of a religious experience that does provide that meaning without which we cannot live and without which we will continue to destroy not only ourselves but also our world.

CHAPTER 13

Fantasy versus Fiction:
Jung's Kantianism Appraised

BY STEPHANIE DE VOOGD

If, as certain modern points of view, too, would have it, the
psychic system coincides and is identical with our
conscious mind, then, in principle, we are in a position to know
everything that is capable of being known, i.e., everything that
lies within the limits of the theory of knowledge. C.G. Jung[1]

How baffling it was to come upon the above sentence for the first time! I had only just begun to read Jung and did not know very much about him and his work. My field was (and is) philosophy and here was a psychologist who spoke of *the* theory of knowledge. I remember drawing a largish question mark in the margin and chewing on my pencil for a while as I wondered which theory of knowledge was meant and why it was spoken of as though no other such theory existed or needed to be taken seriously.

That was quite a few years ago. Since that time I have read and pondered Jung's work more or less continuously. One tiny result of this activity is that I now know Jung had Immanuel Kant's epistemology in mind whenever he spoke of *the* theory of knowledge. Another, perhaps not so tiny result concerns that very identification: I believe Jung's Kantianism to be both self-contradictory and self-defeating and I shall here try to justify my belief. In so doing I shall assume a reader who is familiar with Jung's work but not necessarily with Kant's epistemology. A reader, perhaps, who has wondered from time to time about Jung's many references to, and unquestioning reliance upon, Kant but who has never really known what to think of or do with either. Such a reader deserves to be given fair warning. The full version of Kant's theory of knowledge is to be found in his *Critique of Pure Reason* (published in 1781); a shorter version, which appeared two years later, is entitled *Prolegomena*. Both books (but especially the lengthy *Critique*) are extremely complicated in terms of content and very nearly inaccessible in terms of style. My exposition of Kant's theory will necessarily be far from complete but then my purpose here is not that of explaining the theory in all its details and ramifications but of showing, first, on which part(s) of it Jung relied and, second, why I think Jung was mistaken in so doing.

Thought, including what is called 'seminal' thought such as that produced by Kant, never selects its topics at random. There is always a context and the case of Kant is no exception. The *Critique of Pure Reason* takes up issues raised by Descartes, Newton, Leibniz and Hume, as follows. Descartes had been agonized by the question how he could be sure that the world 'out there' and his own body were real and not just his hallucinations. His own answer to that question had been that the world and his body were God's creation, that God was infinitely good and so could not possibly be constantly deceiving us. Newton and Leibniz quarreled about the ontological status of space. (I observe in parentheses that when philosophers inquire into the ontological status of something they do not do very much more than ask what that something *is*. I would have avoided the phrase if it were not for the fact that I shall have to speak of ontology – a term which can be paraphrased only at the cost of brevity – further on. There is nothing like being prepared.) Newton said space was that in which everything is contained, such that if everything in space somehow disappeared empty space would remain. Leibniz said space was nothing but spatial relations abstracted into the notion of space, such that if all spatial relations somehow disappeared nothing space-like would remain. In each of these instances – that of Descartes, Newton and Leibniz – Kant thought the question appropriate but disapproved of the answer. We shall come back to all this but must first spend some time with David Hume, said by Kant to have 'awakened me from my dogmatic slumber'.[2]

'In all the history of metaphysics, no attack on that science has been more decisive than the one launched by David Hume', writes Kant[3]. It is this attack which awakened Kant from his dogmatic slumber and which now requires our attention. To ask here what Kant meant by the term 'metaphysics' in the sentence just quoted is to invite me to tell the story the wrong way around. In the interest of the reader I decline that invitation. The metaphysics that Hume attacked is not the metaphysics that Kant developed and defended: so much and no more needs to be said now.

In Hume's case worrying about metaphysics chiefly meant worrying about causality. His puzzle was this: (1) The connecting of events in terms of cause and effect is of a *necessary* character inasmuch as the designation of one event A as cause necessarily entails the designation of another event B as effect; (2) however, this connecting of events in terms of cause and effect is not something experience has taught us (since no one has ever observed a cause) but, on the contrary, something in the nature of *a priori* knowledge which human reason somehow possesses and *imposes on* experience (or so, Hume said, metaphysicians would have us believe); (3) yet in that case we must face the fact that it is only the *notion* of cause which implies only the *notion* of effect: but how do we know that what is true of notions in our heads applies as well to actual events designated by such notions? How do we know that, or whether, the existence of certain events (which we call causes) necessarily entails the existence of certain events (which we call effects)? (4) To those who would turn the tables on me (so Hume continued) by asking whether I should prefer to abandon the notion of cause altogether since I seem to doubt its validity or usefulness I reply that I do not question either the notion itself or its validity or usefulness: I question its origin and status. For if the notion of cause is an *a priori* or 'advance' product of human reason, that is, if it is something human reason has produced apart from and in that sense 'ahead of' experience then how does that same reason know that its product *applies to* experience? Then again, if (as I believe) experience offers us only what I call the 'constant conjunction' of certain events (the heating of water and its coming to a boil, say) such that by force of habit we have come to think and speak of them in terms of cause and effect then we must realize that causality is in truth a subjective and *a posteriori* notion falsely labeled objective and *a priori*[4].

'And from this Hume concluded' (writes Kant) 'that all the allegedly *a priori* knowledge produced by reason was in truth nothing but falsely labeled ordinary experience, which was tantamount to saying that metaphysics did not and could not exist.'[5] We shall come back to this point but what, meanwhile, are we to make of this strange thing called *a priori* knowledge? In its widest sense it is knowledge whose truth or falsity is not decided by experience. Compare the propositions 'it is raining' and Kant's own example 'gold is a yellow metal'.[5a] To determine whether the first proposition is true or false you must go outside or at least look out the window. It is only *after* you have done so that you can tell whether the proposition is true or false. 'After' is the key-word here for it translates the Latin *a posteriori*. It is otherwise with the second proposition which tells you nothing about gold (that it is valuable for instance, or sturdy) except *what* it is, how it is defined. Such a proposition is a piece of *a priori* knowledge since it does not concern actual-gold-out-there and the range of its properties but only the definition of gold.

So much for the distinction between *a priori* and *a posteriori* knowledge. A further distinction is that between analytic and synthetic knowledge. Consider the propositions 'gold is heavy' and 'gold is a yellow metal'. The first of these is synthetic, the second analytic. 'Synthetic' literally means 'putting together', 'combining'; in the proposition 'gold is heavy' the notion of heaviness (which is not part of the definition of gold) is put together, combined with the notion of gold, and the result is the synthetic knowledge that gold is heavy. The second proposition, 'gold is a yellow metal', does not combine notions that do not belong together in and of themselves. It merely breaks up, analyzes the notion of gold into the constituent parts 'yellow' and 'metal' that together form its definition.

The reader who wonders at this point whether it would not be sufficient to distinguish between propositions in terms of either *a priori/a posteriori* or analytic/synthetic (since the two distinctions appear to differ only in name) is a reader who is wrong for the right reasons: he or she has understood what has been said so far and fails to take into account only what is yet to come. Note that an analytic proposition is one which is always *necessarily* true or *necessarily* false, that is, it is always either a tautology or a contradiction. If it is a tautology then it is a proposition in which the predicate states explicitly what is implicit in the subject ('gold is a yellow metal'; 'a circle is round'); if it is a contradiction then it is a proposition in which the predicate explicitly negates what is implicitly affirmed in the subject ('gold is not a yellow metal'; 'a circle is not round'). A synthetic proposition on the other hand is always *contingently* true or *contingently* false since it 'puts together' or combines (as subjects and predicates) notions which do not go together in and of themselves so that only contingent experience can tell whether what is combined in words is also combined in fact.

We are now ready for two crucial questions: is all *a priori* knowledge analytic, and is all synthetic knowledge *a posteriori*? (That all analytic knowledge is *a priori* and all *a posteriori* knowledge synthetic is obvious but whether the converse holds is another, indeed *the* other matter.) Hume's answer to both questions was positive and we may now paraphrase his attack on metaphysics as follows. To say that the *notion* of cause necessarily implies the *notion* of effect is very different from saying that an event B occurs necessarily whenever an event A occurs contingently. Yet when we designate the contingent event A as cause we *eo ipso* designate B as a necessary event. I fail to see what right we have to do this. Indeed it seems to me we must make up our minds: *either* the proposition 'There are no causes without effects' is analytic and in that case it does nothing but define the notion of cause, leaving aside the question as to whether that notion has a real counterpart in experience; *or* the proposition is synthetic and in that case it should be replaced by the proposition 'There exists such a thing as the "constant conjunction" of events but this is a contingent datum of experience'.

Now as Kant pointed out (see above) 'Hume concluded from this that all the allegedly *a priori* knowledge produced by reason' was in fact synthetic and hence *a posteriori*. However, the phrase 'all *a priori* knowledge' now turns out to be misleading. Hume was not saying that all knowledge which claims to be both *a priori* and analytic is in fact synthetic and *a posteriori*: that would have been a flat contradiction. He was saying that knowledge which claims to be both *a priori* and synthetic is impossible since all such knowledge is open to objections of the sort he raised in connection with causality. And since the science of metaphysics worked with nothing but synthetic *a priori* propositions it followed that metaphysics was doomed unless someone were able effectively to counter Hume's criticism. Luckily (if only for the story of metaphysics which would otherwise have ended) someone was: Immanuel Kant, 1724-1804, small, frail, bulging blue eyes in an outsized head – Jung's thinking function personified.

His dogmatic slumber a thing of the past, Kant noted two things: that Hume had made an excellent point, and that he had to be wrong. Why did he have to be wrong? Because, for one thing, if he were right then not only metaphysics but mathematics, too, would be at an end, the propositions of mathematics being (according to Kant) without exception synthetic as well as *a priori*. This last point was controversial (it still is) as Kant was well aware. In a passage on the subject he writes that:

The analysts of human reason have so far missed this point entirely, and why? Because, seeing that mathematical reasoning *never violates* the principle of non-contradiction, they have concluded that the axioms of mathematics *arise from* that principle – and here they have been thoroughly mistaken.[6]

Here an explanatory word is in order. The principle of non-contradiction says that any proposition which affirms what it denies or denies what it affirms is formally at fault and therefore necessarily false under any and all circumstances. Conversely, the same principle turns any proposition which affirms what it affirms or denies what it denies into a tautology, that is, a proposition which by virtue of its form is true under any and all circumstances. All analytic propositions thus come under the exclusive sway of the principle of non-contradiction, which is the same as saying that they are either tautologies (necessarily true) or contradictions (necessarily false). Now the propositions of mathematics are also necessarily true or necessarily false and they are furthermore *a priori* but, says Kant, they are not for that reason analytic. His famous example[7] is the arithmetical proposition '7 + 5 = 12', not to be confused with '7 + 5 = the sum of 7 and 5'. The latter proposition is indeed analytic but the *concept of* the sum of 7 and 5 is by no means identical with the number which *is* that sum. If it were we should never have any difficulty pinpointing the sum of any two numbers, 3475 and 8173 for example, but the fact is that when the numbers to be added are of this order we resort to pencil and paper to 'construct' or 'synthesize' their sum.[8] Examples from Euclidean geometry illustrating the same point will be given below.

Yet it is one thing to deny or question the possibility of synthetic *a priori* propositions as such and another to deny or question their applicability in cognitive experience. Had Hume done only the latter Kant would have been quick to point out to him that the application of mathematics in the cognitive experience called physics is a fact. As it happened, Kant pointed it out to himself. And while he was at it he pointed out something else to himself as well: that the science of physics employs principles – such as that every event has a cause, or that matter is quantitatively constant – which are not mathematical but nevertheless synthetic as well as *a priori*. Indeed it was these principles which caused the physicist to approach nature 'not in the manner of a pupil who lets the teacher fill his head with whatever strikes the teacher's fancy, but rather in the manner of a judge who invites witnesses to answer the questions he puts to them'.[9] To put it another way, physics was not just a heap of haphazardly acquired and hence chaotic knowledge concerning the physical world: physics was systematic knowledge systematically acquired, that is, it was knowledge whose acquisition was governed by a set of synthetic *a priori* principles plus the synthetic *a priori* truths of mathematics. And, last but not least, physics worked in the sense that its theories yielded practical results. Now if synthetic *a priori* knowledge worked in physics, why did it not work in metaphysics? Why was metaphysics forever at odds with itself? If someone asked what sort of a science geometry was one could simply hand over Euclid's writings and that would be that – but what of metaphysics? There was not a single book in existence to which one could point saying: 'This is metaphysics, this book tells you how that science proves its knowledge of a supreme being and of life after death, employing for that purpose nothing but synthetic *a priori* principles.'[10]

Of course one difference between physics and metaphysics was immediately evident: physics was able to put its pronouncements to the test of experience and metaphysics was not. A further but related difference was that physics sought to explain phenomena *within* reality whereas metaphysics chose (though not exclusively) reality as such for the object of its knowledge. For example, if in physics the idea was to find causal explanations for phenomena within reality, in metaphysics the idea was to find the cause which would explain reality as a whole. But whereas in physics a synthetic *a priori* principle such as 'every event has a cause' would in each instance of its application lead – via observations made in the context of particular questions – to the development of empirical theories or hypotheses that were subsequently tested by experiment, in metaphysics one synthetic *a priori* principle was employed to prove another such principle, *viz.* that of a *first* cause.

Reflecting along these lines Kant sat down and spent nine years writing his *Critique of Pure Reason*. Note that the genitive in the title is both subjective and objective[11]: reason's critique concerns reason itself, or rather, pure reason's critique concerns pure reason itself. When Kant speaks of 'pure' reason he has in mind the ability of reason to proceed on its own, unhindered, so to speak, by fact or fate. Metaphysics is a product of pure reason and so is mathematics; so, indeed, are all synthetic *a priori* propositions. Now the question which guides reason in the process of its self-examination is, 'how are synthetic *a priori* propositions possible?' – with some emphasis on 'how'. For *that* such propositions are possible is beyond doubt; *how* they are possible, that is, what principles govern their possibility is what needs now to be determined so that we may be in a position to indicate the conditions for, and hence the range and limits of, their application.[12]

Would such an examination decide the fate of mathematics? Of course not. Of physics? Again, no.

But the very existence of metaphysics depends on the answer to our guiding question. For as long as no satisfactory answer to it has been found I shall have the right to dismiss every proposition of metaphysics saying: 'Your utterances are nothing but vain, unfounded philosophy and false wisdom. You employ pure reason and you presume the right to *create* knowledge as it were, in *a priori* fashion: you conjure up a new kind of knowledge which you claim is at once synthetic and yet verifiable without recourse to experience: what prompts you to say such things, how do you justify such claims?'[13]

Kant's next step was to split up his guiding question into three separate questions: (1) How is pure mathematics possible? (2) How is pure physics possible? (3) How is metaphysics possible? I return here to my explanation of the 'how' in these questions (see previous paragraph). There was no need for either Hume or Kant to inquire into the possibility of analytic propositions since these come, as I said earlier, under the exclusive sway of the principle of non-contradiction. The key-word now is 'exclusive' since any proposition whatsoever must *obey* the principle of non-contradiction plus (in the case of non-analytic propositions) whatever other principles or rules are applicable in each instance. The synthetic *a posteriori* proposition 'it is raining', for example, is true *if* the proposition is not self-contradictory (which it is not) *and if* and when it is in fact raining. The proposition 'it is raining and it is not raining' is, however, self-contradictory and therefore false in all kinds of weather. Now in asking how pure mathematics is possible Kant was looking for a principle that would *explain* the synthetic *a priori* propositions of mathematics the way the principle of non-contradiction *explains* analytic propositions. He was not, in other words, denying that the propositions of mathematics must (like all propositions whatsoever) *obey* the principle of non-contradiction; he denied only that the propositions of mathematics are explained by that principle as by their source.

Take [said Kant] the proposition of geometry that two straight lines cannot enclose a space, that is, cannot form a geometrical figure, and try to prove that proposition using nothing but the concept of a straight line and the number two. Or take the proposition that three straight lines *can* form a geometrical figure and see if you can prove that in the same way. All your efforts will be in vain and you will find yourself compelled to resort to visualization which is what geometry, too, does all the time.[14]

Kant was making several points here. The first may be paraphrased as follows: if the propositions of geometry are indeed, as some say, founded on the principle of non-contradiction then they must always be (reducible to) tautologies. In the case of the second proposition above it should then be possible to *derive* the figure we call a triangle from the concept of a straight line and the number three in the same way that one derives the conclusion 'Socrates is mortal' from the premises 'Socrates is a man' and 'all men are mortal'. The fact is, however, that no one is able to do this since the combination of a number plus the concept of a straight line does not imply the concept of a geometrical figure, let alone a geometrical figure *per se*. The proof of the first proposition consists in *showing* that it is impossible to draw two straight lines in such a way that space is enclosed by them; similarly, the proof of the second proposition consists in the visual *construction* of a triangle.

But if a triangle must be seen to be believed, does that mean a triangle is a sense object? If we say that it is we shall have to add that it differs from other sense objects such as starry skies or purring cats in that the latter present themselves to our senses of their own accord whereas triangles do not. And there is more. Our concepts of sense objects are *a posteriori* and so is our knowledge of the empirical world in which sense objects are found. But our concepts of geometrical figures are not and could not be *a posteriori* (we do not run into triangles and circles as we run into animate and inanimate objects) and the same is true of geometrical knowledge. *A posteriori* knowledge is contingent but geometrical knowledge is not: it is necessarily and universally true, that is, *a priori* knowledge.

It is characteristic of all mathematical knowledge that it must present its concepts in an intuition which is *a priori* or pure (i.e. not empirical), since without doing so it cannot take a single step. This explains why its propositions are intuitive and not discursive.[15]

The term 'intuition' is the standard English translation of Kant's term *Anschauung* but its Kantian meaning has little to do with what Jungians and ordinary people in general mean by the word. Literally *Anschauung* means the act of looking at, of 'sighting' something (when I used the word 'visualization' two paragraphs ago I was rendering *Anschauung* in an unconventional way). Kant uses the term to mean the act of sensing, of grasping with the senses whatever the world offers to their grasp. It is true that the words 'sensing' and 'senses' denote more than just the sense of sight, but it is also true that Kant uses the term *Anschauung* in both the restricted meaning of 'sighting' and in the wider meaning of 'grasping with the senses'. Now what Kant was saying in the two quotations on the previous page is that mathematics does not derive its concepts from other concepts in discursive thought: instead, mathematics *constructs* its concepts in an intuition which is *a priori*. However this conclusion promptly confronted him with the further question 'how it is possible for the intuition of an object to precede that object',[16] for that is what the term '*a priori* intuition' implies. Kant's answer to this question touches on the very core of the Kantian theory of knowledge and I therefore quote his train of thought in some detail:

Suppose our intuition to be such as to grasp things *as they are in themselves*: then *a priori* intuition would not occur and all intuition would be empirical. For whatever is part and parcel of an object as its properties I cannot know unless such properties are present and given to me. True, even then it remains baffling how my intuition of an object could acquaint me with that object as it is in itself, it being impossible for the properties of an object to enter my mind. But let us suppose something like this is possible just the same: even then my intuition would not be *a priori*, that is, it could not precede its object. For the relation between my intuition and its object would in that case lack ground. It follows that there is only one single way in which it is possible for my intuition to precede the reality of its object and to occur as an act of *a priori* cognition: *when it involves nothing more than the form of intuition which in the subject within me precedes all the real impressions by which objects affect me*.[17]

Take heart now, and note that Kant proceeds from his point about the *a priori* intuition of mathematics to the question how it is possible for an *empirical* intuition to precede its *empirical* object. The switch serves several purposes, as we shall soon see. The next step consists in the differentiation of empirical intuition in terms of content and form; we are told that obviously the content of an intuition cannot precede the source of that content. But suppose that empirical intuitions with their varying contents are *alike in form*, and suppose furthermore that this form is subjectively predetermined? If that is the case it is not hard to see how *a priori* intuition is possible. For the *content* of an intuition will in that case always come from the object outside (and hence be *a posteriori*), but the *form* that content takes as it is intuited will always be the subject's *a priori* contribution. However if this is correct it follows that we do not grasp things as they are but only as they appear to us: this conclusion and the distinction it involves will concern us in further exposition.

Meanwhile there still is mathematics which 'must present its concepts in *a priori* intuition': but this, too, ceases to be a riddle if it is the case that the propositions of mathematics concern the *form* of our empirical intuition. For if they do concern that form we can see why they are universally and necessarily true of all intuitions; why, in a word, they are synthetic and yet *a priori*. But if this is correct we must realize something else as well: that propositions which concern the form of our empirical intuitions *ipso facto* have no application beyond the range of those intuitions; or – to make the same point in another way – that *a priori* intuition applies to sense experience and to sense experience only. Again, this is a point to be borne in mind as we proceed.

But what *is* the 'form of our empirical intuitions'? Properly phrased that question would read, 'What *are* the *forms* of our empirical intuitions?' Kant's answer was: space and time. He said:

Take your empirical notion of a body and systematically remove from it all that is empirical, that is, its color, its hardness or softness, even its impenetrability: you will still find yourself left with the space your now-vanished body once occupied, and you cannot remove that.[18]

And again:

Space is not an empirical concept abstracted from external experience. For I could not relate an awareness on my part to something whose *location* is other than mine, nor could I be aware of things in general as being *external* to me or *next to* each other if I did not already possess the notion of space. It follows that space is not a concept abstracted from the (spatial) relations between external appearances: on the contrary, space is what makes our experience of such external appearances and their (spatial) relations possible in the first place.[19]

The point of the first quotation above is that we can imagine empty space but not the absence of space. Now if space were, as Newton held, an independent reality this inability on our part would be inexplicable whereas if space is, as Kant holds, the subjective ground for the possibility of spatial experience we see at once why we are unable to imagine space 'away'. The second quotation is Kant's answer to Leibniz whose view of space had the further disadvantage, also noted by Kant, of leaving the necessary and universal character of the propositions of geometry unexplained. Indeed on Leibniz's view those propositions would have to be contingent when in fact they are not.

Space is the subjective ground for the possibility of external (i.e. spatial) experience, or the *a priori* form of human external intuition. Geometry constructs and so concretizes its concepts in that *a priori* form itself. Its propositions are necessary because they are *a priori* and they are synthetic because they concern the form of human external intuition.

That the whole of space (i.e. that space which no longer borders on another space) is three-dimensional and could not have more than three dimensions is based on the proposition that not more than three straight lines can intersect to form right angles at any one point.[20]

Kant's exposition of time as the second *a priori* form of empirical intuition proceeds along similar lines. We cannot imagine the absence of time and time is not a notion abstracted from temporal experience but an *a priori* intuition which makes temporal experience possible in the first place. However whereas space is three-dimensional time has only one dimension, and whereas space is the *a priori* form of external intuition time is the *a priori* form of external and internal intuition.[21] Lastly, time is to arithmetic and pure mechanics what space is to geometry: arithmetic constructs its number concepts by means of the consecutive addition of units in time, and pure mechanics constructs its concepts of motion and change in that same pure intuition.[22] The foregoing is my exposition of Kant's answer to the first of his three questions (see above). Fortunately, as the reader may be relieved to learn, there is no need for us to go into his other two answers in the same detailed fashion; for as I have said we need to get into view only those aspects of the Kantian theory that Jung appealed to and relied upon. The transition from the first to the second question ('how is pure physics possible?') starts with the observation that sense experience by itself does not provide us with knowledge but only with 'raw material' still to be 'processed' into knowledge. It is here relevant to explain that Kant divides the human cognitive faculty into three parts: sensibility (*Sinnlichkeit*), the understanding (*Verstand*) and reason (*Vernunft*). Knowledge properly so called in Kant's view comes in the form of propositions (which he calls 'judgments'). Our spatiotemporal intuitions are the work of sensibility, their transformation into propositional knowledge the task of the understanding. Natural laws are the propositions of the science of physics: but how is it that physics is able to determine the 'lawful' processes of nature? Are natural laws inherent in nature? If they are, then our experience of nature must be such as to tell us not only what is going on and how but also that it is necessarily going on as it is and not otherwise. The fact is, however, that experience acquaints us only with what *happens to*, never with what *must* be going on.[23] This had of course been Hume's point, or that part of Hume's point which Kant thought well taken.

But then the word which requires close attention is not 'lawful' but 'nature'. It can be taken in three ways: (1) as the sum total of all that is; (2) as the sum total of all that can enter human cognitive experience; (3) as the sum total of those processes which are subject to general laws. The first meaning must be ruled out from the start since we do not and cannot know the world as it is (independently of ourselves), limited as we are in our cognitive enterprise by our intuitions which have already transformed things as they are into things as they appear. That leaves the second and third meanings, which belong together as follows. Physics establishes the laws of nature and such laws have objective not subjective validity. But how can this be, when the laws of nature are not inherent in nature? When someone says that the room is overheated another person in the same room may disagree: no matter, these are subjective judgments.[24] But when someone says that heat causes certain materials to expand no one can disagree because this judgment expresses a law that never fails to be borne out by the facts. That is how the two cases differ but there is a similarity between them as well. The person who says that the room is overheated voices a perception. Now perceptions are not natural laws but natural laws certainly involve perceptions such as, for example, those of high temperatures and expanding materials. Kant's point is that that which closes the gap, so to speak, between natural law on the one hand and the perceptions it involves on the other is the *a priori* knowledge that we bring to bear on the latter.

It does not matter which way of putting it I choose. I can say that, but for the law in accordance with which perceptual events are invariably linked to particular previous events (there being a general rule governing their consecutive appearance) no perceptual judgment can count as *experience*. But if I do say that then I am saying no more than that everything of whose occurrence *experience* informs me must have a cause [italics mine].[25]

Obviously the word 'experience' is here used in two senses and an unKantian fantasy may serve to illustrate what is at issue. Suppose you come home one evening and find as you enter that the place looks entirely different from the way you left it. Strange furnishings, carpets, drapes; every wall a hideous green, say, instead of the antique white you distinctly remember; on a couch you never saw in your life, a cat and a dog you never saw in your life, the pair of them staring at you the way such pairs always do. You stand transfixed. Did you enter the wrong house? But how could you have entered the wrong house with the right key? You return to the front door. You check the number and yes it's your number. You return to the street and yes it's your street. You wonder if you are dreaming or going mad. You run into a friend. You tell your tale and it ends with the bewildered question, 'who in the world could have done that?'

Now suppose your friend asks in turn how you can be sure that someone did that, raising the possibility that what happened to your house 'just happened'. If you were then to protest, as you surely would, that things do not 'just happen', that if a wall was white yesterday and is green today somebody must have painted it overnight you would be confirming Kant's point. That is, you would be saying that certain invariable arrangements of our perceptual experience are tacitly agreed upon by all of us, one such arrangement being that which assigns to each and every perceptual event its place in some causal chain. If in the context of a given situation such arrangements are suddenly questioned (as your friend questioned the arrangement of cause and effect) the result is that our very notion of experience is just as suddenly placed in jeopardy. Now these arrangements – which fit what Kant calls 'categories of the pure understanding' – together constitute the synthetic *a priori* knowledge that we bring to bear on our perceptions. And where the latter are of the day-to-day variety, coming and going as they may, the categories are the principles governing the possibility of our day-to-day, shared experience of an objective, spatiotemporal order in which (for example) the question 'what x caused this y?' is thought appropriate by everyone with respect to each and every perceptual event. But where our perceptions are systematic, as they are in science, the categories are those which give rise to questions of the sort that lead us into systematic observation and thence into the insights known as natural laws.

Returning now to the quotation on the previous page we can see that the riddle is solved if we read 'objective experience' the first time and 'perceptual experience' the second. Kant himself does not seem to have been aware (he seldom was) that his wording here might cause confusion though he does say something else in the same paragraph which is worth noting. It is that 'the first way of putting it is after all preferable' because the second suggests that the world – or nature – is somehow there in self-contained fashion so that the question to which we must address ourselves is only how that world subsequently becomes the object of cognitive experience. However, so Kant continues, we cannot speak of the – or a – world apart from our cognitive experience since to do so is self-contradictory. We *can* however speak of our perceptual judgments and of their categorial arrangement and we *can* say that the objectivity of human knowledge is in the last analysis its subjectivity since the 'subject within me' (see the quotation above), that is, the *a priori* part of my cognitive faculty does not differ from the 'subject within all of us' no matter how much all of us may differ as individuals.

Consider here the question raised by Descartes how he could be sure
that the world out there and his own body were real and not just his
hallucinations. As I said, Kant approved of the question but only by
way of approach to the insight that this is the trouble we get into so
long as we speak of a 'world out there'. And so long as we speak in this
fashion there is, according to Kant, no way out of that trouble either.
Does this mean that Kant denied the difference between hallucination
and perception? By no means, his position being a good deal subtler
than that. A person who says 'I am speaking of the world as it is in
itself, independently of what we know about it' is to Kant a person
who says 'what I am speaking of is something of which by definition I
know nothing whatsoever'. Or – to change the wording but not the
point – Kant holds that to speak of the world *is* to speak of our
cognitive experience of the world, just as to speak of our cognitive
experience *is* to speak of the object of that experience. Yes – but were
we not told a little while ago that it is the subject within us which
creates that object, and what is that if not hallucination? Ah – but we
were not told that it is the subject within us which creates that object,
we were told that the objectivity of human knowledge is in the last
analysis its subjectivity. Kant was not saying that there *is* no world out
there, he was saying only that we cannot speak of it without speaking
of ourselves in the same breath. And having made this point he was
ready for his third question, that concerning the possibility of
metaphysics.

Take the proposition 'the world is God's creation' and consider it
not as an article of faith but as the conclusion of a train of thought.
How might such a conclusion be arrived at? As follows: if every event
within the world has a cause then the world as a whole must have a
cause. And the latter cause must itself be uncaused since if it is not I
must go on until I come upon the uncaused cause or God. *Ergo*, the
world is God's creation. Kant's quarrel with this argument is that the
world as a whole is not a perceptual event so that what we witness here
is the causal categorization of – nothing at all. This point requires
elaboration. The categories are employed by the pure understanding
but the guiding hand here is that of reason 'which characteristically
aims at the systematic and unified use of the understanding'.[26] A
degree of tension between the understanding and reason is thus
inevitable. For the understanding is always in Kant's view dependent
on the raw material offered to it by the senses; in the absence of such
material the categories are 'empty, just as intuitions by themselves are
blind'.[27] It follows that our cognitive experience is always *phenomenal*
(we experience things as they appear not as they are) and *partial* (we
intuit spatiotemporally but we do not intuit space and time; we intuit

what presents itself to us in the world but we do not untuit the world as a whole). The objective order we experience and whose laws we seek to discover is thus a phenomenal order whose overall status eludes us. And this goes against reason's grain, the natural impulse of reason being, according to Kant, always toward completion, unification, synthesis and integration. Now since the categories are pure in the sense of being 'in no way determined by the senses' reason is tempted to lift them above every and all experience and apply them to things in themselves, or to 'noumena'.[28] A *noumenon* contrasts with a *phenomenon* as follows.

Remove from your empirical notion of an (im-)material object all the properties that experience has taught you to distinguish in objects, and you will still find yourself unable to remove that which makes you conceive objects in terms of *substance*.[29]

The reader will note the similarity between this quotation and that on p.213. Substance like space is what we cannot imagine away when we are trying to imagine everything away (except our imagining selves). Substance like causality is a category. Without that category we could not experience the phenomenon of change since change requires a background or context which remains unchanged. Substance is that which remains unchanged as temperatures rise or fall, colors fade and resilience wears off into brittleness. Note however that 'substance' and 'object' are not identical: substance is, says Kant, that in whose terms we conceive objects. It is also (but this is saying the same thing in other words) that which persists in time (while properties come and go). Yet just as we employ the category of causality without ever coming across a cause as such, so we employ the category of substance without knowing the substantial as such. We may describe it as the bearer or subject of properties but we do not know that subject. 'Now it may seem that this *substantiale* is to be found in our awareness of ourself as the thinking subject'[30], 'the soul'[31], and that the latter's persistence in time (beyond death) is thus made evident. Kant's objection is that substance is here 'lifted above experience' and treated as a thing in itself or *noumenon* when in fact substance (like causality) is a condition for the possibility of *phenomenal* experience. *That* substance is operative as such a condition is a fact; but *what* substance may be in itself, apart from phenomenal experience is literally anybody's guess.

Did Kant, then, deny the existence of the human soul? Yes, if by existence one means 'phenomenal existence'; no, if 'noumenal existence' is meant. God, the soul and immortality are *noumena*; so is the world 'as it is in itself'; so is the world as a whole; so are 'things in themselves'; so, lastly, is freedom and so freedom must be. For if all experience is ruled by the category of causality there can be no freedom unless we distinguish, as does Kant, between cognitive (phenomenal) experience and moral (noumenal) experience. Kant's *Critique of Practical Reason* (published in 1788, where 'practical reason' means 'reason as a guide to moral action') concerns the latter as his *Critique of Pure Reason* concerns the former. Ask what is the fate of metaphysics in the light of these two *Critiques* and you ask the question which concludes this part of my essay. The answer is that the old, transcendent metaphysics (which would go beyond experience and turn things in themselves or realities beyond space and time into objects of knowledge) comes to an end with Kant's epistemological critique; but Kant himself regarded that critique itself as metaphysics of the new, transcend*ental* variety. Transcendent metaphysics had reasoned from the logically possible to the contingently or possibly actual: but there is a gap here which mere reasoning cannot bridge (as Hume saw). Transcendental metaphysics does the reverse: it reasons from the contingently actual back to the necessarily actual, or from what happens to be the case to what must (in that case) also be the case. In so doing it uncovers the principles which govern (not the actuality but) the possibility of human knowledge and the boundaries which the latter must in consequence respect. 'All that is or ever will be known in fact must be knowable in principle and all that is unknowable in principle is not and never shall be known in fact'. There one has Kant's theory in a nutshell, 'principle' and all. And here we have Jung agreeing with it. But was Jung, or rather, could Jung be a Kantian, given his own work and his own 'principles'? Let us see.

A twentieth-century physicist or mathematician or logician has excellent reasons for considering the foundations of Kant's theory of knowledge wholly outdated. When Kant speaks of physics he means Newtonian physics; when he speaks of mathematics he means Euclidean geometry and arithmetic; when he speaks of logic he means Aristotelian logic. However since Kant's day Newtonian physics has become only one branch of a much broader discipline and Euclidean geometry is today only one kind of geometry just as Aristotelian logic is today only one kind of logic (venerable for its age but not for its sophistication). Yet to call a theory outdated is not the same as calling it repudiated nor as dismissing it out of hand. (The physics, geometry and logic that Kant knew and worked with have not been dismissed either.) It may be that (a modified version of) Kant's theory of knowledge will some day be seen to have its place in a much broader epistemology which takes into account all that has happened since Kant's day in (science generally, and in) physics, mathematics, logic and psychology in particular. But which psychology, whose psychology, how many psychologies? The truth is that I do not know the answer to that question since the only psychology I have studied is Jungian psychology and it is Jungian psychology which (stripped of its apparent Kantianism) strikes me as having a post-Kantian message for epistemologists. There may well be other psychologies of which the same thing is true, but these are not our concern here.

One of the questions that still preoccupy me is how Jung was able to rely on Kant so completely and for so long when his colleagues in other disciplines had no difficulty recognizing Kant's limitations. It would have been different if Jung had appealed to Kant only in his younger or middle years but that is not the case as readers of Jung's *Memories, Dreams, Reflections* (first published in 1962) and of the letters he wrote between 1956 and the year of his death can see for themselves. However there is a general observation to be made here. It is one thing to be critical of Kant's epistemology in view of post-Kantian developments in logic, mathematics and science. It is another to agree that the Kantian taboo on what Kant called 'transcendent metaphysics' must in that case be reconsidered as well. This is true even though logically speaking one cannot be critical of the one and uncritical of the other without exposing oneself to the charge of inconsistency. But of course the fact is that what is impossible in logic is entirely possible in psychology. The fact is also that the mathematicians and scientists of today are no longer Kantians in their professional lives; but they and the rest of us continue to be very much subject to Kant's influence so far as our day-to-day style of consciousness is concerned. And if anyone in this century devoted his efforts to making that style of consciousness visible and questionable it was Carl Gustav Jung: all the more amazing, then, that when the same Jung came under attack for being a 'metaphysician' or 'theologian' he should have sought refuge with none other than Immanuel Kant.

Key notions in Jung's psychology are psychic reality, the archetype and the fourfold function of consciousness. I submit that each of these is exemplary in superseding fundamental Kantian tenets even though I am aware that at least with respect to the first two Jung did what he could either to bring Kant in for support or to make what he had to say sound Kantian and in that sense respectable. In a letter dated 30 April 1952 to Father Victor White, Jung writes (postscript) that 'Buber . . . does not understand psychic reality',[32] Martin Buber having previously voiced the complaint that Jung reduced God to a psychic entity. And the reader who has just sat down to start Jung's *Answer To Job* (first published in 1952) is told under the heading 'Lectori Benevolo' that

Some people believe it to be physically true that Christ was born as the son of a virgin, while others deny this as a physical impossibility . . . They could easily reach agreement if only they dropped the word 'physical'. 'Physical' is not the only criterion of truth: there are also *psychic* truths which can neither be explained nor proved nor contested in any physical way.[33]

Again in a letter dated June 29, 1960 Jung says:

I merely insist on the psychic reality of the God-complex or the God-image . . . What I mean is only the psychic image of a *noumenon* (Kant's 'thing in itself', which is not a negation as you know).[34]

This second quotation (in which the words 'merely' and 'only' are used to assign runner-up status to the very notion which the preceding quotation urges us to take seriously) does leave one feeling that Buber had been hitting at least one nail on the head. Note furthermore Jung's explanation of the term *noumenon*, which is only partly correct. Instead of 'negation' (which is a logical term: 'p and not-p' is a proposition p and its negation) Jung should have said 'negative entity' to indicate that he was making an *ontological* point (he wrote the letter in English). Second, things-in-themselves are indeed *noumena* but noumenal status is also accorded to a transcendent reality or entity such as God. Things-in-themselves are known as they appear, not as they are; but God is (in Kant's view) not an object of knowledge in any way since we can neither intuit God nor even prove his existence. On the other hand it is perfectly true that Kant did not regard *noumena* (in either sense) as negative entities (that is, as non-existent) since we cannot *dis*prove God's existence either and since in order for things to appear to us they must somehow be 'there' in the first place. Be this as it may, Jung clearly distinguishes between the noumenal God on the one hand and the image of God on the other. Now I suggest that in consequence either we are to interpret that image as a Kantian 'phenomenon' or the distinction itself raises more questions than it answers. Yet if we do adopt the Kantian interpretation we are confronted by the difficulty that – as we have seen – a Kantian phenomenon is a spatiotemporal sense datum ordered by the categories. Hence on this view either the 'image of God' is in truth a 'picture of God' (but in that case God must be spatiotemporally present for us to 'take his picture') or the notion of image as well as the broader notion of psychic reality must be said to have nothing to do with the Kantian notion of phenomenal reality – but in that case Jung's distinction between the noumenal God and the image of God becomes pointless as well as misleading.

However there is a deeper anomaly here. Whenever Jung speaks of psychic reality he is of course invoking his theory of an autonomous unconscious psyche which is in part personal and in part transpersonal or collective. At the other end of the spectrum we have Kant declaring the 'impossibility of a psychological darkness such as could not be regarded as a consciousness whose intensity is merely inferior to that of some other consciousness'.[35] Now we might on the basis of this contrast say simply that no depth psychology such as that developed by Jung can be made to fit the framework of an epistemology such as that worked out by Kant even though that is just what Jung tried to do. And we might leave it at that. But to dispose of the problem in this fashion is to dispose of it abstractly and in words only, as though nothing more than a mere contradiction were at issue. The deeper anomaly involves the Kantian and Jungian ontologies or *what counts as real and how* in the views of Kant and Jung respectively. Here it is worth noting that with Kant it is phenomenal reality which is solidly real whereas noumenal entities, for all the verbal respect accorded to them, cannot escape a certain air of unreality given their postulate status and persistent unknowability. In Jung's hands, however, the same phenomenon–noumenon dichotomy is given a twist inasmuch as Jung urges upon us the phenomenal reality of psychic manifestations. In Kantian terms this amounts to nothing less than an invitation to regard the phenomenally unreal as the phenomenally real: I believe we do well to bear this in mind as we observe Jung appearing to be at cross-purposes with himself, insisting on the one hand that psychic manifestations are real and on the other 'only psychic'. A further consequence is that the transcendently noumenal in Jung's work cannot help sounding like the 'real thing' (as against its 'merely psychic' manifestations).

Consider now some observations made by Jung in Part One of his *Psychological Types* (written in 1913-1917, but first published in 1921). The subject is St Anselm's so-called 'ontological' proof of the existence of God and Kant's criticism of that proof. Anselm had argued as follows: (1) I have the idea of a perfect Being; (2) if that Being did not exist it would not be perfect; (3) God exists. Kant's criticism (quoted by Jung[36]) may be paraphrased in two ways: (1) existence is not (like perfection) a predicate but the very condition for the possibility of predication; (2) actual existence (*esse in re*) never follows from possible existence (*esse in intellectu*). In plain language Kant's point is that I can have the idea of a perfect being in my head or intellect and so long as that idea is not self-contradictory such a being may indeed exist as a concrete entity. Still, possible existence is a far cry from actual existence and what is more, actual existence can never be *inferred from* possible existence (which is what Anselm tried to do). Having quoted Kant, Jung writes:

This detailed reminder of Kant's fundamental exposition seems to me necessary, because it is precisely here that we find the clearest division between *esse in intellectu* and *esse in re* . . .From the standpoint of logic there is . . . no *tertium* between the logic either-or. But between *intellectus* and *res* there is still *anima*, and this *esse in anima* makes the whole ontological argument superfluous. Kant himself, in his *Critique of Practical Reason*, made an attempt on a grand scale to evaluate the *esse in anima* in philosophical terms. There he introduces God as a postulate of practical reason. . .[37]

Now it seems to me that Jung's observation '*esse in anima* makes the whole ontological argument superfluous' can be taken in two ways. The first is that *esse in anima* represents a switch from pure reason to practical reason, or to the acceptance of postulates where proofs cannot be had. It is clear from the concluding sentences in the above quotation that this is Jung's interpretation. The second is that *esse in anima* involves a radical departure from reason, proof *and postulate* to fantasy and fantasy images. Oddly and surprisingly, however, we find that this, too, is Jung's interpretation as the following passage shows:

Living reality is the product neither of the actual, objective behaviour of things nor of the formulated idea exclusively, but rather of the combination of both in the living psychological process, through *esse in anima* . . . This autonomous activity of the psyche . . . is, like every vital process, a continually creative act. The psyche creates reality every day. The only expression I can use for this activity is *fantasy* [italics in original].[38]

In contrasting these two interpretations I am not overlooking the fact that Jung describes the switch from pure reason to practical reason as an evaluation of *esse in anima* in philosophical (i.e. not necessarily his own) terms. However my point is that if *esse in anima* is what Jung says it is in psychology then it cannot be what Jung says it is in (Kantian) philosophy. *Esse in intellectu* and *esse in re* are related to one another as idea and entity, that is, as the idea of a concrete entity or state of affairs and the existence of that same entity or state of affairs. In the case of God we cannot argue from the idea of God to the existence of God and so our way out is to postulate that existence: this is Kant's position. But note that both idea and entity – whether conceived in the mind or postulated outside it or really existing there – are literal and concrete and note as well that literal and concrete is precisely what fantasy is not. A postulate is not the philosophical equivalent of a fantasy image any more than the thinking function is the equivalent in consciousness of unconscious imagination. Rather, images are the products of imagination just as postulates are products of the thinking function, but images and postulates are not for that reason in any sense equivalent. It is important here to realize that Kant's objection to transcendent metaphysics is – in Jungian terms – a thinking man's objection to the thinking function overstepping its boundaries by creating, out of the blue and under cover of faulty reasoning, a concrete, literal, non-spatiotemporal world literally peopled by literal entities. It is equally important to realize that the introduction of God as a 'postulate of practical reason' is once again the thinking function at work, but now in self-corrective fashion. Viewed from the perspective of the thinking function, fantasy is tantamount to 'making up' or 'concocting' a literal state of affairs involving literal beings, and postulating, viewed from the same perspective, is doing the same thing but with 'reason' and without the pretense that one is really doing something else. The Cartesian *cogito, ergo sum* apprehended psychologically is nothing if not the thinking function declaring itself supreme (and correspondingly lonely). The entire Kantian analysis including the questions that gave rise to it presupposes this Cartesian reduction of the psyche to the thinking function and the consequent split between a doubting self and an alien, possibly unknowable, possibly hallucinatory world. *Esse in anima* does not (as the Kantian Jung tells us) mediate between *esse in intellectu* and *esse in re* so much as widen their common ground in the act of embracing it and them both, suspending in the process the 'logical either-or' that otherwise keeps them opposed. The paragraph from which we took the last quotation continues:

Fantasy is just as much feeling as thinking; as much intuition as sensation. There is no psychic function that, through fantasy, is not inextricably bound up with the other psychic functions. Sometimes it appears in primordial form, sometimes it is the ultimate and boldest product of all our faculties combined . . . Fantasy it was and ever is which fashions the bridge between the irreconcilable claims of subject and object, introversion and extraversion. In fantasy alone both mechanisms are united.[39]

Thus *esse in anima* does indeed 'make the whole ontological argument superfluous' but not because it mediates between *intellectus, res* and the ontology that goes with (the opposition between) them. Rather, *esse in anima* bespeaks an ontology all its own, where 'arguments' have no place. When Jung said that 'physical' is not the only criterion of truth he was invoking that ontology; but whenever he described non-physical truth as 'only psychic' he was – or so it seems to me – betraying a fundamental, Kant-inspired ambivalence about that same ontology. However if *esse in anima* is a mode of being for which Jung could find no more suitable expression than 'fantasy', and if fantasy so conceived involves all the psychic functions and moreover fashions bridges between otherwise irreconcilable opposites, how shall we recognize it at work? Not by adopting an 'objective' attitude, not by looking for 'facts' and checking these against other 'facts' but by entering the fantasies from which (for example) the very notion of objectivity was born, and again by entering the fantasies that cast light on just these 'facts' at the expense of others. Such fantasies lead us to the root metaphors at work in a given context, the metaphors *in terms of which* we fashion our notions and concepts. A splendid example of such a quest (for the root metaphors inspiring our notions of creativity) is to be found in James Hillman, *The Myth of Analysis*. Under the heading 'An Archetypal Basis for the Notions of Creativity' Hillman writes:

Statements about creativity can also be examined for their root metaphors. The many notions of creativity are comparable to the many notions of any basic symbol (matter, nature, God, soul, instinct). The very existence of so many notions is evidence for the variety of root metaphors by means of which the psyche perceives and forms its notions. The perceptions are filtered through the prism of the psyche. We stand inescapably in the light of one or another color band, giving us a definite perspective and bias.[40]

The ontology that goes with *esse in anima* thus not only recognizes fantasy but even puts it ahead of 'fact'. Such an ontology requires a descriptive model that puts metaphor before concept. Now a consciousness that is post-Kantian in name only holds concepts to be descriptive of 'facts' and 'things' and regards metaphors as mere manners of speaking, poetic sometimes, inaccurate and loose always. The same consciousness is as enamoured of 'facts' as it is fearful of fantasy (which it confuses with fiction, fabrication). But, most importantly, such a consciousness believes in *the* truth, *the* theory, *the* method, *the* epistemology and must do so as long as it believes in 'objective' reality and 'objective' knowledge. It is difficult to tell whether Jung ('whose ontology could be formulated most simply as *esse in anima*'[41] but who also spoke of *the* theory of knowledge when he meant Kant's) would have been startled or pleased by a contemporary philosopher of science saying:

Knowledge. . .is not a series of self-consistent theories that converges towards an ideal view; it is not a gradual approach to the truth. It is rather an ever increasing *ocean of mutually incompatible (and perhaps even incommensurable) alternatives*, each single theory, each fairy tale, each myth that is part of the collection forcing the others into greater articulation and all of them contributing, via this process of competition, to the development of our consciousness [italics in original].[42]

Startled or pleased (or both), Jung would certainly have noted that such language suggests an awareness of *esse in anima* more than an allegiance to Kant. And he might then have undertaken something of which his entire work shows no trace: an evaluation of Kant's epistemology in terms of *esse in anima*, an exercise aimed at seeing through to the fantasies at work in the *Critique of Pure Reason*. 'Sometimes fantasy appears in primordial form', said Jung, which is another way of saying that sometimes fantasy is archetypal. In what is probably his best-known theoretical essay Jung further writes:

The archetypal representations (images and ideas) mediated to us by the unconscious should not be confused with the archetype as such . . . The archetype as such is a psychoid factor that belongs, as it were, to the invisible, ultraviolet end of the spectrum . . . We must . . . constantly bear in mind that what we mean by 'archetype' is in itself irrepresentable, but has effects which make visualizations of it possible, namely, the archetypal images and ideas.[43]

And in an earlier essay we read:

Just as we have been compelled to postulate the concept of an instinct determining or regulating our conscious actions, so, in order to account for the uniformity and regularity of our perceptions, we must have recourse to the correlated concept of a factor determining the mode of apprehension. It is this factor which I call the archetype or primordial image. The primordial image might suitably be described as the *instinct's perception of itself,* . . .[italics in original][44])

Is this bio–psychology or psycho–biology? I do not know, but I do know that something very Kantian is going on when the irrepresentable archetype-as-such is carefully distinguished from its visualizations in the form of images and ideas or from instinctual self-perception. The archetype a *noumenon*, the archetypal image a *phenomenon*: if that is how things stand, who could accuse archetypal psychology (whose sole concern is with archetypal images) of being speculative or 'metaphysical'? Then again, how could an archetypal image ever be a Kantian *phenomenon*? Note, meanwhile, that Jung describes (at least in his theoretical writings) the manifestations of the archetype in visual terms only, thus giving rise to a confusion of

archetypal reality (and) visual imagery . . . But symbolic images are not the only way the archetypes may manifest themselves. We overvalue the study of symbols, believing that we will find archetypal reality there. Iconoclastic breaking of these vessels may be required to free the psyche from this first level of archetypal appearance so that it can perceive fantasy in behavior, in the subtler forms of style, voice, body carriage, and the living enactment of myth.[45]

The *Critique of Pure Reason* contains hardly any images; its style and content are markedly abstract throughout. Now if we follow Jung's implicit rule 'No image, no archetype' we make it impossible for ourselves to approach the book for its (archetypal) fantasy content. But we might also consider *this abstract character itself,* that is, we might look (not for imagery between the book's covers, but) for what is evoked by the enterprise itself which the book represents. In so doing we would be opening a door that Kant did not know was there. Stepping inside we might decide to bypass the rooms where the lectures are given (on space and time; on intuition; on the categories of the pure understanding, and so on) and move toward a spot somewhere in the middle of the house where we can hear all the lectures at once (as we hear music 'at once' even though it is produced by a collection of individual instruments). 'Tuning in' to pick up themes rather than sentences, the general drift rather than specific points we would gradually notice an urgent concern with principle, rule, system, fixity, permanence on the one hand and with contingency, randomness, incoherence, flow and change on the other. From the adjectives used to qualify these two sets of themes we would gather that the first set is being favored in the lecture rooms, the second rejected. We would go on to register the unusual richness of the rejection language (something like seven or eight different idioms for 'nonsense' would reach our ears) and at the same time catch a victorious note in the favoring language. Wearied after a while by the incessant verbal onslaught we might turn our heads a bit to look out the window and into the world. Pondering what we have heard and are still hearing we imagine now a principled, ruled, systematized and 'fixed' world, now one that is random, incoherent, flowing, changing. And we find we cannot opt for either; indeed we feel we must have both. Order, yes; chaos, yes. It does not seem to us a question of choice so much as of proportion. Meanwhile the voices in the lecture rooms drone on. We hear 'order, yes; chaos, no' and we wonder whether they realize in there that Chaos has a child named Eros? We hear them out until the very end. As we leave, order is enthroned, chaos exiled. And Eros, poor child, poor *us*, has gone unmentioned.

This may be the right moment to observe that at least one reason why Jung did not see through Kant is that he did not see through his own allegiance to Kant. However the term 'seeing through' requires explanation.[46] It means seeing *through* a literal context *into* the fantasy at work there. But seeing through a literal context is not the same as dispensing with it or invalidating it or declaring it secondary. Nor does the fact that we can approach a literal context for its fantasy preclude or render superfluous our approaching it in its own, literal terms. Three centuries of Cartesianism have made literalists of us all: we must beware now of becoming 'fantasists' by way of (over-) compensation. The fantasy at work in a theory or pattern or system is not *the* truth about that theory or pattern or system, but a way among other ways of taking each of them. *Esse in anima* is another, not *the* dimension. However to establish it as such outside psychology we shall need to differentiate our notions of 'reality' and 'truth' in terms of 'images' (visual and non-visual) and 'imaginal truth' on the one hand and 'concrete reality' and 'empirical truth' on the other. Underlying such differentiation would be the distinction between the imaginal and the concrete as incommensurable but equal, and equally valid, perspectives. That distinction would put an end to the apparent synonymity of such notions as

imagination	and	delusion
fantasy/dream/myth/metaphor	and	fiction/lie/falsehood/illusion
image/symbol	and	sign
imaginal	and	imaginary
concrete/literal	and	concretistic/literalist

This is to say: we would speak of a concretistic or literalistic perspective whenever the synonymity of the above, paired notions is upheld from the viewpoint of those listed on the right (imagination = delusion, and so on), but we would call 'concrete' any non-imaginal perspective that would respect and leave intact its imaginal partner. By the same token we would describe as 'fantasist' any imaginal perspective that would usurp its concrete partner; where this happens the synonymity of the above, paired notions is again upheld but now from the viewpoint of those listed on the left (delusion = imagination, and so on). We would, in brief, agree neither with the concretist who says that fantasy is fiction and fiction, falsehood; nor with the fantasist who says that falsehood and fiction form part of the fantasy of truth. By the same token we would not follow Jung in defending fantasy by having recourse to an epistemology that separates fact from fiction, but declining to do so we would not forget that it was Jung who opened our eyes to fantasy in the first place.

CHAPTER 14

The Basic Views of C.G. Jung in the Light of Hermeneutic Metascience

BY LAURI RAUHALA

1. Introduction

It has recently come to be realized that the depth psychology developed by Freud and Jung, and the psychotherapeutic practice deriving from it, are clearly distinct from the actual sciences and applications based on them. Hence the philosophical analysis of these fields must also constitute an undertaking of its own.[1-5] The methodology evolved for analysis in the natural sciences is not applicable to an analysis of psychotherapeutic research and its uses. The attempts that have been made in this direction must be considered failures because they have been obliged to regard psychotherapy as one of the objectivistic natural sciences.[6-7] The stagnation currently prevailing in psychotherapy and the continued lack of recognition of this field of work represent a challenge to the philosopher to establish the status of psychotherapy as a scientific discipline.

The so-called hermeneutic approach emerging in European philosophy in recent years would appear to offer new methodological possibilities in the development of a philosophy of psychotherapy. The chief methods now applied in this line of inquiry, those of phenomenological and existential analysis,[8-10] are adequate from the point of view of the problematic of psychotherapy. Psychotherapy appears to involve in a very significant way the problem of understanding (*Verstehen*), and it is precisely with an analysis of the over-all structure of understanding that the two methods in question are concerned.[11] What the hermeneutic philosophy of psychotherapy is or can be will emerge when the principles of hermeneutics have been applied in detail to the problem of depth-psychological research and psychotherapy.

A particularly interesting point of departure for such a philosophical inquiry is provided by the depth-psychological views and therapeutic practice of C. G. Jung. Even a superficial knowledge of Jung's thought gives grounds for supposing that a phenomenological-existential analysis would apply even more fruitfully to his views than to Freudian psychoanalysis, bound as it is in a sense to the natural scientific tradition of research. This is not to say that psychoanalysis is not explicable on a hermeneutic basis, too (see also Rauhala[2]), but the sections to follow will confine themselves to a consideration of the views of Jung.

2. *Intentionality and the Problem of Meaning in the Lived World*

Except in his theory of psychological types Jung did not aspire to a systematic formulation of empirical theory. He sought in his inquiry into consciousness above all to ascertain the general lines of principle involved. His research interests embraced – possibly unknown to himself – a great deal of what is now seen to be the philosophical aspect of the study of any given problem *in toto*. Guided by intuition Jung seems in any case to have concentrated from the outset on problems which, with the subsequent development of the hermeneutic methods mentioned, have become the focus of attention in studies of psychic disturbance. In the light of hermeneutics Jung is thus in a certain sense modern.

The object of interest for Jung is the problem of meaning as it is manifested in the lived world. This of course is precisely the problem Husserl and other phenomenologists have sought by philosophical methods to investigate. Jung saw perhaps more clearly than any other depth psychologist the unique character and logical independence of the problem of mind. In principle he seems to have comprehended, completely in the spirit of phenomenology, that depth psychology and psychotherapy are dealing with the articulation of the lived world or of experience of the world (Husserl's *Lebenswelt*). Such a conception inevitably draws his thought and his practice of psychotherapy into the sphere of intentionality problematics, which is also a point of departure for phenomenology. In phenomenology intentionality is conceived of as the appearance (*Erscheinen*) of sense characteristics (*Sinn*, in Husserl also *Noema*) in experiences of consciousness. Such experience (Husserl: *Noesis*) always intends something outside itself, and is thus according to Husserl experience *von etwas*.[8] Sense cannot be apprehended except by understanding; nor can it be modified except by understanding. Intentionality has no existence in concrete form.

Without employing the terms of phenomenology Jung likewise appears to believe that the lived world is actualized in the structure of intentionality as an appearance of sense. When the sense of something – an object or a circumstance – appears in consciousness, whether correctly and clearly or deficiently, vaguely or in a distorted way, a meaning function has come into being in the lived world. The constitutive principle in this process of organization is the emerging sense characteristic. In meaning relationships the world assumes individualized forms (*Seiendes*), and the human being stands in relation to these beings through the sense characteristics that appear in his consciousness. Meaning functions are the elements of which the lived world is constituted as either normal or neurotic, psychotic or in all possible gradations between these.

Husserl's inquiry is a philosophical one, investigating the constitution of the lived world; Jung is concerned with an empirical study of the organization of the lived world in given contents. Husserl's object is mainly to analyse the constitution of knowledge, while for Jung knowledge is but one type of evidence in which the meaning functions of the lived world are articulated. The distinction is not a decisive one. Husserl, too, spoke of a number of types of evidence and assumed that the lived world must in any case be likewise constituted basically in a variety of evidence types. For both the enquiry was ultimately concerned with the simplest constituents of the lived world, that is, with meaning functions. Thus the primary question for both of them is the same, merely on different levels: how does a meaning function come into being? In Husserl's analysis the constitution of the lived world is assumed to be normal, while for Jung all variations in the organization of the lived world are empirically significant. Nevertheless Husserl's epistemological interest in the assumption of normality by no means excludes the possibility of a phenomenological analysis also of the abnormally constituted lived world or of its organization at the unconscious level. An application of Husserl's principles is precisely the means to bring out the structure of these.

3. Typology

In *Memories, Dreams, Reflections* Jung points out that his typology must be regarded as an attempt to analyse man's mental relationship to the world.[12] It is his initial attempt to outline the main features of the articulation of the world by means of psychological description. In phenomenological terms Jung means by the basic dimensions of his typology, i.e. introversion–extraversion, a dual optionality in which one or the other mode is actualized in the experiencing of the individual human being. In the case of the introverted person the constitution of the lived world is determined more by the organizing dispositions afforded by his own individual existence than by those from the relationality of the external world. On the philosophical level this abstraction must be conceived of as follows.

The axiomatic point of departure for the hermeneutic approach is that all understanding is understanding in context. When an individual understands something new – also in neurosis and psychotherapy – how he understands will be determined by the dispositions already present in him, the context of understanding. For example, a flat, elongated object on the table will immediately be understood by an educated human being as a book. A Bushman, however, might take it for a boomerang that didn't come out right. Phenomenology terms such contexts of understandings 'horizons' (*Horizont*). According to Husserl, horizons are what is already apprehended and known. It is precisely the presence of such horizons in the structure of every act of understanding which explains how the lived world can become distorted and how it can be reconstituted for example on the basis of new horizons brought out and maintained by psychotherapy. In the case of an introvert the horizons making possible the appearance of sense are actualized in a subjectively significant manner. To this type of individual everything new seems to gain its sense characteristics according to what it involves for him, the experiencing subject. For this reason the lived world in such a case will be emphatically individual and private. With the extravert, on the other hand, horizons are so actualized as to bring the subject predominantly into relationship with the external world and other human beings. The consequence is the formation of a lived world in which everyday reality is certainly preserved, but which by reason of its susceptibility to external impulse may involve weakness and lack of delineation in the individual personality concerned. Neither dimension in itself means abnormality, but extreme development in either direction may well imply disturbance.

Jung complements his basic division with four primary functions of understanding: thought, feeling, sensation and intuition. These may combine in various ways in either of the basic dimensions and may assume widely varying manifestations according as they are coloured by one or the other of these. Usually only one of the basic functions is developed and becomes the dominant in the formation of the lived world, two others being evolved to a certain extent and the fourth completely archaistic and diffuse. Jung's basic functions may be regarded as empirical counterparts to the evidence types in phenomenology. The lived world of the everyday is according to Husserl constituted in manifold forms. Although Jung's typology, along with certain others, must be regarded as partly outdated, the modes of understanding he speaks of are still significant for a comprehension of psychic disturbance and psychotherapy. Within the framework of phenomenology they also have their adequate grounding.

The typology is Jung's most integrated and consistent system of thought. He seems however to have realized even prior to its formulation (appearing in 1921) that a mere classification and description of the modes of understanding the lived world would not suffice. An understanding of the structure of the lived world must go much deeper. The phases of emergence of a single meaning function must be traced from as elementary a level as possible. One meaning function is a paradigm of the lived world. Comprehension of its structural organization will shed light on the constitution of the lived world as a whole. In his inquiries along these lines Jung found himself involved with the concepts of archetype and symbol.

4. Archetype and Symbol

Jung's most original attempts to analyse the problem of meaning are contained in his concepts of archetype and symbol. They are at the same time from the philosophical standpoint the most difficult of access in the whole of Jung's thought. In applying these terms he has sought the most fundamental context possible in explanation of the emergence of meaning functions. He nevertheless failed to understand that such fundamental conditions cannot be dealt with solely in psychological terms. It would appear that Jung's idea of archetypes has a great deal in common with Heidegger in his analysis of being (*Sein*). In a philosophical analysis of archetype and symbol it would therefore seem that even Husserl's approach does not suffice; the starting-point must be on a level even more fundamental than that of an analysis of the constitution of the lived world. Heidegger, on the other hand, with his existential mode of analysis, may well offer a model approach to the problem. This existential line of inquiry is, however, an extremely complicated undertaking, and in the present context no more than its most prominent points can be discussed.

In connection with the concept of archetype it is first and foremost essential to ascertain its ontological status, because Jung in applying it also refers to the problem of man in the sense in which philosophical anthropology conceives it. Jung distinguishes on the one hand archetypal experience and on the other the archetype 'as such' (*an sich*). In his definition the 'archetype as such' is 'a mode of experience without definite content'.[13] It is also 'a structure of instinct', he says. Thus defined, the 'archetype as such' is clearly not a psychological concept. Archetypal experience, on the other hand, is a matter of psychology. To judge by the way Jung employed the term 'archetype as such', particularly towards the end of his life, he in fact was referring to the most fundamental ontological conditions of mental experience. This implies that what is examined is no longer the structure of consciousness Husserl is concerned to analyse, but apparently the existential deep structure fundamental to consciousness.

In Heidegger's thought the fundamental undifferentiated initial state from which he sets out to analyse the realization of human existence (*Existenz*) is '*Befindlichkeit*'.[9-10] This is an over-all mood in which existence in the process of realization first comprehends its being. The human being as it were discloses itself in this mood in realized form, in other words understands itself as existing. This primary state is to be conceived of as one in which *Dasein* – the empirically undefined mere possibility of man – encounters (*begegnen*) the real world in an individual life situation. In this encounter existence manifests itself in a so-called 'existential choice', in which a given possibility of existence is realized and other possibilities remain unrealized (e.g. actualization as man or woman, black or white etc. but never as both). In the encounter the world begins to be differentiated as '*Seiende*' and existence comes to stand in relationship with the emerging beings at the points of contact allowed its own life situation. Of special significance from this point are the meaning relationships developing in consciousness, in which the world is organized in the structure of intentionality. The manner in which consciousness is articulated, however, is already preliminarily restricted and directed in the 'primordial understanding' of existential choices (*vorontologische Seinverständnis*). Primordial understanding is the influence upon the realization of existence deriving from existential choice (e.g. all that follows from actualization as woman, for instance the possibility of motherhood).

Jung appears to refer with his 'archetype as such' to the most fundamental conditions of mental existence. Of what else it may constitute the similar conditions, apart from meaning functions, will not be discussed in the present context. In the same way as Heidegger speaks of primordial understanding, Jung refers to understanding prior to consciousness.[13] In this connection he uses the term 'meaning' in a particularly wide sense. The archetype as such, he says, is potentially 'packed with meaning'. It also 'arranges' the contents of consciousness in a certain way without itself being anything but a structural element. According to Heidegger a sense characteristic appearing in a meaning function is, in the last analysis, based on the facticity (*Faktizität*) of the world, where *Dasein* encounters the world as a relational entity (*Bewandtnisganzheit*). Likewise Jung believes that the archetypal experience gains its content from the sphere of life in which the individual lives. Further, Heidegger claims that the fundamental existential choice and the understanding it involves are in the nature of Fate. Jung also speaks of his 'archetype as such' as 'prerational' and as something which cannot be freely chosen. The archetype as such would thus seem to be something which makes the formation of conscious meaning relationships possible, and at the same time restricts and directs it *a priori*. The manner in which this archetypal primordial understanding is present in specific conscious articulation as dreams and psychotic delusions etc. depends according to Jung upon the content of the lived world at a given moment and upon the various phases of its development. In other words, the manifestation of the archetype in those cases is also determined by the horizons of the lived world.

If such a line of thought may be pursued, a more detailed analysis must ask in what manner the 'archetype as such' constitutes the entity of existential conditions of those meaning relationships which Jung considers important. Heidegger requires dozens, if not hundreds, of terms for the investigation of similar questions, and for Jung, too, speaking of the 'archetype as such' is not sufficient. For an elucidation of his thought it would seem necessary to establish greater conceptual differentiation. By means of existential analytics this end might possibly be achieved.

Archetypal experience, or the psychological component in the concept of archetype, is according to Jung the most basic and most primitive state in the organization of consciousness, and the point from which the analysis of meaning functions must set out. Archetypal experience can be regarded as an over-all apprehending relationship to the world. In phenomenological terms this would imply a state in which no specifically articulating horizons are present, the potential sense is not manifested as the sense characteristic of any object, there is merely a conscious condition in which experience and sense (*Noesis* and *Noema*) are as yet one. Reality is not yet or is no longer differentiated into individual beings, there prevails a kind of phenomenal total relationship to the world as a totality. This is precisely the way Heidegger, too, conceives the primary conscious state (*Gestimmtsein, Stimmung*). Jung's archetypal experience and the basic mood described by Heidegger as the most fundamental state of experience are structurally comparable. Nevertheless the general tone of the two conceptions does differ. For Heidegger the over-all primary experience is oppressive (*ängstlich*); for Jung numinous, sacred, blessed, awful, shattering.

Such a phenomenal initial state must of course be taken only as the starting-point for an analysis of consciousness. It may perhaps be assumed after the manner of Piaget that as an empirical fact this condition prevails in the experience of the child in its first days of life. Momentarily it may also appear in adult experience on occasions of profound anxiety, in dreams and perhaps predominantly in psychotic states. Here what is involved is a regression to a primitive mode of experience. The relationship to the world in the organized sense is lost, or as Heidegger puts it, experiencing has 'come off the rails'. Jung's psychological inquiry into archetypal experience proceeds in the opposite direction to Heidegger's fundamental ontological analysis. Heidegger's method can be applied only in the analysis of the 'archetype as such', this being conceived as the existential structure of archetypal experience. The gradual articulation of archetypal experience in the lived world, again, is susceptible to philosophical analysis by means of phenomenological methods.

Jung's limitation in his doctrine of archetypes is that he fails to achieve a more detailed analysis of the initial state of consciousness he envisages. He does, it is true, name a number of different archetypes – *anima, animus*, the Great Mother, the wise old man, the Self and so on – in describing the nature of different primary experiences. In agreement with him it may be held possible that such a capacity for experience is common to man by reason of the brain structure and the broadly similar environmental conditions of the species. In the language of existential analytics we might say that the species possesses a common primordial understanding. It is also possible that this primordial understanding is actualized as such in life situations in which the real horizontal understanding relationships to the world are either meditatively isolated or otherwise suppressed in their function of articulating sense characteristics. This is the case for example in certain states of religious ecstasy, in dreams and in psychoses. This experiential capacity may also manifest itself, as Jung points out, in religious dogma, in art, mythology, ritual and so on. But from the standpoint of philosophical inquiry Jung's analysis is much too indefinite to allow of a rational account of the progressive phases by which experience attains higher levels of articulation.

The next stage in the development from archetypal experience to differentiated apprehension is for Jung the symbol. Every symbol is an archetype, though not every archetype is a symbol, he says. The two are thus closely allied and it is not always easy to distinguish one from the other in Jung's thought. It would clearly be impossible to discuss with adequate precision such an extensive and manifold context as his psychology of symbols without a thorough structural analysis of symbol theory. Nevertheless Jung obviously did not mean by his term 'symbol' merely a representative sign. The symbol, he says, is an experience in which the best possible understanding is achieved of something which otherwise could not be apprehended.

In one particular context Jung says that symbolic understanding is understanding by means of all four primary functions – thought, feeling, sensation and intuition – simultaneously.[14] By sensation man is in general aware that something exists, by feeling he attributes a value to this something, by thought its rational properties, and by intuition its relationality to wider contexts. The overwhelming, imposing, profound and shattering nature of symbolic experience Jung speaks of with such fascination may thus derive from this multidimensional quality of this kind of understanding. The same general tonality prevails likewise in the archetype. The numinous nature of symbolic experience seems to derive its power precisely from this archetypal basic mood. According to Heidegger 'pure being' (*das reine Sein*) as a relationality to the world *in toto* is encountered in this basic mood. It entails the 'sichbefinden (von Dasein) inmitten des Seienden im Ganzen'.[10] This state, in Heidegger's view, cannot be attained, it simply 'befalls' (*überfällt*). Similarly the symbol cannot for Jung be produced or brought about. Man would simply seem to possess a capacity for over-all understanding in certain life situations. Nevertheless Jung does not conceive of the symbol as a diffuse undifferentiated state comparable to the archetypal; something is now being understood. In other words, in symbolic experience the archetypal all-relation has advanced towards elucidation or precision in the relationality of human existence to the world.

Jung would thus appear to refer with the term 'symbol' to the structural phase in which the over-all all-feeling relationality of archetypal experience no longer subsists, but in which differentiation between the cognizing subject and the reality of the external world is taking place. The relation to the world at this structural turning-point is beginning to crystallize in objectivizing meaning functions, which must presuppose the elementary pattern of articulation in the semantic situation: symbolic vehicle, referent, sense of referent object and consciousness for which this sense subsists. What is confusing is the way Jung in various contexts employs the term 'symbol' to refer not only to all these components of the semantic situation together but also to each of them separately. The primitive aspect of the symbol seems mainly to consist in its non-achievement of linguistic articulation. Understanding is still partly lived through. However, once a meaning function is semantically complete, the symbol ceases for Jung to exist. 'It is killed.' In the framework of hermeneutic analysis the symbol is thus located between the non-differentiated state of archetypal experience and the semantically 'complete' meaning function. Its transitional aspect therefore lends it great significance in an analysis of the emergence of meaning. Jung thus sought by means of his symbol concept to establish a hermeneutic derivation of meaning functions from some elementary condition in which they do not subsist in lucid form.

The birth of a symbol presupposes the actualization of a horizon or horizons in the lived world which possess a tendency to differentiate the diffuse archetypal experience into separate meaning relationships.

Here horizons already existing emerge with their potential capacity to develop sense characteristics. The specific nature of symbolic experience might be conceived of as a condition in which the over-all archetypal mood still predominates. Circumstances and contexts, which by reason of the function of horizons are already somewhat differentiated, lend colour to the basic mood: thus that which the existing horizons have *already* specified is nevertheless *not yet* modified.

In Jung's usage the archetype and the symbol are in a curious fashion both primitive and highly advanced. Though understanding is in one respect still totally undifferentiated, in another it is by reason of its coordinative and integrative effect also of great therapeutic significance. Jung's thought on this point must perhaps be taken to assume that in the child, in whom no differentiation of experience has yet taken place, the totality of experience is still at its most primitive. In the adult, on the other hand, where organized relationality has been established, but in whom over-differentiation has perhaps exerted a disintegrative influence, a return to the integrated mode of experience may be favourable, provided the lucidity of relationships already established is not completely lost, as it possibly is in psychoses. The archetypal-symbolic experience is for Jung thus Janus-faced, potentially favourable and unfavourable from the standpoint of the lived world.

Jung sought with his concepts of archetype and symbol to express something very essential from the point of view of the organization of the lived world and also of psychic disturbances. The pre-linguistic primary stages of understanding are at once the most problematic and the most important aspects in the constitution of the lived world, as Husserl has shown in his analysis of so-called passive constitution. Jung's analysis did not, however, arrive at any very significant results. Perhaps the most valuable achievement was that he drew attention to the heart of the matter as regards psychic disturbances and psychotherapy, namely how the organization of meaning relationships of the lived world is to be conceived. Jung's efforts can be said to have shown beyond question at least that depth psychology has difficulty in attaining a sufficiently differentiated and at the same time satisfactorily lucid descriptive terminology without a philosophical analysis of the structure of its concepts.

5. The Topography of Consciousness and Psychic Disturbance

Jung's restriction of his analysis of the lived world to a topographical description of consciousness is a remnant of Freud's thought. It hinders rather than promotes Jung's approach to his ultimate goal. His typology itself – and ever more clearly as his researches proceeded – displays the realization that consciousness or the lived world (what Jung himself terms the psyche) is an entity of meaning functions at various levels of organization. Husserl's conception of different stages of development and clarity in the appearing of sense is of decisive significance for a philosophical analysis of Jung's psychology. It serves to explain how there can exist these various levels of meaning function of which Jung speaks.

Seeking to analyse the constitution of meaning functions, Husserl sets out from the most elementary possible component of sense manifestation given to consciousness. Tracing the articulation of meaning functions from this point he distinguishes two main phases in their constitution, a passive and an active. The former is particularly essential to an analysis of the structure of the unconscious mind. Only in infinitely tiny moments is the mind immediately and absolutely purely in relationship to its object. This relationship can never become conscious as such; only a series of such flashes is consciously manifested. When in these momentary phases the sense characteristic is developed by means of the horizons, the actualization of these horizons and their completive function (*Erfüllung*) is at first spontaneous and independent of conscious guidance. Precisely this aspect Husserl refers to with his term 'passive'. As a result of continuously evolving structural phases the appearance of sense gradually crystallizes, gains precision until finally the stage of conscious meaning functions is reached. The phase in which the meaning function is ultimately categorized in a manner corresponding to everyday reality and becomes linguistically expressible, Husserl calls the phase of active constitution. The conscious manifestation of sense presumes, according to Husserl, the presence of a conscious horizon.

Jung likewise conceives of the appearance of sense as a process, a gradual advance towards clarity and not simply an evenly lucid manifestation on an either-or basis. The personal unconscious comprises for him mainly incomplete, deficient and not-yet-differentiated formation of meaning functions. In fact Jung holds, on the level of the personal unconscious, that what is involved is the organization of suppressed meaning functions which cannot attain consciousness because no adequate horizons are actualized in the conscious mind. On this level Jung also sees a correspondence between psychic disturbance and the unconscious. The manifestations of the collective unconscious, archetype and symbol, are on the other hand genuine and constructive if brought comprehendingly into relation with the lived world. After all the collective unconscious comprises the primordial understanding common to the species. The task for man is to develop the formation of meaning relationships of his lived world on the basis restricted and directed by the primordial understanding of mankind.

Becoming conscious in the sense Jung speaks of it is also explicable in terms of the phases Husserl distinguishes. Attainment of consciousness means for Jung differentiation, organization and development. The condition for cognitive awareness is that a 'receptive' horizon is actualized in consciousness, in which as yet undeveloped and unconscious experience gains the clarity requisite for active constitution. If no receptive system of relationships is afforded there will be no conscious event – in other words new understanding will not take place. Becoming conscious is specifically the attainment of a new sense characteristic in a context already understood.

The instantaneous opposition of conscious and unconscious loses its significance in Jung as compared with what it meant to Freud. Tension for Jung is based on the failure of meaning relationships – as such – to fit each other or the totality of the lived world. This is in keeping with the phenomenological view and represents a philosophically sound conception. No other dynamics, conflicts, contradictions or harmonies can be imagined to prevail in the sphere of the lived world than those based on sense characteristics, so that these concepts are inevitably bound to that of intentionality as Husserl conceives it. Conflicts and ambivalences etc. in the lived world are always conflicts between sense and sense. If a dynamic, attraction, pressure, force etc. is envisaged which does not derive from the structure of intentionality, it must be based on the concretizing mode of thought. But then meaning relationships would have to be attributed concrete form such that tension of the nature of a physical force would act upon them as an adequate influence.

The unconscious is not for Jung in itself anything of a disturbance, nor is consciousness any measure of normality. Absolutely comprehensive cognition is not possible even in principle, because in the process of organization of the lived world there will always from moment to moment be elementary phases which are not in the psychological sense ready for consciousness. In the light of hermeneutics a psychic disturbance comprises an unfavourable state of understanding in the lived world.[1,15] Also for Jung a psychic disturbance is unfavourable understanding arising apparently from either archetypal primordial understanding, or erroneous horizon formation in the lived world, or again of course a combination of both. When archetypal understanding cannot be coordinated with the lived world, however, it is always a question of insufficiency of the horizons of the lived world. In the last analysis a psychic disturbance is thus a function of inadequate or undeveloped horizons. Speaking in his earliest works of what he termed 'complexes' Jung appears to have conceived of their emergence precisely as Husserl does, as a function of horizons. The formation of a complex presumes a certain system of sense-manifesting relationships, the 'nuclear element' as a horizon. In the context this affords the child begins to underestimate its own performance or see it otherwise in an unfavourable light and 'develops a complex'. Also all manner of other negative development of meaning functions, including neurotic and psychotic distortions, are in principle to be understood on this basis. Horizons are representatives of the past in the moments of spontaneous modification of the lived world, and they are mainly what are referred to when we speak of psychogenesis in connection with psychic disturbance.

Although psychic disturbance is in principle regarded as a function of the horizon, there is a great deal left which demands detailed analysis. Account must always be taken of the lived world as an entity. Jung held that a psychic disturbance constitutes in a certain respect the flourishing of one primary function at the expense of others. For example the prominence of thought to the detriment of feeling is always a disturbance of psychic balance. Feeling should, according to Jung, hold complete sway within its own sphere. Although meaning functions may in themselves be well developed and realistic, they must also be balanced among themselves for the lived world to be normal. Of course the mere observation that a given function has acquired undue emphasis is not enough in itself. To comprehend the specific nature of the disturbance we must also know the degree and the content of this over-expansion – in other words the individual meaning functions involved.

6. Psychotherapy

The objective in Jungian psychotherapeutic analysis of the lived world is to understand the various levels and types of manifestation of mental activity as a whole. The analysis is such as to assist the client towards an objectivating understanding of his own understanding. The object of psychotherapy is to correct and develop meaning relationships in such a way that the lived world will attain sufficient integration and harmony. The possibilities this treatment has of promoting conscious understanding and correcting for example neurotic meaning functions are based mainly – to employ the term of structural analysis – on its ability to actualize horizons in which sense appearance may develop along favourable lines. This takes place initially and for the most part at the level of active constitution, although the process may also be reflected in the sphere of passive constitution, as dreams for example demonstrate. The correction of a disturbance entails restraining a given type of meaning function, developing deficiently established ones and bringing the primary functions into equilibrium with each other.

Jung appears to have regarded psychotherapy fully in the spirit of phenomenology. Certain of his disciples and successors are at present developing his views ever more clearly along these lines.[16-18] Assistance to the client is not according to Jung a matter of revealing the 'cause' of the disturbance. Since a disturbance comprises the underdevelopment, distortion and alienation from reality of meaning relationships, their correction and development and their adaptation to the lived world *in toto* is the source of the 'cure'. And this may proceed in widely different ways depending on the case in hand. Husserl says that a meaning function has a long history describable in terms of structural phases. Likewise Jung adopts a historical view for example of the organization of a neurotic lived world. For both scholars the background of a meaning function is extremely complicated. Jung does not assume any single distortive horizon or type of horizon. Hence, too, the development of a meaning function in a new direction may be a very slow and laborious process.

Horizons are not conceived of in phenomenology as a static scheme but as meaning functions of the lived world and thus as subject to constant modification and development. Jung appears to have realized that the psychotherapeutic analyis of the lived world is a unique study in that it is constantly changing its object, the meaning function and the totality of meaning functions. In as much as something new is understood in the context of a neurotic symptom, e.g. father aggression, it follows that subsequently the client's conception of that context, i.e. his father, can no longer be exactly the same. In the next phase the new insight is inevitably present in the horizontal basis. Nothing can be apprehended or understood purely, because there is always present in understanding the function of historically sedimented horizons.

Horizons are present in the psychotherapeutic process in the understanding of both therapist and client. The psychotherapist is not superhuman, he cannot free himself from the basic laws of consciousness. His analysis must thus comprise an examination of matters likewise within given horizons. Indeed he cannot escape these bounds because they represent the *a priori* condition for his analytic approach. Nevertheless he is able to regulate the actualization of horizons. And in this light we may understand why in his work Jung shunned modes of thought and interpretation based on causality. Various series of events in the past may be recreated with comparative authenticity perhaps in their space-time dimensions, but the perfect repetition of a feeling experience is impossible. What is attained in this case is never more than a reconstruction. For example we may feel the disappointments of early infancy in the manner in which, in the context of our present emotional horizons, we feel we felt them as children.

Jung appreciated more clearly than any other of the earliest depth psychologists that psychotherapy is at the same time reduction and construction. The former is not possible without the latter. No vacuum is created, the previous state is gradually modified into another. This serves to explain why Jung paid so little attention to precise theory in psychotherapy. Since meaning functions alter as a result of analysis, a theory as one of the horizons present in the process would modify them in its own direction the more markedly, the more the theory predominated in the treatment. The constructive phase, the phase of becoming something, was a special concern of his in his psychotherapeutic efforts. He seems to have taken for granted that genuine assistance is afforded, *Selbstwerdung* is achieved, best from the basis of the client's own life situation. Change in the psychotherapeutic sense is for Jung precisely a more genuine understanding of one's own life situation. The developmental tendencies of the individual should be evolved out of himself and their autonomous growth safeguarded by the therapist. The application of an established and boldly generalizing theory might in Jung's view only hinder or mislead the process. In this reverence for the individual life situation Jung's conception once more approaches the basic views of Heidegger.

When a better awareness – in a very wide sense – is achieved in psychotherapy of the various types, degrees and relationships of sense appearing, Jung assumes that the analysis will simultaneously open the way for a comparatively unproblematic co-existence of these various components. Discrepancy, conflict and estrangement of meaning functions will be alleviated and the reality of experiencing increased when the individual understands where a sense is from, how it appears just so, how the circumstance whose sense appears comprises part of his particular life situation. The gradual process of elucidation in which this objective is achieved, Jung calls individuation. This process takes place in psychotherapy, but it may also be possible in other modes of self-cognition. The ideal ultimate state to which self-analysis and self-cognition should lead is 'self' (*Selbst*). This is the sublime end Jung, the prophet of individuality, envisages for man's development. Each human being should become just that person who is potentially contained in his own conditions of existence. Jung is well aware that this objective is at very best but imperfectly attained.

7. An Assessment of Jung's Position and Significance

Jung showed at the very beginning of the development of psychotherapy that it can be pursued in more than one way. This is a conception that has since found confirmation from many quarters. However, this multiplicity and apparent disunity may have had a beneficent effect on work in this field. A variety of possibilities have been followed up and it has been possible to take account of demands and expectations placed upon psychotherapy by reason of the diversity of human personality.

While being the main source of this multiplicity and disruption Jung has also paradoxically paved the way for the future integration of psychotherapic research. An understanding of Jung helps to see that the essential core in all psychotherapy is the same, because what is always involved is the problem of meaning in the lived world. The present chapter has sought to show how the current mode of hermeneutic philosophical inquiry is particularly well adapted to an analysis of Jung's depth psychology and psychotherapy. This is because, though he expresses himself in the terminology of early twentieth-century psychology, the model of his thought is fundamentally that of phenomenology and philosophy of existence. Influence exerted on the human entity at the psychic level rests basically on intentionality. Therefore the empirical study of consciousness pursued for example in psychotherapy must be based on a philosophical analysis of consciousness and its existential conditions, which are at present evidently best represented by the hermeneutic approach. The terminology and theory of psychotherapy should throughout be adequate from the point of view of the intentionality structure of the lived world. Only when the whole field has been completely reviewed in the light of this basic requirement can a theory and a practice be evolved on sound philosophical foundations. This was the direction inclined to by Jung's thought. This, in a current assessment of his life's work, must be considered his most valuable contribution. He directed inquiry along lines which will very probably prove rewarding and take development yet another step forward.

CHAPTER 15

The Jungian Interpretation of History and Its Educational Implications

BY JAMES L. HENDERSON

There are layers of time in everything, including ourselves. 'Once upon a time' – that familiar phrase – can lay them bare. When the emphasis is placed on the first of these four words, what stands out is the absolute uniqueness of each person and event: once, and once only, did the light fall just so in a Constable landscape; once, and once only, did Paul see a blinding light on the road to Damascus. About this aspect of each episode there hangs a kind of futile finality, but there is also its complement, where constancy is the keynote. However different the context of time and place and character, 'once upon a time' then promises security, reassurance and renewal. It seems to assert that behind all appearance of change there is a pattern of perpetuation, a quality of indestructibility, which witnesses to a time different from flying sequence.

As an old man introducing his autobiography, Carl Gustav Jung refers to this quality:

Life has always seemed to me like a plant that lives on its rhizome. Its true life is invisible, hidden in the rhizome. The part that appears above ground lasts only a single summer. Then it withers away – an ephemeral apparition. When we think of the unending growth and decay of life and civilizations, we cannot escape the impression of an absolute nullity. Yet I have never lost a sense of something that lives and endures underneath the eternal flux. What we see is the blossom, which passes. The rhizome remains. In the end the only events in my life worth telling are those when the imperishable world irrupted into the transitory one.[1]

Such irruptions do occur and may be studied. They provide the evidence needed to convince us that human striving has a meaning, that it is not transitory and futile – that in fact nothing which has once really lived ever dies.

A common image of the past is of a time which stretches horizontally away behind the back of the present through thousands of years to some undiscovered and perhaps undiscoverable origin.

Scattered along this time-track lie a number of more or less complex
societies, of which Western Civilization is one. These have two
features, the transience of all individual lives and most works and the
durability of certain values. There appears to be a connection between
the durability of those values and the degree of consciousness attained
by the personalities and groups holding them. The quality of that
consciousness cuts clear across the sequential horizontal time-track, to
belong in fact to once 'upon-a-time' in its second sense.

A hypothetical example and its accompanying diagram may serve
to illustrate the point:

Diagram One

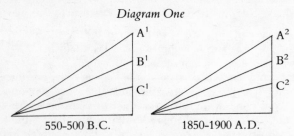

550-500 B.C.   1850-1900 A.D.

Let us assume that there are six men, all of whom lived for fifty years in
the horizontal past, three between 550 and 500 BC (A1, B1, C1) and
three between AD 1850 and 1900 (A2, B2, C2). These all existed for
spans of similar duration, and we may assume also that insofar as they
did not remain unaware of themselves and their environment they did
not remain complete slaves to mere sequence: they somehow acquired
the capacity 'to look before and after', to anticipate and to remember.
Yet the degree of their awareness must also be assumed to have varied
enormously. Although they lived at the same time, A1, whose angle
of awareness to the horizontal time-track is, let us say, 75°, partakes
less of the quality of B1, whose angle is 50°, than he does of the quality
of A2. For A2's angle is also 75°, although it is situated hundreds of
years later in chronological time. A1 partakes even less of the quality
of C1, whose angle is only 25°. In fact, the more acute the
consciousness, the less the time-boundedness.

There is more of a common quality of A1-ishness between Socrates
and Schweitzer, chronologically separated by centuries, than there is
between Socrates and his serving man on the one hand and Schweitzer
and a hack preacher on the other. The degrees of consciousness,
although they do of necessity appear as belonging to a scale of
morality, do so only in a relative way. For what we, by reason of our
involvement in the human predicament, have to assess in terms of
good and evil transcends good and evil in the dimension of pure
consciousness.

A consensus of Eastern and Western wisdom extends the hypothesis to include the idea that after a certain height of consciousness has been attained, the limitations of material incarnation are transcended and may be known to have been transcended. According both to Buddhist and Taoist doctrine it is possible during one life time or more so to cultivate the spiritual principle in oneself as to establish between it and the spirit of pure consciousness a bond which physical death does not dissolve. That, however, is only the case when the consciousness has been raised to a sufficiently high level.

To what, it may next be asked, can be ascribed such varieties of heights and durabilities of consciousness? In suggesting an answer, it will be necessary to adopt another and equally indispensable view of the past, namely a vertical one. In an essay entitled 'Mind and the Earth' Jung supplies a helpful, though admittedly incomplete, analogy between the structure of human personality and an historic site:

. . . we have then to describe and to explain a building the upper storey of which was erected in the nineteenth century, the ground floor dates from the sixteenth century, and a careful examination of the masonry discloses the fact that it was reconstructed from a dwelling-tower of the eleventh century. In the cellar we discover Roman foundation walls, and under the cellar a filled-in cave, in the floor of which stone tools are found, and remnants of glacial fauna in the layers below. That would be a sort of picture of our own mental structures. We live in the upper storey, and are only dimly aware that our lower storey is somewhat old-fashioned. As to what lies beneath the superficial crust of the earth we remain quite unconscious . . .

But the deeper we descend into the past the narrower the horizon becomes, and in the darkness we come upon the nearest and most intimate things, till finally we reach the naked rock floor, down to that early dawn of time when reindeer hunters fought for a bare and wretched existence against the elemental forms of wild nature. These men were still in the full possession of their animal instincts, without which their existence would have been impossible. The free sway of the instincts is not consistent with a powerful and comprehensive consciousness. The consciousness of primitives, as of the child, is of a spasmodic nature; his world, too, like the child's, is very limited. Our childhood even rehearses, according to the phylogenetic principle, reminiscences of the pre-history of the race and of mankind in general. Phylogenetically as well as ontogenetically we have grown up out of the dark confines of the earth.'[2]

Elsewhere Jung remarks:

The psyche is not of today; its ancestry goes back many millions of years, individual consciousness is only the flower and the fruit of a season, sprung from the perennial rhizome beneath the earth; and it would find itself in better accord with the truth if it took the wisdom of the rhizome into its calculations.'[3]

The premise we have just established compels us next to try and correlate the flight of time along the horizontal with the time taken by individuals and groups to grow vertically in consciousness; the attempt will lead us on to a diagonal bisecting the right angle created by the pull of these two arms.

If poetic is more acceptable than psychological insight, reference with regard to this view of the structure of human personality could usefully be made to an observation of Rilke's to the effect that 'our customary consciousness inhabits the apex of a pyramid, whose base in us (and in a sense beneath us) spreads to such breadth that, the further we find ourselves capable of letting ourselves down into it, the more generally do we appear to be included in the given facts, not dependent on time and space, of in the broadest sense worldly experience.' Rilke is convinced that 'at some deeper cross-section of this pyramid of consciousness mere being could become an event for us, that inviolable presentness and simultaneity of all that which, in the upper "normal" apex of self-consciousness it is granted to us to experience as mere sequence.'[4]

Two principles of Jung's Analytical Psychology support the concept just sketched. First, there is the contention that the conscious derives from the unconscious, that the conscious part of human personality is supported and sustained by layers, first individual and then collective, of the unconscious. Above and below, light and dark are in a state of dynamic relationship and polarity to one another. The opposite of what is in the conscious is always found in the unconscious; for example outwardly I smile upon my guest while inwardly I frown, or consciously I detest my rival while unconsciously I love him. This description of personality structure, somewhat mechanistically expressed but not so conceived, is simply posited by Jung as an essential part of his view of human nature. As to the origins of consciousness, he suggest two ways in which it seems to come about:

The one is a moment of high emotional tension comparable to that scene in Wagner's *Parsifal*, when Parsifal in the instant of greatest temptation suddenly realises the meaning of Amfortas's wound. The other is a contemplative condition, where representations move like dream images. Suddenly an association between two apparently disconnected and remote representations takes place, through which a great amount of latent energy may be released. Such a moment is a sort of revelation. In each case it is a concentration of energy, arising from an external or internal stimulus that brings about consciousness.[5]

To anticipate somewhat, we could say that history is the record of such concentrations of energy. Secondly, there is the Jungian concept of the collective unconscious as being constituted of archetypes or primordial images.

The primordial image or archetype is a figure, whether it be a daemon, man or process, that repeats itself in the course of history whenever creative fantasy is freely manifested. Essentially, therefore, it is a mythological figure. If we subject these images to a closer investigation, we discover them to be the formulated resultants of countless typical experiences of our ancestors

The natural man is characterised by unmitigable instinctiveness . . . The heritage that stands in opposition to this condition (i.e. consciousness) consists in the memory-deposits from all the experience of his ancestors. One is inclined to approach this assumption with scepticism because one thinks that 'inherited ideas' are meant. This is not the case. What is meant is rather inherited possibilities of ideas, 'paths', that have been gradually developed through the cumulative experience of the ancestors. To deny the inheritance of the paths would be equivalent to denying the inheritance of the brain. To be logical such sceptics would have to maintain that the child is born with an ape's brain. Since, however, it is born with a human brain, this must grow or later begin to function in a human way, and apparently it will begin at the level of the most recent ancestors. Obviously this functioning remains deeply unconscious to the child. At first he is conscious only of the instincts and all that opposes them is embodied in his visible parents. Thus the child has no idea that what stands in his way may be within himself. Rightly or wrongly, whatsoever interferes with him is projected upon the parents or surrogates . . . Although our inheritance consists in physiological paths, still it was mental processes in our ancestors that created the paths. If these traces come to consciousness again in the individual experience and thus appear as individual acquisitions, they are none the less pre-existing traces which are merely filled out by the individual experience. Every impressive experience is such an impression in an ancient, but previously unconscious, stream-bed.[6]

The archetypes of the collective unconscious may therefore be thought of as continually manifesting themselves in symbolic and conceptual forms on the horizontal, sequential time-track of an individual's or a society's brief span of existence between birth and death. For example, the archetype of death and rebirth, the destiny of spirit's entry into nature's rhythms, takes symbolic form in the myth of Dionysus hundreds of years BC and also in the Stroller figure in Yeats's play, 'The King of the Great Clock Tower', in the twentieth century AD. It is a matter of time-bound expressions of timeless realities.

Such manifestation has the quality of a tension constituted of two opposing forces, an impulse towards conscious personality and individual responsibility and a contradictory impulse towards adherence or return to an unconscious state of irresponsibility. For example, anyone experiencing the challenge of growth must feel ambivalently towards the pain which inevitably accompanies the pleasure attending it: part of him feels the urge to accept and endure it, while another part feels 'I can't bear it' and yearns to return to mother's apron string.

Diagram Two
Angles of awareness – Diagonals of consciousness

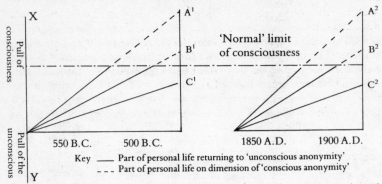

Key ——— Part of personal life returning to 'unconscious anonymity'
    - - - Part of personal life on dimension of 'conscious anonymity'

Diagram Two is intended to illustrate the psychological and historical aspects of this conflict. It should be noted that the ingredients of impulse Y are what Jung calls man's 'Saurian tail', i.e. all those archaic elements of man's instinctual life back to its remotest past, which are still present, for the most part unconsciously, in the individual actually living between 1850 and 1900.

The product of such conflict may, as the diagram helps to suggest, be called the diagonals of consciousness, for example the diagonal of A2. Yet his superior capacity for consciousness, which is the necessary assumption in our original premise, enables him to transcend the limitation of a mere one life-time sequence. The greater strength of impulse X pulling counter to impulse Y results in such an acute A2 angle that the further portion of his diagonal of consciousness escapes, if it may be expressed thus, the gravitational pull of the limited, horizontal time-span and occupies the very dimension which is filled by the further portion of A1's diagonal. Such an achievement is of course only possible for that part of A's personality which has attained a spiritual condition capable of persisting without any longer requiring bodily form. As previously explained, Eastern thought sanctions and some Western psychological investigation suggests the validity of such a concept of a timeless 'communion of saints'. In somewhat less poetic terms this could be defined as that dimension in which every thing that has fulfilled its earthly hypothesis endures.

All the rest of A2 – his corpse that is buried or burnt – simply drops back into the anonymous source from which it derived and possesses no ultimate, historical significance whatsoever. It is in fact all that part of him which has not transcended the secondary characteristic of individual ego-existence by transmutation into spirit-self, independent of time and space. It is what has failed to make the passage from original 'unconscious anonymity' to eventual 'conscious anonymity'.[7] It is all that of Brahman which has not yet got to know itself in Atman. Because it is only a few at any time who have thus disciplined themselves and thus been blessed, there is far more of B2 and C2 to die and suffer corruption than there is of A2 – and far less to survive. The development of the idea of death as a problem occurs only with the increasing growth of ego–consciousness: for it is when the ego becomes aware of itself as a prisoner of that horizontal, linear time, which unrolls from past to future, that the historical consciousness has either to learn how to transcend time or submit to such a de-mythicized version of it as to admit its meaninglessness. That such an effort of transcendence can be made successfully is well demonstrated by R. C. Johnson, who has shown most skilfully how the disciplines of natural science, pyschical research and religion can contribute to the accomplishing of that task.[8]

Before proceeding further, it will be useful to summarise the argument thus far: there is a need, it has been suggested, for two views of the past, a horizontal and a vertical one; these views are countenanced by much traditional wisdom teaching, particularly of the East, by the records of aesthetic experience and by the findings of analytical psychology. The last named provided us with two principles, one the derivation of the conscious from the unconscious and two, the functions of archetypes; their combination indicated a perpetual state of conflict between the pull of consciousness X and the pull of unconsciousness Y, which in historical terms could be called the pull of the future and the pull of the past – the resultant lines of tension being named the diagonals of consciousness.

Thus the combining of sequential, horizontal time with the vertical growth of human personalities produces the diagonal of consciousness as an expression of their inter-relationship. (See Diagram Three). The past needs to be thought of as in us now, as part of our unconscious personality structure and so behind us chronologically in consciousness. Progoff has well indicated the nature of this concept in the following passage:

The psyche has depth downward, but it also extends backwards, across, through time, so that somehow history is latently contained and unconsciously expressed in each individual. This is Jung's great thesis for the study of history in terms of the Psyche. It makes possible a dimension of time-study in which time is a unitary category for personality and social history.'[9]

Up onto the horizontal time-track of A2's fifty years span of life come vertically from below the characteristics of the unconscious; all of man that is making for conscious personality must regard these as belonging to an earlier, more primitive, archaic state, but they are also his very source of life, his roots, his past. An example of the process would be a quite primitive upthrust of lust or greed, originally just instinctual forces but now regarded with disfavour or at least wariness by consciousness. They can then be utilized by A2, according to his capacity, to assist him in the steepening of his diagonal, or more simply be felt by A2 without any advance in his own use of them or be the cause of A2's decline of diagonal into a B2 or C2. The point is that Tarquin's rape of Lucrece in the past and A2's largely unconscious desire to rape his pin-up girl form part of the same 'unitary category', and understanding of the motivation of the former can help to control the latter.

Diagram Three

1850-1900 A.D.

In case such a concept of the nature and function of history should appear startling, it may help to recall here a Hindu sanction for it. The Indian world picture is constituted out of two kinds of time: one is 'curved time', exemplified in cyclical terms of existence emanating from and leading to a timeless state of godhead; in our terminology this would correspond to the horizontal time-track. The other Indian time is that of individual man engaged in working out his Karma, a kind of zig-zag time reflecting his good and evil features, and this would correspond to what in our terminology we have called personality. The link between the two is provided by the diagonal of consciousness. It is tempting to think that it was some such link which the Russian philosopher Berdyaev was seeking to establish when he wrote the following sentence: 'Thus the real goal of the philosophy of history is to establish a bond between men and history, between man's destiny and the metaphysics of history.'[10] ·

Our image of history, time past, is therefore that of a record of the growth of human consciousness on the diagonal of force caused by the tension between the pull of the past and the unconscious on the horizontal and the future and the conscious on the vertical. Our study of history becomes significant, so satisfying the demands of what Whitehead called the 'insistent present', only insofar as we recognise and experience the reality of these diagonals. In other words there has to be a capacity for diagonals in ourselves to respond to the diagonals of others.

The 'dimension of time-study' to which Progoff refers is one in which the essence of the human predicament – the dilemma implicit in being alive at all – never changes, however much the expression of it may vary. It is the archetypes which determine the kind of experience we have, but it is we as individuals who determine what we actually experience. Within its 'unitary category' there are infinite numbers and varieties of manifestations of a certain number of archetypes. When these occur at a high level of consciousness we can, if ourselves sufficiently well-endowed, respond to them wherever they happen to be placed chronologically. Recognising and naming them – a Beethoven sonata – a Socratic dialogue – a Newtonian insight – we call what they represent civilization and are sustained by its perennial truth. When they occur and persist, as is much more often the case, at a low level of consciousness, then too we respond – often very strongly – from our own low levels, but we hardly ever know it or admit it in ourselves, and when we detect it in others we call it barbarism.

I hope that I have expressed with sufficient clarity the image of a relationship between the flight of time and the growth of consciousness. What needs to be held in the mind is the culmination of this relationship in an awareness of real identification with a transcendental and timeless reality, independent of what mortals call death.

'Never the spirit was born, the spirit shall cease to be never.
Never was time when it was not, end and beginning are dreams.
Birthless and deathless and changeless, the spirit endureth for ever,
Death does not change it at all, dead though the house of it seems.'

(Gita)

A full and confident knowledge of this truth is what we exist for: failure in this undertaking can lead only to despair – a plight which two very different writers discerned as the desperate one of post-Christian Western culture catastrophically threatened by the 'death of its house'.

In a poem called 'Vastness' Tennyson wrote:

What is it all, if we all of us end in being
Our own corpse-coffin at last,
Swallowed in vastness, lost in silence, drown'd
In the depths of a meaningless past?
What but a murmur of gnats in the gloom, or a
Moment's answer of bees in their hive?

In an essay entitled 'Rilke and the Concept of Death' William Rose put his finger exactly on the value of that German poet's contribution:

If death is to be absorbed as the final blossoming of life, something to which we are working up and not a running-down of the machine, it must logically be something more than mere annihilation . . . Rilke is absorbed in the problem of death because he regards it as fulfilment of life.[11]

An actual passage from one of Rilke's letters brings the whole challenge to an eloquent climax:

. . . how is it possible to live when the fundamentals of this our life are so completely incomprehensible? When we are always inadequate in love, wavering in our determination and impotent in the face of death? In this book, written under the profoundest inner compulsion, I have not managed to conquer my amazement over the fact that for thousands of years humanity has been concerning itself with life and death (not to speak of God) and yet, even today (and for how much longer?) stands in front of these primary, these immediate tasks (strictly speaking the only ones we have – for what else have we to do?) so helplessly, so pitiably, caught between terror and evasion like the veriest beginners. Is it not incredible? My own amazement over this fact whenever I give way to it drives me into the greatest confusion and then into a sort of horror; but behind the horror there is something else, something so immediate and yet transcending all immediacy, something so intense that I cannot decide with my feelings whether it be like fire or ice. . .

   And so, you see, the same thing happened with Death. Experienced and yet not to be apprehended by us in his reality, always overshadowing yet never quite acknowledged by us, violating and surpassing the meaning of life from the very beginning, he too was banished and excommunicated so that he should not continually interrupt us in our search for this meaning . . . More and more the suspicion grew up against him that he was the anti-thesis, the opponent, the invisible opposite in the air; the end of all our joys, the perilous glass of our happiness from which we may be spilled at any moment . . . Nature, however, knew nothing of this banishment which we have somehow managed to accomplish – when a tree blossoms death blooms in it as well as life . . . And love too, which bedevils our arithmetic so as to introduce a game of Near and Far . . . love too has no regard for our divisions but sweeps us, trembling as we are, into an infinite consciousness of the whole. Lovers do not live from fear of the Actual . . . of them one can say that God is nourishing them and that death does not harm them: for they are full of death because they are full of life.[12]

Any move out of this impasse involves an appeal to the actuality of that part of human personality which, unlike the physical body and the conscious Ego, is in fact deathless. In his book *The Myth of the Eternal Return* Eliade has pointed the way:

The death of the individual and the death of humanity are alike necessary for their regeneration. Any form whatever, by the mere fact that it exists as such and endures, necessarily loses vigour and becomes worn; to recover vigour it must be re-absorbed into the formless if only for an instant; it must be restored to the primordial unity from which it issued; in other words, it must return to 'chaos' (on the cosmic plane), to 'orgy' (on the social plane) to darkness (for seed), to water (baptism on the human plane) . . .[13]

The two most dramatic attempts to break this circle and form history into a kind of linear progressivism have been the pseudo-Messianism of an incomplete Christianity and Marxism, neither of which, however, has been able to save man from what Eliade calls the 'terror of history' – his finding himself literally at a dead end. Yet

Strictly speaking science does not know of death but only of change, for science uses the word death only to connote a natural process, common to every form of life – a part of the cycle of life, to be observed in all nature. Seed, shoot, bud, flower, fruit, seed, is the complete cycle; why regard any of these changes as climacteric?[14]

But so to conceive of death requires of most of us moderns in Western civilisation a tremendous effort to think differently. For, with the decay of genuinely held convictions on Christian lines about human survival, the assumption has crept in that, so far as we personally are concerned, when we die that is the end of everything. Instead of this happening we can learn to adopt a different attitude to death by coming to view it as that part of the historical process, described here already as the disappearance back into 'unconscious anonymity' of all the secondary characteristics of human individuality. Accordingly nothing dies that has attained a certain level of consciousness, and it is towards the attainment of such a level that the 'whole creation travaileth and groaneth'.

CHAPTER 16

Carl Gustav Jung and Musical Art

BY GUNTER PULVERMACHER

In his research leading to the system of 'Analytical Psychology' Carl Gustav Jung extended his studies into fields as diverse as those of medicine, psychology, biology, zoology, archaeology, philosophy, mythology, alchemy, mysticism, religion, orientalism, literature and the visual arts.

Considering his life-long interest in the great cultural movements, in the sciences and in the humanities one finds it rather puzzling that the art of music hardly attracted the attention of Jung's enquiring mind. There are less than twenty references to music in the general index to his Collected Works.

According to Alan Watts's autobiography *In My Own Way*[1] Jung's third daughter, Marianne Niehus-Jung, once remarked that her father had never understood music. Another interesting statement relating to Jung's rare comments on music can be found in the chapter on 'The Therapy of Music' in the book *C.G. Jung Speaking: Interviews and Encounters*.[2] There the reader is informed that Jung supposedly answered a question about his own relationship to music by saying: 'I know the whole literature – I have heard everything and all the great performers' – an astonishingly exaggerated claim, to which he added: 'But I never listen to music any more. It exhausts and irritates me.'

Those two quotations can be accepted as sufficient proof of Jung's particular attitude towards musical art – an attitude which furnishes good grounds for withholding from him the epithet of 'music-lover'. To what extent his daughter's remark justifies the even stronger adjective 'unmusical' is a matter of conjecture.

Jung's psychological research led him to an extensive study of symbolism, especially concerning the symbols of the arts, mythology, religion and magic. Symbols can stand for the most varied contents ranging from natural events to internal psychological processes – contents which can never be fully expressed rationally. There is no doubt that owing to Jung's metaphysical outlook, symbols played an important part in his psychological enquiries, because they come out of that 'between-world of subtle reality which can be adequately expressed through the symbol alone'.[3]

Jung was aware therefore of psychological implications of music, yet he left us nothing but general, rather vague comments. The deeper significance of musical symbols seemed to have eluded him. Those symbols may refer to manifold apsects of music, for example to the material itself, to sound, or to musical form, to musical intruments, to musical notation (often spoken of as 'Augenmusik' – eye music), to melody, harmony, rhythm and still other elements of music.

One of Jung's more explicit if short statements on music is contained in a letter to Serge Moreux dated 20 January 1950.[4] This letter was Jung's answer to Moreux's request for an article on 'The role of music in the collective unconscious' for the Parisian journal *Polyphonie, Revue Musicale*. Jung declined the proposal 'for reasons of age and health'. It is, however, relevant to our point at issue to repeat the main section of this letter:

Music certainly has to do with the collective unconscious – as the drama does too; this is evident in Wagner, for example. Music expresses, in some way, the movements of the feelings (or emotional values) that cling to the unconscious processes. The nature of what happens in the collective unconscious is archetypal, and archetypes always have a numinous quality that expresses itself in emotional stress. Music expresses in sounds what fantasies and visions express in visual images. I am not a musician and would not be able to develop these ideas for you in detail. I can only draw your attention to the fact that music represents the movement, development, and transformation of motifs of the Collective Unconscious. In Wagner this is very clear and also in Beethoven, but one finds it equally in Bach's 'Kunst der Fuge'.

As Moreux asked for an article on 'the role of music in the collective unconscious', Jung disregarded the 'personal unconscious' in his letter, a not altogether unexpected disregard, because he never concerned himself as much with the relatively limited personal unconscious as with the world of the collective unconscious, which he considered to be the abode of archetypes, universal symbols shared by all people everywhere and at all times. But even here, Jung's remarks are evasive and superficial. At least, he admitted that he was 'not a musician' and 'would not be able to develop these ideas'.

Generally speaking, it is true that the psychological study of the visual arts has been accepted far more readily and widely than that of music. This seems to be a paradox, because music is an important part of every culture on earth, especially in the form of song – that is in its combination with language – while the visual arts are not universally present in every cultural setting of man. The psychologist cannot ignore the fact that music is specially receptive of symbols, because it uses the most abstract material: sound, which is invisible, non-

258 *Jung in Modern Perspective*

tangible and transitory. It has always a beginning and an end. Literature, too, makes use of sound which is, however, word-sound which has a linguistic logic with meanings reducible to distinct dictionary definitions. Those meanings have a significance which goes beyond the mere word-sound.

Musical sound, on the other hand, is not bound to definite ideas. It is an end in itself. Moreover, music usually produces a number of sounds simultaneously in the form of harmony and counterpoint. Thus, while literature appeals, before everything else, to the intellect, music is a predominantly emotive art, particularly suited to express mystical, divine conceptions of superhuman powers.

When we remember that sound is actually born out of silence, we can understanding that the Indian Vedas explain the production of sound as the very process of creation. The same idea is expressed in the Book of Genesis of the Bible, where it is written: 'And God *said* "Let there be light", and there was light.' It is, of course, important to remember that exalted or poetic words were never spoken, but always intoned, chanted or sung, especially in ritual use. References to 'creation by word' can be found in numerous other traditions. The primordial sound, therefore, is the divine word-sound through which – according to the first chapter of the Bible – creation began.

The ancient Greeks, too, regarded musical sound as a mysterious material which was not created by human beings, but by the gods. According to Greek mythology musical art was protected by the Muses who inspired the artistic creation of the 'musish', that is 'musiké' arts. The Muses were the daughters of Zeus (the same word as the Latin *deus*), the supreme Greek god, and Mnemosyne, the goddess of memory. The ancient Greeks realized that music could never be appreciated had 'memory' not enabled man to connect already passed sounds with present ones in order to form melodic, rhythmic and harmonic patterns.

There is another aspect in regard to sound which must be of great interest to psychologists, and that is that sound is perceptible through our sense of hearing, and in contrast to our important senses of seeing and touch, hearing cannot go to the object, but comes to the ear. This peculiar 'inward direction' of sound, together with its invisible and intangible characteristics has established – already in ancient times – a relationship of music to the soul, to metaphysics, and to everything that cannot be understood by reasoning.

Nevertheless, those very characteristics of musical sound gave rise to practical objections and philosophical arguments. Pertinent and far-reaching thoughts were expressed by Plato in *Laws* (II, 669), the last of his Dialogues and the crowning work of his old age. There, the great Athenian philosopher condemned pure instrumental music as unworthy of reasonable beings:

For where there are no words, it is difficult to recognize the meaning of melody and rhythm, or to see that any worthy object is represented by them, and we must acknowledge that this kind which aims only at rapid continuity and brutal noise, and uses pipe and lyre not as mere accompaniments of the dance and the song is merely uncivilized.

Europe carried the heritage of this ancient idea for about two thousand years, up to the time of the Renaissance. It is not accidental that the independence of emotive pure instrumental musical sound coincided with man's awareness of his individuality and his discovery of the natural outer and emotional inner world.

It seems inexplicable that C.G. Jung never felt the inclination to pursue his psychological research into the arts further and deeper into the rich, fertile grounds of music, especially with respect to the role of music in what he called the collective unconscious and its contents, the archetypes. Jung found that archetypes can be discovered whenever and wherever man has lived. They are universal symbols which play an important part in our inherited disposition 'which influences our thoughts and feelings and actions'.[5]

Research into archetypal musical sound-patterns produces the interesting fact that there is an astonishing unity of basic conceptions in the varied manifestations of primitive and ancient music cultures.

In the earliest cultures two types of music can be distinguished: one is more closely related to speech and to the limitation of every kind of natural sounds. This type of music is not based upon a fixed tone-system, but on more or less freely intoned melodies.

The second type of music is based upon a systematically arranged series of tones clearly related to one another by consonant intervals.

As a result of the twofold division, voices and instruments may perform in two different tunings, even when sounding simultaneously. Those early melodies were always expressing an idea; they had great significance, and they even were said to exercise magic powers.

The arrangement of the basic musical material in tonal patterns of rising pitches – which vary greatly in different times and countries – is generally known by the term 'scale'. There have never existed scales with less than five notes to the octave (the so-called 'pentatone'.[6] It is an interesting phenomenon that the pentatonic or five-tone scale, a pre-Pythagorean system albeit in various forms, can be found in nearly all ancient music cultures in Asia, Africa, North and Latin America, Europe and even Australia.[7]

At the same time it is notable that ancient music cultures linked many of their musical ideas to cosmological connotations. Already between the fifth and the third centuries BC China related the tone-system by simple arithmetical operations to the order of the Universe.

Similar relations can be found in the musical systems of Babylonia, India, the Islamic countries, ancient Greece and the Christian Middle Ages.[8] Cosmological co-ordinations involve many different concepts such as seasons, cardinal points, months, days, hours, moods, illnesses, parts of the human body, elements, substances and, especially, planets.

Men who lived before the dawn of history watched the stars and wondered what they were, because they affected men in many ways. The sun brought them light and warmth, summer and winter, and measured the time-span of a year. The moon lit up the dark night and its alternating phases marked out intervals of time shorter than those of a year. It was only natural to believe that the other celestial bodies too had certain influences on earth, particularly the planets, as they changed their positions continuously. For thousands of years men saw only five planets moving through the sky: Mars, Mercury, Jupiter, Venus and Saturn. Those heavenly bodies were generally considered to be living deities, and they excited the imagination of ancient men even more than sun and moon, whose paths and correlates could be more easily plotted. Day and night and seasonal changes were regular and therefore not unduly perturbing events. Thus man's unpredictable experiences were always especially linked with the planets.

Already in the Vedas of India, written in Sanskrit ca. 2000 BC, one can read of the cosmological theory of the primordial sound created by the motion of the stars. Similarly, the astronomer–priests of ancient Babylonia, where astronomy was the basis of religion, spoke of the 'voices' of the planets, and many other nations of antiquity agreed that celestial bodies produce sounds inaudible to man.

The identification of cosmic harmony with mystic-religious musical harmony can thus be traced back thousands of years. So, in the oldest music culture known to us, the music of China with its traceable history of about four thousand years, we find a tone system of five notes, a basic pentatonic scale strongly related to cosmological connotations which was an integral part of their musical thought. These five notes symbolized the five known planets, as well as the cardinal points 'north', 'east', 'centre', 'west' and 'south' (besides many other symbolic relationships such as the five elements and the five colours).[9]

Since according to ancient belief all bodies moving in space produce sounds proportioned to their velocity and their distance from the earth, the sounds of the two large luminaries, sun and moon, were added by Babylonians, Chinese and Egyptians to the heavenly harmony long before Pythagoras. The Babylonians already accepted the idea of the 'seven heavens' corresponding to the seven orbital spheres on which each heavenly body was believed to move along. Seven was therefore a sacred number for the Babylonians who by adding two notes to the pentatone enlarged it to the so-called heptatonic scale.

As the countries of the ancient Near East considered seven to be a magic number, it is not surprising that they divided the week into seven days as well. Eventually most parts of the world accepted the septimal rhythm of the week together with the seven note scale as the foundation of their musical cultures. At the same time, they honoured the seven moving stars by naming the days after them:

Sunday: Sun's day
Monday: Moon's day = (Luna): Lundi (French), Lunedì (Italian)
Tuesday: Tiw's day = (Mars): Mardi (French), Martedì (Italian)
Wednesday: Woden's day = (Mercury): Mercredi (French), Mercoledì (Italian)
Thursday: Thor's day = (Jove/Jupiter): Jeudi (French), Giovedì (Italian)
Friday: Frija's day = (Venus): Vendredi (French), Venerdì (Italian)
Saturday: Saturn's day

There is no doubt that when Pythagoras identified cosmic harmony with music, this idea had already been familiar in Eastern countries. Pythagoras, imbued with Egyptian doctrines, regulated harmonic principles only on the proportional harmony of numbers. He was fascinated by mystic numerical experiments, whereby he discovered in his concept of the 'Harmony of the Spheres' remarkable similarities between musical intervals and the spacing of sun, moon and the planets.

According to Egon Wellesz: 'To those tones the names of the seven vowels have been given by the Pythagoreans. The seven vowels, therefore, are also symbols of the planets.'[10]

Moon	alpha		e
Mercury	ĕpsilon		f
Venus	ēta		g
Sun	iota	equivalent tones:	a
Mars	ŏmicron		b flat
Jupiter	ypsilon		c
Saturn	ōmega		d

It is important to remember that the Greeks used the letters of the alphabet as numbers, since they had no cyphers. Thus they used the seven vowels for the planets as well as for the sounds of the celestial bodies.

The Babylonians are usually credited with dividing the day into twelve equal time-periods, the hours, and the Egyptians are said to have doubled the number of hours. This division of day and night into twelve periods each facilitated the observation of the position of the moving stars which, according to ancient teaching, affected men at all times.

As the numbers three and four have archetypal significance (signifying dynamism and stability, respectively, among many other symbolisms), their sum and their multiplication give those important numbers seven and twelve. The division of the year into twelve months is based on the concept of the Zodiac, one of the most wide-spread of symbols, probably originating in the Mesopotamian cultures and to be found in Egypt, Judea, Persia, India, Tibet, China, the Americas, Islamic countries, Greece and Northern Europe. All recognized the symbolism of the zodiacal circle, the origin of which – in various forms – goes back more than two thousand years BC. The word Zodiac is derived from the Greek *zoe* = life and *diakos* = wheel. It is therefore interesting that the signs of the twelve zodiacal constellations bear the names of living creatures (with the exception of Libra), and that they are everywhere – even where the signs differed from those that serve modern astronomy and astrology – archetypal symbols of an ancient animistic pantheism.

The Zodiac – that imaginary belt in the sky along which sun, moon and planets run their yearly circular paths – has its musical equivalent in the twelve tone or so-called chromatic scale. There is no doubt that this scale, known already in ancient Chinese musical theory, was a symbol of the cosmic order, of the Zodiac with its twelve subdivisions. This is proved by the fact that the Chinese have transposed (and are still transposing) their sacred melodies one semitone higher at the beginning of each month in the year. Thus, in our terminology, they sing their melodies in March, the beginning of Spring, in C, in April in C sharp, in May in D, and so on, until they reach B in February and C in March again. The same kind of transpositions, but starting with the New Year, are practised still today in the Byzantine chant of the Greek Orthodox Church.

This sketchy survey of the scale structure of the important fundamental tone-systems has shown that the three most widely used scales are the five tone or pentatonic, the seven tone or diatonic and the twelve tone or chromatic scales. In all three cases cosmological connotations cannot be denied. They are shapes or patterns of musical archetypes which stem from universal images within the human spirit, and as such they appeal to both the conscious as well as the unconscious levels of human experiences.

Whenever Jung, to whom present-day symbology owes so much,

came near cosmology he referred his findings to mythology, mysticism, religion and other related fields, but he never extended his research to music, where the scale patterns are only one of the many musical archetypes worthy of closer investigation. The one brief exception to this rule concerning Jung's attitude to music was the above mentioned letter to Serge Moreux in which the great psychologist specifically refers to Wagner, Beethoven and Bach.

There is no doubt that Wagner gave his musical language intentionally a strong symbolic significance, expecially by means of the so-called *Leitmotifs*. In this regard it is interesting to recall that after discarding the term 'opera' Wagner searched for a suitable classifying name for his dramatic works. In an article in the *Musikalische Wochenblatt* of 8 November 1872, entitled 'Über die Benennung "Musikdrama"' he considered the rather unwieldy designation 'Ersichtlich gewordene Taten der Musik', loosely translated as 'visible manifestations of music'.[11] With this definition he put the emphasis on the 'action' expressed in the music by means of an intricately woven chain of telling leading motives, a procedure which changed opera into a dramatic symphony; and this orchestral symphony was, in turn, converted, so to speak, into visible form on the stage. Although hereby the patterns of Wagner's music have clearly become symbols of analogical emotional, intellectual and bodily patterns, Jung concerned himself solely with the literary side of the music-drama. Robert Donington tried to rectify Jung's omission in his book *Wagner's 'Ring' and its Symbols: The Music and the Myth*.[12] Earlier, in 1959, Deryck Cooke attempted in his *The Language of Music*[13] to unravel the meaning of music. However, he did not come to grips with psychological analyses of musical art.

Jung himself, in his *Essays on Contemporary Events*[14] wrote an article 'Wotan' which although referring superficially to Wagner, deals mainly with the mentality of Nazis in Germany's Third Reich. Again, Jung gave a certain impetus to psychological research into the works of Wagner, but nothing more.

Psychological symbolism in Wagner's music-dramas is comparatively non-problematic on account of allusions to the verbal side of the works. However, when applied to pure instrumental music this kind of symbolic interpretation becomes more precarious.

Dealing with Beethoven, the second composer mentioned in Jung's letter to Serge Moreux, nobody will deny the spiritual significance of his instrumental music, and yet Jung speaks only in broad terms of 'the fact that music represents the movement, development and transformation of motifs of the collective unconscious'.[4] Apparently Jung knew little about Beethoven's 'Poetic Idea'.

Anton Schindler, Beethoven's biographer, violinist, conductor and unpaid private secretary during the last years of the composer's life, reports 'that Beethoven in his later years, complained that people were less able to grasp the meaning of music than they were in his young days, and he even thought of giving poetic titles to his earlier works to supply this deficiency in his hearer's imagination. It is certain, therefore, that Beethoven . . . considered that his music had an extra-musical content.'[15]

It would go far beyond the scope of this article to analyse the musical symbols used by Beethoven in his numerous compositions. However, in connection with Jung's work on 'psychological types', where he attempts to classify human beings into recognizable types and to trace the effects of human behaviour on philosophy, religion, poetry and aesthetics, it will be of interest to mention Beethoven's seventh pianoforte sonata in D, op. 10 no. 3. Anton Schindler as well as Carl Czerny, pianist, composer and pupil of Beethoven, testified that the master answered a question on the meaning of the 'Largo' of the sonata in D, op. 10 no. 3, that he intended to describe *'den Seelenzustand eines Melancholischen mit all den verschiedenen Nuancen von Licht und Schatten im Bilde der Melancholie in ihren Phasen'* (the psychic condition of a melancholic with all the various nuances of light and shade in a picture of the phases of melancholy).[16]

Although Claudius Galenus, the Greek physician, had classified human beings according to four fundamental types already in the second century AD, his descriptive terms of the sanguine, the melancholic, the phlegmatic and the choleric temperaments are still common usage. We call an optimistic, cheerful, ardent or passionate man 'sanguine'; a sad, gloomy or mentally depressed man 'melancholic'; a man sluggish, restrained and not easily roused to emotion or activity 'phlegmatic'; and a man of angry, irascible and hasty temper 'choleric'. One wonders whether Jung realized that those four distinct human temperaments have inspired numerous compositions, and Beethoven's piano sonata in D is supposed to be one of them. The four movements of the sonata are said to express successively the sanguine, melancholic, phlegmatic and choleric temperaments in musical symbols.

True, the ancient descriptive terms of the four different temperaments have been pronounced 'naive' and 'superficial' by modern psychologists, and Jung re-organized the existing distinction by adding the concepts of introversion and extraversion, thereby changing the division of people into an essentially dichotomous classification of types. However that may be, any influence of the age-old concept of the four human temperaments in musical art should have found some reflection in the research of the analytical psychologist whose findings of musical symbolism then would have nothing to do with artistic criticism.

The third and last composer named in Jung's letter to Serge Moreux is Bach. Here Jung is more specific by mentioning 'Die Kunst der Fuge' (the Art of the Fugue), the crowning achievement of Bach's genius. It contains fugues and canons, all on one theme, 20 pieces altogether, in which the master elaborated most ingeniously the devices of imitative counterpoint.

The final fugue, built on three new subjects, is obviously incomplete. Its remarkable feature is that the third subject consists of the theme B A C H, the German terms for the pitches B flat, A, C and B natural.

We have it on the good authority of Johann Nikolaus Forkel (1749-1818) and others, that it was Bach's intention to finish the broken-off music as an imposing quadruple fugue by quite logically bringing in the principal theme which forms the subject of every piece of the 'Art of the Fugue'. In the preface to his 'Uber Johann Sebastian Bach's Leben, Kunst und Kunstwerke' Forkel writes: 'For my accounts . . . I am indebted to the two eldest sons of Joh. Seb. Bach. I was not only personally acquainted with both, but kept up a constant correspondence with them for many years, chiefly with C. Ph. Emanuel.'[17] In chapter IX of Forkel's scholarly biography one can read:

This (last) fugue was, however, interrupted by the disorder in the author's eyes, and as the operation did not succeed, was not finished. It is said to have been his intention to take in the last fugue four themes . . . To make up for what is wanting to the last fugue, there was added to the end of the work the four-part Organ Chorale: 'Wenn wir in höchsten Nöthen seyn' u.s.w., (When we are in direst distress). Bach dictated it a few days before his death to his son-in-law, Johann Christoph Altnikol.

This last composition of Bach was a new version of the chorale-melody in his *Orgelbüchlein* (*Little Organ-Book*). It should be noted that Bach – blind, helpless and on his deathbed – gave it not only a new, most intricate structure, but also a new title chosen from the first line of another stanza of the hymn: 'Vor Deinen Thron tret' ich hiermit' (Before Thy throne herewith I step).

The amazing and to us the most relevant part of this music is its inherent number symbolism. According to the system of the number-alphabet (A = 1, B = 2, C = 3 and so on), the first line of the chorale-melody has 14 notes equivalent to the letter-numbers 'B A C H' (2 + 1 + 3 + 8 = 14). The entire chorale melody has 41 notes which equals the letter-numbers 'J.S. BACH', while 'JOHANN SEBASTIAN BACH' give the figure 158, which corresponds to the number of notes in the setting of the melody of the organ chorale version.

Secret numerical relationships and other tone-symbolisms can be found throughout the history of music. Bach's number symbolism can be discovered in many of his works, but it is certainly of special interest to the psychologist, when it occupied the master's mind in the final hour of his earthly life.[18]-[20]

Even despite the limited reference to only those three composers named in Jung's letter, one has to admit that musical symbolism involves many complicated interpretations, opinions and problems to the investigating analytical psychologist. Whereas the representational and descriptive peculiarities of symbols found in the visual arts bear a kinship to those found in literature, the symbols of music belong to a different, more abstract category, because they are usually not readily amenable to precise definition. Could it be that this fundamental aspect of musical symbolism was a contributing factor for Jung's exclusion of music in his symbolic analyses of the arts?

The content of this chapter seems to be rather negative as regards Jung's own interest in music as a field of research. However, many of his psychological concepts have aroused the interest of some creative musicians as well as music critics, for example Michael Tippett, the English composer (b. 1905), who published in 1959 a collection of fourteen talks and essays under the title *Moving into Aquarius* in which he makes several references to Jung.[21] Already in his Introduction Tippett begins 'I need to make acknowledgement to Jung; not only because of all I have learnt from him . . . '

The great importance of Jung in musical matters lies in the discipline of 'music-psychology' founded in 1931 by Ernst Kurth, the Austrian-born, Swiss musicologist (1886-1946). An essential problem of music-psychology is music-therapy which today is acknowledged practically all over the world. Many music-therapists make use of the psychotherapy of C.G. Jung, and it is in this sphere of musical activity that his influence is reflected most clearly.

Still, here arises another problem: when we discuss music in music-therapy, are we referring to music as an art? Many of the forces that are inherent in tones, in tonal relationships, in the dynamic qualities of tones, in the motion of tones in times and other forces which make music possible are best described as natural phenomena which man has discovered but not invented.[22] In contrast to music as an art, which is created by man, those natural sound phenomena form an indispensable aspect of the musical material used by the therapist who selects his music 'tailor-made' to suit the needs of the patient. Sometimes he improves mere sound effects in order to evoke a desired response. The publications in form of books and recorded tapes by Paul Nordoff and Clive Robbins from the Department of Psychiatry, University of Pennsylvania, Philadelphia provide relevant information.[23]

Admittedly this therapeutic aspect leads to controversial statements and discussions not only on account of either active or passive involvement of the patient, but also on account of difficulties to determine the borderline where music as an art begins or – as some therapists maintain – where the very roots of musical art lie. Here, however, we are confronted with a new set of aesthetic, philosophical and psychological problems which go far beyond the limits of the theme set for this essay – C.G. Jung and the art of music.

Meaning and Order: Concerning Meeting Points and Differences Between Depth Psychology and Physics

BY MARIE-LOUISE VON FRANZ

In his book on synchronicity C.G. Jung introduces two new concepts into depth psychology concerning the world of so-called chance. One is the concept of 'acausal orderedness' and the other that of 'synchronistic events'. The former refers to the regular omnipresent just-so-ness of various constants in nature, such as the specific speed of light, the energy quant, the time-rate of radioactive decay and so on. For such facts we cannot indicate a preceding cause. (Gamov once sketched an amusing scene of what would happen if light speed were much slower than it is.) The acausal existence of these constants make one realize how much the universe is a just-so-story. We generally express this just-so-ness by a number, which is, however, based on an arbitrarily chosen length of space-time. One could theoretically also call an energy quant 1, and then add on 2, 3, 4 and so on, but the exercise would be completely impracticable because of the smallness of h.$\star$ Such acausal orderedness does not only exist in the realm of physics. We find it also in the human mind or psyche. The simplest example is that of the natural integers, because there too we find a just-so-ness in the form of statements we *have* to make about a number. Jung calls this 'the method of the necessary statement'.[1] An example would be the statement that 6 is a so-called perfect number, because 1 + 2 + 3 is identical with 1 times 2 times 3. This is an obvious just-so-ness, for which we cannot indicate a 'cause' which 'produces' this result. We could only say it is so because 6 is the sum of 1, 2 and 3 – but this would be mere tautology.

In the field of dream interpretation this method of necessary statements is the same as that which Jung more frequently calls

---

$\star$ This is a constant in Max Planck's equation $E = h \times \nu$, where E is the quantum energy and ν the frequency of an oscillator. The actual value of h has been calculated to be 6.625×10^{-27} erg sec.

'amplification'. In it we also do not proceed arbitrarily, letting our imagination run free, but we use what Jung calls 'disciplined imagination' to find the associations to a symbolic image. For instance, we cannot say that Circe in *The Odyssey* is a benevolent mother figure, because the very context refutes this. In the realm of the natural integers, statements of connections, such as $2 + 2 = 4$, seem to be even more cogently 'necessary' statements than those about mythological images. Hence connection of these with logical and mathematical reasoning. Modern mathematicians did indeed try to make their discipline as logically watertight as possible against psychological implications, because they regarded the latter as purely subjective,[2] while they thought that mathematical logic concerns a purely objective, true, non-psychological reality.[3] It deals with a truth which serves all observers.[4] For Frege, for instance, the statements $1 + 1 = 2 = 6/3 = \sqrt{4}$ are all absolutely identical! They are seen as the result of a formulated *relation*, and it is the latter that counts. Even if I say in mathematics this number is 4, I imply 'nothing else than four'. Numbers themselves cannot be defined, they are 'logically simple'.[5]

In the year 1931, Kurt Goedel dashed all these former attempts to constitute some ultimate, safe formulations for mathematics.[6] He showed: 'that any logical system within which arithmetics can be developed is essentially incomplete. In other words, given any consistent set of arithmetical axioms, there are true arithmetical axioms which are not derivable from the set.'[7] Goedel's proof is too complicated to explain here. But in short, he arithmetized all formal statements of mathematics into unique specific numbers. The result showed:

. . . that Arithmetic is incomplete in the transparent sense, that there is at least always one arithmetical truth which cannot be derived from the arithmetical axioms and yet can be established by a metamathematical argument outside the system. Contrary to previous assumptions the vast 'continent' of arithmetical truth cannot be brought into systematic order by way of specifying once and for all a fixed set of axioms from which all true arithmetical statements would be derivable.[8]

However our creative reasoning could always establish new mathematical propositions by 'informal' meta–mathematical reasoning. In other words the natural integers, the basis of arithmetics, are a partly irrational basis for our rational reasoning. Concerning the series of natural numbers which are the foundation of all mathematics, Weyl therefore remarks that, to our surprise, it has an aspect of obscurity, though we believe it to be only a construct of our mind.

This element of obscurity in numbers (meaning that they are not logically wholly diaphanous) is based, in Jung's view, on the fact that they are archetypal symbols.[9] They are also individuals and have an aspect of acausal just-so-ness, which one can ignore, as mathematicians mostly do, but which exists in our mind all the same. Viewed from this angle most of the former mathematicians were something like the theologians of the number gods. They shared their resistance to psychology with the 'other' theologians! They argue along the 'necessary statements' induced by the archetypes, but ignore the concomitant psychological experiences which they consider to be purely subjective. Jung goes one step further and calls numbers '*an archetype of order which has become conscious*'.[10] This number archetype is thus the 'predestined instrument for creating order, or for apprehending an already existing, but still unknown, regular arrangement or "orderedness"'.[11]

From the time of Archimedes on, and to a much greater degree, since Galileo, physics has concentrated on exploring the *measurable* aspects of the outer, so-called natural, reality, and thus on its mathematization. And it works! The mathematical forms of order which the mind of a physicist manipulates coincide 'miraculously' with experimental measurements. The absolute differential calculus, for instance, which was born in the fantasy of the mathematician Rieman, became later *the* mathematical tool for Einstein's theory of relativity and its applications.[12]

This event led Eugène Wigner to speak of an 'unreasonable effectiveness of mathematics in science'.[13]

Nowadays physicists have become mainly interested in the concept of order, and they are also fully realizing that it is inseparably related to the functioning of their own mind. Their equations are no longer perceived to be an objectively accurate reflection of material reality, but only a structurally accurate relationship-connection. Like the mathematicians, the physicists have little use for numbers but mostly use algebra and topology as their tools, because these are the logical abstractions drawn from number *relations* and less irrational than the number individuals themselves. They mostly express relationships which are true for *all numbers*. (For instance, if $a + b = c$, then $a = c - b$.) Seen from this angle, algebra is a kind of group psychology of numbers and topology is concerned with their possible spatialization by viewing them as arrangements of points and their connections in a manifold.

However, an archetypal representation also always contains meaning, and if number is an archetype of order which has become conscious, this would mean that it possesses a preconscious, latent, psychic reality which would be indefinable. Only when it becomes conscious do we feel motivated to call one 'unity, *the* unity, the All-oneness, individuality, non-duality, counting unit' and so forth, or do we have to say about two that it is the 'halved, the doubled, duality distinctness, non-uniqueness' and so on. Our mind is in no way free to speculate just anything about a specific number; what we say about it is determined and limited by the conceptions of one-ness, two-ness and so on, and their implications.[14]

Among these 'necessary statements' which are engendered by number, only one part is what one calls the statements of mathematical logic. (The latter uses, for its operations, for instance, only the statement: one is a counting unit – and ignores the others.) We could say that mathematics deals with the 'acausal orderedness' in our own mind, which is based on number, and physics, among other themes, deals with the 'acausal orderedness' in nature, such as the speed of light and the rate of radioactive decay, which could also be designated by number. But do they also have meaning? Jung writes:

> The concept of 'order' is not identical with the concept of 'meaning'. Even an organic being is, in spite of the meaningful design implicit within it, not necessarily meaningful in the total nexus. For instance, if the world had come to an end at the Oligocene period, it would have no meaning for man. Without the reflecting consciousness of man the world is a gigantic meaningless machine, for in our experience man is the only creature who is capable of ascertaining any meaning at all.[15]

Jung uses here the term 'order' as a sub-term of 'meaning', order being a partial fact – a meaningful design, for instance, which can be found in all mathematically or biologically organized phenomena – but 'meaning', on the contrary, rather concerns a holon, or rather *the* holon, the Unitas (in the sense of the gnostics of Princeton) and simultaneously it concerns that *one* individual who realizes it. This does not imply that man creates the meaning,[16] he only realizes it or lifts it into consciousness; but it is already latently existent in nature itself, independent of our conscious realization.[17]

As I mentioned at the outset, Jung subdivides the principle of synchronicity into two sub-terms: acausal orderedness, which concerns 'all . . . *a priori* factors such as the properties of natural numbers [and] the discontinuities of modern physics';[18] and, secondly, *synchronistic events* as a particular instance of general acausal orderedness, 'namely, of the equivalence of psychic and physical processes where the observer is in the fortunate position of being able to recognize the *tertium comparationis*',[19] namely, its meanings.[20] Synchronistic events are 'acts of creation in time',[21] but they are *not caused* by any archetype, they merely let its latent meaning become visible. Thus the contingent would be 'partly . . . a universal factor existing from all eternity – a just-so order – and partly . . . the sum of countless individual acts of creation occurring in time'.[22] Although these acts probably occur all the time in nature, they only become *meaningful* coincidences when an individual experiences them.

In the case of the foregoing which Jung reports as an example in his paper, his patient dreamt of a scarab and most surprisingly a *Cetonia aurata* flew into the room while the dream was told. If nobody had seen the inherent meaning, there would have been only a *similarity* between the outer and inner events; only if one knows that in Egypt the scarab is a symbol of the reborn Sun-god rising in the morning, i.e. a rebirth of consciousness, does the event become meaningful – and it did in fact have a healing impact on the dreamer. Thus synchronistic events constitute moments in which a 'cosmic' or 'greater' meaning becomes gradually conscious in an individual; generally this is a shaking experience. One is moved because one feels, like a primitive, that a higher force, a ghost or god, aims at you, often by playing you a trick. But such an interpretation regresses to the level of magical causal thinking, which Jung sought to avoid. The archetype does not magically *cause* such events but becomes manifest in them without that any antecedents seem to exist. As Jung points out, such events can also occur without anybody seeing their meaning, but it is latently present there all the same. But there also exists a 'danger that meaning will be read into things where actually there is nothing of the sort',[23] or that one misinterprets the meaning. Let me give an example.

A man who suffered from a psychotic idea that he was the savior of the world attacked his wife with an axe in order to 'exorcise the devil out of her'. She called for help. At the very moment when a policeman and a psychiatrist entered the house, the only lamp, which lit up the passage where they all stood, exploded. They were plunged into darkness, covered with glass splinters. The sick man exclaimed: 'See . . . this is like it was at the crucifixion of Christ! The sun has eclipsed.' He felt confirmed that he *was* the Savior. But if we amplify this symbolism correctly with 'necessary statements', i.e. with 'disciplined imagination', there appears a completely different meaning. A light bulb is *not* the sun, that symbol of numinous source of cosmic consciousness; it only symbolizes a 'little light' made by man, i.e. his ego-consciousness. So the event means a 'blackout' of that man's ego-consciousness, the disruption of his ego, which is exactly what happens in the beginning of a psychotic episode. When I saw the man and his wife two days later, *I* saw the meaning and was able to show it to them, which had a positive, sobering effect on the poor man. The correct interpretation of a synchronistic event is essential and can only be done by a sober and disciplined mind which keeps to the necessary statements and does not run off into arbitrary assumptions.

Another amusing example of misinterpreting the meaning of a

synchronistic event can be found in old annals of the T'ang period in China.[24] Once after an earthquake a new lake was formed and in its middle a mountain arose. The wife of the emperor, called Wu Tse t'ien, said that this was a lucky sign and named the mountain 'Mountain of Luck'. But a citizen of the capital wrote her a letter, saying:

Your servant has learned that cold and heat become disturbed when the breath of Heaven and mankind are not in harmony, and that hills and mountains arise when the breath of the earth is disturbed. Your majesty as a woman takes over the role of the male principle Yang on the throne . . . That means to exchange the strong for the weak . . . Your majesty should practise penance and fear in order to answer to the admonition of Heaven. Otherwise I fear that there will be misfortune.

The Empress got furious and banished the poor outspoken citizen from court.

Now the Empress's interpretation of 'lucky mountain' was purely arbitrary. The citizen, on the contrary, used the classical Chinese archetypal associations. For Ken – the mountain – is male and Tui – the lake – is female, as we know from the *I Ching*. The animus-possessed Empress was overpowering her weak husband and the outer event was a meaningful coincidence. This coincidence has no thinkable causal connection. The volcano did not arise because of the wrong attitude of the Empress (to assume that would be magical thinking), nor did the Empress behave in such an overpowering manner because of the volcano. The connection of the two events lies purely in the meaning of the coincidence. In old China one thought that all unusual events in the Empire were thus revealing the psychological situation at the Emperor's court. The citizen was 'in Tao', to use Chinese language, and thus he saw the true meaning of the event.

We know from the *I Ching* that: 'the kind man discovers Tao and calls it kind. The wise man discovers it and calls it wise. The people use it day by day and are not aware of it . . . The Tao of the universe is kindness and wisdom, but essentially the Tao is also beyond kindness and wisdom.'[25] The sages of ancient times 'put themselves in accord with Tao', in order to build the oracle.[26] And the same holds true in order to understand it.

Here we can see again, as I have already mentioned, that in contrast to order 'meaning' has to do with the ultimate, the Whole of existence, in other words it points to a connection with what we call the Self.

Viewed naively and more superficially: synchronistic events seem to be meaningful coincidences between one inner and one or more outer events. But, as Jung pointed out, the awareness of the coinciding outer events is ultimately also a different psychological condition.

Therefore a synchronistic event is, in fact, this: 'One (psychic state) is the normal, probable state (i.e. the one that is causally explicable), and the other, the critical experience, is the one that cannot be derived causally from the first.'[27] It is a content of 'immediate knowledge' or 'immediate existence' which suddenly irrupts into the ordinary state of mind, generally accompanied by a strong emotion which causes an *abaissement du niveau mental* and makes the irruption of that other abnormal state of awareness possible.[28]

In the unconscious there seems to be an *a priori* knowledge or immediate presence of events which has no cause and which from time to time irrupts into our 'normal' state.[29] Jung stresses that:

Synchronicity in space can equally well be conceived as perception in time, but remarkably enough it is not so easy to understand synchronicity in time as spatial, for we cannot imagine any space in which future events are objectively present and could be experienced as such through a reduction of this spatial distance.[30]

We know now, however, through Einstein, that space and time are somehow inseparable entities: there seems nevertheless to be a difference, in that the annihilation of time or even its reversal in the psyche is more easily possible than the annihilation of space. We must therefore look at time a bit more closely from a psychological angle. Measured time, or clock time, as we know, is only a Western culturally specific way of thought. Psychological time is rather to be seen as the flow or stream of inner and outer events. As I tried to show in a paper two years ago, the archetypal image of that time-stream of events is always associated with each culture's highest god-image, or image of the Self. Time is, so to speak, engendered by the motion of the Self archetype. So, for instance, Tao is the nameless still void, but also 'the begetter of all begetting' and, in this latter aspect, it is called 'change', says the *I Ching*.[31] 'It is something that sets in motion and maintains the interplay of forces. Tao brings this about without ever becoming manifest.'[32]

In the Aztec religion the highest god, Omote'otl, is the Lord of Time. In the *Bhagavadgita* the Indian highest god, Vishnu, calls himself Time and so is Shiva called by his adorers. Only in the Judeo–Christian religion is God timeless and only creates (not emanates) time. He is the unmoveable mover, outside time-space. But even here time is closely linked with the idea of the supreme godhead and its creative activity.

Now, if synchronistic events are what they seem to be, they point to the fact of a continuous creation going all along with the stream of time and that would also imply that meaning (in the sense of concerning the Unitas or the Holon) uses time as a vehicle of its realization in man. 'Time', says G.J. Whitrow, 'is the mediator between the possible and the actual.'[33]This is just another aspect of the concept of 'continuous creation'. It needs a flow of outer and inner events to actualize the latent meaning of archetypal patterns in the form of sporadic synchronistic events. Each time such an event takes place, the Holon of existence is changed. What I call Holon or Unitas, in using a word of the so-called gnostics of Princeton, is the same as that which Jung calls the Unus Mundus, the One World, which transcends the duality of psyche and matter.

The mandala, Jung pointed out,[34] is the inner psychic counterpart of the Unus Mundus and synchronistic phenomena the parapsychological equivalent of it. How these two factors can be combined in so-called divinatory double mandalas I have tried to show in my book on *Number and Time*, and cannot discuss here, but I would like to probe a little deeper into the experience of meaning as it is conveyed to us by synchronistic events. As Jung already remarked, synchronistic events sometimes appear like something arbitrary or like something having a purpose. That is why they were understood in the past as the action of a god or a ghost, a saint or devil, or whatever, who wanted to demonstrate something by it. Only in China was the Tao not viewed as being personal, but beside it the old Chinese also conceptualized the so-called 'Will of Heaven', which could be benevolent or annoyed, like a human being.

Our Western civilizations seem to have believed predominantly in a personal god to whom they have attributed, at least in the past, personal, even anthropoid, psychological reactions. Synchronistic events were seen as miracles performed by God or the Devil. But even in our Western world the highly personal god, Jahweh, and the Christian god were imagined to be a sphere, which is a symbol of mathematical order, not of some partial order but of a total order, a world-formula, so to speak.

Why should God not reveal himself also in mathematics, Novalis asks? The history of this symbolic idea is actually very old.[35] It began with Empedokles, who called God 'an infinite sphere which enjoys its eternal circling'. For Parmenides too the true Existence is circular and infinite. For Plato the totality of the world of ideas is irrepresentable, but its replica in matter, the universe, is a geometrical sphere. But the more explicit description of God as a perfect but infinite sphere stems from Plotinus.[36] For Plotinus' God is one *omnipresence* in the multiplicity of concrete things. Plotinus illustrates his point with a threefold sphere (see diagram):

The outer sphere is the cosmic sphere of the many things, the middle sphere is subdivided by the radii into the different ideas[37] and represents the world soul; and finally the central sphere represents the *compact one-ness* of all ideas. This central sphere is without movement.

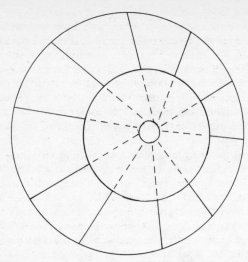

Its centre is 'the soul's most genuine nature, the idea of its inner unity, uniformity and totality'. This image, however, is only an incomplete schema, compared to what is really meant, for there is absolutely no difference between the smallest and the bigger spheres. In other words, there is no real extension at all. One could just as well call it a single point.

The next important continuer is Salomon ben Gebirol (ca. AD 1020-1070), whose main work was translated into Latin as *Fons vitae* (*Source of Life*). Gebirol calls the godhead for the first time a '*sphaera intelligibilis*' – a spiritual sphere. His book was translated into Latin in 1150 in Spain and influenced Wilhelm of Auvergne, John Duns Scot, Albert the Great and many others. Another continuation of this tradition is the so-called theology of Pseudo-Aristotle, which originally was a Syrian-Arab excerpt of the last three of Plotinus' *Enneads*, where God is seen mainly as the non-dimensional center, but also as the all-embracing circular periphery of all Existence.[38] God emanates into all things and remains simultaneously a unity without any subdivision into space and time.[39] And last there is an anonymous 12th century *Liber XXIV philosophorum* which sums that view up in the famous sentence: '*Deus est sphaera infinita, cuius centrum est ubique circumferentia nusquam.*' And this famous sentence went on to be quoted by Alanus de Insulis as a saying of Hermes, because another title of the treatise was *Liber Termegisti de regulis theologiae.*[40]

The next most famous theologian who took up this symbolism was Meister Eckhart. 'God is an immeasurable and unmeasured circle which embraces the widest mind of man in the form of a point which is

– compared to God's incomprehensible measurelessness – so small that one cannot even name it.'[41] Christ as the Incarnation of God is the squaring of the circle, because 'Christ is quadrangular', and because the squaring of the circle can be only an infinite approximation. We find similar ideas in the works of mystics like Ruysbroeck and Tauler and Seuse. Eckhart added certain new aspects to the old symbolism: namely, that in God all is equal, there is no plus or minus: '*Deus est sphaera intellectualis infinita, cuius tot sunt circumferentiae quot sunt puncta*', or: '*cuius centrum est ubique et circumferentia nusquam*', or: '*qui totus est in sui minimo*'.

But it is the mathematician-mystic Nicolas of Kues who most frequently made use of this simile of the godhead.[42] In this 'sphere' the straight and the curved become one in an infinite process of approximation,[43] whereby God is more the curved, his creation more the straight aspect. Thus the infinite sphere is also, in a way, a straight line (*infinita circularis est recta*). The circumference is the Holy Ghost.

From there we reach next Johannes Kepler, who, however, wanted God to be more the centre of the sphere than the surface, Christ the surface (the becoming visible of the center) and the Holy Ghost the radii. Kepler's model of the planetary spheres is a 'play of nature' which imitates God's 'play' and the human mind must imitate this spherical play in its search for the truth.[44]

Nicolaus Copernicus also was inspired by the sphere of Cusanus,[45] and Valentin Weigel later postulates that because the centre of the sphere is everywhere, it is also at the bottom of the human soul.[46] Where 'I am God and God is in me, I am the heavens and the heavens are in me'.[47]

I will pass over such intermediary adherents to this idea as Johannes Reuchlin, Pascal, Bovillus Zozzi, Boehme and Henri More,[48] and come to Leibniz, who taught that from all monads (souls) God is the most primary monad 'le centre primitif' from which all others are 'fulgurated' (are produced by an act of lightning). He continues: 'On a fort bien dit qu'il est comme un cercle dont le centre est partout mais la circonférence n'est nulle part'; and 'All monads, and thus also our own psyches, are all psychic centres which express the infinite circumference of the cosmos'.[49] These centres are not only passive 'collecting' points but active centres which radiate forth a spontaneous individual representation of the universe.

We pass over a few more philosophers to end up with the German philosopher J.G. Fichte, who saw this image of the infinite sphere as a symbol of the creative absolute Ego in our psyche, in contrast to our accidental ego,[50] and these egos are all united by universal love into the great All-Sphere, where God and man are one. From there – as we see – the step to Jung's interpretation of the sphere as a symbol of the Self is not a big one.

In modern mathematics one could compare this old 'sphera intelligibilis' with the non-dimensional point and space as conceived as an infinite manifold. (The so-called Hilbert-space, on the contrary, contains already *one* limitation because its vectors are an infinite series of real numbers whose quadratic sums are convergent.[51]) This geometrical symbol has been, one could say, the god of the mathematicians and in it prevails the intuition of all-embracing cosmic order, which has also a meaning though the latter is interpreted slightly differently throughout the ages.

The geometrical god-image, the mandala, is as a whole a relatively *static* symbol of order, even if it can include an internal rotating movement. As a whole it is represented as standing still. And what is more important, it is something completely *impersonal*. One can admire a mandala or be moved by its harmony, but one cannot talk to it or quarrel with it. That is why in most existing religions the godhead is also represented by a personal Being. Krishna can speak to man, as we see in the *Bhagavadgita*, though he is inhumanly terrible in his true form. The Judeo-Christian God is a person. The advantage of a personal god-image, Jung says, 'lies in making possible a much better objectification of the *vis-à-vis*'. Its 'emotional quality confers life and effectuality' upon it. 'Hate and love, fear and reverence enter the scene of confrontation and raise it to a drama. What has merely been "displayed" becomes "acted". The whole man enters the fray with his total reality.'[52] This comment implies again that meaning is more total, more a 'holon', than order, and also that there is no meaning except for *me*, for that very individual which is 'hit' by it. The realization of order suggests a wise adaptation to it, but entails a kind of stoic or epicurean fatalism which, as Raymond Ruyer points out, is the average attitude of nowadays among leading American physicists. But there is no *feeling* confrontation. Meaning, on the contrary, implies feeling reactions and ethical decisions; it contains a personal nuance.

Originally, as we saw in the example of the sphere, meaning and order were combined; only with the development of modern science did they become separate. The tearing apart of order and meaning also becomes visible in another symbol, in the idea of a cosmic machine, i.e. the idea that the universe is like an enormous machine, preferably conceived as a clock. The first clocks were mostly used in monasteries and cathedrals and one attributed to them a kind of religious meaning. Nicolas Cusanus, for instance, says in his *Vision of God* (1453): 'Let then the concept of the clock represent eternity's Self, then the motion of the clock representeth succession. Eternity therefore enfoldeth and unfoldeth succession, since the concept of the clock which is eternity doth alike enfold and unfold all things.'[53] One sees here a close relation of the clock to the idea of the divine sphere.

Only in post-cartesian sciences and philosophies did the symbol of the clock as an image of the universe become the image of a soulless autonomous mechanism which stupidly ticks on into all eternity towards its entropy-death. This mechanistic view prevailed until some thirty years ago. Man forgot that no clock can exist without a clockmaker, a purposeful intelligence behind it. If we look at the symbolism of machines, how it appears in dreams and unconscious phantasies, it generally points to the existence of such a purposeful intelligence working behind it in the unconscious. Such a dream, for instance, is the world clock vision which Jung published in *Psychology and Alchemy*. Another dream is the following:

I am in a deep cellar, together with a boy and a man. The boy has been given an electric installation for Christmas: a large copper pot is supended from the ceiling and electric wires from all directions make it vibrate. After some time there are no more wires, the pot now vibrates from atmospheric electric oscillations.[54]

For us this dream is a symbol of the Self. In a letter about it, Jung comments:

What is so peculiar is the symbolization of the Self as an apparatus. A 'machine' is always something *thought up*, deliberately put together for a definite purpose . . . The Tantrists say that things represent *the distinctness of God's thoughts*. The machine is a microcosm that Paracelsus called the 'star in man'. I always have the feeling that these symbols touch upon the great secrets, the 'magnalia Dei' ('the great things of God').[55]

Distinctness is *the* characteristic of order. If the modern physicists mainly search for order in matter, they really look out for distinctness in the chaotic dance of sub-atomic particles. Let us look closer therefore at the problem of distinctness. For us it is an achievement of consciousness. The archetypes in the collective unconscious have no distinctness; they contain or are only a latent preformed order. Jung saw them surrounded by a 'diffuse cloud of cognition'.[56] Only when an archetype becomes conscious in us does it manifest in a more distinct image, but in fact never in *one* image alone but in a large number of images. The archetype of the Great Mother, for instance, can become manifest in mother goddesses. Paradise, the Kingdom of God, the Heavenly Jerusalem, the Church, city, country, heaven, earth, the woods, the sea, the still waters, matter, the moon. All these can be mother symbols, likewise all places of fertility, such as the cornucopia, the ploughed field, the garden. The archetype can also be associated with a rock, a cave, a tree, a spring, a deep well, various vessels such as the baptismal font, the Grail, or with flowers such as the rose or the lotus, and various animals such as the cow, the hare, the bear and so on.[57] In this way what we think to be a distinct archetype is empirically only graspable by a whole bundle of archetypal images. And this is true for all archetypes such as the hero (think of Campbell's *Hero with a Thousand Faces!*), the life tree, the divine child, and so forth. If we attribute meaning to an archetype it is therefore something very indistinct. Jung says quite rightly that what 'that factor which appears to us as "meaning" may be in itself we have no possibility of knowing.'[58] The Chinese equivalent or cosmic meaning is their concept of Tao.[59]

Incommensurable, impalpable,
Yet latent in it are forms;
Impalpable, incommensurable,
Yet within it are entities.
Shadowy it is and dim.

Tao Te Ching, Chapter XXI[60]

Tao does not manifest in the world of the senses but it is somehow its organizer.

Because the eye gazes but can catch no glimpse of it,
It is called elusive.
Because the ear listens but cannot hear it,
It is called the rarefied.
Because the hand feels for it but cannot find it,
It is called the infinitesimal . . .
These are called the shapeless shapes,
Forms without form,
Vague semblances.

Tao Te Ching Chapter XIV[60]

Now if number is an archetype, as I tried to show before, it shares this ungraspable vagueness with everything else in the unconscious. It becomes only 'number' in the usual distinct sense of the word when its latent orderedness has become conscious. We effect this by trying to make those 'necessary statements' about each number which I mentioned before. Then number reaches the state of definite distinctness in our mind and even becomes the foundation of mathematical logic, but it does not lose completely its obscurity, as Hermann Weyl saw correctly, or as he remarked once jokingly: 'God exists because mathematics are consistent but the Devil too exists because we cannot prove this consistency.'[61]

Now we have to turn to the question of how the archetypes of number relate to the other archetypes which we generally discover at the bottom of mythological images and collective ideas. Are they something different or not? If we look at different cultural traditions we see that the first numbers were frequently associated with certain archetypal images. The number 1, for instance, with the supreme godhead, the total *unus mundus*, the singled-out individual and so on. The most impressive system of such combinations is the *I Ching*. It uses number, as it says, because 'the language of communication with suprahuman intelligences was believed to be based "on number" '.[62] There Heaven is the ultimate unity, the Creative is 1; Earth, the feminine, the receptive, is 2; Heaven encompassing the Earth (1 encompassing 2) is also 3. However, Heaven is not just Heaven; it is round, the prince, the father, jade, metal, cold, ice, deep, red, a good horse, an old horse, a lean horse, a wild horse, fruit. The Receptive is earth, mother, cloth, a kettle, frugality; it is level, it is a cow, a calf, a large wagon, the multitude, a shaft, various kinds of soil; it is black.[63] We have here the same cloud of cognition or bundled images we saw before in the example of the mother. In spite of this vagueness one can feel that there is a kind of meaning in this bundle of images, of which the number association appears to be just one among others.

But number, when it is conscious, seems especially to be 'order'. What more special kind of order is it then? Western mathematics chose an order of quantity and of the logical relations of number sets. The Chinese, on the other hand, chose a *temporal* order, an active dynamic form of order. Thus a commentary to the *I Ching* says: 'The Changes have no consciousness, no action; they are quiescent and do not move. But if they are stimulated, they penetrate all situations.'[64] It (the *I Ching*) 'serves for exploring the laws of number and thus for knowing the future.'[65] The Changes use number as *a time-phase indicator* of dynamic processes. Jung too saw in numbers such a time factor, for he says: 'The first ten numbers represent – if they represent anything at all – an abstract cosmogony derived from the monad.'[66] This statement means, for instance, that the All-One-God or Unitas comes necessarily before the Two-God, etc.

Now the Chinese used number especially to express qualitative time-phases. For them there are one-ness moments, so to speak, times of duality, times of fourfold-ness. The whole *I Ching* is nothing more than a most impressive symbolic system of such a play or order of possible archetypal moments, expressed in the form of numerical permutations of lines. This makes use of something we know but tend to forget: archetypes are not only relatively permanent structures in the unconscious psyche, they are dynamisms; and if they are dynamisms, that is, if they are in movement, they enter time. We can actually observe such time-phases in the constellation of an archetype. In most cases when any archetype constellates, it first manifests as *one* archetypal image in a dream. When it moves towards the threshold of consciousness it generally appears doubled, as two identical or nearly identical images, two people, two dogs, two trees. We take this as a sign that the unconscious content is beginning to reach the threshold of consciousness. That would be the two-phase of its 'time'. Three groups of beings symbolize that that very archetype is actively possessing the ego, forcing upon it actions or thoughts. That is why fate gods are so often triadic. When the same content appears in its four-phase it has reached its best possibility for being realized in our consciousness (namely, through the four functions).

Seen from this angle, number is not only quantity but has also a *temporal* quality. One would be the quality of origin, beginning point; two the quality of polarization or symmetry; three of directed action, movement; four of confinement, consolidation, and so on.

Dr. Capra has asked me the relevant question: Why are we so interested in number and not so much in geometry, or rather, in topological structures? This is, I think, because synchronicity seems more connected with time than with space. For, as Jung pointed out: 'It is not easy to understand synchronicity in time as spatial, for we cannot imagine any space in which future events are objectively present and could be experienced as such through a reduction of this spatial distance.'[67]

Let us take an example. I dream that a friend in America dies. Twenty-four hours later this actually happens. It is thinkable that the image of the friend's death already exists in my unconscious psyche, which is outside time and space, and that the synchronistic event takes place in America a little later (that would mean a contractibility or relativization of time); but it is difficult to think that the friend already died somewhere far away in space, on the moon for instance, and that I perceived it there at the time of the dream and that he then died closer, in America (that would be a contractability of space). That is why Jung got more interested in number as time-phase indicators than in topological structures. Since Einstein, however, we know that time and space as an observable factor are inseparable. It seems to me that the difference of arithmetics and topology resembles that between music and the visual arts. Number has more to do with rhythm and with processes in time, the visual arts more with the mysteries of space. But a combination of the element of order and of meaning probably exists in both. But time, seen not as a vector or empty frame of reference, as the physicists do, but seen in the Chinese way as a succession of *qualitatively* distinct phases in which a specific amount of inner and outer events coincide, would be something slightly different from space, being more closely connected with the unconscious psyche than the latter. Spatialization would be derived from time, not *vice versa*.[68] Perhaps the fact that time-inversion (operation T) resists being reduced into perfect symmetry has to do with this fact (whilst operation P, spatial mirror inversion, and operation C, is more frequent and less absurd than is operation T).[69]

In his paper on S-matrix theory,[70] which he had the kindness to send me, Dr. Capra points out that in S-matrix theory physicists abandon 'the idea of fundamental building blocks of matter and accept no fundamental entities whatsoever'.[71] The universe is rather 'seen as a dynamic web of interrelated events'.[72] Each network of events which we observe 'in an experiment is nevertheless structured according to definite rules. These are the conservation laws. Only those reactions can occur in which a well defined set of quantum numbers is conserved.'[73]

Only those reactions would be possible which show a *flow*[74] of quantum numbers exhibiting the patterns associated with quarks, i.e., the 'two-ness' characteristic of mesons and the 'three-ness' characteristics of Baryons together with the various flavours that can combine to form the quantum numbers of the observed hadrons.[75] As a layperson in physics I cannot judge the implications of this position, but it seems to me that in this more dynamic view of the reality of matter we could find a rapprochement to Jung's dynamic view of the archetypes in the unconscious psyche. Certainly not only topological stuctures but numbers appear also as a quality of matter – just as they appear as a quality of psychic contents. The only difference, it seems to me, would lie in an interpretation of quality only as order or also, as we do in psychology, as having a meaning. Up until now most physicists certainly do not associate consciously any meaning with order. The 'two-ness' of mesons has no special 'meaning', if I understand them rightly.

We therefore touch here upon the differences between the two fields of knowledge. Let me amplify it in the language of some modern physicists. According to R. Ruyer's book on *La gnose de Princeton*,[76] some modern physicists see reality in the following way.

We have a direct consciousness of ourselves consisting of a certain amount of direct information. This is not our body, but our 'I'. But if we look at another being or object we can in fact not truly see it because we see only its body, its outer appearance, which we call matter, and not its 'inwardness', which is its true nature.[77] The corporeal existence is only an illusion, or a by-product of our sense perception. We have two modes for acquiring information: by observation and by participation.[78] The latter consists in participating in trans-spatial 'themes', as they put it. This is very similar to Jung's idea of a collective unconscious, which is, by his definition, partly trans-spatial and trans-temporal; its themes are what we call the archetypes.[79] God, for instance, is a participable, more than an observable.[80] Ruyer also calls some of the themes superindividual domains and part of a Universal Consciousness. In contrast to 'observables', participables, however, are postulated to be outside space.[81] But the very 'participables' have a timeless aspect which causes time, as Ruyer formulates, to be more than a functioning of spatial structures; they give time a direction in the sense of time's arrow and a *meaning*. Science 'reveals' the world of participation but it sees it only in its observable 'other' side.[82] The universe makes 'meanings' manifest by its very existence, form and life.[83]

To such modern speculative ideas of some physicists, we analytical psychologists come very close. For Jungian psychology is mostly an attempt to describe participables, or man, as a holon of meaning, in contrast to certain schools of psychiatry which look at man only as an 'observable', not allowing any empathy or communication of meaning. Aniela Jaffé rightly called Jung's myth the myth of meaning. But there are still also great differences, because although the physicists in question believe in God as a superdomanial ultimate intelligence with which we can play, so to speak, by making scientific experiments, this intelligence or cosmic mind does not, or rather only partially, comes to meet us in our soul. That is why these physicists mostly do not believe in incarnation and in Christ. For Jung, on the contrary, the dramatic encounter of man with the personified god-image in his psyche is *the* essential meaning of man's existence. The Princeton physicists imagine God as a cosmic domanial supra-intelligence far transcending the intelligence of man, so it seems not concerned with details. We, also, would say: Yes, the Self is a supra-*intelligence* far transcending that of man (Jung calls it 'absolute subjectless knowledge, consisting of images'), but it is the intelligence of the collective unconscious. It is vast but not focussed. On this planet at least man has most probably the most focussed consciousness; he can experience definite realizations of meaning which are more 'real' than these latent 'clouds of cognition' in the unconscious. Jung writes:

> Since a creation without the reflecting consciousness of man has no discernible meaning, the hypothesis of a latent meaning endows man with a cosmogonic significance, a true *raison d'être*. If . . . the latent meaning is attributed to the Creator as part of a conscious plan of creation, the question arises: Why should the Creator stage-manage this whole phenomenal world since he already knows what he can reflect himself in, and why should he reflect himself at all since he is already conscious of himself? Why should he create alongside his own omniscience a second, inferior consciousness – millions of dreary little mirrors when he knows in advance just what the image they reflect will look like?
>
> . . . He is just as unconscious as man or even more unconscious, since according to the myth of the *incarnatio* he actually felt obliged to become man and offer himself as a sacrifice.[84]

The God of modern physicists resembles more the god-image of Hinduism, or generally of the Far East, and has, as Ruyer points out, actually been influenced by it. Jung's view stands closer to Western Christianity, though he thought it incomplete and in need of a further unfolding of its myth. This does not mean that one is more 'true' than the other. What one believes in this respect is more a matter of temperament.

To Western man, the meaninglessness of a merely static universe is unbearable. He must assume that it has meaning. The Oriental does not need to make this assumption; rather he himself embodies it. Whereas the Occidental feels the need to complete the meaning of the world, the Oriental strives for the fulfillment of meaning in man, stripping the world and existence from himself.[85]

Jung, as one can see from this quotation, sees it as the task of man to complete the meaning of nature by his efforts to become conscious. '*Quod natura relinquit imperfectum, ars perficit*', as the old alchemists said. Jung was not at all sure that meaning would prevail. At the end of his life he wrote in his *Memories*:

The importance of consciousness is so great that one cannot help suspecting the element of *meaning* to be concealed somewhere within all the monstrous, apparently senseless biological turmoil, and that the road to its manifestation was ultimately found on the level of warm-blooded vertebrates possessed of a differentiated brain – found as if by chance, unintended and unforeseen, and yet somehow sensed, felt and groped for out of some dark urge.[86]

The world into which we are born is brutal and cruel, and at the same time of divine beauty. Which element we think outweighs the other, whether meaninglessness or meaning, is a matter of temperament. If meaninglessness were absolutely preponderant, the meaningfulness of life would vanish to an increasing degree with each step in our development. But that is – or seems to me – not the case. Probably, as in all metaphysical questions, both are true: Life is – or has – meaning and meaninglessness. I cherish the anxious hope that meaning will preponderate and win the battle.[87]

Here Jung reaches out into realms which lead far away from a strictly scientific outlook. He did it quite consciously because the meaningful but rather vague language of myth is in his view more appropriate for the description of psychological facts. Only so can it include the vagueness of meaning and the feeling function. This, I think, will always keep psychology separate from physics. If we try, all the same, to meet, it is for the reason that in its fringes, where psychology reaches over to other fields of science, there should exist – if possible – no fundamental contradictions. A psychology which does not keep pace with the findings of the other sciences seems to me no good. I think that Jungian psychology meets nuclear physics on a fringe via the concept of order, especially closely in the view that number is an archetype as well as a property of material phenomena, as in quantum numbers or patterns of particle interactions. Dr. Capra writes: 'When the particles are arranged according to the values of their quantum numbers they are seen to fall into very neat patterns, hexagonal and triangular patterns, known as octets and decuplets.'[88] Very similar patterns appear in the archetypal structures produced by the unconscious psyche, but in contrast to the aspect of order alone we have in psychology also to search for their 'meaning'. Number, it seems to me, unites both: order and meaning, and is therefore, together with its topological spatializations into 'patterns', a possible meeting point for the two fields of science. In dealing with 'participables', however, psychology has to transcend the hitherto delineated limits of science, because it cannot exclude 'meaning' and the feeling function from its way of describing its object. That seems to be the specific value but also the limitation of psychology. The search for order appeals to the function of sensation, thinking and also sometimes intuition. But to include feeling values and thus the 'whole', the vagueness of 'meaning' forces us to go beyond science and leads us back to the older way of mankind for expressing itself: to myth. That inevitably leads to antinomies and an obscuring of scientific clarity. It makes understandable why the 'theologians of number' do not like us and why the gnostics of Princeton feel that we are occultists. But because we have to deal with the human individual as a whole, we are forced into this outlook. To me this is something positive because I would regret it if physics as it is would swallow up psychology or vice versa – it seems more fruitful to me that both fields keep their own field of thought and action but exchange their views in those fringe areas where we can creatively meet.

Notes and References

The *Collected Works of C.G. Jung* (18 volumes, eds H. Read, M. Fordham and G. Adler) referred to throughout are published by Routledge Kegan Paul (London, 1969) and Pantheon Books (New York, 1969).

CHAPTER 1

1. W. Stekel 'Die verpflichtung des namens' *Zeitschrift für Psychotherapie und medizinische Psychologie*, no. 3, Stuttgart, 1911.
2. C.G. Jung (1950) 'Concerning rebirth', *Collected Works*, 9. (1).
3. C.G. Jung (1944) 'Psychology and alchemy', *Collected Works*, 12.
4. C.G. Jung (1946) 'The psychology of transference', *Collected Works*, 16.
5. C.G. Jung (1907) 'The psychology of dementia praecox', *Collected Works*, 3.
6. C.G. Jung (1958) 'Schizophrenia', *Collected Works*, 3.
7. C.G. Jung (1902) 'On the psychology and pathology of so–called occult phenomena', *Collected Works*, 1.
8. C.G. Jung (1951) 'On synchronicity', *Collected Works*, 8.
9. C.G. Jung (1958) 'Flying saucers: a modern myth', *Collected Works*, 10.
10. C.G. Jung (1952) 'Answer to Job', *Collected Works*, 11.
11. C.G. Jung *Memories, dreams, reflections* (Routledge Kegan Paul, London, 1963).
12. W. James 'The divided self' in *The varieties of religious experience* (Fontana, London, 1960).
13. N.G.L. Hammond and H.H. Scullard (eds) *Oxford classical dictionary* (Oxford University Press, 1970). Ref. pp. 843-4.
14. E. Jones *Sigmund Freud: life and work*, vol. 2 (Hogarth Press, London, 1955).
15. C.G. Jung (1942) 'Paracelsus as a spiritual phenomenon', *Collected Works*, 13. Ref. p. 117.
16. F. Yates *Shakespeare's last plays: a new approach* (Routledge Kegan Paul, London, 1975).
17. C.G. Jung (1957) 'The undiscovered self', *Collected Works*, 10. Ref. p. 303.
18. C.G. Jung (1954) 'Transformation symbolism in the mass', *Collected Works*, 11.
19. C.G. Jung (1958) 'A psychological view of conscience', *Collected Works*, 10. Ref. p. 453.
20. C.G. Jung (1912) 'Symbols of transformation', *Collected Works*, 5. Ref. p. 132n.
21. H. Hesse *Steppenwolf* (Penguin Books, Harmondsworth, 1927). Ref. pp. 70-1.

CHAPTER 2

1. Karl Abraham 'Traum und Mythos' in *Schriften zur angewandten Seelenkunde*, Heft 4, Franz Deuticke Verlag, Bern, 1909.
2. Hedwig von Beit *Symbolik des Märchens*, Francke Verlag, Bern, 1952.
3. Charlotte Bühler and Josephine Bilz *Das Märchen und die Phantasie des Kindes* (Johann Ambrosius Barth Verlag, München, 1961).
4. Hans Dieckmann 'Der Individuationsprozess in orientalischen Rahmener-zählungen' in *Praxis der Kinderpsychologie*, Jahrgang 12, Heft 2, 1963.
5. Hans Dieckmann *Märchen und Träume als Helfer des Menschen* (Adolf Bonz Verlag, Stuttgart, 1966).
6. Hans Dieckmann 'Der Wert des Märchens für die seelische Entwicklung des Kindes' in *Praxis der Kinderpsychologie*, Jahrgang 15, Heft 2, 1966.
7. Hans Dieckmann 'Das Lieblingsmärchen der Kindheit und seine Beziehung zu Neurose und Persönlichkeitsstruktur' in *Praxis der Kinder-psychologie*, Jahrgang 16, Heft 6, 1967.
8. Hans Dieckmann 'Zum Aspekt des Grausamen im Märchen' in *Praxis der Kinderpsychologie*, Jahrgang 16, Heft 8, 1967.
9. Hans Dieckmann 'Das Lieblingsmärchen der Kindheit als therapeutischer Faktor in der Analyse' in *Praxis der Kinderpsychologie*, Jahrgang 17, Heft 8, 1968.
10. Marie-Louise von Franz 'Bei der schwarzen Frau' in *Studien zur Analytischen Psychologie*, C.G. Jungs II. (Rascher Verlag, Zürich, 1955).
11. Sigmund Freud (1900) *The Interpretation of Dreams* in *Standard Edition*, vols 4–5 (Hogarth and the Institute of Psychoanalysis, London).
12. Sigmund Freud (1913) *The Occurrence in Dreams of Material from Fairy Tales* in *Standard Edition*, vol. 12 (Hogarth and the Institute of Psychoanalysis, London).
13. Erich Fromm *Märchen, Mythen und Träume* (Diana Verlag, Konstanz-Stuttgart, 1957).
14. Wilhelm Hauff *Sämtliche Werke* (Griesbach Verlag, Gera, 1896).
15. Paul Heyse 'Das Ratsel der Spinx' zit. nach F. v.d. Leyen '*Traum und Märchen*' (sehe unten).
16. Jolande Jacobi *The Psychology of C.G. Jung* (Routledge, Kegan Paul, London, 1942).
17. Aniela Jaffé 'Bilder und Symbole aus E.T.A. Hoffmanns Märchen "Der goldne Topf"' in *Gestaltungen des Unbewussten* (Rascher Verlag, Zürich, 1950).
18. C.G. Jung *Mysterium Coniunctionis* in *Collected Works*, vol. 14 (Routledge, Kegan Paul, London, 1955).
19. St. B. Karpman 'Fairy Tales and Script Drama Analysis' in *Transactional Analysis Bulletin*, vol. 7, 26 April, 1968.
20. Wilhelm Laiblin *Märchenforschung und Tiefenpsychologie* (Wissenschaft-liche Buchgesellschaft, Darmstadt, 1969).
21. Friedrich von Leyen 'Traum and Märchen': der Lotse, Band 1 u. 2, 1901.
22. Erno Littman (Übz.) *Die Erzählungen aus den 1001 Nächten* (Insel Verlag, Wiesbaden, 1953).
23. Erich Neumann 'Die Erfahrung der Einheitswirklichkeit' in *Der Schöpferische Mensch* (Rhein Verlag, Zürich, 1959).

24. *Pantschatantra* Müller und Kiepenheuer Verlag, Bergen II, 1952.
25. Otto Rank *Das Inzestmotiv in Dichtung und Sage* (Deuticke Verlag, Wien, 1926).
26. Ottokar Wittgenstein 'Das Reifungserleben im Märchen' in *Das Kraftfeld des Forschers un Menschen Gustav Richard Heyer*, Festschrift zum 65. Geburtstag, Kindler Verlag, München, 1955.

CHAPTER 3

1. J.F. Rychlak (ed.) *Dialectic: Humanistic rationale for behaviour and development* (S. Karger, Basel, 1976).
2. J.F. Rychlak *The psychology of rigorous humanism.* (Wiley-Interscience, New York, 1977). Refs. pp 8–31, p. 283.
3. Aristotle *Physics* and *Topics*, in R. M. Hutchins (ed.) *Great books of the western world (Vol. 8)* (Encyclopedia Britannica, Chicago 1952). Ref. pp. 276-7.
4. F. Bacon *Advancement of learning*, in R. M. Hutchins (ed.) *Great books of the western world (Vol. 30)* (Encyclopedia Britannica, Chicago, 1952).
5. J. Locke 'An essay concerning human understanding', in R. M. Hutchins (ed.), *Great books of the western world (Vol. 35)* (Encyclopedia Britannica, Chicago, 1952). Ref. p. 369.
6. I. Kant 'The critique of pure reason', in R. M. Hutchins (ed.), *Great books of the western world (Vol. 42)* (Encyclopedia Britannica, Chicago, 1952).
7. S. Freud 'Contributions to a discussion of masturbation', in J. Strachey (ed.) *The standard edition of the complete psychological works of Sigmund Freud (Vol. XII).* (Hogarth Press, London, 1962). Ref. p. 247.
8. E. Jones *The life and work of Sigmund Freud: The last phase (Vol. 3).* (Basic Books, New York 1957). Ref. p. 345.
9. C.G. Jung (1957) 'Psychiatric studies', *Collected Works*, 1. Ref. p. 521.
10. C.G. Jung (1960) 'The psychogenesis of mental disease', *Collected Works*, 3.
11. W. McGuire (ed.), *The Freud/Jung letters* (translated by R. Manheim and R. F. C. Hull) (Princeton University Press, 1974). Refs. pp. 251-2, p. 382.
12. C.G. Jung (1954) 'The development of personality', *Collected Works*, 17. Refs p. 375, p. 91.
13. J. F. Rychlak *A philosophy of science for personality theory* (Houghton Mifflin, Boston 1968).
14. J. F. Rychlak *Introduction to personality and psychotherapy: A theory-construction approach* (Houghton Mifflin, Boston 1973).
15. J. F. Rychlak *Discovering free will and personal responsibility* (Oxford University Press, New York 1979).
16. E. Cassirer *The problem of knowledge* (Yale University Press, New Haven, 1950). Ref. pp. 91-3.
17. P. Rieff *Freud: The mind of the moralist* (Viking Press, New York 1959). Ref. p. 26.
18. J. Bradley *Mach's philosophy of science* (Athlone Press of the University of London, 1971). Ref. p. 53.
19. S. Freud 'A case of successful treatment by hypnotism', in J. Strachey (ed.) *The standard edition of the complete psychological works of Sigmund Freud*

(Vol. I). (The Hogarth Press, London 1966). Refs. p. 117, p. 471.

20. C.G. Jung (1961) 'Freud and psychoanalysis', *Collected Works*, 4. Refs. p. 337, p. 293.

20a. C.G. Jung (1957) 'Symbols of transformation', *Collected Works*, 5.

21. C.G. Jung (1964) 'Civilization in transition', *Collected Works*, 10. Refs. p. 147, p. 141.

22. C.G. Jung (1959) 'The archetypes and the collective unconscious', *Collected Works*, 9, (1). Refs. p. 40, p. 109.

23. C.G. Jung (1954) 'The practice of psychotherapy', *Collected Works*, 16.

24. C.G. Jung (1960) 'The structure and dynamics of the psyche', *Collected Works*, 8. Refs. p. 125, p. 332, p. 31.

25. C.G. Jung (1958) 'Psychology and religion: West and east, *Collected Works*, 11. Refs. p. 554, p. 305.

26. C.G. Jung (1959) 'Aion', *Collected Works*, 9. (2). Refs. p. 226. p. 61, p. 5.

27. C.G. Jung (1953) 'Two essays on analytical psychology', *Collected Works*, 7. Ref. p. 60.

28. G. Adler and A. Jaffé (eds), *C. G. Jung letters* (translation from the German by R. F. C. Hull) (Princeton University Press, 1975). Ref. pp. 500–2.

29. C. G. Jung *Memories, dreams, reflections*. (Pantheon Books, New York and William Collins, London 1963). Ref. p. 357.

CHAPTER 4

1. G. Adler (ed.) *C.G. Jung Letters: Vol. I: 1906-1950* (Routledge Kegan Paul, London, 1973).

2. G. Adler (ed.) *C.G. Jung Letters: Vol. II: 1951-1961* (Routledge Kegan Paul, London, 1976).

3. D. Bakan *S. Freud and the Jewish mystical tradition* (van Nostrand, Princeton, 1958).

4. D. Bakan *The duality of human existence* (Rand McNally, Chicago, 1966).

5. E.A. Barber (ed.) *Lidell, Scott and Stuart Jones' Greek-English lexicon: a supplement* (Clarendon Press, Oxford, 1968).

6. G. Bateson (1970) 'Form, substance and difference', in *Steps to an ecology of mind* (Paladin, London, 1973).

7. T. Benfey *Sanskrit-English dictionary* (Longmans & Green, London, 1866).

8. S. Blanton *Diary of my analysis with Sigmund Freud* (Hawthorn Books, New York, 1971).

9. E. Bleuler *Dementia praecox or the group of schizophrenias*, tr. J. Zinkin (International Universities Press, New York, 1950 [1911]).

10. V. Brome *Jung: man and myth* (Macmillan, London, 1978).

11. P. Chantraine *Dictionnaire étymologique de la langue Grecque. Histoire des mots* (Éditions Klincksieck, Paris, vol. I. 1968. vol. II. 1970).

12. E. Christou *The logos of the soul* (Dunquin Press, Zurich, 1963).

13. E.D. Cohen *C.G. Jung and the scientific attitude* (Philosophical Library, New York, 1975).

14. Hannah S. Decker 'Freud in Germany: revolution and reaction in science 1893 – 1907', *Psychological Issues, Monograph* 41, I.U.P., New York, 1977.

15. J. De Greef 'Philosophy and its "Other",' *International Philsophical*

Quarterly, 10, 1970.

16. H. Ellenberger *The discovery of the unconscious* (Basic Books, New York, 1970).

17. M. Fordham 'The evolution of Jung's researches', *The British Journal of Medical Psychology,* 29, 1956.

18. M. Fordham *Jungian psychotherapy: a study in analytical psychology* (John Wiley and Sons, New York, 1978).

19. H.W. Fowler and F.G. Fowler (eds.) *The concise Oxford dictionary of current English* (Clarendon, Oxford, 1964).

20. E. Freud (ed.) *The letters of Sigmund Freud and Arnold Zweig,* tr. W.D. Robson-Scott (Hogarth, London, 1970).

21. S. Freud (1901) *The psychopathology of everyday life,* in *Standard Edition,* vol. 6 (Hogarth and the Institute of Psycho-Analysis, London).

22. S. Freud (1905) *Three essays on the theory of sexuality.* in *Standard Edition,* vol. 7, *ibid.*

23. S. Freud (1910) *Five lectures on psychoanalysis,* in *Standard Edition,* vol. 11, *ibid.*

24. S. Freud (1910b) 'Leonardo da Vinci and a memory of his childhood, in *Standard Edition,* vol. 11, *ibid.*

25. S. Freud (1911) *Psycho-analytic notes on an autobiographical account of a case of paranoia,* in *Standard Edition,* vol. 12, *ibid.*

26. S. Freud (1912) 'Postscript to "Psycho-analytic notes on an autobiographical account of a case of paranoia"', in Standard Edition. vol. 12, *ibid.*

27. S. Freud (1912b) 'Recommendations to physicians practicing psycho-analysis', in *Standard Edition,* vol. 12, *ibid.*

28. S. Freud (1913) 'The claims of psycho-analysis to scientific interest', in *Standard Edition,* vol. 13, *ibid.*

29. S. Freud (1914) *The history of the psycho-analytic movement,* in *Standard Edition.* vol. 14, *ibid.*

30. S. Freud (1915) 'The unconscious', in *Standard Edition,* vol. 14, *ibid.*

31. S. Freud (1923) 'Two encyclopaedia articles: the libido theory; in *Standard Edition,* vol. 18, *ibid.*

32. S. Freud (1925) *An autobiographical study,* in *Standard Edition,* vol. 20, *ibid.*

33. S. Freud (1926) 'Psycho-analysis', in *Standard Edition,* vol. 20, *ibid.*

34. Barbara Hannah *Jung: his life and work; a biographical memoir* (Putnam, New York, 1976).

35. M. Esther Harding *The 'I' and 'not I': a study in the development of consciousness* (Princeton University Press, Princeton, 1965).

36. J.W. Heisig 'The VII sermones: play and theory', *Spring,* 1972.

37. Judith Hubback 'VII sermones ad mortuous', *Journal of Analytical Psychology,* 11, 1966.

38. Jolande Jacobi *Complex/archetype/symbol in the psychology of C.G. Jung,* tr. by R. Manheim (Routledge Kegan Paul, London, 1959 [1957]).

39. Aniela Jaffé *C.G. Jung: word and image* (Princeton University Press, Princeton, 1979).

40. J.L. Jarrett 'The logic of psychological opposition – or how opposite is opposite?', *Journal of Analytical Psychology,* 24, 1979.

41. C.G. Jung (1902) 'On the psychology and pathology of so-called occult phenomena', in *Collected Works*, vol. 1, ed. H. Read, M. Fordham and G. Adler (Routledge Kegan Paul, London).

42. C.G. Jung (1905) 'Cryptomnesia', in *Collected Works*, vol. 1, *ibid*.

43. C.G. Jung (1906) 'Association, dream and hysterical symptom', in *Collected Works*, vol. 2, *ibid*.

44. C.G. Jung (1907) *The psychology of dementia praecox*, in *Collected Works*, vol. 3, *ibid*.

45. C.G. Jung (1908) 'New aspects of criminal psychology', in *Collected Works*, vol. 4, *ibid*.

46. C.G. Jung (1908b) 'The Freudian theory of hysteria', in *Collected Works*, vol. 2, *ibid*.

47. C.G. Jung (1909) 'The family constellation', in *Collected Works*, vol. 2, *ibid*.

48. C.G. Jung (1909b) 'The significance of the father in the destiny of the individual', in *Collected Works*, vol. 4, *ibid*.

49. C.G. Jung (1911) 'A contribution to the psychology of rumour', in *Collected Works*, vol. 4, *ibid*.

50. C.G. Jung (1912) *The psychology of the unconscious*, tr. B.M. Hinkle (Kegan Paul, Trench, Trubner & Co., 1919).

51. C.G. Jung (1914) 'Some crucial points in psychoanalysis: a correspondence between Dr Jung and Dr Löy', in *Collected Works*, vol. 4, *ibid*.

52. C.G. Jung (1916) *Septem sermones ad mortuous: the seven sermons to the dead written by Basilides in Alexandria, the city where the East toucheth the West*, tr. H.G. Baynes (Stuart & Watkins, London, 1967).

53. C.G. Jung (1916b) 'The structure of the unconscious', in *Collected Works*, vol. 7, *ibid*.

54. C.G. Jung (1919) 'Instinct and the unconscious', in *Collected Works*, vol. 8, *ibid*.

55. C.G. Jung (1921) *Psychological types: or the psychology of individuation*, tr. H.G. Baynes (Routledge Kegan Paul, London, 1923).

56. C.G. Jung (1928) 'The relation between the ego and the unconscious', in *Collected Works*, vol. 7, *ibid*.

57. C.G. Jung (1929) 'Commentary on *The secret of the golden flower*', in *Collected Works*, vol. 13, *ibid*.

58. C.G. Jung (1934) 'The development of personality', in *Collected Works*, vol. 17, *ibid*.

59. C.G. Jung (1935) 'The Tavistock lectures', in *Collected Works*, vol. 18, *ibid*.

60. C.G. Jung (1943) 'On the psychology of the unconscious', in *Collected Works*, vol. 7, *ibid*.

61. C.G. Jung (1944) 'Introduction to the religious and psychological problems of alchemy', in *Collected Works*, vol. 12, *ibid*.

62. C.G. Jung (1946) 'Analytical psychology and education', in *Collected Works*, vol. 17, *ibid*.

63. C.G. Jung (1946b) 'The psychology of transference', in *Collected Works*, vol. 16, *ibid*.

64. C.G. Jung (1952) 'Religion and psychotherapy: a reply to Martin Buber', in *Collected Works*, vol. 18, *ibid*.

65. C.G. Jung *Memories, dreams, reflections*, recorded and edited by Aniela

Jaffé, tr. R. and C. Winston (Collins, London, 1963).

66. G.S. Kirk and J.E. Raven *The presocratic philosophers* (Cambridge University Press, Cambridge, 1971).

67. J. Lacan *The language of the self*, tr. A. Wilden (Johns Hopkins University Press, Baltimore, 1968).

68. J. Lacan *The four fundamental concepts of psychoanalysis*, tr. A. Sheridan (Hogarth, London, 1977).

69. J. Lacan *Écrits. A selection*, tr. A. Sheridan (Tavistock, London, 1977b).

70. Anika Lemaire *Jacques Lacan*, tr. D. Macey, (Routledge Kegan Paul, London, 1977).

71. H. G. Liddell and R. Scott *A Greek-English lexicon* (Clarendon Press, Oxford, 1901).

72. J. Lustman 'On splitting', *The Psychoanalytic Study of the Child*, 27, 1972.

73. J. Macmurray *Persons in relation* (Faber & Faber, London, 1961).

74. W. McGuire (ed.) *The correspondence between Sigmund Freud and C.G. Jung*, tr. R. Manheim and R.F.C. Hull (Hogarth, Routledge Kegan Paul, London, 1974).

75. G.H. Mead *Mind, self and society* (Chicago University Press, Chicago, 1934).

76. V.W. Odajnuk *Jung and politics: the political and social ideas of C.G. Jung* (Harper & Row, New York, 1976).

77. S. Ramfos *The kale psyche and its other* (in Greek) (Kedros, Athens, 1978).

78. O. Rank *The double: a psychoanalytic study*, tr. H. Tucker jr. (University of North Carolina Press, Chapel Hill, [1914] 1971).

79. O. Rank *Beyond psychology* (Dover, New York, 1941).

80. L. Rauhala 'Intentionality and the problem of the unconscious', *Anales Universitatis Turkuensis*, Turku, 1969.

81. L. Rauhala 'Analytical psychology and metascience', *Journal of Analytical Psychology*, 21, 1976.

82. L. Rauhala 'The basic views of C.G. Jung in the light of hermeneutical metascience' (in this volume).

83. J. Redfearn 'Romantic and classical views, of analysis – primal relationship or working relationship', *Journal of Analytical Psychology*, 25, 1980.

84. M. Robert *From Oedipus to Moses: Freud's Jewish identity*, tr. R. Manheim (Anchor, Garden City, [1974] 1976).

85. J.F. Rychlak *A philosophy of science for personality theory* (Houghton – Mifflin, Boston, 1968).

86. J.F. Rychlak *Introduction to personality and psychotherapy* (Houghton – Mifflin, Boston, 1973).

87. J.F. Rychlak 'Carl Gustav Jung as dialectician and teleologist' (in this volume).

88. G. Ryle *The concept of mind* (Penguin, Harmondsworth [1949] 1963).

89. J.P. Sartre *The transcendence of the ego* (Noonday, New York [1937] 1957).

90. S.T. Selesnick 'C.G. Jung's contribution to psychoanalysis', *American Journal of Psychiatry*, 120, 1963.

91. W. Stekel *The autobiography of William Stekel: the life story of a pioneer psychoanalyst* (Liveright, New York, 1950).

92. P.E. Stepansky 'The empiricist as rebel: Jung, Freud and the burdens of

discipleship', *Journal of the History of Behavioral Sciences, 12,* 1976.

93. E.W. Strauss 'Norm and pathology of I – world relations (1961)', in *Phenomenological psychology: selected papers* (Tavistock, London, 1966).

94. T. Szasz 'Freud as a leader (1963)', in F. Cioffi (ed.) *Freud: modern judgements* (Macmillan, London, 1973).

95. J. Szczepanski 'The Other', *Dialectical Humanism, 6,* 1979.

96. L. van der Post *Jung and the story of our time* (Pantheon, New York, 1975).

97. Marie-Louise von Franz *C.G. Jung: his myth in our times,* tr. W.H. Kennedy (Hodder and Stoughton, London, 1975).

98. A. Wilden *System and structure: essays in communication and exchange* (Tavistock, London, 1972).

99. L. Wittgenstein *Tractatus logico-philosophicus,* tr. D.F. Pears and B.F. McGuinness (Routledge Kegan Paul, London [1912] 1961).

CHAPTER 5

1. C.G. Jung (1955) 'Mysterium coniunctionis', *Collected Works,* 14. Ref. para. 749.

2. C.G. Jung (1921) 'Psychological types', *Collected Works,* 6. Refs. paras 712–14; pp. 440-2.

3. C.G. Jung *Collected Works,* 9.

4. C.G. Jung *Collected Works,* 2.

5. C.G. Jung *Collected Works,* 9. I owe this historical data to manuscripts that Dr. Elisabeth Ruf, editor of *Gesammelte Werke,* kindly made available to me and to a study of R.F.C. Hull *Bibliographical Notes on Active Imagination in the Works of C.G. Jung* (Spring, New York, 1971). Ref. pp. 115-120.

6. C.G. Jung *Memories, dreams, reflections* (Routledge Kegan Paul, London, 1963). Ref. Ch. 6.

7. C.G. Jung (1957) 'The Transcendent Function' *Collected Works,* 8. Refs. p. 78, p. 83, p. 84.

8. C.G. Jung (1955) 'Mysterium Coniunctionis' *Collected Works,* 14. Ref. para. 706.

9. For example the dialogues with the anima in *Memories, dreams, reflections.* op. cit.

10. Example cited by M.L. von Franz 'Meditation in Religion and Psychotherapie' in a collection of readings edited by W. Bitter (Stuttgart, 1958). Ref. pp. 136-48.

11. C.G. Jung (1955) 'Mysterium Coniunctionis', *Collected Works,* 14. Ref. para. 446.

12. C.G. Jung (1955) 'Mysterium Coniunctionis', ibid. Refs. paras 333, 705.

13. C.G. Jung (1955) 'Mysterium Coniunctionis', ibid. Ref. para. 446.

14. C.G. Jung (1929) 'Commentary on the Secret of the Golden Flower', *Collected Works,* 13. Ref. paras 20-3.

15. C.G. Jung (1955) 'Mysterium Coniunctionis', *Collected Works,* 14. Ref. para. 749.

16. C.G. Jung (1955) 'Mysterium Coniunctionis', ibid. Ref. pp. 752-3.

17. cf. André Loupiac on The Imago.

18. C.G. Jung (1952) 'Interpretation of Visions', *Collected Works,* 6. Ref.

Lecture I, 4 May 1932, p. 3, from the notes of Mary Foote mimeographed in 1940.

19. C.G. Jung & C. Kerényi *Introduction to a science of mythology* (Routledge Kegan Paul, London, 1951). Ref. p. 228f.

20. C.G. Jung (1955) 'Mysterium Coniunctionis', *Collected Works*, 14. Ref. p. 756.

21. L.P. Clark 'The Phantasy Method of Analysing Narcissistic Neuroses' *Psychoanalytic Review*, vol. 13, 1925, pp. 225-232; and *Medical Journal and Record*, vol. 123, 1926, pp. 143ff.

CHAPTER 6

1. The material of this chapter is extracted from a thesis submitted by the author to the Faculty of Psychology, Catholic University of Louvain, for the degree of Doctor in Psychology, under the mentorship of Mme Depuydt-Berte: L. Jadot *Contribution á l'étude théorique et expérimentale de la structure héroïque de l'imaginaire*, in two volumes, unpublished, 1973.

2. R. Alleau *De la nature des symboles* (Flammarion, Paris, 1958).
   E. Cassirer *La philosophie des formes symboliques* vol. 3, (Editions de Minuit, Paris, 1972).
   G. Durand *L'imagination symbolique* (P.U.F., Paris, 1964).

3. C.G. Jung *Collected Works*, 5. Ref. pp. xxiv-vi.

4. C.G. Jung *Collected Works*, 5. Ref. p. xxiii.

5. C.G. Jung *Collected Papers on Analytical Psychology* (Baillière Tindall, London, 1916). Ref. author's preface, first edition.

6. This point of view, however, is no longer rigidly supported by a number of contemporary authors who are preoccupied with the critique of sciences. One of the culminating points of this debate has been taken up by J. Monod in his work *Chance and Necessity*. On this question one should consult J. Ladrière's article where he proposes a concept of finality which fits better with the modern critique, concerning an 'integration within a totality' (in *Revue Philosophique de Louvain*, vol. 67, 1969, pp. 143-181); see also: J.F. Rychlak: 'Causality and proper Image of Man in Scientific Psychology' in *Journal of Projective Techniques*, no. 5, 1971, pp. 403-419; and S. Lupasco *Les trois matières* (Julliard, Paris, 1960) on causality-finality. Refs. pp. 43-46, pp. 95-100, pp. 151-156.

7. G. Durand *L'imagination symbolique* (P.U.F. Paris, 1964). On reductive hermeneutics see pp. 38-57; on instaurative hermeneutics see pp. 58-81.

8. G. Bachelard *La poétique de la rêverie* (P.U.F., Paris, 1960).

9. E. Cassirer *La philosophie des formes symboliques*, 3 vols (Editions de Minuit, Paris, 1972).

10. M. Eliade *Images et symboles* (Gallimard, Paris, 1952).
    H.R. Zimmer *Mythes et symboles dans l'art et la civilisation de l'Inde* (Payot, Paris, 1951).
    H.R. Corbin *L'imagination créatrice dans le soufisme d'Ibn'Arabi* (Flammarion, Paris, 1959); *Terre céleste et corps de résurrection* (Buchet/Chastel, Paris, 1961); *Avicenne et le récit visionnaire* (Maisonneuve, Paris-Téhéran, 1964).

J. Starobinski 'Remarques sur l'histoire du concept d'imagination' in *Cahiers international du Symbolisme*, no. 11, 1966; *L'Oeil vivant II, la relation critique* (Gallimard, Paris, 1970).

J. Ricoeur 'Structure et Herméneutique', in *Esprit*, Nov. 1963. 'Le Conflict des Herméneutiques' in *Cahiers internationaux du Symbolisme*, no. 1, 1962. 'Le Symbolisme et l'explication structurale' in *Cahiers internationaux du Symbolisme*, no. 4, 1964.

G. Durand: *L'imagination symbolique* (P.U.F., Paris, 1964); *Les structures anthropologiques de l'Imaginaire* (P.U.F., Paris, 1963).

11. S. Freud *Introduction à la Psychanalyse* (Payot, Paris, 1947). *L'Interprétaton des Rêves* (P.U.F., Paris, 67).

J. Lacan *Ecrits* (Seuil, Paris, 1966).

G. Dumezil *L'Héritage indo-européen à Rome* (Gallimard, Paris, 1949). *Mythes et dieux des Germains* (P.U.F., Paris, 1953).

C. Lévi-Strauss *Anthropologie structurale* (Plon, Paris, 1958). Refs chapters XI and XI. *La pensée sauvage* (Plon, Paris, 1962).

12. G. Durand *L'imagination symbolique* (P.U.F., Paris, 1964). Ref. p. 82f.

13. P. Ricoeur 'Le conflit des herméneutiques, épistémologie des interprétations', in *Cahiers internationaux du Symbolisme*, no. 1, 1962.

14. G. Durand *L'imagination symbolique* (P.U.F., Paris, 1964). Ref. p. 104.

15. The angel: see E. Souriau *L'ombre de Dieu* (Paris, 1955). Ref. pp. 133–67; see also G. Durand, op. cit., refs. p. 13 and pp. 31–37. 'The Angel of the Work' is an 'aura', 'in the beyond', 'mediator', 'creative freedom of a meaning'.

16. G. Durand *L'imagination symbolique* (P.U.F., Paris, 1964). Ref. pp. 105–106.

17. G. Durand ibid., Ref. p. 107.

18. P. Ricoeur 'Le conflit des herméneutiques', in *Cahiers internationaux du Symbolisme*, no. 2, p. 183, 1962.

19. G. Durand *L'imagination symbolique* (P.U.F., Paris, 1964). Ref. pp. 108–9.

20. G. Durand ibid. Ref. pp. 82–110.

21. G. Durand *Les structures anthropologiques de l'imaginaire* (P.U.F., Paris, 1963).

22. The word is Bachelard's.

23. G. Durand *L'imagination symbolique* (P.U.F., Paris, 1964). Ref. pp. 109–10.

24. G. Durand *ibid*. Refs. p. 67 and pp. 83–85.

25. S. Laupasco *Les Trois Matières* (Julliard, Paris, 1960). Ref. p. 88.

26. P. Ricoeur 'Structure et Herméneutique', in *Esprit*, Nov. 1963. Ref. pp. 626–627.

26. A. Lalande *Vocabulaire critique et technique de la philosophie*, (P.U.F., Paris, 1951). Ref. article 'Symbole sens', no. 2.

27. G. Durand *L'imagination symbolique* (P.U.F., Paris, 1964). Ref. p. 6.

28. C.G. Jung (1921) *Collected Works*, 6. Ref. p. 474f.

29. G. Durand *L'imagination symbolique* (P.U.F., Paris, 1964). Ref. pp. 7–8.

30. Ibid, p. 9.

31. P. Ricoeur *Finitude et culpabilité, II, la symbolique du mal* (Aubier, Paris, 1960). Ref. p. 18.

32. On the etymology of symbolon, see R. Alleau *De la nature des Symboles*

(Flammarion, Paris, 1958). Ref. pp. 11–17.

33. G. Durand *L'Imagination symbolique* (P.U.F., Paris, 1964). Ref. p. 9.
34. E. Cassirer *An Essay on Man*, p. 57.
35. G. Durand *L'imagination symbolique* (P.U.F., Paris, 1964). Ref. p. 10.
36. G. Durand op. cit. Ref. p. 11–12.
37. H. Corbin *L'Imagination créatrice dans le Soufisme d'Ibn'Arabi*, (Flammarion, Paris, 1958). Ref. p. 13.
38. G. Durand *L'imagination symbolique* (P.U.F., Paris, 1964). Ref. p. 12.
39. Ibid. Ref. p. 14.
40. On the 'method of convergence' see G. Durand *Les structures anthropologiques de l'imaginaire* P.U.F., Paris, 1963). Ref. pp. 33-3.
41. On the coherence of hermeneutics see P. Ricoeur 'Le conflit des herméneutiques', in *Cahiers internationaux du Symbolique*, no. 1, 1962.
42. Lacan J. *Ecrits* (Seuil, Paris, 1966). Refs. pp. 443-5, p. 468, pp. 550-6.
43. J. Laplanche et J. Pontalis *Vocabulaire de la psychanalyse* (P.U.F., Paris, 1967). Ref. symbolisme, pp. 476–80.
44. Ibid. Ref. p. 476.
45. Ibid. Ref. p. 476.
46. Ibid. Ref. p. 479.
47. Ibid. Ref. p. 479.
48. J. Laplanche et J.B. Pontalis *Fantasmes originaires*, Ref. pp. 157-9.
49. J. Laplanche et J.B. Pontalis *Vocabulaire de la psychanalyse* (P.U.F., Paris, 1967). Ref. symbolisme, pp. 477-8.
50. O. Rank *Le traumatisme de la naissance* (P.B. Payot, Paris, 1968).
51. See the titles of chapters: Ch. 3: Sexual satisfaction; Ch. 5: Symbolic adaptation; Ch. 6: Heroic compensation; Ch. 7: Religious sublimation; Ch. 8: Artistic idealisation; Ch. 9: Philosophic speculation.
52. J. Laplanche et J.B. Pontalis *Vocabulaire de la psychanalyse* (P.U.F., Paris, 1967). Ref. symbolique, p. 475.
53. J. Lacan *Ecrits* (Seuil, Paris, 1966). Ref. p. 445.
54. J. Lacan ibid. Ref. p. 468.
55. J. Lacan ibid. Ref. p. 468.
56. J. Laplanche et J.B. Pontalis *Vocabulaire de la psychanalyse* (P.U.F., Paris, 1967). Ref. imaginaire, p. 196.
57. Ibid. Ref. symbolique, p. 474.
58. Ibid. Ref. symbolique, p. 475.
59. Lévi-Strauss 'Introduction à l'ouvrage de M. Mauss' (*Sociologie et anthropologie*, P.U.F., Paris, 1950).
60. G. Durand *L'imagination symbolique* (P.U.F., Paris, 1964). Ref. pp. 11–12. On the gestural, linguistic, iconographic relations, see above.
61. J. Laplanche et J.B. Pontalis *Vocabulaire de la psychanalyse*, (P.U.F., Paris, 1967). Ref. imaginaire, p. 195.
62. Ibid. Ref. p. 195.
63. Ibid. Ref. p. 196.
64. F. de Saussure *Cours de linguistique générale* (Payot, Paris, 1955).
65. C1. Lévi-Strauss 'Introduction à l'ouvrage de M. Mauss' (*Sociologie et anthropologie*, P.U.F., Paris, 1950).
66. F. de Saussure *Cours de Linguistique générale* (Payot, Paris, 1955).

67. S. Lupasco, *Qu'est-ce qu'une structure?* (Bourgois, Paris, 1967).

CHAPTER 7

1. A. Rifflet-Lemaire *Jacques Lacan* (Deggart, Bruxelles, 1970).
2. When the words are used in strict relation to Lacan's theory, I have preferred to leave the French terms.
3. I have translated with negation the French word used by Rifflet-Lemaire. The exact meaning of negation in this context does not correspond therefore to the psychoanalytic definition.
4. A. De Waelhens 'Introduzione a Demoulin P.', *Nevrosi e psicosi*, S.E.1., Torino, 1970.
5. The references to symbolism which follow are related to symbolism as theorized by Lacan. This does not correspond therefore to Jung's symbolism.
6. This might be the major reason why the dreams of an analysed patient often follow the direction given by the analyst's interpretation. It is well known that patients in Freudian analysis dream differently from those in Jungian analysis, and so on. The unconscious, according to this evidence, could be allowing those contents to rise to the surface which the patient feels may possibly be communicable to the analyst.
7. L. Binswanger *Tre forme di esistenza mancata* (Il Saggiatore, Milano, 1964).
8. J.W. Perry 'Acute Catatonic Schizophrenia', *Journal of Analytical Psychology*, vol 11, no. 137, 1957.
9. See Demoulin P. under note 4 above.

CHAPTER 8

1. C.A. Meier *Ancient incubation and modern psychotherapy* (Rascher, Zürich, and North-Western University Press, Evanston, 1949).
2. W.A. Jayne *The healing gods of ancient civilisations* (University Books, New York, 1962).
3. M-L von Franz 'Archetypal patterns in fairy tales', lecture privately circulated at the C.G. Jung Institute. Ref. p. 8.
4. L. Senghor, quoted in *Contemporary leaders in Africa*, by A. J. van Rensburg (H.A.U.M., Cape Town, 1975).
5. E.L. Rossi 'Growth, change and transformation in dreams', *Journal of Humanistic Psychology*, vol. 11, no. 2, 1971.
6. C.G. Jung (1926) 'Two essays on analytical psychology', *Collected Works*, 7.
7. C.G. Jung (1913) 'Symbols of transformation', *Collected Works*, 5.

CHAPTER 9

1. W.D. Hammond-Tooke *Bantu speaking people of Southern Africa* (Routledge Kegan Paul, London, 1974).
2. M. Vera Bührmann 'Xhosa diviners as psychotherapists', *Psychotherapeia*, vol. 3, no. 4, 1977.
3. Ibid 'Dream therapy through the ages' *Psychotherapeia*, vol. 3, no. 1, 1977.

4. Ibid 'Tentative views on dream therapy by Xhosa diviners', *Journal of Analytical Psychology*, vol. 23, no. 2, 1978.
5. Axel-Ivor Berglund *Zulu thought patterns and symbolism* (C Hurst & Company, London, 1976). Ref. p. 197.
6. Ibid. Ref. p. 127.
7. M. Vera Bührmann '*Xhentsa* and *Inthlombe*: a Xhosa healing ritual', *Journal of Analytical Psychology*, 26 (1981), pp. 187–201.
8. C.G. Jung *The structure and dynamics of the psyche* (Routledge Kegan Paul, London, 1960). Ref. p. 44.
9. C.A. Meier *Antike inkubation und moderne psychotherapie* (Rascher, Zürich, 1949). Ref. p. 74.
10. Marie-Louise von Franz *Interpretation of fairy tales* (Spring, Zürich, 1975).
11. C.G. Jung *Psychology and alchemy* (Routledge Kegan Paul, London, 1953). Ref. p. 65.
12. C.G. Jung *Symbols of transformation* (Routledge Kegan Paul, London, 1950). Ref. pp. 167–8.
13. C.G. Jung *Symbols of transformation* (Routledge Kegan Paul, London, 1950). Ref. p. 210.
14. Oshar Pfister 'Instructive psychoanalysis among the Navahos', *Journal of Nervous and Mental Disorders*, no. 76, 1932.
15. I would like to acknowledge the financial help I received in this project from the Human Sciences Research Council in Pretoria. I would like also to thank Mr. Joseph Gqomfa for his invaluable work as interpreter, and the *amagqira* for their trust.

CHAPTER 10

1. We thank Thelma McDowell and Pamela Eriksen for their comments and advice on the manuscript.
2. C.G. Jung (1969) 'Psychological Commentary on the *Tibetan Book of The Dead*', *Collected Works*, 11. Ref. p. 511.
3. C.G. Jung, (1969) 'Yoga and the West', *Collected Works*, 11. Refs. pp. 530–3, p. 535.
4. C.G. Jung (1969) 'Foreword to Suzuki's *Introduction to Zen Buddhism*', *Collected Works*, 11.
5. C.G. Jung Commentary, in R. Wilhelm and C.G. Jung *The Secret of the Golden Flower* (Routledge and Kegan Paul, London, 1972). Ref. p. 86.
6. C.G. Jung *Commentary on Kundalini Yoga* (Spring, New York, 1975). Ref. pp. 1–32.
7. H.R. Zimmer *Philosophies of India*, in J. Campbell (ed.) (Princeton University Press, 1951). Refs p. 421, p. 324.
8. M. Eliade *Yoga: Immortality and Freedom* (Routledge Kegan Paul, London, 1969). Refs. p. 423, p. 45, p. 36.
9. C.G. Jung (1960) 'The Real and the Surreal, *Collected Works*, 8. Ref. pp. 382–4.
10. C.G. Jung (1949) 'Definitions', *Collected Works*, 6. Refs. pp. 535–6, p. 540, p. 536, p. 613, p. 616.
11. C.G. Jung (1960) 'Spirit and Life', *Collected Works*, 8. Refs. pp. 325–6, p. 323

12. C.G. Jung (1971) 'Conscious, Unconscious and Individuation', *Collected Works*, 9 (1). Refs pp. 283, 286.

13. R.E. Ornstein, *The Psychology of Consciousness* (Freeman, San Francisco, 1972).

14. I.K. Taimni *The Science of Yoga* (Quest Books, Wheaton, 1972) Refs. p. 7, p. 67, p. 214, p. 278, p. 32, pp. 103–5, p. 131, p. 108.

15. C.G. Jung (1951) 'The Ego', *Collected Works*, 9 (2), Ref. p. 3.

16. C.G. Jung (1972) 'On the Psychology of the Unconscious', *Collected Works*, 7.

17. C.G. Jung (1971) 'The Concept of the Collective Unconscious', *Collected Works*, 9 (1). Ref. p. 79.

18. C.G. Jung (1960) 'On the Nature of the Psyche'. *Collected Works*, 8. Refs. p. 201, p. 213.

19. C.G. Jung (1960) 'Instinct and the Unconscious', *Collected Works*, 8. Refs. p. 137–8, p. 136.

20. C.G. (1969) 'A Psychological Approach to the Dogma of the Trinity', *Collected Works*, 11. Ref. p. 149.

21. J. Jacobi *The Psychology of C.G. Jung* (Routledge Kegan Paul, London, 1968). Ref. p. 60.

22. C.G. Jung (1972) 'The Function of the Unconscious', *Collected Works*, 7. Ref. p. 173.

23. M.-L. von Franz 'The Process of Individuation', in C.G. Jung (ed.) *Man and His Symbols* (Aldus Books, London, 1972). Ref. p. 161.

24. C.G. Jung (1971) 'The Psychology of the Child Archetype,' *Collected Works*, 9 (1). Ref. p. 159.

25. C.G. Jung (1971) 'The Phenomenology of the Spirit in Fairytales', *Collected Works*, 9 (1). Ref. p. 215.

26. C.G. Jung *Analytical Psychology. Its Theory and Practice* (Routledge and Kegan Paul, London, 1968). Ref. p. 194.

27. C.G. Jung (1971) 'Psychological Aspects of the Mother Archetype', *Collected Works*, 9 (1).

28. C.G. Jung (1954) 'Some Aspects of Modern Psychotherapy', *Collected Works*, 16.

29. C.G. Jung (1954) 'Analytical Psychology and Education: 3 Lectures', *Collected Works*, 17.

30. C.G. Jung (1971) 'Concerning Rebirth', *Collected Works*, 9 (1). Refs. p. 129, p. 142.

31. C.G. Jung (1964) 'What India Can Teach Us', *Collected Works*, 10. Ref. p. 527.

32. W.Y. Evans-Wentz *The Tibetan Book of the Dead* (Oxford University Press, 1960).

CHAPTER 11

1. Dr. James Kirsch was in large measure responsible for leading me to an understanding of Jung's religious and theological significance, an understanding which Jung himself personally corroborated.

2. See A.J. Ayer *Language, truth and logic* (Dover Publications, New York,

1952) for a brilliant expositions of this theory.

3. Raymond Hostie *Religion and the psychology of Jung* (Sheed & Ward, New York, 1957).

4. C.G. Jung (1969) 'The practice of psychotherapy', *Collected Works*, 16. Refs paras 524 and 537.

5. C.G. Jung (1957) 'Symbols of transformation', *Collected Works*, 5.

6. C.G. Jung (1960) 'The structure and dynamics of the psyche', *Collected Works*, 8. Ref. para. 388.

7. C.G. Jung, *Collected Works*, 16 (3).

8. C.G. Jung *Memories, dreams, reflections* (Routledge Kegan Paul, London, 1963).

9. Ibid. Ref. chapter 4.

10. Werner Heisenberg *Physics and philosophy: the revolution in modern science* (Harper & Row, New York, 1958). Ref. p. 200f.

11. C.G. Jung *Memories, dreams, reflections* (Routledge Kegan Paul, London, 1963). Ref. p. 351f.

12. *The Bible*, Ephesians, 6:12.

13. C.G. Jung *Collected Works*, 8. Ref. para. 409.

CHAPTER 12

1. James W. Heisig 'Jung and theology: a bibliographical essay' in *An Annual of Analytical Psychology and Jungian Thought* (Spring, New York, 1973). Ref. p. 204.

2. Theodore Jennings *Introduction to theology: an invitation to reflection upon the Christian mythos* (Fortress, Philadelphia, 1976).

3. Heije Faber *Psychology of religion* (SCM, London, 1976)

4. Morton T. Kelsey *The other side of silence* (Paulist Press, New York, 1976).

5. C.G. Jung *Collected Works*, 11. Refs. pp. 365, 8, 32, 47, 459, 168.

6. C.G. Jung *Collected Works*, 13. Ref. p. 6.

7. C.G. Jung *Memories, dreams, reflections* (Routledge Kegan Paul, London, 1963). Refs. p. 56, p. 197, p. 326.

8. Victor White *God and the unconscious* (Fontana, London, 1960). Refs p. 259, p. 18.

9. Karl Barth *Der   Römerbrief (The Epistle to the Romans)* (Oxford University Press, 1933).

10. Rudolf Otto *Das Heilige (The idea of the holy)* (Clarendon, Oxford, 1931).

11. G.B. Caird, *Principalities and powers: a study in Pauline theology* (Clarendon Press, Oxford, 1956).

12. C.G. Jung *Collected Works*, 12. Ref. p. 12.

13. C.G. Jung *Modern man in search of a soul*.

14. Jolande Jacobi *The way of individuation* (Hodder and Stoughton, London, 1967).

15. Jolande Jacobi *The psychology of C.G. Jung* (Routledge Kegan Paul, London, 1969).

16. R.C. Zaehner *Mysticism: sacred and profane* (Oxford, 1961). Refs p. 202, p. 119.

17. C.G. Jung, *Collected Works*, 9. Ref. p. 37.

18. Frieda Fordham *An introduction to Jung's psychology* (Penguin, Harmondsworth, 1973).
19. H.M.M. Fortmann *Als ziene de onsienlijke* (3 vols) (Paul Brand, Hilversum, 1968).
20. Henri Frankfort *The intellectual adventure of ancient man* (University of Chicago Press, 1946).
21. Stephen Neill *The interpretation of the New Testament, 1861-1961* (Oxford, 1964).
22. Mircea Eliade *Myths, dreams & mysteries* (Harvill Press, New York, 1960).
23. John Hick *Evil and the God of Love* (Macmillan & Co, London, 1966). Ref. p. 59f.
24. John Hick 'The concept of divine goodness and the problem of evil', *Religious studies*, vol. II, no. 1, March 1975.
25. Antonio Moreno *Jung, gods and modern man* (Sheldon, London, 1974).

CHAPTER 13

1. C.G. Jung *Collected Works*, 8. Ref. para. 362.
2. 'Prolegomena', in *Kants Werke* (Akademie Textausgabe, Berlin, 1968), vol. IV, p. 260. All English translations and paraphrases of Kant's text are my own. In each instance I have to the best of my knowledge been faithful to Kant's meaning but I have altered and/or abbreviated his wording whenever a literal translation produced anything but the desired clarity or succinctness.
3. 'Prolegomena', in *Kants Werke* (Akademie Textausgabe, Berlin, 1968). Ref. p. 257.
4. My rewrite, with minor additions, of Kant's paraphrase, 'Prolegomena'. Ref. pp. 257-60.
5. 'Prolegomena'. Ref. p. 258.
5a. Ibid. Ref. p. 267, section 2b.
6. Ibid. Ref. p. 268 (my italics).
7. Ibid. Ref. p. 268.
8. Ibid. Ref. p. 269.
9. *Kritik der reinen Vernunft* (Critique of Pure Reason), second or B–edition, *Kants Werke*, vol. III, B XIII (references are to B paragraphs).
10. 'Prolegomena'. Ref. p. 271.
11. See H. Vaihinger, *Kommentar zu Kants Kritik der reinen Vernunft*, (Stuttgart, 1881) vol. I. Ref. pp. 116-22.
12. 'Prolegomena'. Ref. p. 276.
13. Ibid. Ref. p. 277 (my italics).
14. *Kritik* B64-65 (see note 9 above).
15. 'Prolegomena'. Ref. p. 281, section 7.
16. Ibid. Ref. p. 282, section 8.
17. Ibid. Ref. p. 282, section 9.
18. *Kritik* B6 (see note 9 above).
19. *Kritik* B38-39 (my italics). (See note 9 above).
20. 'Prolegomena'. Ref. p. 284, section 12.
21. *Kritik* B46-48 (see note 9 above).

22. 'Prolegomena'. Ref. p. 283, section 10.
23. Ibid. Ref. p. 294, section 14.
24. In the sense of 'personal', 'private'. Kant himself uses the term in two senses (cf. the last lines of the quotation on p. 212).
25. 'Prolegomena'. Ref. p. 296, section 17 (my italics).
26. Ibid. Ref. p. 350, section 56.
27. *Kritik* B74–76 (see note 9 above).
28. 'Prolegomena'. Ref: p. 332, section 45.
29. *Kritik* B6 (see note 9 above).
30. 'Prolegomena'. Ref. p. 334, section 46.
31. Ibid. Ref. p. 334, section 47.
32. C.G. Jung *Letters*, vol. 1 (Routledge Kegan Paul, London, 1975). Ref. p. 61.
33. C.G. Jung *Collected Works*, 11. Ref. para. 553.
34. C.G. Jung *Letters*, vol. II (Routledge Kegan Paul, London, 1975). Refs. p. 572, p. 573.
35. 'Prolegomena'. Ref. p. 307, section 24.
36. C.G. Jung *Collected Works*, 6. Ref. para. 65.
37. C.G. Jung *Collected Works*, 6. Ref. para. 66.
38. C.G. Jung *Collected Works*, 6. Ref. paras. 77, 78.
39. C.G. Jung *Collected Works*, 6. Ref. para. 78.
40. James Hillman *The Myth of Analysis* (Evanston, 1972). Ref. p. 41.
41. *Ibid*. Ref. p. 165.
42. Paul Feyerabend *Against Method* (NLB London, 1976). Ref. p. 30.
43. C.G. Jung (1954) 'On the Nature of the Psyche' *Collected Works*, 8. Ref. para. 417.
44. C.G. Jung (1948) 'Instinct and the Unconscious' *Collected Works*, 8. Ref. para. 227.
45. James Hillman *The Myth of Analysis* (Evanston, 1972). Refs. p. 188, p. 189.
46. See Hillman, *Re-Visioning Psychology* (Harper and Row, New York, 1975). Readers familiar with Hillman's exposition of 'seeing through' will note that my view differs from his. However, it is doubtful if I could or would have developed my own position if I had not come across Hillman's 229 pages of brillant if unmeasured prose.

CHAPTER 14

1. L. Rauhala 'Intentionality and the problem of the unconscious', *Annals of the University of Turku*, 1969.
2. L. Rauhala 'The hermeneutic metascience of psychoanalysis' *Man and World*, vol. 5, no. 3, 1972a.
3. L. Rauhala 'Wissenschaftsphilosophie der Tiefenpsychologie', *Zeitschrift für Analytische Psychologie und ihre Grenzgebiete*, vol. 4, January 1973.
4. P. Ricoeur *Freud and philosophy* (New Haven, 1970).
5. A. Lorenzer *Sprachzerstörung und Rekonstruktion: Vorarbeiten zu einer Metatheorie der Psychoanalyse* (Frankfurt am Main, 1971).
6. A Ellis 'An operational reformulation of some of the basic principles of psychoanalysis', in *Minnesota Studies in the Philosophy of Science*, vol. 1, eds

Herbert Feigl and Michael Scriven, Minneapolis, 1965.
7. E. Nagel 'Methodological issues in psychoanalytical theory', in *Psychoanalysis, Scientific Method and Philosophy*, ed. Sidney Hook, New York, 1959.
8. *Husserliana I-XI* (Den Haag, 1950-63). Especially *III*, pp. 216-54.
9. M. Heidegger *Sein und Zeit* (Tübingen, 1963).
9a. M. Heidegger *Einführung in die Metaphysik* (Tübingen, 1963).
10. M. Heidegger *Wegmarken* (Frankfurt am Main, 1967).
11. G. Raditzky *Continental schools of metasciences I-II* (Göteborg, 1968).
12. A. Jaffé (ed.) *Memories, dreams, reflection* (Routledge Kegan Paul, London, 1963). Ref. p. 211.
13. C.G. Jung *Collected Works*. Especially 11, p. 307; 9 (1), p. 48, 8, p. 482, p. 493; 9 (1), p. 13; 11, p. 149, 9 (1), p. 79; 11, p. 518.
14. C.G. Jung (1921) 'Psychological Types', *Collected Works*, 6. Ref. pp. 647-8.
15. L. Rauhala 'The myth of mental illness', *Psychiatrica Fennica*, 1972b.
16. G. Adler 'Die Sinnfrage in der Psychotherapie', in *Psychotherapeutische Probleme*, Studien aus dem C.G. Jung Institut, Zürich, 1964.
17. L. Frey-Rohn *Von Freud zu Jung* (Zürich, 1969).
18. A. Jaffé *The Myth of Meaning* (London, 1971).

CHAPTER 15

1. C.G. Jung *Memories, dreams, reflections* (Routledge Kegan Paul, London, 1963).
2. C.G. Jung *Contributions to analytical psychology* (transl. by H.G. Cary F. Baynes, London, 1928, 1942, 1945). Ref. pp. 118-9.
3. C.G. Jung (1952) 'Symbols of transformation', *Collected Works*, 5. Ref. p. xxiv.
4. Rainer Maria Rilke *Letters*, vol. 2 (New York, 1945). Ref. p. 342.
5. C.G. Jung *Contributions to analytical psychology* (transl. by H.G. Cary F. Baynes, London, 1928, 1942, 1945). Ref. p. 365.
6. Ibid. Ref. p. 246, pp. 60-1.
7. I am indebted to G. Adler for the phrases 'conscous' and 'unconscious anonymity'. See Adler's *Studies in analytical psychology* (London, 1948). Ref. p. 127.
8. See R.C. Johnson *The imprisoned splendour: an approach to reality based upon the significance of data drawn from the fields of natural science, psychical research and mystical experience* (London, 1953).
9. I. Progoff *Jung's psychology and its social meaning* (London, 1953). Ref. p. 32.
10. Berdyaev *The meaning of history* (London, 1936). Ref. p. 17.
11. William Rose *Rainer Rilke: aspects of his mind and poetry* (London, 1959).
12. Rainer Maria Rilke *Selected letters 1902-1926* (transl. R.F.C. Hull, London, 1946). Ref. pp. 264-5.
13. M. Eliade *The myth of the eternal return* Ref. p. 88.
14. M. Plowman 'What does death mean to you?' in *The Right to Live* (London, 1942). Ref. p. 299.

CHAPTER 16

1. Alan Watts: *In my own way* (New York 1972). Ref. p. 394.
2. *C.G. Jung speaking: interviews and encounters*, edited by William McQuire and R.F.C. Hull (London, 1977). Ref. chapter 'The Therapy of Music', p. 273 ff.
3. Quoted from Jung's 'Integration of the personality' in Dr. Jolande Jacobi's *The psychology of C.G. Jung* (Routledge Kegan Paul, London 1942). Ref. p. 91.
4. *C.G. Jung's letters*, vol. 1, edited by G. Adler (Routledge Kegan Paul, London 1973). Ref. p. 542.
5. C.G. Jung (1954) 'Psychological aspects of the mother archetype' in *The archetypes and the collective unconscious*, Collected Works, 9 (1). Ref. para. 154.
6. A.H. Fox Strangeways in Grove's *Dictionary of music and musicians*, vol. VI, Ref. p. 618.
7. Curt Sachs *The rise of music in the ancient world: east and west*, (Dent, London, 1944).
8. For a detailed account of primitive and ancient music cultures see *The new Oxford history of music*, vol. I 'Ancient and oriental music' edited by Egon Wellesz (Oxford University Press, London, 1937).
9. Curt Sachs *The rise of music in the ancient world: east and west* (Dent, London, 1949).
10. Egon Wellesz *A history of Byzantine music and hymnography* (Clarendon Press, Oxford, 1949). Ref. p. 58.
11. *Richard Wagner's Gesammelte Schriften*, vol. 13, 'Uber die Benennung "Musikdrama"' (Kapp, 19). Ref. p. 119.
12. Robert Donington *Wagner's 'Ring' and its symbols: the music and the myth* (Faber, London, 1963).
13. Deryck Cooke *The language of music* (Oxford University Press, London, 1959).
14. C.G. Jung (1946) 'Essays on contemporary events', Collected Works, 10.
15. J.W.N. Sullivan *Beethoven* (Penguin Books, Harmondsworth, 1949). Ref. p. 37.
16. Anton Felix Schindler *Beethoven as I knew him*, translated by Constance S. Jolly (Faber, London, 1966). Ref. p. 406.
17. Johann Nikolaus Forkel *Uber Johann Sebastian Bach's Leben, Kunst und Kunstwerke* (1802), translated into English by Stephenson under the title *On Johann Sebastian Bach's life, genius and works* (1808); reprinted in *The Bach reader*, ed., Hans T. David and Arthur Mendel, (Dent, London, 1946). Ref. section six, pp. 294f.
18. M. Jansen 'Bach's Zahlensymbolik', *Bach-Jahrbuch XXXIV*, 1937.
19. Karl Geiringer *Symbolism in the music of Bach* (Washington, 1956).
20. Hans Brandts Buys *De Passies van Johann Sebastian Bach* (L. Stafleu, Leiden, 1950).
21. Michael Tippett *Moving into Aquarius* (Routledge Kegan Paul, London, 1959).
22. Victor Zuckerkandl *Sound and symbol in music and the external world*

(Routledge Kegan Paul, London, 1956). Ref. chapter XX.
23. Paul Nordoff and Clive Robbins 'Improvised music as therapy for autistic children' in *Music as therapy* ed. E. Thayer Gaston (Macmillan, London, 1968). Ref. chapter 14.

CHAPTER 17

1. C.G. Jung *Memories, dreams, reflections*. (Routledge Kegan Paul, London, 1963). Ref. p. 310.
2. Cf., for instance, G. Frege, *Grundgesetzder Arithmetik* (Olms, Hildesheim, 1962). Ref. p. vii, p. xivf.
3. Ibid. Ref. p. xvii, p. xviii.
4. *Function, Begriff, Bedeutung* (Vandenhoeck, 1975). Ref. pp. 44–45, 17–18; cf. also p. 83.
5. Ibid. Ref. p. 67.
6. See H. Weyl, *Philosophy of mathematics and natural science* (Princeton University Press, New Jersey, 1949).
7. Quoted from E. Nagel and T.R. Newman 'Goedel's proof', *Scientific American*, June, 1956, p. 81. I owe the knowledge of this article to the kindness of Dr. W. Just.
8. Ibid. Ref. p. 86.
9. C.G. Jung *Memories, dreams, reflections* (Routledge Kegan Paul, London, 1963). Ref. p. 310.
10. C.G. Jung (1952) 'Synchronicity: An acausal connecting principle', *Collected Works*, 8. Ref. para. 870.
11. Ibid.
12. Cf. T. Danzig *Number, the language of science* (New York, 1934). Ref. p. 234.
13. *Symmetries and reflexions* (Cambridge, Mass., 1970).
14. C.G. Jung *Memories, dreams, reflections* (Routledge Kegan Paul, London, 1963). Ref. p. 310f.
15. C.G. Jung *Letters*, Vol. 2 (Princeton University Press, New Jersey, 1976). Ref. p. 494.
16. As A. Jaffé erroneously asserts.
17. C.G. Jung, *Letters*, Vol. 2 (Princeton University Press, New Jersey, 1976). Ref. p. 495.
18. C.G. Jung 'Synchronicity: an acausal connecting principle', *Collected Works*, 8. Ref. para. 965.
19. Ibid.
20. My addition.
21. Ibid.
22. Ibid. Ref. para. 968.
23. C.G. Jung *Letters*, Vol. 2 (Princeton Univercity Press, New Jersey, 1976). Ref. p. 495.
24. Liu Guan-Ying 'Die ungewöhnlichen Naturerscheinungen in den T'ang Annalen und ihre Deutung', in *Symbolen*, ed. I. Schwabe. Vol. II (Basel, 1961). Ref. pp. 32f.
25. *I Ching, or Book of Changes*, ed. R. Wilhelm, trans. C. Baynes (Routledge

Kegan Paul, London, 1968). Ref. p. 321.

26. Ibid. Ref. p. 281.
27. 'Synchronicity: an acausal connecting principle', *Collected Works*, 8. Ref. para. 855.
28. Cf. ibid. Ref. para. 856.
29. Ibid. Ref. para. 856.
30. Ibid. Ref. para. 855.
31. *I Ching*, op. cit. Ref. p. 322.
32. Ibid. Ref. p. 320.
33. G. J. Whitrow *The natural philosophy of time* (London, 1960). Ref. pp. 295–6.
34. C.G. Jung (1956) 'Mysterium Coniunctionis'. *Collected Works*, 14. Ref. para. 662.
35. I base the following representation on D. Mahnke *Unendliche Sphaere und Allmittelpunkt* (Stuttgart, 1966).
36. Ibid. Ref. pp. 230/5, p. 215f.
37. Ibid. Ref. p. 273.
38. Ibid. Ref. p. 199.
39. Ibid. Ref. p. 202.
40. Ibid. Ref. p. 175.
41. Ibid. Ref. p. 167.
42. Ibid. Ref. p. 141f.
43. Ibid. Ref. p. 141.
44. Ibid. Ref. p. 139.
45. Ibid. Ref. p. 127.
46. Ibid. Ref. p. 125.
47. Ibid. Ref. p. 123.
48. Ibid. Ref. p. 18.
49. Ibid. Ref. p. 17.
50. Ibid. Ref. p. 8, p. 10.
51. Cf. Marie-Louise von Franz, *Number and time* p. 122.
52. C.G. Jung *Memories, dreams, reflections* (Routledge Kegan Paul, London, 1963). Ref. p. 337.
53. Cf. F.C. Haber 'The Darwinian revolution in the concept of time', in *The study of time I*, ed. Fraser-Haber-Müller (Springer, Berlin, 1972). Ref. p. 383.
54. Cf. C.G. Jung, *Letters*, vol. 1, (Princeton University Press, New Jersey, 1976). Ref. p. 325.
55. Ibid. Ref. p. 326.
56. *Memories, dreams, reflections*, op. cit. Ref. p. 308.
57. Cf. C.G. Jung Collected Works, 1. Ref. p. 81.
58. C.G. Jung 'Synchronicity: an acausal connecting principle', op. cit. Ref. para. 916.
59. Ibid. Ref. para. 917.
60. Quotes ibid. Ref. para. 921.
61. Quoted from Morris Kline 'Les fondements des mathématiques', *La Recherche*, vol. 6, no. 54, 1975. Ref. p. 207.
62. *I Ching*, op. cit. Ref. p. 282.

63. Ibid. Ref. pp. 295–6.
64. Ibid. Ref. p. 339.
65. Ibid. Ref. p. 323.
66. *Memories, dreams, reflections*, op. cit. Ref. pp. 310–11.
67. 'Synchronicity: an acausal connecting principle', op. cit. Ref. para. 855.
68. This is the view of the *I Ching*: Heaven Spirit has Time as its field of action, Earth as a derived principle has space as its field of realization.
69. Cf. Ruyer, 1.c., pp. 120/121.
70. Fritjof Capra 'Quark physics without quarks: a review of recent developments in S–Matrix theory', preprint (ready 1978) submitted to *The American Journal of Physics*, June, 1979.
71. Ruyer, p. 29.
72. Ibid.
73. Ibid. Ref. p. 10.
74. My italics.
75. Ibid. Ref. p. 17.
76. Fayard, 1974.
77. Ibid. Ref. p. 34.
78. Cf. ibid. Ref. p. 123f.
79. Ruyer compares them too with the patterns of behaviour of animals, *ibid*. Ref. p. 124.
80. Ibid. Ref. p. 129.
81. Ibid. Ref. p. 128.
82. Ibid. Ref. p. 130.
83. Ibid. Ref. pp. 131–2.
84. C.G. Jung *Letters*, vol. 2, op. cit. Ref. pp. 495–6.
85. Quoted from *Memories, dreams, reflections*, op. cit. Ref. p. 317.
86. Ibid. Ref. pp. 338–9.
87. Ibid. Ref. pp. 358–9.
88. Fritjof Capra, 'Quark physics without quarks', op. cit. Ref. p. 7.

Index

abaissement du niveau mental, 12, 176, 274

abasia-astasia syndrome, 24-6

Abraham, Karl, 23, 288n, 290n

active imagination, 33, 89-108, 175-80

Adler, Gerhard, 6, 38, 45, 287n, 290n, 292n

Aesculapius, 139, 144

affect, affective, 65-6, 97, 120, 131

Agrippa of Nettesheim, 13

Alanus de Insulia, 276

Albert the Great, 276

alchemy, alchemical, 6, 13, 15, 47, 92, 102-3, 171, 193, 202, 279

Alexander the Great, 71

Alice in Wonderland, 27

amagqira, see igqira

analysis, 7, 10, 16-18, 23, 71, 93-6, 99-108

Anaximander, 35-6

Andersen, Hans, 25-8, 31-2

Angelus Silesius, 13

anima, 79, 85, 92, 236

animals, 93, 104, 153-4, 161, 201, 262, 279-80

animus, 32, 85, 101, 143-4, 158, 162, 236, 273

Anselm, St, 222

Answer to Job, 6, 193-4, 197

Aquinas, St Thomas, 191

archetypes, 2, 12, 18, 34, 141, 143-4, 153-4, 164, 170-2, 179-81, 188-9, 225-6, 248-9, 257, 262-3, 270-2, 279, 282-3, 286, and fairy tales 23-33, and the Other, 82-8, and the Imaginary, 110-18, and psychotics, 119-34, and symbols, 233-40

Archimedes, 270

Aristotle, 35-7, 39-40, 52, 191, 219, 289n

Aristotelian Society, 85

Aschaffenburg, Professor, 67

association(s), 24, 32, 43, 62-7, 88, 97, 102, 105, 147

Atman, 168, 178, 198, 251

Augustine, St., 191, 201

Ayer, A.J., 185, 301n

Bach, J.S., 263, 265-6

Bachelard, Gaston, 110-1, 295-6n

Bacon, Sir Francis, 13-14, 38, 289n

Bakan, D., 56, 71, 290n

Barber, E.A., 55-6, 290n

Barth, Karl, 195, 301n

Basilides, 82-3

Bateson, Gregory, 78, 290n

Becquerel, 184, 187

Beethoven, Ludwig van, 253, 257, 263-4

behaviourism, 3, 16, 33, 40, 42

Beit, H. von, 23, 33, 288n

Benfey, T., 55, 290n

Ben Gebirol, Salomon, 276

Berdyaev, 252, 304n

Bhagavadgita, 253, 274, 278

Bible, biblical, 191-3, 258, 301n

Bilz, J., 23, 288n

Binet, 89

Binswanger, L., 129, 298n

Bion, 119

Black Book, 77

Blanton, S., 70, 290n

Bleuler, Eugen, 43, 65-6

body, 19, 66, 91, 107, 115, 126, 154

Boehme, 277

Bohr, Niels, 187

Brahman, 168-9

Brahmanism, 165, 199, 251

Brentano, 27

British Broadcasting Corporation, 191

HALLUCINOGENS

CROSS-CULTURAL
PERSPECTIVES

MARLENE DOBKIN DE RIOS

Hallucinogens
Cross-Cultural Perspectives
Marlene Dobkin de Rios

THIS book surveys the uses of mind-altering plants in eleven societies in the Americas, Asia, Africa, Australia, and New Guinea, ranging from the hunter-gatherer level to the complex ancient civilizations of the Aztec, the Maya, the Nazca, the Mochica, and the Inca. Some of the data are derived from the author's research in modern Peru, where plant hallucinogens are used in folk healing. Many other data have been assembled from a variety of scientific and anthropological publications. The lay reader with a general interest in primitive ritual, religion, and healing will find a great deal of information in this concise volume, which is illustrated with drawings of the various plants that can produce altered states of consciousness and with reproductions of ancient Peruvian art that the author sees as drug-related.

Several themes emerge from de Rios's cross-cultural examination of sacred plants. She argues convincingly that plant hallucinogens, which have been used from time immemorial, influenced human evolution. She also discusses religious beliefs that may have been influenced by the mind-altering properties of particular plants, and she focuses on the ways hallucinogens have influenced ethical and moral systems.

MARLENE DOBKIN DE RIOS is professor of anthropology at California State University.

8½ x 5½, 256 pp
Full colour cover
Line drawings and tables
1 85327 061 X Paperback

SACRED PLANTS, MYSTICISM
AND PSYCHOTHERAPY

Edited by
CHRISTIAN RÄTSCH

Gateway
to Inner Space

*Sacred Plants, Mysticism
and Psychotherapy*

ED. Dr. Christian Rätsch

IN recent years there has been
considerable debate about the
visionary experiences induced by
hallucinatory plants — often
regarded as sacred in shamanic
societies — and the related use of
psychedelics in contemporary
psychology.

This fascinating work consists of
essays by many leading researchers
in the field of altered states of
consciousness — presented to honour
Dr Albert Hofmann, who first
discovered the extraordinary effects
of LSD in 1943.

Featured here are writings on the
medical use of psychedelics, the
controversial issue of 'molecular
mysticism', the relationship of
sacraments to Gnosis, death and
rebirth themes in shamanism,
comparisons between meditative and
psychedelic experiences and states of
tryptamine consciousness.

Among the many distinguished
contributors to this remarkable
volume are Dr Stanislav Grof,
Terence McKenna, Dr Ralph
Metzner, Professor Hanscarl Leuner,
Dr Claudio Naranjo, Claudia Müller-
Ebeling and Dr Christian Rätsch.

DR CHRISTIAN RÄTSCH is an authority
on sacred plants and the culture of
the ancient Mayans. He has
published extensively in German —
his books include *Chactun — die
Gotter der Maya* and *Bilder aus der
unsichtbaren Welt.*

*8½ x 5½, 256 pp
Full colour cover
1 85327 037 7 Paperback*

EXPLORING THE
PARANORMAL

PERSPECTIVES ON
BELIEF AND
EXPERIENCE

EDITED BY DR. G.K. ZOLLSCHAN,
DR. J.F. SCHUMAKER & DR. G.F. WALSH

Exploring the Paranormal

Perspectives on Belief and Experience

EDITED BY Prof. G.K. Zollschan, Dr J.F. Schumaker and Dr G.F. Walsh

THIS important anthology brings together some of the world's leading authorities in their fields and presents frameworks for understanding paranormal belief and experience. It describes special applications of the scientific method and also features debates between believers and unbelievers in the paranormal. There are chapters on mind-expanding drugs, the near-death experience, mysticism and meditation, an evaluation of the contribution of biology to the study of the paranormal, and an examination of 'miracles'.

Contributors to this far ranging book include such internationally acclaimed figures as Charles Tart, Stanley Krippner, Harvey Irwin, Anthony Flew, and John Beloff as well as many other distinguished researchers from the United States, Britain and Australia.

The three editors also differ in their views. *ZOLLSCHAN* is a sociologist and practising Jewish mystic. Formerly an assistant to Sir Karl Popper he has taught in the USA, Canada, Britain and Australia. *SCHUMAKER* is a clinical psychologist and is an "absolute unbeliever" in the paranormal. *WALSH* is a social scientist and Roman Catholic with an interest in how inter-denominational differences affect belief in the supernatural.

8½ x 5½, 400 pp
Full colour cover
1 85327 026 1 Paperback

Sentics

The Touch of the Emotions
Dr Manfred Clynes

INTRODUCTION BY
Yehudi Menuhin

SENTICS reveals how emotions are communicated early in life and in music, painting and sculpture. It is a revolutionary, new scientific discipline which examines the biological basis of emotion. Its discoverer, DR MANFRED CLYNES, is the inventor of the Sentograph, an ingenious device which measures emotional responses through the fingertips. Clynes' research has also uncovered genetically programmed brain and nervous system patterns for such basic emotional states as joy, anger, hate, grief and love. Moreover he has developed the so-called 'Sentic Cycles', an exercise technique for the emotions, which anyone can learn and which can lead to a profound sense of well-being.

The author is one of the most creative, multidisciplinary minds working in science today. He holds advanced degrees in neuroscience, engineering and music. He is a university lecturer and has toured Europe as a concert pianist.

"This breakthrough could only have been achieved by a musician . . . a scientist who remains a musician at heart." Yehudi Menuhin.

8½ x 5½, 284 pp
Full colour cover
1 85327 025 3 Paperback

The Celtic Twilight

Myth, Fantasy and Folklore
W.B. Yeats

ALTHOUGH renowned as one of the most famous poets of the 20th century, *WILLIAM BUTLER YEATS* 1865-1939) was also a devoted exponent of the western mystical and magical traditions. Yeats met with students of the occult in Dublin in the 1880s and was later introduced by his friend Charles Johnson to the Theosophical Society. Yeats subsequently left the Theosophists and in 1890 was initiated as a ceremonial magician of the Golden Dawn — arguably the most influential esoteric order in the western magical tradition — and for a time became its leader.

Yeats exercised a profoundly Celtic influence on his fellow occultists and his love of Irish folklore is reflected in this book, which was first published in 1893. THE CELTIC TWILIGHT brings together many of Yeats' most enchanting and mystical tales — a dazzling array of sorcerers, faeries, ghosts and nature spirits which draw their inspiration from the visionary heart of Irish folk tradition.

This book is a special tribute to the memory of W.B. Yeats and is published fifty years after his death.

8½ x 5½, 128 pp
Full colour cover
1 85327 029 6 Paperback

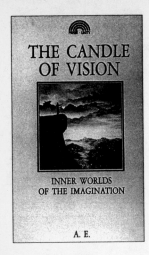

THE CANDLE
OF VISION

INNER WORLDS
OF THE IMAGINATION

A. E.

The Candle
of Vision

*Inner Worlds
of the Imagination*

A.E. (George Russell)
FOREWORD BY Nevill Drury

FIRST published in 1918, this book is one of the classics of modern western mysticism. While it may seem that such concepts as 'creative visualisation' and 'imagining our own reality' are recent innovations of the human potential movement, they are also found here — in a very lucid and eloquent form.

The author was a distinguished writer, artist and poet and believed that each of us can use the creative powers of the imagination as a pathway to other worlds. The imagination can transport us to an awesome, mystical universe and we then sense the vastness of the Infinite. This is the true nature of the visionary inspiration.

A.E. was the *nom de plume* of *GEORGE RUSSELL* (1867–1935). Russell was a major literary figure in the Irish Renaissance and a friend of W.B. Yeats. Like Yeats, Russell was strongly influenced by theosophical mysticism and by the beauty of Celtic mythology. He was the author of several works, including *Song and its Fountains* and *The Avatars*, but CANDLE OF VISION is widely regarded as his masterpiece.

8½ x 5½, 112 pp
Full colour cover
1 85327 030 X Paperback

REINCARNATION

ANCIENT BELIEFS
AND MODERN EVIDENCE

DAVID CHRISTIE-MURRAY

Reincarnation

*Ancient Beliefs and
Modern Evidence*

David Christie-Murray

R EINCARNATION is a fascinating
concept. What happens when we
die? Reincarnation and related
subjects (such as former lives) are
increasingly discussed in the media
but how can the ordinary reader,
unversed in theology or psychical
research, decide whether there is any
truth in the theory?

DAVID CHRISTIE-MURRAY has
gathered and assessed the evidence,
theories and views of reincarnation
from the religions of the East and
West, recollections of adults and
children, mediumistic communications, *déjà vu* experiences, regressive
hypnosis, Christos experiments, and
the results of meditation techniques.

His purpose is to inform, not to
convert, and after reading this book
readers should be able to reach their
own conclusions.

*8½ x 5½, 288 pp
Full colour cover
1 85327 012 1 Paperback*

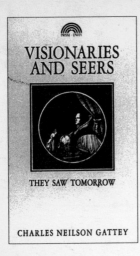

VISIONARIES
AND SEERS

THEY SAW TOMORROW

CHARLES NEILSON GATTEY

Visionaries and Seers

They Saw Tomorrow
Charles Neilson Gattey

8½ x 5½, 288 pp
Full colour cover
1 85327 020 2 Paperback

I N this unique book, Charles
Nielson Gattey recounts the
stranger-than-fiction life-stories of
the most astounding seers and
sorcerers of all time. Such well-
known characters as Nostradamus
and Cheiro are here in all their
brilliant and bizarre detail —
including the former's visions of the
Second World War and a bleak
outlook for Britain towards the end
of the 20th century and the latter's
predictions of Edward VIII's romance
and abdication — as well as such
lesser-known but equally intriguing
figures as Mlle Lenormande,
clairvoyante and confidante of the
Empress Josephine and Ernst Krafft,
alleged by some to have been Hitler's
personal astrologer.

Primitive Magic

The Psychic Powers of
Shamans and Sorcerers
Ernesto de Martino

THE idea of magic challenges our basic concepts of reality and the natural order of things. But for native shamans and sorcerers magic is as tangible and 'real' as science is in our modern 'civilisation'. The Australian Aborigine, for example, will die if pierced by an arrow that has been 'sung' — no matter how superficial the wound.

This astounding book describes societies where magic is a way of life, where sorcerers, shamans, diviners and fire walkers form powerful bonds with the psychic realities of Nature.

PRIMITIVE MAGIC is itself an initiation — into the enthralling world of ancient mysteries.

'There is no such thing as unreality; there are only various forms of reality' — Eugene Ionesco

ERNESTO DE MARTINO lives in Rome and is Professor of the History of Religions at Cagliari University. He has a long-standing interest in the links between parapsychology and anthropology and is the author of several works in this field, including *South Italy and Magic* and *Death and Ritual in the Ancient World*.

8½ x 5½, 192 pp
Full colour cover
1 85327 021 0 Paperback

MODERN
RITUAL MAGIC

THE RISE OF
WESTERN OCCULTISM

FRANCIS KING

Modern Ritual Magic

The Rise of
Western Occultism

Francis King

THIS is the inside story of the Hermetic Order of the Golden Dawn and associated occult offshoots — told in its entirety for the first time. The author's researches into the conflict between W.B. Yeats and Aleister Crowley are described in detail, as well as the full story of Yeats' early magical training and practices. Francis King also relates the often difficult relationship between Yeats and the influential Kabbalist, Macgregor Mathers.

However, it is not only the student of the Golden Dawn who will find this book absorbing. King also describes Rudolph Steiner's attempt to take over English occultism and links Bengali Tantricism with the magic of the American Mulatto. All the major figures in modern western magic feature in this book, which since its first publication in 1970, has been rightly regarded as one of the major histories of the western esoteric tradition.

FRANCIS KING is also the author of *Magic: the Western Tradition, Sexuality, Magic and Perversion* and *The Secret Rituals of the O.T.O.* He co-authored *Techniques of High Magic* with Stephen Skinner.

8½ x 5½, 224pp
Full colour cover
1 85327 032 6